Where Have All
the Horses Gone?

Where Have All the Horses Gone?

How Advancing Technology Swept American Horses from the Road, the Farm, the Range and the Battlefield

JONATHAN V. LEVIN

McFarland & Company, Inc., Publishers
Jefferson, North Carolina

LIBRARY OF CONGRESS CATALOGUING-IN-PUBLICATION DATA

Names: Levin, Jonathan V.
Title: Where have all the horses gone? : how advancing technology swept American horses from the road, the farm, the range and the battlefield / Jonathan V. Levin.
Description: Jefferson, North Carolina : McFarland & Company, Inc., Publishers, 2017. | Includes bibliographical references and index.
Identifiers: LCCN 2017020796 | ISBN 9781476667133 (softcover : acid free paper) ∞
Subjects: LCSH: Horses—United States—History. | Horses—Social aspects—United States.
Classification: LCC SF284.U5 L48 2017 | DDC 636.100973—dc23
LC record available at https://lccn.loc.gov/2017020796

BRITISH LIBRARY CATALOGUING DATA ARE AVAILABLE

ISBN (print) 978-1-4766-6713-3
ISBN (ebook) 978-1-4766-2837-0

© 2017 Jonathan V. Levin. All rights reserved

No part of this book may be reproduced or transmitted in any form or by any means, electronic or mechanical, including photocopying or recording, or by any information storage and retrieval system, without permission in writing from the publisher.

Front cover: Street scene in Merna, Custer County, Nebraska (Library of Congress)

Printed in the United States of America

McFarland & Company, Inc., Publishers
 Box 611, Jefferson, North Carolina 28640
 www.mcfarlandpub.com

To my grandchildren
Benjamin, Natan, Talia, and Esther

Table of Contents

Preface — 1

Introduction — 3

One: America's Horses Go to War — 11

Two: What Did You Do in the War, Dobbin? — 28

Three: On the American Road — 63

Four: On the Farm — 103

Five: On the Range — 123

Six: Recreation — 131

Seven: Racing — 142

Eight: Polo — 151

Nine: Unwanted Horses — 174

Conclusion — 185

Appendix (Tables 1–10) — 187

Chapter Notes — 199

Bibliography — 217

Index — 231

Preface

I recall that when I was a boy playing on the street in New York, our game had to be interrupted every little while to let a horse and wagon go by—milk wagon, iceman, vegetable man, or old clothes man. We took it for granted and resumed our game, usually punch ball or stick ball, after its passing.

Some few years ago, I became curious about what had happened to all those horses. Where had all the horses gone?

No one I spoke to had a satisfactory answer. Nor could I find one in other sources I looked into. This led me further into the subject. What had the horses done and how had they been replaced? I found the subject engrossing and full of surprises. It drew me back in time to when and how the horses had become involved in the functions they had come to carry out, and into the origins of the technologies that came to replace them.

I became convinced that it is really one long, diverse story and an important one, dipping into military history and the different sectors of the civilian economy that make the country work. Having put together the pieces from sources very distant from each other, I am pleased to present it as one story, tying together the many fragmented answers to the question of what happened to the horses.

I am grateful for the assistance I received from the several libraries I inhabited, primarily the Department of Agriculture Library, which introduced me to *The Breeder's Gazette, the Yearbook of Agriculture,* and the series of Agriculture Department studies and statistics that kept track of the horses until they were too few to be counted separately from the mules. My thanks are due also to the Library of Congress, to the library of the Census Bureau, and to the staff of the United States Polo Association. I am grateful to Mark Nerenberg for the good advice on cable cars and fire horses and his information on the fire horse memorial. I take pleasure in thanking my friend the Honorable Norbert Ehrenfreund for the valuable contribution on his experience in the twilight years of Army horses. I should like to express my appreciation to Carin Millman for her careful comments on the manuscript, to Anne Gordon, who pointed out to me that this was the first account of changing technology from the point of view of the horse, and to Xingchi Wang for reformulating the tables. I am grateful to my son Daniel for his valuable help with the computer.

    I wish to thank Houghton Mifflin Publishing Company, which reserves all rights, for permission to publish excerpts from *Memoirs of My Service in the World War, 1917–1918,* by George C. Marshall, copyright 1976 by Molly B. Winn. I also thank Peter Burford of Burford Books for permission to publish excerpts from *Over There,* by Frank Freidel; to Penguin Random House UK and New York Review Books for permission to publish material from "Akenfield: Portrait of an English Village," by Ronald Blyth, copyright 1969, 1999, included in *The Book of Horses,* published by William Morrow & Co.; to the Germans from Russia Heritage Collection, North Dakota State University Libraries, Fargo, www.ndsu/grhc, for permission to publish material including the horse sweep; and to Lyn Macdonald for permission to draw upon *1914.* I am indebted to the authors and officials whose writings and reports helped me understand and bring together the many parts of the story. My thanks are due finally to my wife and family for tolerating my isolation and distraction for the thirteen years it took me to put the book to bed.

Introduction

Over the past century technology has transformed the American economy. An important part of this transformation has been the disappearance of the working horses. Horses were an important working part of the American economy. Their disappearance is significant in itself and as a reflection of the technological changes that affected the whole of the economy. This book examines each of the American horses' careers and the particular technologies affecting them. In a sense, it examines the history of technological change from the horses' point of view.

The book opens with a description of the ubiquitous presence of horses on the scene in 1915, the point at which the American horse population reached its peak along with the wide-ranging human involvement in their maintenance and use, which raises the question: Where have all the horses gone?

The first place they went was to war, as the Allies purchased almost a million American horses and shipped them across the submarine infested Atlantic to World War I. There, in a foretaste of the century ahead, technological advances prevented the horses from carrying out the functions for which they had been recruited. Nineteenth century advances in firepower, machine guns, and barbed wire produced an overwhelming predominance of defense that forced the armies into the stalemate warfare of the trenches, which stretched in two opposing lines for 475 miles from the Swiss border to the North Sea. Here the horses' cavalry functions could not be carried out. What the horses were called upon to do, how the American forces entering the war coped with their inability to obtain sufficient horses, and the fate of the American horses when the war ended makes an interesting, and somewhat surprising, story. The Army's continued recruitment of horses in the interwar period, and the account of one participant in the twilight of the horses' use at the beginning of World War II brings that chapter of military horses to a close.

In civilian life, on the road, the important task of people-moving fell to the horses. Historically this function had been affected by technological changes in the wheel—solid wood, then spoked, and iron-rimmed; the pavement—Roman, cobblestone, macadam, asphalt, cement, and steel-rail; and the vehicle the horse had to pull—cart, stage coach, omnibus, horse car, and carriage. Hastening efforts to find a replacement for the horses was the epidemic of equine influenza—the epizootic—which came down from Canada in October 1872, and incapacitated horses throughout the United States, Mexico, Central America and the Caribbean. In New York, immigrants were hired to pull the horse cars. The first technological innovation to replace the horses was quick to appear. This was the cable car, made possible by the new open hearth process of steel-making facilitating the production of steel cables five miles long that could be placed in underground conduits and gripped to move vehicles on the surface. The first American cable car system was installed in San Francisco in 1876 to move the vehicles up its steep hills. By 1886 there were 59 cable car street railways in the U.S., totaling 360 miles in length.

Technology moved quickly, however, and the cable car boom was soon ended. With the discovery of electricity—the dynamo and the electric motor—earlier in the century, a number of partially successful efforts to adapt it for the movement of vehicles were undertaken. The first successful trolley car line was installed in Richmond, Virginia, in 1888, was soon adopted by Boston, and spread rapidly to other cities. By 1902, 97 percent of U.S. street car trackage was electrified, and the force of 100,000 animals that had powered the horse cars in 1886 was reduced to fewer than 9,000.

That left private carriages, which the self-propelled internal-combustion engine vehicles hustled off the streets and highways beginning in the 1890s. Moving freight remained a horse-and-wagon function a little longer, as it took the short hauls in denser city traffic, while the competing trucks took on the longer hauls away from dense traffic with greater speed. The horse and wagon survived into the 1940s, moving the retail trade for ice, milk, fruit and vegetables, and the junk man. Though horse advocates, organized as a horse publicity organization in 1919, urged governments building highways with pavement too slick for horses to leave a pathway alongside for the slower horses, the horses' road career was ending.

One interesting earlier example of the interaction between road horses and technology was the sixty-year episode of the fire horses. With the invention of the first successful steam fire engine in 1852, firemen who had been pulling the lighter hand pumps had to call in the horses. The horses were moved into the bottom floor of the fire houses, had the harness lowered onto them seconds after an alarm sounded, and went charging through the street, the clanging, smoking engine behind them, to arrive at the fire scene within minutes. All that was to end with the invention of the motorized fire engine around 1900. Sent off with departure ceremonies in some cities, the horses had to go.

On the Farm

On the farm, still the major component of the American economy, the horses were fully occupied, with a seemingly promising career. Reviewing the nature and long history of farming, the book notes that the horse came late to farming, having awaited invention of a harness that did not choke it. Then, thanks to the shift to gunpowder, which released the large knight-bearing horse for plowing, the horse became the star of farming in Europe and subsequently in America. In eighteenth century Britain and then in the nineteenth century U.S., a horse-led agricultural revolution greatly increased output and released manpower for application elsewhere, as one new horse-drawn implement after another increased the flow of produce. Then came the McCormick reaper, with a revolving reel pressing wheat stalks against a cutting blade. The expanded flow of wheat coming from the field brought invention of the mechanical thresher. Its need for rotary power sent the horse into a merry-go-round-like horse sweep, moving in a circle instead of the straight line to which it had been accustomed. When that did not suffice, steam was drafted. The steam engine, rolled out on a platform from farm to farm, took over from horses the provision of rotary power for the seasonally busy thresher teams. The horses were not idle, though. They hauled the steam engine until it was able to self-propel and steer—and even then ran hitched in front of the engine so as not to frighten other horses—and they had to bring to the steam engine the large volume of fuel and water it needed to operate.

By 1890, the new horse-drawn technology and then the steam engine had brought an immense economizing in human labor. From then on, however, technology proceeded to work the farm horse out of a job. The steam plow, despite its great weight, gained wide usage, 70,000 by 1910, after which it was soon replaced by the lighter, internal combustion engine tractor. Though focused on plowing, tractor manufacturers gradually devised improvements that took over other functions that horses performed on the farm. Trucks came along to take on the off-farm hauling functions. Farmers purchased tractors not only to replace horses, but to reduce their need for hired labor, whose wages had risen for several causes, among them their reduced availability following the 1920s immigration laws. The labor saving and the reduced need to care for horses meant also a reduced need for children, so that the size of farm families declined. The number of horses on the farm declined by 90 percent between 1910 and 1974; the number of people on the farm by 70 percent. Around the farms, the small towns that had provided them with goods and services declined as well. The result was a partially depopulated countryside, with the younger people leaving for work in the cities, so that the small towns were left with an older population, ironically paralleling the aging population of farm horses that the reduced pace of horse breeding had produced. An interesting conclusion to the story of technology and the farm horse.

On the Range

To the west, another horse career arose, blossomed, and diminished in the wake of technological change. Transplanted from the western edge of Europe, to which spreading agriculture had pressed it, horse-mounted cattle herding was practiced in the Caribbean with the progeny of cattle Columbus had transported, and was carried to Florida, Mexico and its northern Texan and Californian extensions. The escaped cattle, five million strong, and the wild, mustang descendants of conquistadors' horses, were gathered by Texans beginning in the 1860s and trailed north to the new railheads for shipment east to market. The cowboy, or vaquero, culture shaped the horse-led cattle industry first on the open range and then on the ranches and leased public lands grazing areas.

Changes challenging the horse's role came first with the barbed wire fencing, which reduced the need for far-ranging round-ups, then with the ranch pickup and cattle trailer, which could move horses and cattle to and from the field, and finally with the feedlots, which took the cattle off the range at a young age and brought them more rapidly to maturity with grains now raised more cheaply on land no longer needed to feed the diminished national horse population. The surviving ranch culture focused on cow-and-calf ranching, raising the calf for about eight months before weaning, sending it to a backgrounding facility preparing it for bunk feeding, and then to the feedlot to live for eighteen to twenty months, in contrast to the four or five years under the previous regime. The result was fewer cattle and fewer horses needed for duty on the ranch.

Recreation

As each of the horses' careers affected by technological change faded away, a new set of career opportunities appeared, like a mirage, on the horizon. The array of advancing technologies that had eliminated the horses' careers had operated also on the rest of the economy. Freed from many of their time-consuming duties, people filled their new free time with leisure and recreation, areas in which horses could contribute. Some activities which had previously been work were now recast as play. With the west popularized, perhaps romanticized, by dime novels, Wild West shows and movies, people flocked to dude ranches, rodeos, and western horse shows. Rodeo contestants competed in time trials for staying on a bucking bronco, and, in partnership with their horse, cutting a cow from the herd, and lassoing and tying up a calf. Horse lovers groomed and showed their animals in the ubiquitous weekend horse shows in the western or English hunting traditions. Millions enjoyed pleasure riding on the trail and grooming their horses for relaxation at home or at the neighborhood training barn. Perhaps most striking on the new leisure horse scene, outside of the rodeos, was the prevalence of females, almost 90 percent of riders and horse owners.

Some of the horses' roles in the new leisure age were a continuation of previous sporting activity. Horse racing, particularly by thoroughbreds, continued its dependence on on-track and then off-track betting, but faced new problems with competition from other forms of gambling and entertainment and the drug culture threatening other high-pressure sports. The all-embracing culture surrounding horse racing was reflected in the statistics-filled *Daily Racing Form* and the long training regime that made a thoroughbred into a racehorse.

Another long-standing horse sport, polo, faced the challenge of expanding from its origin as an exclusive elite sport. The cost of maintaining multiple ponies for the break-neck speed play on the huge pitch raised questions as to whether the sport could be sustained through the long, sometime economically depressed, years from its 1880 introduction into the U.S. Its survival to its more recent expansion was probably attributable in part to Army participation up to World War II and to its role as a varsity sport in eastern and western universities, with ROTC support in many cases.

With attitudes shifting toward viewing the horse not as a beast of burden but as an athletic teammate or social companion, there emerged in the post–World War II era concern over treatment of the mustangs, wild horses subsisting on mostly public western lands. After treatment as wildlife open to hunting and removal to clear grazing land for domestic stock in the early years, their removal for slaughter raised increasing opposition later in the century. This led Congress to mandate their preservation by the Bureau of Land Management on the public lands they inhabited, in the Wild Free-Roaming Horse and Burro Act of 1971. Controversy did not stop, however, as the mustang population, undisturbed by any predator other than man, grew beyond the land's holding power. As a result, pending more effective population control efforts, and despite a successful adoption program, the majority of mustangs were kept in BLM holding areas under contract with servicing ranchers.

Debate persisted on whether the wild horses were feral or escaped from human ownership, which might have had some influence on their legal status. Meanwhile wild horse populations continued to inhabit western public and Indian lands and, in smaller numbers, scattered public lands on the barrier islands and outer reefs of the Atlantic Coast. Facing the Atlantic, across which their originating ancestors came and others were taken to war, never to return, these horses form perhaps a footnote to the long history of horses that were an integral part of the American economy, interacting with each technological advance, until their careers faded away as the economy was transformed by technological advances

Yet hardly a century has passed since the American horse population peaked at 25 million; in 1915, the mule population, primarily in the rural South, approaching its 1925 peak of 6 million. In the course of the nineteenth century, which has been called the golden age of the horse,[1] American horses helped produce fundamental changes in both the farm and the city. Horses powered the mechanization of agriculture with the seed-drill, the reaper, the harvester, the header, the binder, and the thresher.[2] In the city, the horse-drawn omnibus, followed by the rail-borne horse car, made it possible for people to commute to work so that separate residential districts could develop, apart from commercial, industrial, and retail districts.[3]

While horses were indispensable for the movement of people and freight, they were in turn dependent upon a vast complex of human resources. Urban stables, some five stories high, occupied valuable city real estate. Besides the teamster to move the team, a hostler, or groom, was needed to care for the horses, along with farriers, blacksmiths, veterinarians, wheelwrights, carriage painters, draymen, livery men, makers of saddles, harnesses, whips, blankets and other horse accouterments, as well as manure transporters, and rendering workers. To feed the city horses, hay and oats were raised in a grain belt around each city, requiring roughly four acres to produce forage for each horse. Besides the farmers who raise the crops, a network of hay and grain dealers was needed to transport the bulky forage and market it in the city. Though horses provided the country with a transportation system sustained by a renewable source of energy, half the country's crops were raised to feed its animals.

Overarching all this activity was the horse trade itself, the moving of the thousands of horses from the four-and-a-half-million farms where they were raised. Roughly one-tenth were sent to cities, with the rest going to industrial or other users. Though they move by the thousands, each horse was sold only after examination of its individual qualities and condition. Some horses, exhausted from pounding city pavements, and perhaps fully depreciated by large-scale city users, were returned to the country for farm labor. Others did not survive their city labor and were claimed by the horse disposal services for rendering plants and hides processing.

On the edge of New York City, along the shore of Dead Horse Bay, stood the Barren Island horse-rendering plant, with a smokestack belching an acrid plume that raised complaints miles away.[4] Heavily engaged also were public sanitation services. In New York City alone, for example, horses contributed 500,000 pounds of manure and 45,000 gallons of urine each day.[5]

But all this was not to last. Over the previous century one after another of the horse's functions had been taken over by other providers. Steam-driven railroads had replaced the stagecoach, the covered wagon, and the freight wagon. Horse-borne rapid communication, as embodied by the short-lived pony express, launched on April 3, 1860, was replaced by the telegraph as the first telegram to California was transmitted on October 24, 1861.[6] Electricity, by 1890, replaced the horse car and cable car with the trolley car.[7] Finally, invention of the internal combustion engine in the late nineteenth century and its incorporation in automobiles, trucks and tractors over the past decade (the Model T Ford in 1908), now posed the greatest challenge to the horse's transportation function.[8]

Between 1910 and 1930 the number of horses on U.S. city streets shrank by 90 percent, from three million (3,182,789) to 300,000, taking with it the vast infrastructure of supporting services. On U.S. farms, from its 1915 peak of 21,421,000 the number of horses fell by half (to 10,444,000) in 1940, and by half again (to 5,548,000) by 1950.

In four areas, elements already at work in 1915 were reversing the growth of the American horse population: a distant battlefield, the road, the farm, and the range. Each area was different from the others. What linked them together was the role of the horse and an advancing technology displacing it. In what follows each of these is examined in turn to answer the questions:

Where have all the horses gone?
Where have all these changes come from?
How have all these new technologies developed, affecting the role of the horse?

One

America's Horses Go to War

The first place they went was to war, the First World War, 1914–1918. On June 28, 1914, the Crown Prince of Austria was assassinated in the then Austrian city of Sarajevo, near the Serbian border. Austria accused Serbia of instigating the crime and, after an unsatisfactory exchange of notes, declared war on Serbia on July 28, 1914. Reflecting their alliance commitments, Germany declared war on Russia August 2 and on France August 3. On August 4, Great Britain declared war on Germany when it became evident that Germany's attack on France was advancing through Belgium and violating her treaty regarding Belgian neutrality. Soon, Great Britain, France, Russia, Belgium, Italy, and Serbia, the Allies, faced Germany, Austria, and Turkey, the Central Powers.[1] The impact on American horses was not long in coming.

Previous wars had left their impact on the American horse population. During the Civil War the Federal Government bought over 800,000 horses,[2] during 1864 requiring more than 500 horses a day to replace losses.[3] The depleted supply kept prices firm until the early 1870s.[4] With the Spanish-American War, 1898, and the Boer War, 1899–1902, during which the British Government bought over 100,000 horses in the U.S.,[5] and lost 350,000 dead out of the 520,000 remounts supplied in South Africa,[6]

> buyers began to scour the country for cavalry mounts. Nearly all of these came from the West, and from that time on a buying movement started that finally swept the ranges bare of horses.... The West that for years sent branded horses by the thousands to the East and Middle West is now [1919] devoid of them, and never again will contribute them in numbers as of old.[7]

In the years before the outbreak of the World War there were 2 million horses in the United Kingdom, 3.2 million in France, 1 million in Italy, 4.5 million in Germany and 1.8 million in Austria. The United States and European Russia (including Poland), in contrast, had about 23 million horses each.[8] Each of the continental powers had built national breeding and army remount establishments—Austria's dating back almost a century, France with nine remount depots, three in Algeria, Germany with a national bureau, and England "boarding out" government horses maintained by citizens for their work. But with the coming of the World War the horses supplied by these programs proved inadequate.[9]

Drafting British Horses

The coming of the war and its impact on horses emerges in reports sent to the *Breeder's Gazette*, the American weekly devoted to livestock developments. As war loomed in Europe in the summer of 1914, a British correspondent wrote: American visitors "hit England just at the right time to observe a nation making ready for war."

He wrote that American visitors would witness remount officers and veterinary surgeons moving through the show yards, the hunter rings, the Shire horse stalls, street corner cab ranks, and outside railway stations, sifting the wheat from the chaff and dispatching their selections to the seat of war. Particularly hard hit were the owners of pure bred stock horses. In one case, a hunting friend of his had to sacrifice three of his best horses, for which he usually paid $1,500 to $2,000 apiece, for $250 each. Ten of the Prince of Wales' polo ponies were commandeered, and the Household cavalry received six horses from the Princess Royal.[10]

Another report stated:

> In England's recent preparations for war no sight was more interesting to the visitor during the first week of hurried mobilization than the commandeering of horses in the city streets. An officer charged with this duty, bearing a certain number of orders for horses, rode through the streets, and when a horse of the proper size, build and color was found a halt was ordered, the driver being asked to unhitch in the name of the Royal Service. After a hurried examination of the horse, which was usually a satisfactory one, the Government's brand of a broad arrow was burned on the animal's hoof, and the owner's name and address was taken, with the assurance of a subsequent settlement, if the Government's veterinarian accepted the horse. Without further ado the horse thus taken was then the property of the Government, and the army officer rode away, leaving the former owner standing on the curbstone...."[11]

Buying American Horses

The impact on American horses was soon to appear. The outbreak of the World War in August 1914 came upon a U.S. horse market hungry for demand. Col. John S. Cooper, in a communication to *The Breeder's Gazette* in December 1915, recalled a year later that though the first half of 1914 witnessed a particularly good trade in all sorts of horses, "...by the end of July last year the horse business was as dead as the proverbial doornail...." It continued to deteriorate through the end of August, city teamsters, for lack of work, sacrificing their horses regardless of loss.

Then came news of British buying. Col. Cooper recalled:

> On the last Sunday of that month—the Sunday during the Iowa State Fair—I received a long telegram from "Jimmie" Johnstone, who was at the big Des Moines show, telling me that the British government had placed orders for cavalry and artillery horses and that the Guyton-Harrington federation, which had supplied Great Britain many thousands of horses and mules during the Boer rebellion, once more had had the call. That was the first word we had of the new move. Buying had begun the day before (Saturday) at Creston, Ia., and never had the market been in a more disorganized condition. During the first few days horses of equal merit would often be bought $40, $50 or even more apart, according to the anxiety or necessity of the holder to sell. Never was a more magnificent opportunity offered to any big buyer to purchase horses of the type required well within their real value.

Shortly thereafter, he recalled, came news that the French government had begun buying in the south, reportedly under a tentative agreement that Great Britain purchase in the north and ship through North Atlantic seaboard ports while the French operate in the south and west and ship through Gulf of Mexico. This arrangement was soon abandoned, however, after one load of horses put aboard in New Orleans was sunk by enemy cruisers and two boats coming in to load were burned.

The two countries followed different purchase practices. The British, buying horses on "orders" they could abrogate on two weeks' notice, would take delivery on acceptance and arrange their own transportation. The French purchased by contract for delivery of the horses at some designated "home" port.[12]

Soon other nations' agents were buying horses in the United States. Near the Fort Worth stockyards one reporter for the *North Fort Worth News* could often count among the buyers as many as fifteen uniforms from as many nations.[13]

Beginning in September 1914, U.S. horse exports rose rapidly, going from 804 in August to 7,146 in September, 12,091 in October, 28,071 in November and 30,687 in December. They reached a peak of 47,380 in July 1915 and did not fall below 18,000 a month till July 1917.[14]

In the four years ending June 30, 1918, U.S. horse exports rose from 111,456 in the previous four years to 1,101,332, with 67 percent, or 734,311 horses going to the United Kingdom and France. Over the same period U.S. exports of mules expanded from 15,213 in the previous four years to

343,271, with some 57 percent, or 197,215, going to the United Kingdom alone.[15]

Even before they reached the ports and became exports, however, about 10 percent of the horses purchased by the British died, mostly of influenza and shipping fever. The French and Italian losses were even greater.[16] In addition, purchased horses encountered various mishaps. In June 1915, 5,000 horses intended for the Allies were stampeded by a storm in Alton, Illinois.[17] In December 1915, a consignment of 533 animals for the French Government drowned in the Hudson River when the barge *Virginia* sank. Delays in raising the barge and ascertaining the cause enabled possible conspirators to escape.[18]

Hostile action at sea included both sabotage and submarine losses. In November 1914, the horse shipment aboard the S.S. Rembrandt was reported burned by German spies.[19] In March 1916, barbed steel "oats" were placed in shipments for Europe and a German plot was suspected.[20] Thousands of horses were lost on transports torpedoed by submarines. In 1917, for example, the Georgic was sunk with 1,200 horses aboard.[21]

Bacterial Sabotage

Damage came also from another source. Unknown at the time and for a dozen years thereafter, was an episode of bacterial sabotage aimed at the horses and mules purchased by the British and French. In early October 1915, 31-year-old Dr. Anton Casimir Dilger, Virginia-born but educated in Germany, arrived in the U.S. with four glass vials of anthrax and glanders bacilli. They were to be used for infecting American horses and mules on their way to Germany's French and British enemies in the war.

Son of a German-American Civil War hero, Anton Dilger was raised on the family's Greenfield Farm in Front Royal, Virginia, a part of which was sold in 1911 to become part of a U.S. Army Remount Depot. At ten, he went to live with his sister and brother-in-law in Mannheim, Germany. He attended Heidelberg University Medical School, where his medical thesis was entitled: "Concerning *In Vitro* Tissue Cultures: With Special Consideration of the Tissues of Adult Animals." An expert on the growth of bacteria, he put this skill to work in the basement of a house he rented in the Chevy Chase section of Washington, D.C., six miles from the White House. There he set up a laboratory growing anthrax and glanders bacilli.

To distribute the material, he was assisted by Captain Frederick Hensch of Norddeutsch Lloyd's Neckar steamship, tied up in Baltimore harbor, who operated under sabotage paymaster Paul Hilken. Hensch carried the anthrax and glanders vials from Chevy Chase and distributed them to stevedores recruited by stevedore foreman Eddie Felton to be administered to horses and mules in British and French animal corrals at ports up and down the U.S. East Coast. At the British Remount Service's massive Newport News corrals, for example, stevedore John Grant, working for Felton, in late December 1915, injected horses and mules for several hours and poured the remaining liquid into the animals' water basins and feed troughs. Signs of glanders appeared in horses within a week after infection.

Operation of the Chevy Chase laboratory continued for about nine months. It was under Dr. Dilger's supervision until his departure in late January 1916, and was operated by his brother Carl and fellow German-American Fred Herrmann until August 1916, when alarm raised by the July 30, 1916, Black Tom explosion in New Jersey brought the decision to close "Tony's Lab." Herrmann helped another associate set up a germ laboratory in St. Louis, site of the Midwest stockyards, but operations were shut down in November when the cold killed the cultures.

Anton Dilger went on to become the Prussian War Ministry's principal spy in Mexico, under the alias Dr. Albert Delmar, before departing for Spain where, under the alias Alberto Donde, he died in the influenza epidemic in a Madrid hospital on October 17, 1918.

It was a dozen years before the anthrax and glanders sabotage operation emerged from secrecy in testimony by Hilken, Herrmann, and stevedores Hensch had hired. They testified before the German-American Mixed Claims Commission settling disputes over German responsibility for wartime damage, most notably for the Black Tom explosion. No one connected with the biological sabotage was ever punished, at least in North America, as the statute of limitations had run out and the nature of any crime was unclear, the U.S. not having been at war at the time.[22]

Getting the Horses to Europe

With the heavy volume of French and British purchases and the effects of submarine warfare, a limiting factor in horse and mule exports became the shortage of ocean transport. One portrait of a wartime horse transport is available in an account written by a veterinarian, W.J. Ratigan, who participated in one such horse transport, which was published in *The Breeder's Gazette* of August 5, 1915.

Arriving in Galveston, Texas, with U.S. troops following their evacuation of Vera Cruz, Mexico, W.J. Ratigan found a great deal of talk of the European war. Emissaries from various countries were in the city buying

American horses and shipping them to Europe through the port. Going to New Orleans, from where the French and British were exporting horses, he met a Londoner who was financing French horse purchases and had train loads of horses coming in from Memphis. He agreed to take charge of the arriving 1,200 horses and he made several trips to the French consul "marked by a great demonstration of stealth and a painful sense of quiet."

Security for departure was intense. Crewmen had to carry passes signed by the captain, two watchmen were on duty day and night, and supplies were watched from the time they left the warehouse till they were placed on the ship.

The horse transport was the Rembrandt of Liverpool. On its previous trip from Baltimore it had started to burn at sea on its third night out and had to head back to Newport News to extinguish the fire. With 500 animals dead, a number from pneumonia due to the smoke, the ship had gone back out to sea to cast the dead horses overboard. Ship's officers were convinced of the fire's incendiary origin and were aware the horses were being poisoned the first day out, which explained the security in New Orleans.

The Rembrandt left New Orleans with the veterinarian, a physician, eighty-odd hostellers, and three foremen of hostellers aboard, besides the regular crew. It cost $71 a head to carry the horses from New Orleans to France, each horse having cost about $200, with insurance issued by Lloyds of London. Like other large horse transports, the Rembrant carried extra horses by means of its deck load. With a shed built all round the top. Each stall, both within the ship and on deck, could hold one standing horse, with not enough room to lie down. If a horse fell, exhausted, the front of the stall was unbolted and the horse dragged out.

Though some horses had arrived in New Orleans with influenza or pink eye, they were all taken aboard, and by the second week out it had spread to the whole load. Keeping to the South Atlantic as long as possible because of the sick horses, they were fortunate to lose only fifty-three. Cast overboard, the horses sank rapidly. Only hay was fed the first week out, but grain was added thereafter when the ship struck rough weather, and started to roll, which gave the horses exercise, facilitating their digestion.

For security the ship carried two wireless men, who only listened and did not transmit, and all lights were covered at night. They were convoyed at time by a French cruiser. At one point, close to France, they encountered an English battleship fleet, including many super dreadnaughts. At St. Nazaire harbor, arriving before the four o'clock curfew, they lay in the harbor for two days awaiting a dock, so that the horses were on the water for a total of 23 days. The marine police cutter that greeted the ship was manned by old men, there being a great absence of young men, with all kinds of manual work, including running the street cars, performed by women.

German prisoners readied the bridges for unloading the horses, but were not allowed close to the ships. French soldiers led the horses off the ship and turned them over to the German prisoners. The horses joined the 7,000 horses already in the port that were recent arrivals.

Several times as the horses were unloaded, the French commandant of cavalry observing their arrival, turned to the veterinarian, W.J. Ratigan, and declared: "Your horses are beautiful."[23]

To the north, British forces had already moved, with their horses, across the English Channel to France. Though this was a far shorter crossing than the trip across the Atlantic, it was not without incident. While officials in mid–August 1914, reported that the British Expeditionary Force had been safely landed in France with no casualties, Lyn Macdonald's book entitled *1914* points out that this was not the case with the horses.

Though the British papers repeated the official report that the British Expeditionary Force had crossed the Channel with no casualties, this was not the case with the horses, some of whom, unboxed, had died of heart attacks. Hoisted from the deep holds by means of slings under their bellies, they experience vertigo and terror as they swung high above the deck, quivering and screaming, before being lowered onto the cobblestone at the quayside. One groom, who, in his concern for his charges, had spent the passage in the dank and fetid hold below the water line, with the horses tightly tethered, swaying with the ship, stamping, sweating, and trying to keep their footing. As the ship docked in France, he came up on deck but couldn't continue with the troop.[24]

British officials reported that during the war 411,473 horses and 205,231 mules were shipped from America to the United Kingdom, besides 7,601 horses and 64,224 mules shipped from America directly to France. Those lost by sickness at sea were 1.18 percent of the horses and .89 percent of the mules. Over two-thirds of the horses shipped to France from the United Kingdom were draft animals. The highest total of animals in France with the British armies was reached in June 1917 at 460,000.[25]

The massive exit of American horses abroad was not without objection. Addressing the August 1916 meeting of the American Veterinary Medical Association in Detroit, Veterinarian David E. Buckingham declared:

> Imagine my feelings as I saw beautiful 1300 to 1600 pound half-grade and three-quarter bred Percheron mares going to the Italian Army at $50 per head more than we are paying for little 14.2 900 pound militia cavalry horses according to class. And these grand animals are leaving the country—they are the very fountain and source of our future supply. ... every mare exported averages three colts less on

Remount station corrals, Camp Kearny, California, December 1917—100,000 head of stock (Library of Congress).

American farms and now that so many hundreds of thousands are gone we shall need every first class brood mare to replenish our stock.

Our government should stop the exportation of mares for whatever purpose on account of economic and agricultural reasons.[26]

The U.S. Enters the War

Then the U.S. entered the war. On April 6, 1917, after growing dissatisfaction over loss of American lives as the result of Germany's unrestricted submarine warfare, the United States declared war against the Imperial German Government.[27] Like the European powers that had entered the war almost three years earlier, the United States faced the challenge of mobilizing men, horses, and materials. In Germany, every male 17 and older had been eligible for conscription well before the start of the war, and in France three-year service had been required of men ages 20 to 45. In England, however, there had been no draft and the small, professional regular army was virtually destroyed in the first four months of the war. This was succeeded by the all-volunteer "New Army" or "Kitchener's Army" which reached three million men before the first conscription bill was enacted on January 6, 1916, a full 16 months after England's entry into the war.[28]

Unlike England, which immediately drafted horses but, for 16 months, not men, the United States did not draft horses, but immediately drafted men. In the United States, just three weeks after its entry into the war, on April 28, 1917, a selective service law for the conscription of men between the ages of 20 and 30, both inclusive, was passed.[29] In 1914 the United States had a regular army of only 127,588 and a national guard of 181,620. By the end of World War I 2,149,000 draftees and 198,000 volunteers had served in the Army.[30]

Buying Army Horses

On May 12 and June 17, 1917, Congress appropriated $53,000,000 for the purchase of about 250,000 horses and mules.[31] To carry out the extensive inspection and purchasing program this required, the Army greatly expanded its network of remount stations. The United States was divided into four zones, with offices for the Central Purchasing Zone in Kansas City, Missouri, the Northern at Fort Keogh, Montana, the Southern at Fort Reno, Darlington, Oklahoma, and the Eastern at Fort Royal, Virginia.[32] In May 1917, the creation of 39 auxiliary remount depots was authorized, one for each Army, National Guard, and Regular Army division, along with animal embarkation depots and field remount depots with a capacity of 5,000 animals each.[33] At each auxiliary remount depot and animal embarkation depot there were schools for horseshoers, teamsters, packers, saddlers, and stable sergeants, with instruction covering four months for horseshoers and two months for packers and teamsters.

In establishing auxiliary remount depots, the Army drew on its experience in the management of horses and mules in the 1916–1917 Punitive Expedition into Mexico in pursuit of Francisco (Pancho) Villa following his raids into the U.S. In March 1916, two auxiliary remount depots had been established to accommodate the 55,000 animals the Army was authorized to purchase.[34] That experience had demonstrated the need to condition the animals before issue to troops. When shipped from point of purchase to destination, an estimated 90 percent of all animals had contracted shipping fever or influenza at the stockyards and stock pens where they had been unloaded to comply with the law requiring release for feed and water every 28 hours.

Shipped direct to the using organizations a considerable number had died. To receive animals purchased and shipped, care for them properly and condition them prior to their issue to troops, the network of remount depots was established in the U.S. and later in France. The organization and training of field remount depots, later called remount squadrons, for overseas duty was carried out at Camp Joseph E. Johnson in Florida. Each squadron consisted of four Quartermaster Corps officers, one medical officer, I veterinary officer, 150 Quartermaster Corps, 4 Medical Corps, and 3 Veterinary Corps enlisted men.[35]

For the inspection and purchase of animals for the war, quartermasters in each zone appointed purchasing boards headed by men who had owned, bred and shown horses, usually wealthy men, including in one purchasing zone, for example, half a dozen millionaires. Purchasing boards consisted of six men: the purchasing officer, usually a captain, two assistants from the new veterinary corps, two civilian clerks, and a messenger. The record for each animal included its age, sex, distinguishing marks, height, weight and class. Each animal was branded with the letters U.S. on the left front shoulder, and beneath it either C for cavalry, A for artillery, or, in the case of heavy siege gun horses, another A on the hip. Later in the war the number of the man in charge of the inspection board was also branded.[36]

The Remount Service was greatly expanded. From one officer and four men in Washington and a few purchasing agents at its remount depots at the time of U.S. entry into the war, it grew to 300 officers and 11,000 enlisted men by February 1918. The veterinary force was increased from 64 officers and enlisted men to 1,000 officers and 12,000 men.[37]

Besides putting in place the physical and administrative infrastructure for the intake of horses, the Army had to decide, if it was not to conscript horses, how it would purchase them. Could the sudden great increase be accommodated by existing purchase methods? Before entering the war, the Army had purchased horses in large lots from dealers submitting bids in an auction. Advertisements had been inserted in newspapers and livestock journals and announcements had been sent to interested breeders and dealers inviting bids for the sale to the Army of horses meeting certain specifications. A contractor successful in the competitive auction had to arrange for the buying and shipping of at least 300 animals to a place of inspection, usually designated by the contractor, where he was responsible for receiving, stabling, and sheltering the animals until the date of inspection.[38]

A minor flow of horses had come from the system of breeding horses conducted by the Bureau of Animal Industry of the Department of Agriculture. It furnished the services of a government stallion to suitable mares owned by farmers and breeders who contracted to sell the resulting colt to the government at a set price when it was three years old. If they chose to keep the colt, the owners paid a service fee of $25. If the foal died or the government chose not to purchase it, no service fee was charged. While holding promise for future supply, if expanded, this source of army horses was still minor.[39]

To meet the suddenly expanded needs of the war while engaging the interests and cooperation of potential suppliers, clearly some changes in purchase procedures would have to be made. Suggestions for how this was to be done were not long in coming.

New Purchasing Procedures

Writing in *The Breeder's Gazette* of May 3, 1917, Wayne Dinsmore, secretary of the Percheron Society of America and a prominent member of the horse trade community, wrote that since the army had only 70,000 horses and mules, it would have to buy about 350,000 horses and mules during the next six months. He noted that no information had been released regarding how the purchase would be made, but stated that in the judgment of experienced horsemen the purchase of so many horses and mules in so short a period would best be accomplished by setting a definite price to be paid by the army for the different animals that would pass inspection for their respective classes, and by establishing ten or fifteen inspection points where horses and mules could be inspected. This would permit large and small dealers, or even farmers, to consign their horses directly to inspection points knowing what they would receive for them if they pass inspection. He saw no good reason why the producers of horses should not be permitted to sell them directly to the government, if they pass inspection, rather than being required to sell them through an intervening contractor. He hoped, in conclusion, that the army officials would decide on some such general plan.[40]

Three weeks later, another horseman, W.W. Anderson, of the Kentucky Experiment Station, wrote, similarly, that since the War Department would soon be in the market for army horses, the greatest benefit to farmers would be for the department to arrange to buy these horses directly from the breeders. If the farmer had to sell to a small dealer and he in turn to a larger one, who would then sell to the contractor, one of two things would be certain: either the department would have to pay $40 to $100 more than the horses were worth, or the farmer would have to sell his horses for $40 to $100 less than their value.[41]

By mid-summer[42] the Army was ready to put a new purchase policy into operation, moving, in effect, from a contract system to a system of open-market purchase. It invited

> Any responsible dealer, breeder, or farmer, who is capable of supplying the Government with one or more carloads of animals at a sanitary place, suitable for feeding, inspecting, branding, and loading them on cars, to furnish purchasing officers a list of the number of mature specification cavalry and riding horses, light artillery horses, heavy artillery horses for siege batteries, (6 to 10 years of age, none white, and up to 15 percent mares,) wheel mules, lead mules, or pack mules (5 to 10 years of age, without regard to sex) he is ready to supply at what price and place of delivery.[43]

To accommodate farmers and breeders with smaller numbers of horses, at least one purchasing board in each zone was to be reserved for the inspection of animals offered by farmers and breeders in not less than carload lots.[44] By reducing the minimum delivery to twenty animals (one carload) from 300, this opened the way for direct purchase from farmers, but left it to suppliers to offer their prices.

The pricing policy was again altered, however, in November 1917, when the Quartermaster-General announced a new plan under which a tentative minimum price was established for direct purchases from farmers $20 below the price the Government paid dealers. This, it was explained, recognized the dealer's extra expense of collecting, shipping to inspection points, financing and sustaining losses from accident, disease and rejection. It was also designed to obviate the competition between dealers and Government agents.[45]

Though the minimum purchase had been reduced from 300 to 20 horses, however, rejection rates of sometimes more than 50 percent often obliged farmers to cooperate with neighbors to meet the 20-horse limit, or in reality to become a contractor to assemble sufficient animals.[46]

The open purchase policy brought still other changes in the market. Writing on February 28, 1918, Lieut. George H. Conn reported that while the Government was securing the largest number of animals from the large markets, such as Chicago, St. Louis, Kansas City, Omaha and Sioux City, a large number of smaller dealers had taken small contracts to furnish from 50 to 200 head and were going to the country districts to buy their horses. The larger contractors usually had a number of buyers whom they sent all through the country to buy horses and mules for them. Other large contractors had nearly all their animals consigned to them by individuals who bought them at their own risk and held contracts giving them so much per head for every one that was accepted.

The Army, Lieut. Conn wrote, found it cost just as much to go out and inspect and accept one carload of animals as it would to inspect four or five carloads. Though it was the hope that small inspections would help the Army secure horses more rapidly, "in our experience," he wrote, "it has been a dismal failure." He suggested instead that "it might be good policy to make a minimum contract of 500 animals and then require the contractor to fill this number in not more than five inspections." The one advantage he cited in buying animals from private parties and small contractors was that with the avoidance of the large holding centers, where severe sanitation problems had arisen, the mortality among the purchased animals was much less.[47]

In the end, despite inspection problems with the various innovative arrangements which the open-market purchase system had stimulated, efforts to meet the Army's needs were successful. The Quartermaster-General's Report concluded: "This plan of purchase proved satisfactory in every way and was still in operation at the close of the War."[48] Between June 1917, and March 1, 1918, the Army purchased more than 300,000 horses and mules.[49] Open-market purchase innovations, mobile purchasing boards, and a wide network of remount depots had permitted the army to meet its suddenly massive needs, not without side-effects, however.

To meet one of the side-effects on farmers, in May 1918, the Quartermaster Department contracted for the sale of 3 million tons of manure from Army posts and cantonments to replace the absence of horses on the farm and farmers' wartime loss of commercial fertilizer, which was hindering crop production. This product from cavalry, artillery and transport horses and mules had previously been disposed of through burning.[50]

Getting Horses to the American Expeditionary Force

The purchased horses and mules served with the assembled draftees and volunteers training in Army camps in the United States. By mid-1918, however, a million men were moving to Europe. Could the mules and horses they had trained with accompany them?

Facing this issue, the Army could draw on its logistic experience in the management of horses and mules in the 1916–1917 Mexican border campaign, led by General John J. Pershing. General Pershing had served earlier in Cuba with the 10th Cavalry and was to command the American Expeditionary Force in France, with a full appreciation of the role of horses and mules.[51] The Mexican campaign, however, had not had to contend with overseas transport. This was to be the major obstacle to the employment of U.S. Army horses in Europe.

The unrestricted submarine warfare that had caused U.S. entry into the war posed a major obstacle to the movement of U.S. forces, their equipment and horses, to Europe. In the five months ending June 30, 1917, unrestricted German submarine warfare, begun in February 1917, had destroyed three and a quarter million tons of Allied shipping.[52] Though ship building increased, in 1917 as a whole twice as much tonnage was sunk as was built. As one analyst wrote, the accumulated deficit at the beginning of 1918 meant that even if the Allies had twice the tonnage they actually possessed they would still have been "far short of supplying Europe's needs and transporting the American army."[53] Increased ship building and the tightening of the convoy system with the aid of U.S. destroyers sent to British waters[54] succeeded in stanching the net shipping losses so that by June 30, 1918, the Admiralty could report to Commons that Allied and neutral tonnage was no worse than it had been at the beginning of 1918.[55]

In May 1917, soon after the April 6, 1917, U.S. entry into the war, the Allies dispatched a special mission to America, the British sending General Bridges and Lord Balfour, the French sending Marshal Joffre and M. Viviani. They came to say the Allies needed material, supplies, and gold, but mostly men.[56] Marshal Joffre made a special request that a combat division be sent at once to Europe "as visual evidence of the American purpose to participate actively in the war."[57] On June 15, 1917, the French Government cabled its military attaché in Washington to make the War Department a concrete offer of enough animals to equip the First Division to go overseas, 4,850 horses and 2,100 mules.[58]

At the time of its entry into the war, the U.S. had no military organization higher than its regiments, and they were scattered throughout the country. There was no organized division that could be sent overseas prepared to take the field. So, a division was assembled of regular regiments, transferred officers, men and recruits to reach the required strength. Though it was clear to all commanders that the division could not be actively employed for some months, it was sent to France in June 1917. The first U.S. troops were dispatched directly from along the Mexican border and reached France in late June, General Pershing coming directly from his San Antonio headquarters.[59] The first ships arrived at St. Nazaire June 26, 1917, to be the visible sign of U.S. participation in the war and a parade of some of its elements in Paris on July 4th caused great enthusiasm.[60]

On July 1, 1917, a letter received from the French Ministry of War offered to supply the American Expeditionary Force (A.E.F.) with 7,000 animals per month to begin in September. The War Department consequently cancelled plans for shipping any more animals abroad, ceased converting ships into horse transports, and diverted horse tonnage to other purposes. No animals were shipped, therefore, between July and November 1917.

On August 23, 1917, however, the French Government announced that owing to the needs of the French Army, it found itself unable to supply any animals beyond the number required for the First Division, then already in France. It agreed to "loan" the A.E.F. 4,000 draft horses for the Artillery Brigade of the 26th Division, expected to arrive shortly, with the understanding that they would be replaced by November 1, 1917, by importation from the U.S. On December 18 the U.S. pointed out that replacement from America would require the conversion of cargo and passenger ships into horse transports and would delay the movement of American troops and French supplies from the U.S. An August 1917 study by the A.E.F. had estimated that the shipment of animals by sea required eight to ten tons of shipping per head, or 101,992 tons for a division's requirements and 1,019,920 for 10 divisions. France agreed, so that the animals already provided were sold outright to the Americans.

By December 25, 1917, 12,414 animals had been provided by the French and 9,550 imported from the U.S. On January 29, 1918, with the five U.S. divisions in France only 50 percent complete as far as animal strength was concerned, the French were approached with a proposal that animals be purchased in the open market, a practice not previously resorted to. This was meant to ease the tonnage problem and eliminate the risk of sickness during the period of acclimatization following a sea voyage. To meet projected A.E.F. needs, the French agreed to carry out open-market purchases and turn over to the U.S. during the five month period of March through July 100,000 horses, later reduced to 80,000, at purchase price plus 30 percent.[61] With this bright prospect, the lack of shipping, and the scarcity of forage in France, A.E.F. headquarters recommended to the War Department that shipments of horses be discontinued, and all shipments were stopped in April.[62] Purchases in the U.S. were ordered cancelled on March 27, 1918, and a number of officers on duty with purchasing boards in the U.S. were ordered abroad to purchase animals in France and Spain.[63]

Open-market purchases proved disappointing, however, for, as General Pershing wrote: "The farmers in general simply would not sell, and one reason given was that they had the idea that we would thus be compelled to make a large importation of horses, which would give them an opportunity to buy cheaply after the war."[64] Up to June 1918, open-market purchases had yielded the A.E.F. only 31,589 animals,[65] and on May 31st the French advised the U.S. that due to military developments on the Western Front the government had issued orders suspending the purchase of any additional animals for the American forces. General Pershing then pointed out to the French the extent to which the failure to supply animals would immobilize a considerable portion of the American forces. The French then agreed to adopt a system of enforced requisition throughout France which extended from June 20 to August 15. It was estimated that there were approximately 3,000,000 animals in France not in military service, of which 300,000 to 400,000 would be of suitable type and would yield some 160,000 through the requisition. Of these, 80,000 were promised to the Americans.[66] When difficulties were encountered, the French agreed that beginning July 20 all animals requisitioned would go to the American forces. As a result, 77,520 animals were provided to the Americans, including 3,450 from French remount depots and other sources, about 70 percent of the total obtained in the requisition.[67]

The ten U.S. divisions training with the British Expeditionary Forces received 18,883 animals from the British, plus 2,376 obtained subsequently. Efforts to purchase animals in Spain were interrupted by a Spanish embargo due to German influence, lifted following diplomatic efforts, and yielded a total of 21,259 animals.[68]

On September 4, 1918, as the American Army prepared for the Argonne offensive, with roughly half of its required animal strength, Marshal Foch directed that 13,000 of the French army's animals be immediately placed at the disposal of the A.E.F. About 8,000 were supplied in September and somewhat over 4,000 in October.[69]

Faced with the great shortage of animals, the A.E.F. took steps to reduce the divisional allowance of animals. The August 1917 allowance of 8,777 was reduced on January 14, 1918, to 8,277 by dismounting certain officers and men, substituting bicycles for horses, and motorizing certain units. As these allowances exceeded supply, a priority schedule was established on

January 18, 1918, to assure active combat divisions of sufficient animals to maintain their mobility. This proved inadequate, however, and on June 4, 1918, further adjustment of divisional allowances yielded a net reduction of 499 animals. On August 25, 1918, further reductions were authorized, applying to divisions to be motorized. This brought the authorized division strength to 6,093 animals. This did not relieve the situation appreciably, however, as the necessary motorization was not immediately available.[70]

In the summer and fall of 1918, A.E.F. headquarters, realizing the critical shortage of animals, cabled several times to Washington requesting substantial shipments of animals and the transformation of numerous vessels into horse-boats. So crippled was the Animal Transport Service by the shortage of boats, however, that the resumption of shipments, discontinued in April, brought only three horse-boats in September and three in October, for a total of 4,409 animals.[71] With 139,571 animals serving the American combat troops against requirements of 245,774, the A.E.F. was only 57 percent complete so far as animal strength was concerned.[72]

Over the 19 months of U.S. participation in the war, from April 6, 1917, to November 11, 1918, the date of the Armistice, shipments of horses to the A.E.F. took place in eight months. The total number of animals acquired by the A.E.F. from the various sources was as follows[73]:

Source	Horses Cavalry	Horses Draft	Mules Draft	Mules Pack	Total Supplied	Percentage Share
United States	5,937	32,835	28,399	553	67,725	27.9
France	21,450	105,472	3,955	5,037	135,914	55.0
England	2,862	10,780	6,674	943	21,259	8.6
Spain	1,400	423	13,347	3,292	18,462	7.6
Total	31,650	149,510	52,375	9,825	243,360	100.0

Two

What Did You Do in the War, Dobbin?

Close to a million American horses, then, were to go to war in Western Europe. They formed part of the 1,500,000 horses and mules that served the Allied cause in France.[1] To the east, the Austrian army mobilized 600,000 horses, the Germans 715,000 horses, and the Russians—with twenty-four cavalry divisions—over a million. Staff officers estimated the horses to men proportion as one to three.[2]

This was not a new role for horses historically, for, before their application to transportation and agricultural tasks, horses were instruments of battle. From the plains of Northern Asia to the chariot rider[3] of the classical Middle East and the knights of Medieval Europe horses had been applied to war.[4] More recently their role had expanded beyond cavalry to the transport of artillery. On the Western Front of the First World War, however, their role was to change and many of their previous functions were phased out.

This change may most clearly be seen in the contrast with the American Civil War. During that conflict, in which Confederate cavalrymen brought along their own horses, and received per diem for their use, while Union forces organized massive purchase and supply facilities, cavalry performed a number of important functions. These included cavalry charges, flank attacks, sweeps leading to attacks from the rear, surveillance of enemy forces and positions, picket duty, protection of rail lines and supply trains, raids against enemy rail lines and supply trains, and the carrying of messages. Besides the cavalry, horses hauled the guns, ammunition wagon trains, the ordinary supplies, and most officers.[5] Many such functions were performed during the first four months of World War I on the Western Front, as German forces swept through Belgium and western France. These traditional practices ceased, however, as the war of movement gave way to the static warfare of stalemate behind parallel lines of trenches stretching 475 miles from the North Sea to the border of Switzerland.[6]

But what was responsible for the introduction of trench warfare? Primarily the spectacular growth of artillery and firepower during the nineteenth century. These stemmed from a number of technological advances: metallurgical progress, the rifling of gun barrels, the pneumatic absorption of recoil, smokeless gunpowder in the form of gelatinized gun cotton invented by Vieille in 1884,[7] invention of the machine gun and barbed-wire, and the use of limbers hauling the guns and carrying a ready supply of ammunition.[8] The result was the overwhelming dominance of defense, against which attacking armies battled in vain, at the cost of many thousands of lives before retreating, exhausted, to the long lines of defensive trenches. Between these trenches many more lives would be lost in the more than three years of stalemated warfare before the final months of the war.

The Loss of Cavalry Functions

In these conditions, against overwhelming firepower, barbed wire and trenches, there was no opportunity for cavalry charges. The last cavalry charges, in fact, had taken place "in 1866 in the Austro-Prussian War when 56,000 cavalrymen armed with lance and saber went up against guns and rifles, and a few years later during the Franco-German War 96,000 men rode into the field similarly armed in the last massed charge in military history."[9] Replacing the cavalry charge and the use of cavalry to demoralize the enemy before an infantry assault in World War I, was the development of the creeping barrage, fire dropped in front of advancing troops.[10]

Besides the cavalry charge, other cavalry functions previously carried out, as in the U.S. Civil War, were no longer feasible in the siege and attrition conditions of trench warfare. With the long line of trenches stretching from the North Sea to the Alps, there could be no sweep around for flank attack and no need for picket duty to protect against flank attack. Nor was there the possibility of cavalry raids against railroads or supply trains in enemy-held territory beyond the line of trenches. So too was there no role for cavalry defense of rail, supply, or communication lines, which was so critical during the Civil War.[11]

Discontinued also was the cavalry's messenger function carried out during the Civil War, though supplemented then by the telegraph.[12] During the World War telephone lines were laid to permit instant communications but were frequently cut by artillery fire. Messages were also carried by messengers on horses, by dispatch riders on motorcycles,[13] and at times by messenger pigeons.[14] In the last weeks of the war, during the Americans' Meuse-Argonne offensive, three troops of the 2d Cavalry did carry out courier duties between the flank divisions and the front, delivering messages, though the existence of trenches made it difficult to maneuver.[15] Other means of communications predominated, however. A British cavalry division in 1917 had four wireless sets, 18 combination telegraph and telephone sets, 18 motorcycles, several bicycles, flags, carrier pigeons, several Aldis and Lucas lamps, and four miles of wire on pack animals.[16] The horse's messenger functions were rarely important.

Perhaps most dramatic, however, was the loss of the cavalry's reconnaissance and surveillance function, so important in the Civil War and operative also in the initial, pre-trench, months of the World War, when British cavalry detected the strength and direction of the German army's sweep through northwestern France.[17] With the continuous line of trenches laid down thereafter, however, there was no opening to a flank through which cavalry surveillance could be launched. Instead, surveillance came through the air, initially by tethered balloons and soon thereafter also by airplanes. Tethered balloons had been used to a limited extent during the Civil War by Union forces to observe distant Confederate positions. This came initially through the personal intervention of President Lincoln, who took the aeronaut, Thadeus Lowe, by the hand and brought him in to conservative army commander General Winfield Scott, who had refused to see Lowe though he had a note from the President.[18]

Behind the trenches in the World War, tethered balloons carrying observers were important instruments of reconnaissance and artillery-spotting for both Allied and German forces. At the start of the war German forces took the lead in balloons, with eight Prussian and two Bavarian observation field units, each with 280 officers and men, 194 horses, and thirty-five carriages. The 21,000-cubic-foot balloons were able to rise to 2,500 feet, with later, larger balloons ascending to 3,500 feet. These were followed by Allied balloons launched by French, Belgian, and British forces and later by U.S. forces.[19]

Operating British balloons was a

> ground crew winching the balloons up and down on their steel hawsers. Each balloon was accompanied by a tender truck and a winch truck and a ninety-man crew, including two dozen men operating as three-man lookout and machine gun crews, who formed a defensive circle around the balloon to deter or attack enemy aircraft trying to shoot it down. Dangling in wicker baskets below the hydrogen-filled "blimps" at a height of up to 3,600 feet was perilous work for the observers—many of whom jumped or plunged to their deaths as their balloons collapsed in flames—but far less hazardous for the ground crews.... Four or five miles behind the front lines, [they] would occupy as safe a position as any could be in a war zone.[20]

When the heavier-than-air aircraft took to the skies, their functions were at first restricted to obstruction of enemy observation balloons, defense of their own forces' balloons, and reconnaissance—the identification of enemy gun positions, the mapping of enemy entrenchments, and the detection of any movement of troops.[21] Only later were they engaged in the attack of opposing forces and aircraft. As early as March 1915, in preparation for the Neuve Chappelle offensive, British forces used aerial photography for the first time to detail the enemy's trench system.[22] German views of Western Front battlefields from balloons tethered at 1,000 meters were executed by a General Headquarters artist who had them published after the war.[23] The value of air reconnaissance and spotting was stressed by a quoted French official who concluded "...They are not liable to be stopped like cavalry by the uninterrupted lines of trenches. They fly over positions and batteries enabling our forces to aim with accuracy."[24]

Though cavalry was active on the Eastern Front, in the West, throughout the period of trench warfare from late 1914 to the spring of 1918, cavalry could not fulfill its traditional functions. Some cavalry divisions were held in reserve by the British army in the hope that they could be used to follow through on an infantry breakthrough of the German line. In January 1918, the British Commander-in-Chief was obliged by a Cabinet edict to disband two of his remaining five cavalry divisions.[25] The German army concentrated its cavalry on the Eastern Front,[26] but there too most of the cavalry was dismounted as the war progressed. Of those not retained for escort duty, about 80 percent were grouped into dismounted units called Kavallarie-Schutzen by war's end.[27]

Only in the last few months of the war, when movement succeeded static warfare, was cavalry attack attempted, with considerable losses, however. One American was quoted as saying: "You can't have a cavalry charge until you have captured the enemy's last machine gun."[28] Though the cavalry at the battle for Le Cateau had achieved some success, the British Official History wrote:

> ... the cavalry had done nothing that the infantry, with artillery support and cyclists, could not have done for itself at less cost; and the supply of the large force of horses with water and forage had gravely interfered with the sending up of ammunition and the rations for the other arms, and with the allotment of the limited water facilities.[29]

What role could the horse play, then, in the years of trench warfare? Did the need for horses diminish? No.

The Horse in Trench Warfare

As the frenetic pace of movement warfare during the first few months of the war gave way to stalemate, with ammunition exhausted and Germany shifting troops to its Eastern Front and digging in for a defensive posture in the West, the use of horses did not diminish. The British 46th Division coming through Le Havre in March 1915, counted in its supply column 200 wagons, 600 men and as many as 550 horses.[30]

But what was to be the principal function of horses during the three years of trench warfare? It was supply. As one historian put it:

> For strategic mobility, the crucial transport arm was the railway.... However, for short and medium distance mobility, despite the fact that by 1914 a British division included nearly 900 motor vehicles, all armies relied on the horse to an extent that is now difficult to appreciate. And on the battlefield itself, all armies moved on foot. The disparity between strategic mobility and relative tactical immobility was a technological paradox whose implications had not impressed themselves on any observer in 1914.[31]

United States military authorities, on entry into the war in 1917, found that trench warfare had enormously increased the tonnage of supplies required by troops.[32] Both the British and French armies maintained a system of daily distributions of food supplies for men and animals provided automatically, with no need for reauthorization.[33] A similar system was instituted by the American Expeditionary Force so that combat units would not be burdened with a single day's stores above the authorized standard reserves. This prevented the accumulations at the front, which would be exposed to the danger of destruction or capture and might indicate intentions to the enemy. However, this system placed a heavy burden on the railroads, which had to deliver the equivalent of 25 French railway carloads of supplies daily at a point within reach of motor or horse-drawn transportation for each combat division.[34]

For the three-and-a-half million Allied combatants in place at the time of U.S. entry into the war, the burden of daily moving this volume had fallen on the railroads in northwestern and central France. To supply its forces, the A.E.F. selected the comparatively unused south-Atlantic ports of France and the railroads leading from them to the northeast. For all practical purposes, General Pershing's report stated, the American Expeditionary Forces were based on the American continent, facing three thousand miles of submarine-menaced ocean, unknown quantities of shipping tonnage, and 400 miles of communication from the ports to their probable front.[35] To accommodate the added needs for U.S. and Allied supplies, the U.S. forces constructed 80 new berths at the selected ports and 1,002 miles of standard-gauge railroad tracks, brought in from the U.S. 20,000 railroad cars and 1,500 standard-gauge locomotives, and repaired 57,385 French railroad cars and 1,947 French locomotives.[36]

A British captain asked about the work of the horse at the front is quoted as saying: "Why at the front the whole damned thing is the horse." They found from bitter experience, that beyond a certain zone—they had railroad transportation, and beyond that was another zone in which they used very large motor trucks, and beyond that was another zone where they used horses, and where they had to.[37] A contemporary account declared:

> This is a war in which the horse has upheld his place as chief baggage and transport agent against all comers. Motors and railroad locomotives there are in France in abundance, but their effectiveness ceases where the roads end—about 6 miles from the front line trenches. Over the last 6 miles the horse and mule are practically the only means of transportation. They carry food and ammunition to the boys in the trenches; they haul the guns to their positions. There are no roads in a battlefield and the only way to forward supplies is by means of a carrier that can travel up hill, across ravines and swamps, through mud-soaked and rock-bound country. Here none of the inventions of man can take the place of the horse.[38]

The unsung task of carrying each day's food to the front fell to the mules and horses hauling the ration wagons. A private in the Supply Company of the U.S. 16th Infantry wrote:

> For a few days now, I and one of the other clerks have been riding the wagons going for rations early in the morning, as the other men are all too busy, and we must have two men on each wagon. The mule "skinners" will probably never be cited for great bravery, and may be ridiculed as too cowardly to go to the front, but it will be most unjust if such does happen, for, when others take to the dugouts, he must remain with his "jar-heads," exposed to view; and he does it with no great notion of his bravery. Good weather or bad, he must steer these crazy mules up to the very edge of what may be the great divide for him; but still, I believe, you would find less bucking and kicking in the supply outfit than in any other.[39]

Similar sentiments were expressed by George C. Marshall in his *Memoirs of My Service In The World War, 1917-1918*:

> During this period of our service, the most dangerous duty probably fell to the Quartermaster Sergeants and teamsters who went forward each night with the ration carts to revictual the infantry. Confined to roads and anticipated by the enemy, they had to make their way along the most heavily beaten zones in the sector. The casualties among these men and the poor mules who hauled the carts were very heavy. No publicity or glory attached to this service, but those who carried it through always had my profound admiration. Apropos of these unsung heroes, I found one day an elaborately decorated grave in a woods where the supply echelon of an infantry regiment was located. Over the grave was a large wooden cross with the following inscription:
> Here lies poor Nelly of the Supply Company of the Sixteenth Infantry.
> Served in Texas, Mexico and France.
> Wounded and killed near Villers Tournelles.
> She done her bit.
> Nelly was an army mule.[40]

In some areas where rations were brought forward by trucks, motors were stalled during the wet season, and troops in the trenches were supplied with rations only by the prompt substitution of horsepower.[41] In some circumstances, emergency rations had to be rushed forward. Following a night attack by mustard gas, one regiment's food was ruined by the gas and it became necessary to reach them with a new supply of rations before dawn.[42]

In May 1918, noting that the gasoline consumed by an American division had been as high as 2,000 gallons a day compared with 500 gallons consumed proportionally by French troops, A.E.F. headquarters ordered that when the railhead or refilling point was within fifteen to eighteen miles, animal transport should be used. It suggested that wagon transportation should be stationed midway between the railheads and the kitchen of the foremost units to be supplied, and take two days for the trip, stopping overnight at its station. The wagon unit would be divided in half, the second half alternating with the first. Motor trucks, it stated, should be used only for perishable supplies, such as meat.[43]

The last mile to the front-line trenches could not be reached by the ration carts, however. This was because of the geography of the trench system. There were generally three lines of trenches. The front line trench was fifty yards to a mile from its enemy counterpart. Several hundred yards back was the support trench. And several hundred yards further back was the reserve line. Coming up from the rear these trenches were reached through a communication trench, perpendicular to the three trenches, sometimes a mile or more long and gradually deepening until it was well below ground. At the front lines there were only fighting men. Back from the front lines, in the next zone, semi-immune from shell fire, were the ancillary services, Army Service Corps, casualty clearing stations, possibly some heavy guns, and horse lines, where horses were tied up between activities. Above ground activities took place at night, hidden from enemy detection. "By day the roads were deserted; but as soon as dusk fell they were thick with transport, guns, ammunition trains, and troops, all moving up to take their positions in or behind the lines."[44]

Marshall recalled one sector where the vicious and continuous shelling forced regimental officers to confine all their movements to periods of darkness.

> Reconnaissances, visits of inspection, transportation of food and reliefs were carried out under the cover of night. Breakfast was usually served late in the evening, after which the personnel went about their active duties which generally occupied the remainder of the night. Dawn being the hour most propitious for attack, everyone was held on alert at that time, and later would have dinner. With the coming of broad daylight most of the garrison would go to sleep, and it was not until evening that the current activities of the sector were resumed.[45]

In this setting, mules and horses hauling the ration wagons could not possibly approach the front line trenches. For the last mile or so the rations had to be carried by the men. The A.E.F.'s Baker Board, assigned to study French and British experience when the U.S. entered the war, stated in its report in May 1917:

> One of the greatest difficulties of transportation is to be found in forwarding food, fuel and ammunition to the trenches. An enormous amount of manpower is consumed in the work. The matter was discussed with officers of both the British and French Armies, all of whom pronounced as to the present unsatisfactory means of forwarding those supplies to the trenches, and the great waste of manpower.[46]

In the American army, with the company kitchens normally some distance behind the lines, hot food was carried by hand to the forward trenches in insulated "marmite" cans for the solid food and in milk cans for coffee. The "Marmites Norvegienne," or fireless cookers, consisted of a solid wooden case about one-third larger than an inner container with the space between packed with shavings or crumpled paper. Food boiled for 15 minutes was immediately placed in the case, hermetically sealed, and ordinarily kept in the cooker for four or five hours.[47] The marmite kept the food hot for several hours and solidified alcohol was supplied for heating the coffee. Water was brought to the front in water carts, a vehicle new to the American service. Only one animal could be spared to haul the water carts, which were redesigned to reduce the 2,500 pound weight for 150 gallons to 748 pounds for 100 gallons.[48]

It was the soldiers, then, who were obliged to carry the rations, ammunition and supplies along the communication trench deepening to the below-ground level as it approached the front trenches. However, the horses were able to carry ammunition directly to the artillery, as artillery was stationed behind the lines, and this proved to be a major function dependent upon the horses.

The Horses' Artillery Functions

As the horses' cavalry functions declined, the need for more artillery service increased. With opposing forces dug in behind their long line of trenches, their employment of artillery and ammunition reached staggering proportions. French heavy artillery organized in regiments, for example, was increased from 300 pieces in August 1914 to 6,000 pieces in June 1917. Demolition fire for the destruction of every 100 meters of trenches was estimated to require 300 shells of the 155-millimeter guns. Daily consumption of projectiles by the batteries of a single, two-division army corps amounted 1,200 tons at times.

Launching these munitions were various kinds of artillery, with different missions requiring their location at different distances from the enemy lines. Trench mortars, used to batter the enemy's front line, were usually in or near the second trench line of the first position. The light field artillery, located behind the first position, was used to dismantle enemy trenches, support assaulting waves of infantry with barrages, and repulse enemy counter-attacks. The heavy artillery was located further to the rear, depending on size and range, and was employed for demolition fire to destroy the enemy works, deep shelters, redoubts, and communications.

By 1916 a revolution in theory had taken place. A 1913 view had held that artillery had only a minimum effect against an under-cover enemy, which had to be compelled to expose itself by attacking infantry, which conquered and held the ground. By 1916, French General Petain declared: "In the warfare of the present, the artillery conquers the ground, the infantry occupies it."[49]

In the periods of mobile warfare during the opening and closing months of the war, it was the principle function of the horses to move the guns, which were attached to two-wheel limbers pulled by horses, three pairs of horses for a 3-inch gun, four pairs for a 4.7-inch gun, and five pairs for a 6-inch gun, with one driver mounted on the off horse of each pair[50] until put in place. Some horses were even reported to have corrected their artillerymen when the guns were not spaced properly.[51] In the three years of static, trench warfare, however, there was less movement of the guns, which were set in their place behind the lines and often did not move when their parent unit was shifted.[52]

The horses' responsibility for the transportation of the ammunition to the guns took on immense importance, as the volume of ammunition fired reached enormous proportions. The priority of this function had been clear in previous wars. In the Civil War, for example, a photograph of an ammunition train passing through as other wagons pulled aside is accompanied by an explanation that

> the ammunition train had the right of way over everything in the army, short of actual guns and soldiers, when there was any possibility of a fight.... Its wagons were always marked, and were supposed to be kept as near the troops as possible. Soldiers could go without food for a day or two if necessary; but it might spell defeat and capture to lack ammunition for an hour.[53]

Similarly, in the conditions of trench warfare in the First World War, a critical factor for the outcome of a battle was the supply of ammunition brought forward to the guns from the railhead or closest truck stop by pack or wagon, by horse or mule. The Baker Board examining British practice in May 1917, reported:

> The ammunition is delivered from the base to the railheads, whence it is taken by rail to the ammunition depots. It is then sent in motor trucks or by narrow gauge railroads to distributing points from which it is taken by the horse-drawn ammunition columns to the batteries.[54]

The Baker Board reported that in the French service the order of precedence for the movement of supplies on the light railways was 1st, ammunition, 2nd, engineering supplies, and 3rd, food supplies.[55]

The delivery of ammunition to the artillery was quite perilous. One American officer manning a sector as part of the 1st French Army wrote:

> Last night I had an urgent order for 40 truck loads of 155 mm shells and I went on ahead to arrange for dumping it. We delivered it at a point 1½ miles from the trenches. Whether the Boche were trying to get the Corps dump or merely strafing the roads, I know not. Perhaps the shells that fell all around us were merely wild shots, primarily intended to reach our infantry. At any rate that is one reason why the service of ammunition is particularly hazardous; we are always exposed to shell fire, whereas if we were up at the front we would of necessity remain under bomb proof cover. Be that as it may, the brilliant flares, the signal rockets, the whining 75s, the roaring 155s, the clatter of horse batteries on the roads is enough to make any one sit up and take notice.[56]

An appreciation of the importance attached to this role of horses can be gained from the conduct of the Battle of Arras, in April 1917. By 1917, the British had recognized the importance of counter-battery fire—the destruction and neutralization of enemy guns—to the success of the infantry. By 1917, too, the use of gas warfare—chlorine, phosgene, and then mustard gas—was widely employed, following its introduction by the Germans in the second Battle of Ypres on April 22, 1915.[57] On April 9, 1917, in the Battle of Arras, as the British began their attack on a 14-mile front, their bombardment included the heaviest concentration of gas thus far in the war in order to kill or immobilize large numbers of horses and prevent German transport of shells to the front.[58] A German document captured after the Battle of Arras reported that gas injuries to horses had impeded the flow of ammunition to the guns, and suggested that mechanical transport be substituted for the horses.[59] Photographs of horses on the Western Front show them wearing "nosebag" style respirators designed to protect them from gas attack.[60]

Horses and mules in enemy service were regarded as military objectives. An early account of French and British reconnaissance airplanes' activities listed among other incidental successes the killing of artillery horses.[61] In the long history of enemy horses and mules as military targets, a Civil War account provides a particular example. In the capture of a Union wagon train by a Confederate raid, "…men were detailed to set fire to the wagons and kill the mules, since it was impossible to escape with the livestock."[62]

Late in the First World War, in 1918, the horses' vital role in bringing up ammunition was supplemented in an important innovation. The R.A.F. successfully dropped 100,000 rounds of ammunition to Australian machine gunners advancing to capture enemy positions in the Battle of Hamel, their machine guns having already devoured vast quantities of ammunition.[63]

The End of Trench Warfare

For three years the Western Front was locked down in trench warfare, a war of position rather than of movement. What brought it to an end?

The first step, in German reaction to the violent shocks of Allied offensives, was the gradual transformation from the thin, hard-crusted front line to a deep defensive system, with the chief resisting-strength drawn back towards the rear.[64] The British too moved to a more elastic defense, with the forward trenches more lightly manned and supported mainly by automatic weapons. Two to three miles back was the more fully defended "battle zone," foreshadowing a shift to a warfare of movement.[65]

The most substantial change, however, came with the German launch of attack by infiltration, by-passing the heavily-weaponed high ground and strong points while reaching for the softer spots and speeding reserves through the openings to the enemy's rear to cut off further resistance. This method was introduced by Germany's General Oskar von Hutier in the Eastern offensive around Riga and with great success against the Italians at Caporetto.[66] Initiated on the Western Front with more massive artillery and gas attacks, it provided each infantry battalion with eight portable 76-millimeter artillery pieces, which could be mounted on two wheels and drawn by one man or hung on shafts and carried by four men in pairs to traverse the furrowed ground of no-man's land.[67] The breakthrough was made possible by the invention of the Bergmann maschinenpistole 18 (MP18), the first practical, widely used submachine gun. Weighing just over ten pounds, it fired 9-mm rounds from a 20-round box magazine or a 32-round drum magazine. Its development came as John Talieferro Thompson in America was working on his "trench broom" submachine gun, which was later called the Tommy Gun and was used extensively in World War II.[68]

Employed in a counter-attack blunting the British advance in the Battle of Cambrai in November 1917,[69] the new German tactic had its greatest success in the three March 21-to-June 2, 1918, offensives, driving deep wedges 60 kilometers into Allied territory.[70] It was halted at this point for lack of

Two. What Did You Do in the War, Dobbin?

a mobile force for further exploitation of the breakthrough, the Germans having kept their cavalry on the Eastern Front and using only nine tanks, four of their own and five capture British Mark IVs; never, in fact, having more than thirteen tanks in use on any single occasion.[71]

The Allied offensive which followed made use of the same infiltration tactics but also tanks—called "the cavalry of this war" in *The Stars and Stripes* of October 25, 1918[72]—to crush the barbed wire entanglements, silence machine gun nests and enfilade enemy trenches.[73] Benefiting from the unified command of Marshall Foch as Allied Commander and the added strength of American manpower, the Allied offensive succeeded by coordinating attacks all along the Front, so that the Germans could not rush reserves to any single crisis point requiring reinforcement as they had done before, and culminated in the Armistice of November 11, 1918.[74]

Tanks

Tanks followed the medieval example of giving protection to the soldier by encasing him in armor.[75] Development of the tank, Britain's chief tactical innovation of the war, was the work of Sir William Tritton.[76] It combined the caterpillar tracks of commercial heavy equipment with the road-bound armored car, and the spark ignition engine devised by Gottlieb Daimler in 1885 and advanced to a compact 100-horsepower power plant by 1915.[77] Unlike armored cars and trucks, the tank could go off the road on rough open ground, where it rarely averaging more than 1 or 1.5 miles an hour, however.[78]

The first British tanks, three-dozen 30-ton machines, went into action at dawn on September 15, 1916, in the Battle of the Somme,[79] the French tanks on April 17, 1917, in the fighting in the Aisne.[80] In the Battle of Cambrai, November 20 to 29, 1917, the British massed 409 tanks.[81]

To manufacture in the United States copies of France's Renault light tank, the American Expeditionary Force in February 1918, sent Lieutenant Elgin Braine to the U.S. to act as liaison with tank production. Arriving with the tank's plans and assorted tank components, he encountered a maddening bureaucratic nightmare that blocked production. As a result, it was not until November 20. 1918, nine days after the Armistice was signed, that two American-built Renault tanks reached the American Tank Corps in France, eight more following in December.[82]

In the last days of the war, as American infantrymen advanced against German lines west of the Meuse River, tank support was scarce. George C. Marshall wrote:

Instead of a proper complement of about five hundred tanks, to protect the doughboys against excessive losses in such an advance, we were only able to muster 18, and these were all employed against the little village of Landres-et-St.-Georges. Here was a commentary on the price of unpreparedness to be paid inevitably in human life. With America the master steel-maker of the world, American infantrymen were denied the support and protection of their land battleship.[83]

American tank forces did not fare well after the war. In June 1920 Congress dissolved the Tank Corps as a separate entity and assigned all units to "Infantry (Tanks)." One congressman explained: "I am unable absolutely to see any reason during peacetime for the creation of the overhead that would have to be established to give you a separate organization."

Wartime tank leaders moved to other fields. In August 1920, George S. Patton, who had spearheaded tank development in the American Expeditionary Force, transferred to the cavalry. There he served until taking over the newly formed 2d Armored Division's 2d Armored Brigade in July 1940. Dwight D. Eisenhower, who had commanded tank force training in Gettysburg during the war, was rescued from the down-sized tank center at Fort Meade in January 1922, by assignment to an infantry brigade in Panama. The U.S. virtually ignored the tank during the 1920s and early 1930s, leaving development of new tactics and strategic concepts for the employment of armored vehicles to England, France, and Germany.[84]

Forage

Though horses had lost many of their warfare functions in the trench war years, they were essential to the supply function and still needed to eat and drink. Adequate forage, in fact, had long been a critical element in horse-drawn warfare before the coming of railroads. Then, advances launched from frontier supply points carrying soldiers' rations and horses' forage could go only about seventy miles, or five days' march, before dependence on pre-stationed supplies or roadside pasture began. This often meant waiting for spring and new grass before attacks could begin. Movement through territory without adequate forage, as in Napoleon's advance to Moscow through the scorched earth left behind by retreating Russian forces, could prove disastrous.[85]

Though trench warfare did not involve movement away from sources of supply, the concentration of horses along the front and the destruction of nearby pasturelands by the war meant that forage would have to come from further back. Potatoes and vegetable gardens were cultivated in close-by rear areas by soldiers,[86] but delivery of soldiers' rations, horses' feed, and other supplies depended on the railroads. For horses this was a substantial load, each horse needing to eat about 2 percent of its weight—roughly 20 pounds—and drink 10 gallons of water daily.[87] A.E.F. General Orders called for feeding horses three times a day and watering them as often as was practicable.[88]

The supply of forage for A.E.F. horses was a source of continual concern, however, on account of the lack of shipping and the shortage of forage in France.[89] Initially, the daily rations set by Army Regulations (Par. 1077) were for heavy draft horses 17 pounds of hay and 14 of oat, for light draft horses 14 pounds of hay and 12 of oats, and for mules 14 pounds of hay and 9 of oats. Over the winter of 1917–1918 the French Army rendered assistance by supplying the A.E.F. with hay. With the expectation that the 1917 French oat crop would permit Americans to purchase much forage locally, forage shipments from the U.S. were curtailed. The crops fell short of expectations, however, and on January 25, 1918, daily rations were reduced to 10 pounds of hay and 10 of oats for horses, and 10 pounds of hay and 8 of oats for mules.[90]

This led to increased shipments from the U.S., so that by May 27, 1918, daily rations could be increased to 14 pounds of hay and 12 of oats for heavy draft horse, 14 pounds of hay and 10 of oats for light draft horses, and 12 pounds of hay and 8 of oats for mules.[91]

The early 1918 shortage was aggravated by the diversion of rail resources to the south for the sudden movement of British and French troops to reinforce the Italian Army after the defeat at Caporetto. For a time the supply of forage for the U.S. First Division was completely cut off. George C. Marshall recounts:

> The country was covered with snow and ice, and I recall receiving word one night that a battalion of artillery in a little village nearby was without forage for their animals and without rations for the men. The horses were too weak to be moved and the division did not then possess transportation which could be utilized to haul rations to the men of this unit. The question to be decided was whether the animals would be left to starve while the men were marched to some point where there were rations, or was there any way we could devise to transport the necessary food. Unfortunately, I do not remember just what was done, but I have a distinct recollection of the dilemma in which we found ourselves at Division Headquarters regarding this incident.[92]

With the resumption of supply, regular delivery was provided by the French Authorities. American receiving officers finding any discrepancy between the actual weight and the weight shown on tags of bags of French hay were required to prepare a report in quadruplicate, to be signed by a French officer or military interpreter present, and sent to headquarters so that the proper deductions could be made upon presentation of the bill by the French Government.[93]

Water for A.E.F. horses was provided at "water points," sometimes through pipelines. Special engineer troops in the Army's Water Supply Service were responsible for investigating water sources, developing the water supply, and constructing and operating the works necessary to make water available at "water points." This included conveniences for the watering of animals, filling water carts, water-tank trains, buckets, canteens, and other containers. Tactical units were responsible for transporting water from the water points to the final point of consumption.[94]

Horses fed or watered in some towns were subject to the payment of "octroi duties," a toll which French law authorized certain towns to collect on foodstuffs, fodder, fuel, building materials, gasoline, etc., consumed or utilized within the town. By agreement with the various octroi towns, the octroi duties were commuted for the A.E.F. to a flat payment per man or per animal, or both, per year. In cases where horses were to be paid for, all animals fed within the octroi limits of the town had to be included. The quartermaster making payment multiplied the daily return of horses and mules by the number of centimes representing the daily octroi dues.[95]

Care

The problem of wartime care for the horses' health began long before their arrival at the battlefront. It arose first with the diseases that came to characterize their mass transportation. Foremost among these was what came to be called shipping fever, a variation of influenza or pneumonia. As noted earlier, even before U.S. entry into the war, British purchases in the U.S. suffered 10 percent losses while still in the U.S. and French and Italian losses were even greater.[96] Of the almost 250,000 U.S. Army horses purchased which were not sent overseas some 7½ percent were lost while still in the U.S.[97] To combat shipping fever, medical treatment and vaccination were not effective. However, sanitary measures, such as disinfecting cars and stockyards, improved quarters, and the establishment of veterinary hospitals at railhead centers helped the U.S. Army to reduce the death rate from five of every 1,000 a week to two per 1,000 head a week. Also important for both stateside and European horse care was the expansion of the Army's veterinary force from the original group of 64 officers and no enlisted men to 1,000 officers and 12,000 men.[98]

A persistent health problem both in the U.S. and France was glanders, a highly contagious and fatal horse ailment detected with an ophthalmic test which consisted of introducing a few drops of concentrated mallein, made from the product of the glanders germ, into the eye. Horses and mules having the disease developed a severe inflammation of the mucous membrane. Quarantined, tested every 21 days, and subjected to a laboratory blood test, animals with confirmed glanders were destroyed and their carcasses burned. There was no cure for the disease, which was transmissible to man, in whom it produced death.[99] Evidence of shipping fever and glanders was present in W.J. Ratigan's account, above, of his 1915 journey aboard a horse transport going to France.[100]

In France, mange afflicted many A.E.F. horses. A highly contagious skin disease caused by parasites, its outbreaks were increased by lack of proper and thorough grooming, unsanitary surroundings, reduced rations, excess of work and general neglect. Contagion took place directly through contact with infected animals, or indirectly through contact with bedding, blankets, harness, grooming kits and other objects. This called for extensive disinfection.[101] Medicines and the necessary facilities were scarce, however. Because mangy animals were sometimes kept with organizations after they should have been evacuated, a large percentage became unfit for further service. As a result, mange accounted for more disability among A.E.F. horses than any other disease.[102]

On the battlefront, illness was compounded by the trying, primitive conditions horses had to endure and by the poor care at the hands of soldiers with no previous experience in caring for animals. The increased purchase of U.S. Army horses had early on emphasized the serious lack of enlisted men acquainted with proper horse care. A high Army officer was quoted as saying:

> The man who knows how to take care of animals in this country has become very scarce. We must provide thousands of men capable of taking care of animals and who can shoe a horse, drive a team and adjust a pack saddle. You cannot train a horseshoer in less than four months; you can teach a man to pack or drive a team in about two months. Without horseshoers, packers and teamsters we cannot have an army. The men who handle machine guns will be of little service unless they are taught to take care of mules. Without teamsters we cannot have an army.[103]

A 1916 British cartoon illustrated the problem of city men unfamiliar with proper horse care. It shows an officer advising a soldier struggling with a horse: "Don't beat him; talk to him, man—talk to him!" and the soldier replying: "I come from Manchester."[104]

References to the problem of care persisted throughout the war. At the war's end, in December 1918, a month after the Armistice, a U.S. Army Bulletin stated that: "Reports of inspectors regarding the condition of animals in the A.E.F. indicate serious neglect or lack of knowledge of the care of animals on the part of responsible officers." It ordered that all animals be fed three times a day, and groomed twice a day, before starting work in the morning and after work in the evening. It found many animals in poor condition or sick through overwork and lack of care and ordered that they be given special care and attention, with only light work or exercise.[105]

A month later, to stimulate interest in the proper treatment of animals, the A.E.F. initiated a program of horse shows, with division shows to be held during January and February, corps shows during March, army shows during April, and the A.E.F. shows thereafter. All divisions still in France on March 1, 1919, which had not held a show were to report in writing to A.E.F. headquarters giving the reasons therefore.[106] The Final Report of the Assistant Chief of Staff, G-1, in April 1919, concluded:

> The results of the horse shows have justified them from every point of view. The rewards for the best entries and penalties inflicted on organizations having animals showing lack of proper care have brought into play a spirit of competition which has done more than any one thing to instill in the minds of both officers and men an interest in the proper care of animals.[107]

Besides the incentives provided by the horse shows, increased knowledge of horse care was disseminated by means of schools for the care of animals established in A.E.F. divisions, corps, and armies soon after the Armistice. The result was a marked improvement that reportedly took place in the condition of the animals.[108]

Beyond the level of individual care, there was the need for organized institutions to care for sick horses and horses injured by enemy action. This was the first war in which specialized veterinary hospitals were established.[109] For the first time in history, sick and wounded animals could be evacuated to field and base hospitals where they received treatment comparable to that given to soldiers.[110] During the American Civil War, there was no adequate provision for taking care of sick horses. Treated by horseshoers, they were taken along with the rest of the command until they could no longer travel. At this point they were abandoned, since horses unfit for use were a hindrance to the movement and efficiency of their regiment.[111]

The need for organized horse care was also met in the warring nations by the buildup of a voluntary, civilian auxiliary, fashioned after the Red Cross, to back up the veterinary corps and veterinary hospital system.[112] Among these were the Blue Cross and Royal Society for the Prevention of Cruelty to Animals in Great Britain and the Red Star Animal Relief in the U.S. The Blue Cross was originally founded in Great Britain in 1912 under the aegis of Our Dumb Friends' League.[113] It was recognized by the French Minister of War and was later given sole authority to care for the war dogs and horses in the kennels and hospitals of France. By November 1917, it had twelve hospitals in France together with supply depots and branch hospitals manned by veterinarians. Wounded horses arriving at the hospitals were given a drink of water and undisturbed rest, and the following day were washed, their wounds cleaned, inspected and treated. The badly wounded were taken to the hospital and, after operation, sent to the Blue-Cross pastures for recuperation and convalescence.[114]

Besides its hospital work, the Blue Cross supplied provisions to army units in France and Italy. This included "Veterinary Chests" containing a supply of instruments, bandages, rugs, and wither and sheepskin pads. More expensive gifts included portable forges, clipping machines, chaff-cutters, poultice-boots, canvas water troughs, fomenting pails, and special waterproof rugs for winter use.[115]

Also present at Blue Cross hospitals at the front were war dogs, suffering from broken legs, effects of gas, liquid-fire burns, deafness, or shell-shock. Blue Cross dogs working with the Ambulance Corps sought out the wounded soldier on the field, hurried to the stretcher bearers, and conducted them to his side.[116]

In England, soon after war broke out in 1914, the Royal Society for the Prevention of Cruelty to Animals went to the aid of the army veterinary corps, raising money and rushing experienced horsemen to France. By July 1918, Britain had in Flanders hospital accommodations for 48,000 horses, one-fourth of which were built and equipped by the Royal Society. The hospital work was in two sections, the base section, and the mobile section, operating portable hospitals in tent form, located near the front line and moving from one place to another on the borders of the danger zone. Animals generally remained in the portable hospitals not more than 48 hours and as soon as possible were transported by motorized two-horse ambulances or by specially constructed railway cars to sidings adjoining the base hospitals. With wards for contagious diseases and for the non-contagious, operating theaters, a dispensary, forage barns, cooking kitchens, a disinfecting tank, and individual stalls, there were accommodations for more than 2,000 animals at some base hospitals.[117]

In the U.S., the Red Star Animal Relief grew out of a 1916 suggestion by U.S. Secretary of War Newton Baker to the American Humane Society that it render organized aid to injured animals in time of war.[118] In August 1917, it launched a campaign to raise $250,000 for the relief work of caring for sick and wounded horses and mules both in the new army camps rising in the U.S. and behind the battle lines. It stated that it stood ready to erect one or more veterinary hospitals, equipped with the necessary shelter tents, ambulances, and supplies, with motor trucks for transportation purposes and a large number of veterinarians to look after the work.[119] To correct with education the poor care army horses were getting in some camps, the Red Star issued a booklet entitled "First Aid for Horses," which met with extensive demand so that a fourth edition had to be rushed into print.[120]

Comprising both government and voluntary organization facilities, at the time of U.S. entry into the war, the French and English were reported to have a veterinary hospital every eight miles along the more-than-400-mile Western Front, with about 28 percent of the horses in the hospitals there for sickness and 72 percent because of injuries.[121] Of the 2,562,549 horses and mules admitted to British forces' hospitals in France, 78 percent were cured and returned to service.[122]

In Great Britain, an R.S.P.C.A. plaque "records the death by enemy action, disease, or accident of 484,143 horses, mules, camels and bullocks, and of many hundreds of dogs, carrier pigeons, and other creatures on the various fronts during the Great War."[123]

American veterinary hospitals were attached to each remount depot,[124] of which there were 38 in France by the time of the Armistice.[125] A corps level mobile veterinary hospital was staffed by two veterinarians and 35 enlisted men, including four farriers, a horseshoer, and two wagoners. It had twelve riding horses for general use of the hospital and six draft mules for use with its two-mule animal ambulance and four-mule escort wagon.[126] The working basis in the Veterinary Corps was one commissioned officer and sixteen enlisted men for each 400 horses or mules.[127]

As Private O. Mensing of the 117th Sanitary Train wrote home on November 1, 1918:

> Ten days ago I was on detailed service with the Tennessee Ambulance Co. with my mules. I had to haul patients from the front to the dressing station where the Motor ambulances relay them to the hospital. It was raining constantly while I was there, and it was impossible for motors to get through, so the mule ambulances were kept very busy.... The road that I had to drive four mules over was simply a trail through war devastated country, and many shell holes which I had to dodge.... We had four mules killed and two drivers were blown up out of the Company on this front.[128]

By agreement with the French in February 1918, American animals left with the French or straying into French zones would be assured of proper care and treatment, whether left in French military establishments or with French civilians.[129] A.E.F. regulations in March 1918 set daily reimbursement for the care of American animals at Fr. 2.60 for French civilians, Fr. 3.15 for the French Army, and Fr. 5 for treatment (including medicine) in a veterinary unit of the French Army. This was increased to Fr.5, Fr. 5, and Fr. 8.5, respectively, effective October 1, 1918, because of increased forage costs.[130] The A.E.F.'s shortage of horses increased the burden of horse sickness, as some units retained animals only partially fit for duty rather than evacuate them, since the unit would otherwise be without proper facilities for movement.[131] This was a sharp contrast with British forces, which had sufficient horses so that a horse was sent to the hospital the moment it got sick.[132]

An interesting insight into the operations of an army veterinary hospital is afforded by an account of a German veterinary hospital organized in East Prussia early in the war, in November 1914, in vacated cavalry barracks. Staffed by four veterinarians, two assistant veterinarians, each assisted by two men trained for the veterinary sanitation service, and a farrier, it had the services also of 148 men of the German Landsturm, mostly with a long practice in the handling of horses. Of the 1,995 horses received in the hospital during its first six months, 973 were returned to their units as cured, 108 affected with glanders were killed, 128 were sold to horse slaughterers, 92 died or were killed because of suffering, 49 were handed over to other depots or detachments, 12 mares in foal were handed over to the Chamber of Agriculture, 84 were sold to farmers as unfit for military service or not worth the expense of fodder, and 554 remained in the hospital at the end of the period. The account concluded:

> By employing all the available resources, a veterinary hospital such as this is able to cure a considerable number of invalid horses and, by surgical operations, to make a great many wounded ones fit again for war use, which otherwise would unavoidably be doomed to death at the slaughterer's hand or by a welcome bullet.[133]

Horses in Soldiers' Memoirs: The Opening Months

Though horses, of course, could leave no testimony of their wartime experiences, revealing glimpses of their role can be gained from mention in various soldiers' memoirs. These reflect the marked difference between experiences during the war of movement in the opening months of the war, the three years of stable trench warfare, and the final months of movement that ended the war.

In the very earliest days of the war, as British forces embarked on the French coast and rushed to meet the German advance in Belgium and northwestern France, horses played an important part in the movement of the artillery.

Author Lyn McDonald described one episode. As the army moved to the battle by train, unloading the horses on the narrow ramps to the rails on the three gangways available took a long time. Harnessing the horses in total darkness, attaching them to the wagons and guns, and guiding them across the series of rails to the road proved most difficult. Then, a wheel on the last wagon dropped into a deep depression between the tracks as it missed the crossing. Unknowing, the rest of the battery had moved off, leaving Lt. R.A. (Rory) Macleod and his wagon behind, to press through the darkness trying to join them.

Lt. Macleod reported that besides the darkness in the dank and stuffy night, they had to contend with a raging thirst and the need to water the horses. As a young officer he had been told repeatedly to first take care of the horses, then the men, and only then himself. Eventually they found water for the horses, before the long march to the front, during which several horses collapsed and had to be shot.[134]

The placement of the guns was quite different from what it would have been a dozen years earlier. Then the guns were placed on the front line, ahead of the infantry, where they could see the enemy and fire on them directly. The Boer War had demonstrated that with the new rifles the enemy could see the gunners and could pick them off from as far as a thousand yards away. Now the guns were placed in the rear, needing only a well-placed forward observer, range finders, and faster, more accurate shells to zero in on the enemy. A scientific and mathematical background prepared artillery officers for their duties, rather than the riding to the hounds.

Lt. Macleod described the preparation of the artillery for battle. As practiced in their many exercises, the two Brigades of Artillery, with 36 guns, 36 limbers, a dozen ammunition wagons, and more than 500 horses, dashed over the slopes, guns and horses swinging from their chains. He thought it to be a sight to behold, but the sleepy infantrymen, holding a line of trenches a third of a mile away, were too occupied to cheer. Within seconds, the guns disappeared into the landscape. The horses and limbers were taken back to the wagon lines for their protection by the grooms. As expected, "It was a textbook demonstration. No one had expected anything less."[135]

Far different from the orderly placement of artillery in anticipation of battle was the hasty withdrawal and redeployment in conditions of retreat. Lieutenant Macleod wrote of being awakened at half-past three in the morning with the order to withdraw, getting the men together, hooking up the guns and limbers, and retreating as fast as they could, the men fed up with having to leave their position after all the work they had done. Getting to the rendezvous point was difficult, and with the shelling intense. They got the horses down the steep hill to Petit Wasmes, but then had to keep them calm in the midst of constant explosions and bullets zinging above their heads and ricocheting off the rooftops. As the weight of the guns was bearing down on the horses, the drivers pulled hard on the reins, the brakesmen sweated and strained and the horses neighed and whinnied, their hooves struggling to keep a foothold on the slippery cobblestones.[136]

The importance of maintaining access to the horses that had been moved to the rear while the guns were in action was demonstrated by the experience of a German artillery group retreating in the early, movement phase of the war.

The German troops, defeated at Nery, in their haste had to leave behind their ammunition wagons. They had manhandled their four remaining guns, but with no shells, having left their ammunitions wagons behind, the guns were useless. So they left them behind in the woods, to be found by the British Tommies, who gleefully took them over.[137]

By late October 1914, as huge losses on both sides marked the last stages of the war of movement, British hussars, cavalrymen who dismounted to go into battle as infantrymen, were thrown into the battle. The Northumberland Hussars were relieved and pulled back into reserves. As they walked back to fetch their tethered horses and then clopped wearily down the road, the grooms came behind with the string of horses whose riders lay dead in the wood.[138]

In the difficult British retreat, horses served various purposes. One driver, J. Low, wrote that he was greatly shaken by the retreat since they were getting no food. With no rations, they had to live on the land, getting what they could from the farms. Because it was getting cold at night, and raining, and there was no shelter, he used to put his hand in the horse's mouth and play with the tongue in the back. The horse's warm breath warmed his hand and since the horse knew him and didn't mind, he was not afraid."[139]

A gunner, A. Cook, wrote that because rations were scarce and could not reach them, they had to resort to looting. With most shops and houses evacuated, French families left behind them a choice of a rabbit in a hutch or a duck in the pond. To be able to cook them, they had to form groups, those doing the looting sharing with those that held the horses. Their horses were very useful in another way. Since grapes grew plentifully up the fronts of the houses, the gunners riding single horses were able to ride up to the grapes and just pick a few bunches off, which they had to share with those driving on the guns and other vehicles. For some time they did very well, until the sad order came saying *Looting must stop*.[140]

Rifleman E. Gale wrote of being saddled up, hauling a water cart, twenty-four hours a day for ten days with no more than an hour's sleep at a time. The other drivers were so sick of riding in the saddle that they got off and walked at the head of their horses. The water carts had two poles that were strapped to the shafts. When they had a chance to stop, the drivers would unstrap the poles let them down to the ground, and take the weight off the horses' backs.

Rifleman Gates recalled the case of a fellow who during the entire retirement did not bother about the horses at all. When the saddle was finally pulled off, half the horses' skin came away from their backs. The fellow was removed from the transport and sent back to the Battalion when they linked up with them. In those days your horse used to come before you, he recalled. You could get a soldier for a shilling a day but a horse cost a hundred pounds.[141]

Horses in Soldiers' Memoirs: The Closing Months

From the time of the American Expeditionary Force's arrival in April 1917, General John J. Pershing, its commander-in-chief, was uneasy with the training of American troops by the French and British concentrating on the lessons of trench warfare. He stressed the need for aggressive training in the warfare of movement.[142] With the German breakthrough of March-June 1918, discussed above, the war of movement had arrived.

American artillerymen rushing to the banks of the Marne in July 1918, experienced this. Lieutenant Bledsoe, of Battery A, 7th Field Artillery, serving with the 1st Division, wrote to his sister:

> Of course we had to come into position at night. I'll never forget it! It took two and a half hours to travel the last half-mile. The roads were literally blocked, jammed and packed with men and carriages of every description—caissons, caissons, little guns and big guns, motorcycles, autos, hundreds of horses—men fighting and swearing at them; add to this two or three hundred tanks, a night as black as Hell itself, and over all a drizzling rain, and you can imagine what a tangled mess it must have seemed. However, we reached the battery position at 3 A.M., "layed" the guns and had a bite of "iron ration."[143]

To prepare for their participation in the coming offensive, American artillerymen trained with horses obtained from the British and French, their own horses having been left behind in the U.S. at their port of embarkation. This sometimes presented language problems, as one American artilleryman recounted. Promptly, the morning after their arrival, they drew French horses, guns, and caissons, and set to work breaking the horses to harness. But the horses didn't understand English, which they had to teach them.

He wrote:

> Some of the fellows had brought French grammars over with them, and they tried out some of the French words on the horses. But their pronunciation was so punk

Two. What Did You Do in the War, Dobbin?   51

that the nags didn't savvy at all. As driver of the lead piece, I had my troubles, as you can well imagine.

I gave orders that nothing but United States [English] be talked to the horses, and every time I caught a Frenchy "parlevoing" to them I blew up and asked him what in thunder he meant by butting in on my educational system. I guess the first United States words the nags learned were "damn" and "hell," for I confess I used both pretty freely at the start of the instruction.[144]

While the A.E.F.'s desperate need for horses for its late 1918 offensive was partially met by contributions from its French and British Allies—bringing its horses to only half of full strength—this was not without its cost to its Allies. John Terraine wrote of this period of movement that followed the years of trench warfare that it was still a largely horse-drawn war and that the severe shortage of horses affected not only the Americans, whose plight was worst of all, but also the British field artillery, which, having parted with two out of each of its six-horse teams to supply the Americans, found that in the heavy going of a wet autumn the four-horse teams were often too weak for their new active role.[145]

As U.S. troops were pulled off the line to recover before embarking on the Allied counter-offensive in the spring of 1918, concern focused also on the horses, worn down by duty at the front and facing new strains in the war of movement for which they were being trained. George C. Marshall recounts an incident in April 1918, when the U.S. First Division passed under the control of the French Fifth Army, headed by General Michler, who was greatly concerned that the American horses had not yet fully recovered from the hardships of the fall, and arrived to inspect the Division's artillery regiment.

Marshall wrote:

> General Summerall, who commanded the Artillery Brigade, had been strenuously endeavoring all winter to condition his horses and he was not prepared at this time to acknowledge the existence of any weakness which might delay our entry into the fight. As he assured General Michler that the teams could do their work, a mounted orderly passed close by and his horse—as though he had overheard the conversation—sank to the ground and expired in our presence. Even this did not faze General Summerall, who is one of the greatest living exponents of the principle that much more can be done than ever seems possible, if there is the will to do it.[146]

Not untypical was the experience of Captain Harry S. Truman of Battery D of the 129th Field Artillery. He later recalled:

> Our regular battery positions were in the Herrenberg forests in the Vosges Mountains. Somebody took a notion to fire three thousand rounds of gas at the Germans. So we had to move to another position and put the batteries into place to fire five hundred rounds at seven o'clock. The horses were sent back. As soon as the

last round was fired they were to come with the horses. They were twenty or twenty-five minutes late. I got on a horse to see what was going on. He fell in a shellhole and rolled over on me. The German batteries began to fire on us. The sergeant gave the men by the wrong flank and two of our guns got stuck in the mud. While we were working to release them the Germans fired very close to us and this sergeant hollered, "Run, boys, they got a bracket on us." ... I got up and called him everything I knew.... Pretty soon they came sneaking back.... The Major and the Colonel wanted me to court-martial the sergeant. I didn't but I busted him and afterwards I had to transfer him to another battery. Later [in] the war, he stood firm under the fiercest fire.[147]

George C. Marshal, recalling the final month of the war, wrote:

The culmination of the northward advance of the First Army was a typical American "grandstand finish." The spirit of competition was awakened in the respective divisions to such an extent that the men threw aside all thoughts of danger and fatigue in their efforts to exceed their neighbors. There were numerous cases where soldiers dropped dead from exhaustion, wonderful examples of self-sacrifice and utter devotion to duty. It requires far less of resolution to meet a machine-gun bullet than it does to drive one's body to the death. The men in the Sixth Division, which lacked thousands of draft animals, substituted themselves for the missing horses and mules and towed the machine-gun carts and other light vehicles.

He wrote that though the Army had achieved "a wonderful and inspiring feat of arms by driving the Germans beyond the Meuse from Sedan to Verdun, a 38-kilometer gain in six days, the American people failed to fully appreciate this, having been focused on President Wilson's exchange with the German Government."[148]

Regarding the war's final battles of St. Mihiel and the Meuse-Argonne, Marshall wrote:

Another problem ... was keeping accurate track of the status of the horses in the artillery brigades. Our losses in animals had been tremendous. I believe there were more than forty thousand casualties after the opening of the St. Mihiel, principally in the artillery regiments, from exhaustion, shell fire, and gas. It became necessary in some cases to tow the guns and caissons of artillery regiments out of action with trucks, there not being enough horses left for this purpose. Our men knew little about the care of draft animals and it took them a long time to learn.[149]

General Pershing wrote:

In these last days of the fighting some of our troops, including the 81st, operated with a serious shortage of animals, which made it impossible to employ all their artillery in close support of the infantry, and often required the men to drag their guns by hand. The 6th Division (Gordon), which unfortunately did not get into the battle, pulled a large part of its transportation many miles by hand in attempting to reach the rapidly moving front south of Sedan, where it was planned to use this division in case of necessity.[150]

The loss of horses was heavy too on the German side. Covering the German retreat during the final weeks of the war, *Stars and Stripes* reporter Sergeant Alexander Woollcott wrote:

> But by no means all of the guns captured were sacrifice pieces. Whole batteries were found hooded and mute, abandoned in the haste and confusion of flight that was not made any easier by the fearful slaughter which our artillery wrought among the enemy horses. Dead horses carpeted the battlefield.[151]

Results

In the nineteen months between the April 6, 1917, U.S. declaration of war and the November 11, 1918, Armistice, 243,360 animals served with the American Expeditionary Forces in France, 181,160 horses and 62,200 mules. Of these, 56,603, or 23 percent, died in service.[152] Disposal of their bodies was a particularly difficult problem. As the Report of the A.E.F. Assistant Chief of Staff stated:

> There was without a doubt a demand for dead animals by salvage units, but there was difficulty experienced in getting the carcasses to the rendering plants, as the railroads refused to accept them for shipment. The only recourse was to dispose of the carcasses in the most convenient manner on the spot. In some instances they were turned over to neighboring American or French salvage units; in other cases they were given to local inhabitants who in turn for the hides agreed to remove and dispose of them.[153]

Over the four years of British participation in the war, their contingent of horses in France, which included those purchased in the U.S., suffered losses of 256,000. Of these, only 58,000, or less than a quarter, were officially classified as destroyed by enemy action. The chief cause of the losses was officially given as "debility," brought about by exposure that lowered the animals' resistance. "Picketed out in the open in the Flanders winter, often standing in liquid mud over the fetlocks," many rapidly lost condition and succumbed to lung and digestive troubles.[154]

The A.E.F. faced the problem of disposing not only of dead animals but also of debilitated animals, condemned as unfit for further military service. The first action taken by the A.E.F. was to dispose of them locally at auction. Then, a contract running from June 5, 1918, to September 30, 1918, was entered into with a wholesale butcher in Paris for the taking over of condemned animals for butchery purposes. As the French believed that many animals were being butchered which might be fit for agricultural purposes, it was agreed on October 5, 1918, that the French Government would take over all condemned animals at a flat rate of 450 Francs each, regardless of condition. In exceptional cases, where a badly injured animal had to be killed immediately, the French granted permission to turn the animal over to the local butcher. Of the 14,465 condemned animals, 6,896 were sold by the A.E.F. to butchers and 4,569 turned over to the French.[155]

British forces, serving in Flanders closer to home, had more time to develop a solution. In late 1916, two years after British entry into the war, a London horse-slaughtering firm was commissioned to help dispose of unwanted animals, and Army Waste Products Ltd., a military trading company appointed by the Army Council, was charged with the task of disposing of horse carcasses in an efficient manner. Horsemeat was sold in London and Liverpool and between September 1916, and March 1919, nearly forty thousand horse and mule hides were shipped to England.[156]

Survivors

What of the horses that survived? Were A.E.F. surviving horses to be sent home to the States? Basically, no.

There was apprehension in the U.S. that animals serving with the A.E.F. might be returned to the States and carry some disease or infection acquired abroad. Reacting to reports of a return order in preparation in the Quartermaster General's office, W.H. Butler, president of the Ohio Percheron Breeders' Association, wrote to the War Department:

> It is a well-known fact that there are many diseases now raging in the remount camps on the other side and the return of war animals would no doubt result in the spread of an epidemic in this country among the horses.... It would be most discouraging and disastrous to permit the return of these animals with a chance of a country-wide spread of numerous diseases they are exposed to. The need of horse power on the other side and the high prices there makes it possible for the Government to dispose of the animals over there at a good figure and in this way eliminate the chance of a serious epidemic. Therefore, on behalf of the Ohio breeders I ask that you do all within your power to stop enactment of this order.[157]

On January 30, 1919, the War Department directed that: "No public animals belonging to the military forces will be imported from Europe to the United States." It was directed, however, that up to two hundred private mounts of officers could be imported, subject to ninety days quarantine in Europe, shipment in isolation, and a further ninety days quarantine in the U.S. In addition to veterinarian certification, an officer was required to certify that he was the bona fide owner of the mount and that it was acquired for his personal and official use as an officer of the army.[158]

For horses other than officers' mounts, shipment to the States was not to be.

Following the Armistice, as A.E.F. units were released to return to the States, their animals were not returned with them but were transferred to the Remount Service. The best were selected to replace animals in other divisions that were not in top condition. While surplus animals were not suitable for condemnation, their forage and maintenance costs made it necessary to dispose of them as soon as possible. The French Government, anxious to have the sales conducted under its auspices, selected 5,000 of the best animals in the depots and sold them at auction. Concerned that the French auctioneers did not attempt to push the bidding beyond a very low figure, in many cases probably not over half what the Americans might get, the A.E.F. in March 1919, obtained French agreement for the Remount Service to hold its own auction sales. The Remount Service was able to obtain better prices at 600 public auctions it held in various parts of France and in private sales to farmers and dealers at all Remount depots. It disposed of 113,098 animals between March 1 and June 30, 1919.

The U.S. Liquidation Commission, in charge of the disposal of A.E.F. assets, authorized the sale of surplus animals in Belgium and Luxemburg, but the shortage of forage there was so acute that the civilian population was able to buy only a very small number of animals. More animals were sold to governments. The French Government purchased 33,045 animals on its own account for distribution to inhabitants of its devastated regions. The Polish government bought 5,500 horses and Belgium bought 400 cavalry horses. Other purchases came from England, Serbia, Switzerland and Czechoslovakia.

The Third Army, assigned to Luxemburg and occupation duty in the German Rhineland, was provided with 50,430 animals. It sold its condemned animals for butchering in the occupied German territory. To hasten disposal of remaining surplus animals, the sale of surplus animals in occupied Germany was approved in March and April 1919, on condition that every animal was to be retained in that territory with a record of its location so that it could be easily collected again in case of emergency. By October 1919, the Third Army was reduced to one brigade's strength. It had disposed locally of all its surplus animals and retained only about 600 horses and mules.[159]

Demobilization at Home

Returning British Expeditionary Forces, crossing only the Channel and not the Atlantic, were able to bring back army horses and return them to civilian life. Over the previous four years an estimated 17 percent of Great Britain's working horse population had been taken to the war. The remaining British Army horses in France were thought to include 27 percent that were sound and under eight years old and 44 percent between nine and twelve years, with most of the others either over twelve years or unsound. Only the best of horses, from the class of sound horses under twelve years, were to be returned as soon as they could be released by the army of occupation. It was announced in January 1919 that 25,000 of the best surplus horses would be listed for sale in the British market within a month and that the authorities planned to bring horses back from the army as fast as business and farm work required them.[160]

Within the United States, with all but 200 of the American Expeditionary Forces' horses and mules staying in Europe, there remained in army hands the large stock of animals bought for the war but never shipped overseas. With the demobilization of most of the armed forces, the great majority of these animals would not be needed. To meet the Army's needs, the better animals were retained in the service. Many of the surplus animals were old, of poor type, or with defects and blemishes from hard use.

The Remount Division of the Army announced at the beginning of 1919 that 44,455 surplus animals, including cavalry and artillery horses, and draft and pack mules, would be offered for sale at army camps in a series of auctions beginning the following four Tuesdays.[161] Crowds of farmers attended the auctions of about 1,000 animals each at of the remount depots.[162] Though the auctions were open to all, the Army Quartermaster General quoted estimates that 90 percent of the animals sold were bought by dealers. This, it explained, was due to the fact that the animals sold in the auctions were not guaranteed and that farmers desired a guarantee or the opportunity to try out animals before making a purchase.[163]

Like the Army's attempt to deal with farmers directly with its open market purchasing policy in 1917, when the 30-horse minimum and the nearly 50 percent rejection rate proved a serious obstacle, the no-guarantee auction sales procedure again brought in the dealers to serve an intermediating function between the Army and the farmers. This was in sharp contrast to the Army's sale of surplus food in 1919, which was successfully carried out through retail stores set up in different cities and through orders placed with local postmasters.[164] Clearly, sale of standardized food commodities differed from sale of horses, each of which could differ in many respects.

From the beginning of January to June 30, 1919, 189 sales were held at 39 different places and 170,355 surplus animals were sold, bringing in

$19,073,544.37, or 60 percent of the original cost. The highest percentage of original cost came from the sale of pack and riding mules, 90 percent, and the lowest from sales of cavalry horses, 44 percent.

Animal Sales, January–June 1919[165]

Class	Number	Average Price	Total Value	% Original Cost
Cavalry horses	53,836	$71.30	$3,845,649.66	44
Artillery horses	51,981	$103.86	$5,398,697.71	54
Draft mules	56,951	$153.14	$8,721,257.26	70
Pack mules	7,487	$147.98	$1,107,939.74	90
Total	170,355	$111.96	$19,073,544.37	60

The Quartermaster-General reported that the amount of feed saved to June 31, 1919, as a result of these sales was $12,147,969.80, with savings of labor and overhead costs of a further $7,019,693.60.[166]

The sale of surplus animals was completed in December 1919 with the sale of an additional 14,381 animals, including 5,092 horses and 9,289 mules. This brought the total to 184,737 animals sold for a total of $21,295,524 and a recovery rate of 62 percent of original cost.[167]

On June 30, 1920, with the surplus sales completed, the Army had on hand 89,156 animals as follows[168]:

	Horses	
	Cavalry	38,190
	Draft	13,831
	Pack	125
	Mules	
	Draft	30,127
	Pack	6,883
	Total	89,156

Over the war, therefore, the Army purchased 300,802 animals in the U.S.,[169] shipped 67,725 overseas to the A.E.F.,[170] sold 184,737 of those remaining at home at war's end, and had 89,156 in its hands on June 30, 1920.[171]

The exact statistics vary, however. An April 3, 1919, article in *The Breeder's Gazette* reports that the total number of horses bought by the U.S. Army on both sides of the ocean was 458,653; 152,386 bought abroad and 67,984 shipped over, for an overseas total of 220,284. Losses overseas from all causes were 44,359, or 22 percent, and in the U.S. 7½ percent, for a general average of 14.7 percent.[172]

In 1921 there was erected in the State, War and Navy Department Building in Washington a memorial tablet to commemorate the services of American horses and mules in the war, 243,133 having been employed, with a casualty list of 62,862, besides some 700 that were lost at sea.[173]

Postwar Remounts

Convinced by its wartime experience that horses required in time of war would have to be produced in peacetime, the Army in 1919 created the Remount Board, and in 1921 launched an Army horse breeding and purchasing program. The country was divided into remount areas, with a headquarters in each that procured the best available stallions—generally about 700 in all—and placed them in the hands of the best civilian breeders. The Army's Remount Purchasing and Breeding Program was to operate for 28 years, during which 230,000 foals were produced. About 75 percent of the Army's procurement of horses in these years was the produce of sires placed with agents under the breeding program.[174]

Army purchases were in the 1,500 to 2,500 per year range during the 1930s. By 1940 horses had been replaced completely by motor transport in most military units. The remaining animal-using transport and cavalry units had an authorized strength of 16,800 horses and 3,500 mules. Remount Branch procurement rose to 24,000 horses in fiscal 1941 in anticipation of greater demand, but dropped to 2,900 horses in fiscal 1942, four in fiscal 1943 and none through V-J Day, as units going overseas were dehorsed for lack of shipping space and large scale dismounting of Army and National Guard units was completed by March 1944. Throughout the period only 49 horses were shipped from the U.S. to the armed forces overseas. Within the U.S., the greatest demand came from the Coast Guard, which took 3,900 riding horses for its beach patrols protecting U.S. shores from landings by hostile submarines.[175]

Mules Supply

A contrasting record was presented by mules. Experience with the need for animals in the rugged mountain terrain of Italy and Burma, where few if any roads existed, led to a preference for mules as surer of foot and hardier than horses. As a result, while the remount service purchased only four horses after fiscal 1942, it procured 25,545 mules in these years. Of the 30,523 it purchased in 1941–1945, however, only 7,800 were shipped to the armed forces abroad, and another 3,500 to the United Kingdom under lend-lease. Most of the mules used by the Army in Italy and Burma were procured locally, 11,500 in Italy, for example.[176]

The supply of mules was essential to the Army's Italian campaign. Men holding the high ground in the Apennine Mountains, obtained at the cost of many lives, had to be supplied with ammunition and rations by pack mules. The Remount Service in the U.S. shipped twenty-nine hundred mules and most arrived only in the last weeks of the war. Turning to other, local, sources, the Army purchased two Sardinian mule trains of six hundred mules each. Then, U.S. forces, together with the British, obtained seven Indian, five Cypriot, six Italian, and eight French mule trains, totaling more than ten thousand mules. Remount Depots, with veterinarians treating wounded mules, processed newly purchased mules and those captured from the Germans on a continuous basis and distributed them to the advanced units.[177] When light-colored mules attracted German fire, the quartermasters sprayed them with a 5 percent solution of potassium permanganate, darkening them for about two months.[178]

American forces made extensive use of mules also in their campaign in Tunisia and Sicily. In Sicily they rented horses and donkeys for a dollar a day, with agreement to compensate for killed or disabled animals at $150 per mule, $120 per horse, and $40 per donkey.[179]

Mules proved particularly important in the China-Burma-India Theater of the war. The British under Brig. Orde Wingate, and the Americans under Gen. Joseph Stilwell and Brig. Gen. Frank Merrill (Merrill's Marauders), moved equipment and supplies from India to China over mountains and through jungles. Of 700 mules en route to Merrill's Marauders, 340 were lost on a ship torpedoed in the Arabian Sea.[180]

Like many of the horses shipped off to Europe in World War I, U.S. mules shipped to India in World War II embarked at New Orleans. They were brought down from Camp Hale and Camp Carson in the Colorado Rockies and went off in converted Liberty ships carrying 300 to 400 mules each.[181] They traveled through the Panama Canal and past Guadalcanal and Australia, where they picked up a total of another 4,000 horses and mules. They arrived at Calcutta, from where the Remount Service's three major depots and three sub-depots moved them from the port to the front lines. By war's end the Remount Service had supplied some 18,000 horses and mules to Chinese and U.S. combat forces. Some 10,000 were furnished by the British Remount Directorate, 4,000 Missouri mules directly from the States, and 4,000 relayed from the South Pacific where they had previously served. This was in addition to the animals the Chinese had recaptured from the Japanese and added to their supply.

While the American mules turned out to be well suited for the needs of the Army's field artillery battalions and Quartermaster pack troops, and were used by the Chinese to carry large gun loads, the horses did not do as well in the mountain terrain and jungle climate.

By war's end, all but 4,000 of the 18,000 animals handled by the Remount Service, had been either lost to disease or enemy action or transferred to China. The last were driven in a group of 900 from Lashio to Kunming, a 2,300 mile walk, travelling 15 to 20 miles a day along the old Marco Polo caravan trail and the Stilwell Road.[182]

Back in the U.S., the closing chapter of the American horses' military career was playing out. In contrast to an earlier history of rapid cavalry movement on the plains, the horse had come to focus on the difficult terrain of front-line mud in World War I, beach sand in World War II, and, along with the mule, on mountainous terrain in World War II.

The Army's Horse Breeding Program was transferred in 1948 to the Department of Agriculture, which liquidated the program and sold all stocks at public auction of 100,000 horses, later reduced to 80,000, the following year.[183]

The massive drain on America's horse population which was set off by World War I and tapered down with diminishing military use over the following years, thus came to an end some three decades later.

The Twilight of Army Horses

An interesting personal perspective on the twilight of American army horses is found in the experience of one man, Norbert Ehrenfreund,[184] at the beginning of World War II:

> In September 1939 I enrolled in the University of Missouri and was immediately placed in the Army Reserve Officers Training Corps (ROTC) which at the time was mandatory for all male students. That was the same month and year that Hitler invaded Poland to start World War II so we were pretty serious about the program. We knew we would eventually get into the war. The Missouri program was focused on horse-drawn artillery which meant we had to learn to ride horseback, hitch the horses up to artillery caissons and howitzers and drive the horse teams over rough territory. At the time we used teams of six horses, two behind two behind two, to pull the caissons and the artillery weapons. We had no jeeps or trucks and relied solely on the horses for transportation. One man would drive the lead team, another man would have the middle team, and another the third team which was closest to the object being pulled, all harnessed together. So it was three men driving six horses. Obviously we all had to move in unison or we couldn't move.
>
> I remember one time I was driving the lead team and we had to cross a little ditch. The ditch was wide enough and deep enough that I had to jump my team

across it. When I jumped my horses the team behind me balked and held back which yanked my team back from under me and I went flying head over heels forward over my horse. I was thrown to the ground on the other side of the ditch. There being no one to drive the lead team, the horses all got excited and started rushing forward without a leader. I was on my back and looking up at six horses coming right at me pulling this heavy caisson behind them. I was scared because it seemed like they were about to roll right over me. Fortunately I was able to scramble to the side and get out of the way while they ran right past me.

While we were learning to ride that first year a debate arose among the ROTC higher-ups as to which saddle we should use. It was said on one side that the Western saddle was better because it was more comfortable and easier to stay in the saddle; on the other side it was said that the smaller English saddle was better because the rider could last longer in that saddle in a long ride. The English saddle won out and that's the one we always used from then on. After about a year the Army suddenly decided that horses were obsolete, especially for combat in Europe, so they got rid of the horses and brought in jeeps and trucks. We all had to learn to drive which I couldn't do very well. It made me sad because I loved the horses. They were something you could get attached to. They were warm and goodhearted and had beautiful eyes. We had to say goodbye to them and I wondered what would happen to them. I remember kissing them on the nose before they were taken away. The vehicles were cold and impersonal. What's to love? You couldn't love a truck.

After graduation and a three-month course at Officers Candidate School (OCS) I longed to get back to horses if I had the chance. So when I got out of OCS as a second lieutenant the Army gave me the chance to choose what kind of outfit I wanted. It was now 1943. As far as I could tell there were no more horses in the cavalry. No more horse-drawn artillery. The infantry didn't use horses. Where had all the horses gone? The closest thing to a horse outfit was the mule pack artillery which involved mules carrying parts of 75 millimeter howitzers through the mountains along with ammunition and the other necessary supplies. So that's what I chose and that's what I got. But before I could join a mule pack battery I had to pass a thirty-day equestrian course at Fort Sill, Oklahoma.

It was an exhilarating experience. There were about ten of us in the course. Each of us was assigned our own horse for the month. We had to get down to the stable every morning and groom and wash our horse and make sure they were fed properly and clean out our horse's shoes, then saddle up, and head out together across the Oklahoma plains, the same grassy fields where the famous Indian fighter Geronimo used to ride against the white intruders. We'd ride all day, sometimes in a line in a narrow lane through the woods, sometimes the ten of us abreast if we were in a big open field, hooting and yelling and waving our arms as if we were a cavalry platoon going into battle. The only thing missing was a flag up front flapping in the wind. We knew the old days of horses in battle were dying out and that we were the last vestige of those old glory days so often pictured in the movies. We knew we might be the last of the horse-back riding officers in the American army and we were determined to make the most of it.

On the last day came the final examination. We had to gallop as fast as we could to keep up with our leader, jump high hedges, leap off a cliff into a lake with our horse and then swim our horse across the lake to the other shore. There was only one test given, whether you passed or not. If you were still on your horse at the end of the grueling eight-hour ride, you passed. If not, you failed. It was that simple. I fell off twice but got back in the saddle each time and so I passed.

Then I was assigned to Battery B, 607th Field Artillery Battalion, 71st Infantry Division, a mule pack battery stationed at Camp Carson, Colorado, in Colorado Springs. I had hoped there would be at least a few horses in my new outfit but there were none. Only mules. Nevertheless while the mules did not have the personality and charm of horses, you could still pat them and talk to them and in some cases even love them. They had a reputation for being stubborn and not as smart as horses but in some ways they were smarter than horses. For instance when a mule got too tired he would stop and refuse to go on until he rested while a horse would keep going until he dropped. The mule packers were a rough and ready bunch. They took pride in how tough they were, always on their feet, never riding, each man walking beside his mule, cursing them and singing to them. We climbed Pike's Peak from the western slope, the side opposite the tourist trail. The mules turned out to be good climbers and sometimes we had to grab their tails on steep cliffs to keep from falling back.

We were told we were being trained for combat in the mountains of Burma or Italy. The Army wanted to see what the mules could do in long marches over rugged terrain similar to what we would have to face in those foreign lands. So they took us out of Colorado and sent us off on maneuvers in central California near San Lucas. We arrived during the height of the rainy season and had to slog through the mud and rain and quicksand. At night we would huddle around the fire and sing the mule pack song:

> I'd rather be a soldier, with a mule and a mountain gun,
> Than a knight of old, with spurs of gold,
> A Roman, Greek or Hun.
> For when there's trouble brewing
> They always send for me,
> To start the fun with a mountain gun
> In a mule pack battery.

Then the plans changed. The generals decided they needed us in Europe and suddenly the same thing happened that happened in ROTC with the horses. They took the mules away and gave us vehicles instead. I knew that this time we were motorized for good. The romance with horses and mules was over. So was our association with the mountain gun—the 75 millimeter howitzer. It was late 1944. We were sent overseas to France with 105mms and immediately went into combat on the western front.

In the spring of 1945 the story of horses in World War II came to a bitter end for me. For all the talk about the blitzkrieg and so on the German army still relied heavily on horses for transportation. They still had horse-drawn artillery and used horses to pull their wagons whereas we did not. Even the German infantry used horses extensively whereas we were mostly mechanized with jeeps and trucks and tanks. As the Germans retreated in Europe they left behind hundreds of their dead horses slain by our artillery and air raids. It was a gruesome sight. I saw horses lying in the roadside, some with their guts split open, some lying in pools of blood, innocent victims of the war and man's aggressive nature.

Three

On the American Road

Far from the battlefields of the First World War, along the roads of the nation, the horse was facing a different challenge. Even as the American horse population was reaching its peak in 1915, the long history of horse-drawn vehicles was winding down.

The marriage of the wheeled vehicle to the horse came some four thousand years ago. Over the millennia, three things were to change in the technology surrounding the life of the horse on the road: the wheel, the road, and the vehicle. In the end, it was the vehicle, which came to be self-propelled, that brought the life of the horse on the road to a close.

Wheels

The critical importance of the wheel was evident at the start. Chronologically, the cart came before the horse, as the A-frame two-wheeled vehicle—the cart—was drawn first by the donkey-like onager, or wild ass, a native of northwest India.[1] This was followed by the more cumbersome four-wheeled wagon in use in Mesopotamia around 2,800 BCE and weighing half a ton. It could be pulled only by oxen since harnessing horses to such a heavy load remained a problem.

Both the two-wheeled and four-wheeled vehicles made use of solid wooden wheels. To reduce the wear on the wheels' running surface, leather tire coverings were introduced and then protruding iron nails. As the wheeled vehicles came into use in Europe and the Middle East, the spoked wheel was invented by the Celts, fastening together a series of C-shaped segments, formed by bending heated timber. With the lighter spoked wheel, the two-wheeled cart, and particularly the two-wheeled chariot, could be pulled by horses.[2]

Horses came to be associated with the chariot—a light open vehicle with two spoked wheels, drawn by horses yoked on either side of a draught pole, as represented on Syrian seals dating from the eighteenth century BCE.[3] Chariots continued in use well into Roman times. Wheeled vehicles, however, were dependent on terrain. War chariots were especially vulnerable over muddy or rocky ground but could attain remarkable speeds over smooth and even surfaces.[4] This was evident in the popular chariot races in the Roman circuses and hippodromes and was the basis also for the solidly paved network of Roman roads.

Iron came to be used for building the vehicle bodies about 1500 BCE, and iron tires were built by bolting or riveting iron segments to the wooden wheel. The process was simplified by the Celts about 400BCE by building an iron tire smaller than the wheel, heating it to expand, and shrinking it into place around the wheel as it cooled.[5]

Metal surfaced wheels were to continue in use into the nineteenth century—and even today in some areas—when solid rubber tires came as an improvement, with Charles Goodyear's discovery of the practical vulcanization of rubber in 1839.[6] The final improvement, perhaps too late for the horse, was the pneumatic rubber tire, invented in 1888 by the Scottish veterinarian John Dunlop, specifically for the use of the bicycle.[7] Earlier in the nineteenth century came the flanged iron wheel to fit the rails of the railroad and of the urban horse cars within the cities.[8]

Pavement

Roman roads, bordered on both sides by longitudinal drains, were built up with an earthen structure using material excavated from the drains, covered with a leveling bed of sand, and topped off with a layer of flat stones. Then came a cement-stabilized or mortared course of small stones followed by a similar layer of smaller broken stones or brick material. Well compacted, this was covered with carefully fitted hexagonal flat stones.[9]

In the centuries following the decline and fall of the Roman Empire, the knowledge and resources for the construction and maintenance of roads of Roman quality were gone. The demand for roads in Europe declined, reflecting the decline of trade and of organized military activities. Roads that were built for trade were narrow, wide enough only for pack animals, not wheeled vehicles.

Then, with increasing population and trade, there came a dramatic increase in wagon and coach travel between 1550 and 1750, calling attention to the need for improvements in the conditions of the roads.[10] A number of ambitious efforts at improved road construction were undertaken in the seventeenth and eighteenth centuries. One widely followed innovation in the eighteenth century was by the Scottish stonemason and bridge builder, Thomas Telford. Built over the large flat blocks at the bottom were vertically set oblong stones, placed on edge, with smaller stones hammered into the interstices, and covered with a layer of pebbles and broken stones.[11]

These efforts were capped by a new departure, introduced by John Loudon McAdam (1756–1836). He determined that it was unnecessary to have large stone blocks at the bottom to ensure stability. A bed of sharp, broken stones, firmly tamped down together was just as firm. Above this, a firmly tamped down bed of smaller broken stones—with sharp edges, as distinguished from rounded-edge gravel—drained, and kept relatively dry, would provide a better running surface.[12] The surface stones, it was stressed, were to be smaller than the width of the common iron coach tire.[13] One drawback of the open graded course, however, was that it was easy for horses' hooves to dislodge surface stones.[14]

This macadam road set the widely adopted standard for road building in the decades that followed. The immediate consequence of the new paving in England was that the speed at which the Royal Mail coaches could travel was limited not by the road but by the ability of the horses.[15]

The need for improvement of macadam roads, particularly for urban traffic, led to a number of innovations. One was the use of bitumen, the heavy, viscous component of petroleum, sometimes referred to as pitch, for waterproofing and as a glue for the top layer of stones.[16] Mixed with sand and fine stone and called mastic, it was also used for footpath construction.[17] The mixture of bitumen and limestone in its native formation as asphalt, called natural asphalt, varied in composition at different sites around the world. It was found slippery and abradable in mid-nineteenth century European tests. Instead, stone blocks were used in Paris and wood blocks in London.[18] Tests of natural asphalt in the U.S. in the 1870s found it relatively durable but excessively slippery, though advocates claimed it caused less injury to horses when they fell and was more resilient underfoot.[19]

With the extraction of coal gas from coal and its use for street lighting early in the nineteenth century, tar became available as a by-product at a very cheap rate. It soon came to be used as filler, replacing the sand, stone, dust, and soil being used to fill the open spaces in the macadam surface. Pouring the melted tar to seep down between the stones as a binder gluing together the course of stones, and later improved as road tar, proved to be effective, particularly for rural roads, and came to be referred to as tar macadam or tarmac.[20]

Pouring cement, made of burnt limestone or dolomite, together with water and sand, over the underlying mix of stones produced a form of concrete, a composite that includes stones.[21] Below the running surface, the structural courses could make use also of concrete, a Roman usage forgotten over the centuries and rediscovered at the end of the eighteenth century. With the introduction of improved concrete mixes and continuous concrete mixers, concrete came to be used extensively in the late nineteenth century in the underlying road structure. It was less appropriate for surface use since its smooth impervious finish made it slippery and impractical for iron-shod animal traffic.

Subsequently, the combination of natural asphalts from different sites, with other additions, including sand, finely crushed limestone, and bitumen, gained some success.[22] Resistance persisted, however, to mixtures that were not the natural product and controversy over the best additions and the proportion to be used continued well into the following century.

Variations in the macadam surface started with the introduction of smaller materials to fill the voids, then pitch, or bitumen, as mortar between the stones, and then tar, for what came to be called tarmac.[23] Finally came asphalt, which produced, however, a slippery surface.

The horse-drawn vehicle of the nineteenth century posed a dilemma for the pavement engineer. Good surface traction and resilience were needed to accommodate the horses, while the hard iron-tired wheels needed a smooth and rigid surface.[24]

While McAdam regarded compaction by traffic to be adequate for the stone courses, others, particularly in France in the 1830s, considered rolling a necessary element of compaction. Horses, however, could not pull rollers heavy enough to result in adequate compaction. A British roller maker used a steam traction engine, available in 1842, to substitute for horses pulling the roller, and by 1850 a combined tractor engine and roller in a single unit was in use in Paris. In Calcutta, a new steam-powered roller replaced the bullocks that had been pulling the road roller. While thirty-ton rollers were found to crush the stones and defeat the necessary interlock, twenty-ton rollers were found to be satisfactory. Though steam rollers were retired after decades of service in the 1960s, their diesel replacements continued to be referred to as steamrollers.[25]

Horses and oxen were essential in earthworks for road construction, pulling plows, scoops, scrapers, spreaders, leveling drags, and carts. By the 1880s, wide scoop-like devices pulled by four horses could shift a cubic meter of material an hour and soon the material could be mechanically lifted into carts by special machines pulled by further teams of horses. Horses were replaced in road construction by steam-driven tractor engines introduced in 1885 and by gasoline-powered crawler tractors with self-laying tracks introduced in 1904. Stimulated by the example of the tanks in World War I, tractor use expanded in the 1920s, with the introduction of the bull-dozer, followed by the coming of diesel-powered equipment in the 1930s.[26]

Even as advanced equipment arrived to build and maintain the more modern roads, other roads continued to serve with the pavements of an earlier age. One early alternative to beaten earth was the cobblestone. Uncut, with rounded corners, it was embedded with the largest surface vertical in a bed of sand, lacking mortar until late in the nineteenth century. Smaller than the contact surface of wheels and hooves, cobblestone surfaces were free-draining, inert and strong, but uneven, noisy, and slippery.[27] They did not have the problem of large, flat slabs, which tilted or cracked under heavy wheel loads near the edge.

To accommodate wheeled traffic, flat-faced cubicle stone, called stone setts, were adopted, with the spaces in between filled with sand, mortar, pitch, or tar. Setts made of Belgian granite, for example, were used for New York City pavements. Setts were generally limited in size to less than the width of horses' hooves. To improve traction, urban horses' shoes were often built with small protuberances called calks. Though setts were far costlier than the broken stones of macadam surfaces, worn main street setts would be taken up, redressed, and re-laid on minor streets.[28]

One alternative to stone, was the use of timber blocks, with the tough end-grain facing traffic. They were sometimes set on a structural course of crushed rock and sand, sometimes covered with tar and sand. Rotting was a major problem with wood blocks, however, partially alleviated with creosote impregnation. The creosote-soaked wooden streets caught fire in the 1871 Great Fire in Chicago, as they had previously in San Francisco and New York. Hardwood blocks remained a preferred option, however, with London experience showing fewer horse accidents with wood blocks than with asphalt or granite setts.[29]

One alternative meeting the requirements of both the iron-tired wheeled vehicles and the iron-shod horses pulling them was the cartway. Laying narrow, smooth flat stones only on the wheelpaths on both sides provided a smooth wheel track for the cart or wagon and left a better traction surface between for the horse pulling the cart or wagon. The smooth surface for the wheels permitted the horse to pull a much greater load. A cartway between Albany and Schenectady operated from 1834 to 1901.[30]

Studies in the late nineteenth century of the resistance of various surface types to iron-tired wheels showed clearly the effect of the changes that had been made in road surface. The pull a horse needed to exert, as a fraction of the weight being pulled, was one-seventh on deep, loose sand, one-fifteenth on dry earth and gravel, one-thirty-fifth on cobblestone, one-seventieth on well-packed dry macadam, one-ninetieth over brick, and one two-hundred and fiftieth on stone trackway or steel plate.[31] With so considerable an advantage for steel, cities followed the example of railroads and laid tracks on their streets for horses to pull passengers on horse cars.

Vehicles

The third technology to change and affect the life of the horse on the road was the vehicle the horse was to pull. The earliest vehicle was the two-wheeled cart, an important example being the chariot, discussed above. There was no problem steering the two-wheeled cart since it could turn around the bottom contact point of the two wheels. With the four-wheeled wagon, however, the fixed axles did not permit the vehicle to turn at sharp curves. The solution came in the attachment of the front axle to a vertical axis around which it could swivel. The front wheels, in addition, had to be small enough to pass under the floor of the vehicle when they turned. Fully steerable wagons were not prevalent in Europe until the Middle Ages or later, with a greater dependence on carts.[32] Trade moved overland in large part by pack horse, and mainly by river or sea. Later, in the era of canals, horses could haul a barge with twenty times the load they could pull in a cart or wagon, though at half the speed.[33]

The width of a cart or wagon, that is the distance between its wheels, was limited from earliest times by the width of the road and by the practice of wheel-rutting, that is the cutting of ruts in the surface of the road to fit the distance between the wheels.[34] Vehicles were also limited as to the weight they could carry and the width of each wheel. Concern over the damage to road surfaces by heavy loads borne by iron-tired wheels led to limiting loads, based on how much each horse could haul. Wagons drawn by more than two horses were banned in Paris in 1508, for example, as were vehicles drawn by more than five horses on English roads in 1629.[35] In shogunate Japan two hundred years ago, on the Tokaido, one of the five main roads maintained for official purposes, stations were set up to provide travelers with horses, runners, and palanquin bearers, but wheeled vehicles were prohibited because of the ruts they would cause.[36] Ruts created by America's covered wagons, travelling with no roads in pioneer days were still visible from the air at the end of the twentieth century.[37]

Over the centuries, the use of four-wheeled vehicles to carry passengers advanced. Brakes controlling downhill hazards permitted their use in hilly terrain. To tamp down the jarring jolts from riding rigidly connected to the axles, straps and chains were used to suspend the passenger compartment from wooden corner posts. Next the suspension came from the top of C-shaped iron springs. Finally, in the early nineteenth century, the passenger compartment could rest on the newly invented horizontal elliptical springs. With a lower center of gravity and the lighter construction, coaches could carry more passengers more comfortably and, with more horses, travel at greater speeds.[38]

Over the centuries, passenger service between cities became better organized and more regular. Coaches traveled in stages between houses posted along the route—post houses—that provided fresh teams of horses. France had introduced a private stage system, in which travelers supplied their own two-wheeled carts, known as chaises, or shays, and hired horses from post houses along the way.[39]

Within cities, new variations of both two-wheeled and four-wheeled vehicles evolved. In earlier centuries, most cities were small enough to allow their residents to reach destinations within the city by foot.[40] With industrialization and the growth of city sizes, stagecoach services were extended to within cities with some variations. Rather than the coaches' entry from the side, the longer, horse-drawn city omnibuses had their entry from the rear. The pace of the omnibus through the city streets was quite slow, the horse moving at a walk. London omnibus operators, in fact, offered the passengers free newspapers and books to read in transit, a practice cited by some as the first free library.[41]

Operation of omnibuses on city streets was generally subject to rules set by government authorities. Early experience in London included the licensing and numbering of omnibuses, permission to pick up and set down passengers on city streets at specified stops, rather than at riders' houses, the charging of set fares, and requirements that drivers and conductors be licensed and wear numbered badges.[42] One reported daily London omnibus routine was the veterinarian examination of each horse every morning.[43]

Improving roads and new lighter two-wheel and four-wheel vehicles brought a new role to American horses. During the first half of the nineteenth century "a network of well-engineered roads began snaking across America ... and [Americans] climbed out of the saddle and into the driver's seat."[44] Mid-nineteenth century historian Frank Forester noted that five out of six people he passed on the road were driving, not riding. Great numbers of new types of stylish, well-sprung vehicles were produced: the buggy, barouche, coach, cabriolet, randem, berlin, Victoria, surrey, herdic, hansom, rockaway, cariole, britzka, tilbury, chaise, phaeton, sluggy, gharry, coupe, curricle, trap, growler, gig, dos-a-dos, landau, limber, brougham, vis-à-vis, and whim.[45] The horse and wheeled vehicle had been reunited on a grand scale.

The spread of fast-moving horse-drawn vehicles generated great enthusiasm for the sport of harness racing, in which horses running at either of two gaits, the trot or the pace, pulled a two-wheeled rig called a sulky, generally for the distance of a mile. "For the final fifteen years of the nineteenth century, and the first fifteen of the twentieth.... America had a passionate fling with the light harness horse, or Standardbred, as he is more formally known, ... and followed his sport more fervently than any other."[46] Americans enjoying their own fast buggies speeding along the road could identify with the horse-drawn sulky speeding around the track.

But the unhorsed vehicles were soon to intrude upon this scene. In microcosm, this scenario was played out in New York's Central Park.[47]

In Central Park, a mecca of stylish carriage exposure in the decades since its establishment in 1859, the rivalry came first in the form of bicycles. In 1880 bicycle traffic was banned from the park as an uncontrollable disturbance to horses' equilibrium. Bicycle-riders, organized in 1880 as the League of American Wheelmen (LAW), challenged the ban, first by appeal to the Park Commissioners and then by violating the ban and carrying their case to the New York Supreme Court. Testimony before a referee centered on whether bicycles frightened horses and could lead to dangerous runaways if admitted to the park. The judge ruled, however, that whatever the merits of the case, the law gave the commissioners the widest discretion and that no court would be justified in setting aside a provision made by them for the regulation of the parks except in the clearest cases.

In April 1884, the Commissioners allowed bicycles to use the park at certain hours, though reportedly not the pleasantest and most convenient hours. Failing in a December 1886, appearance before the Commissioners seeking to have all restrictions lifted, the Wheelmen turned to the State Legislature. There, in May 1887, a bill was passed stipulating that the bicycle was a carriage and could not be excluded from any roadway where pleasure vehicles were admitted. Following wide-ranging debate, the bill was signed by the governor. It became law in June 1887, and bicycles were admitted to the park.

Next came the automobile. The first sale of an automobile in the United States took place in 1896 and in 1899 the Automobile Club of America was founded in New York. It soon turned its attention to seeking approval for automobiles to operate in Central Park. Pressing a test case in which a club officer was arrested for driving in the park, it secured a magistrate's ruling that automobiles qualified as "pleasure carriages" so that, under provisions of the 1887 bicycle law, automobiles could use the park. On December 16, 1899, after considerable deliberation and experimental drives, the Park Commissioners issued a permit to the club officer specifying that he may "enter upon and pass over the drives of Central Park with an open electric pleasure carriage (phaeton) operated by an experienced motorman."[48]

Outside the park, across the nation, governments were beginning to face the presence of automobiles on the roads, and they too were concerned with the effect on horses. Initially, motor vehicles were simply subjected to the same laws that applied to the ownership and use of horse-drawn vehicles. About the turn of the century, however, separate automobile ordinances were passed, but at the local level. This gave way to state regulation, led by compulsory automobile registration in New York State in 1901, followed by eight other states in 1903.[49]

Maryland's first automobile legislation, in 1904, besides setting speed limits of six and ten miles an hour, took special care to protect the horse. It provided:

> That the person in charge of said motor vehicle at the signal or request of any person riding a horse, or any person leading or driving a horse or other animal, or at the indication of such horse or horses or other animals becoming alarmed by said motor vehicle, shall go as far as practicable to the side of the road and remain stationary until said horse or horses or other animals have passed to a safe distance, in the meantime making as little noise as possible with the steam.[50]

The next automobile law, in 1906, while raising the speed limit to twelve miles an hour, provided that on meeting a horse and buggy driven by a lady or child, the motorist was required to use every precaution to avoid frightening the horse, and if requested to do so, to stop the motor vehicle, alight, and lead the horse by the vehicle.[51]

The same law, to protect motorists from attacks that had been occurring, made it a misdemeanor "to hurl stones or other missiles at [any automobile] or at the occupants thereof."[52]

Such measures could not stop the increasing difficulties of automobiles speeding alongside slower horse-drawn vehicles. By 1911, one observer, signing himself Manhattan in communications to *The Breeder's Gazette*, wrote:

> Road driving, which was very popular for many years prior to the coming of the automobile, exists now in memory, and this is due to the fact that people will not run the risk of broken limbs and death on the automobile-infested roads where machines run riot with speed ordinances, and injure, maim, and kill seemingly as they choose.[53]

In 1913, viewing the situation in Central Park, he wrote: "It seems only a short time ago ... that horses outnumbered automobiles more than 2 to 1. Now there are fully forty automobiles to 1 horse."[54] However, "If the automobile has practically put the fast-stepping road horse out of commission," he noted, "it has not detrimentally affected the saddle horse in the community. In Central Park the bridle paths fairly swarm with riders.... It is estimated that fully 2,000 horses per day are used for park riding, a large part of which comes from the riding academies located near the park entrance."[55]

Outside the park similar changed were taking place. He wrote:

> It is doubtful if any other place in the country has undergone such a radical change in livery and boarding stables during the past ten years as the city of New York. The American Horse Exchange, at Broadway and 50th street, the California Stable in 58th street, the Decernea, the Colorado, and one or two other stables in 58th street, the Tichenor-Grand Horse Exchange in 61st street, and the Dwyer Stable in 142d street, are among the places where a few years ago horses could be hired or boarded and that have been converted to other uses. With the exception of the riding academies, where only horses are boarded and kept for hire, there is scarcely a place on Manhattan Island today that can properly be called a livery and boarding stable in which such business is exclusively conducted.
>
> One does not have to look very far to ascertain the cause of this transformation. In the days when the livery and boarding stables were prosperous, the road horse was at the height of his popularity and the public stables were crowded with fast driving horses and vehicles owned by the sport-loving people, who experienced much pleasure in speeding along the streets and avenues in the suburbs of the city and dining at the popular road houses which were at that time everywhere abundant. Now there is scarcely a road house patronized by road drivers within ten miles of Madison Square Garden and it is exceedingly rare that a road horse hitched to a road wagon or a light vehicle of any kind is seen upon the streets or in the parks and the most unsalable horse in the market is the once famous roadster.[56]

By 1919, cars were going much faster—the Maryland speed limit had been raised to 35 miles an hour[57]—and the builders of new roads gave little thought to horses. Experience during World War I, trying to move men and materials to the East Coast by truck convoys over rutted dirt roads in the face of inadequate railroad facilities, had convinced Federal authorities that major trunk lines, "defense highways," were needed. The Federal Aid Road Act of 1916 had left the choice of where to build roads to the states with Washington bearing half the cost and overseeing the projects.[58]

In these circumstances, one objective of the new Horse Publicity Association of America, meeting for the first time in 1919, was: "to see to it that the public highways are so constructed as to afford safe and adequate roadways for horse-drawn vehicles."

"As you know," temporary chairman Fred M. Williams told the group,

> the roads now being constructed at public expense are almost worthless, so far as the horse is concerned. Legislators seem to think they have performed their full duty to the public when they have provided a smooth, hard, narrow strip or race course for the automobile. Under certain weather conditions it is impossible for the horse to pull a load on these roads.
>
> We contend that if the public is to build roads which at present seem to be constructed for the exclusive use of motor-driven vehicles, the law should at least provide for a strip on either side for horse-drawn loads.... Surely the highways which are paid for from the public treasury should be for the people and not for a favored frenzied few.[59]

Through the rest of the twentieth century the riding academies providing riding horses for Central Park continued on a dwindling scale. The last to go was the Claremont Riding Academy on West 89th Street, which closed its doors on April 29, 2007. Its owner explained that it had become too costly to run the stable and that the bridle paths in Central Park had gotten too crowded—with humans, not horses. *The New York Times* lamented its passing and wondered "whether the city wasn't more human still when we shared so much more of it with horses." All that was left of the once great urban herd, it commented, were the carriage horses in the park and the police horses in Midtown.[60]

However, the carriage horses too faced opposition. By 2014, some 220 carriage horses living in four stables hidden away in three-to-four story buildings on Manhattan's far west side, would wend their way through up to two miles of city traffic to put in their nine-hour shifts in Central Park.[61] Their presence was the subject of controversy and political advocacy. Opponents stressed the trips through city traffic and the horses' lack of green space. Supporters pointed to the good care the horses received, their annual five-week vacation mandated by the City Council, and the carriage rides' attraction to tourists from the United States and abroad.[62] One compromise, proposed by a former parks commissioner, was to convert several structures within Central Park to stables, so that the horses and carriages would never have to leave the park.[63]

Stagecoach, Omnibus, Horsecar

While the family buggy was being crowded off the road by the growing traffic of automobiles, horse-drawn public transportation was ceding its place to the railroad, the cable car, and the trolley.

A pioneer of horse-drawn public transportation was the stagecoach. A closed-in four-wheel coach, it carried eight to fourteen passengers, baggage and mail on a fixed route and schedule between stages or stations. Typically drawn by four or six horses, that were changed for fresh horses at the stations along the route, coaches would travel twelve to eighteen hours a day and cover forty miles a day in summer and twenty five miles or more a day in winter. The stagecoach flourished mainly during the first half of the nineteenth century, when improved roads made the use of wheeled vehicles, rather than horseback, practical in Europe and America. In 1785, for example, stagecoach lines began carrying passengers, baggage and mail between London and Edinburgh and between Albany and New York.[64] Post roads, the route of some early stagecoaches, came to play a

Last trip of the famous Deadwood stagecoach, South Dakota, 1890. Photograph by John C.H. Grabill (Library of Congress).

prominent role in America during this period, increasing from 1,905 miles in 1792 to 115,176 miles in 1830.[65]

With its coach supported lengthwise by two leather straps to diminish jolts felt by the passengers, the stagecoach was the mainstay of public transportation in the Eastern states and the pioneer American West before the coming of the railroad. Completion of the transcontinental railroad in 1869, however, replaced the cross-country stagecoach, and shorter branch railroads phased out shorter stagecoach runs except in remote areas which railroads did not reach.

On the urban scene, short-run stagecoaches carried passengers from outlying suburbs into the city early in the nineteenth century. By the 1820s, however, horse-drawn omnibuses, which had evolved from the stagecoach with a longer body, made their appearance. Carrying twelve to twenty passengers along a fixed route and schedule, omnibuses were in use in Paris, London and New York. Inspired by a Paris omnibus, a low-slung vehicle resting on elliptical springs producing a more comfortable ride and an easier pull for horses was introduced in New York, which came to be called "The City of Omnibus."[66]

School children in a horse-drawn car, Washington, D.C., circa 1899. Photograph by Francis Benjamin Johnston (Library of Congress).

Laying tracks along the omnibus route made the ride even smoother and easier for the horse to pull. Running on tracks, the omnibus became the horsecar. By 1859, horsecars, on tracks, were operating in New York, New Orleans, Brooklyn, Boston, Philadelphia, Baltimore, Pittsburgh, Cincinnati, and Chicago, though Washington public transit still consisted of only one line of horse-drawn omnibuses.[67] Elsewhere in the 1880s, horses

> hauled open wooden cars with bench seats along steel tracks on muddy streets at a mere six miles an hour—not much faster than a person could walk. [These] required prodigious numbers of horses, which were expensive, survived only four to five years in their grueling labor, and were prone to maladies....[68]

The search for some alternative to horses for hauling city horse cars was stimulated by two factors coming from abroad. One was the sudden arrival of Peruvian guano, a more effective fertilizer, which made the manure, previously a valuable by-product of street railway stables, a liability which required payment for its removal. The other was the Great Epizootic of 1972, a respiratory and lymphatic disease, in which 18,000 horses were

Horse-drawn street car, between 1915 and 1925 (Library of Congress).

killed or disabled in New York in three weeks, stopping all street car operations for several weeks, and leading New York horse car operators to hire teams of immigrants to move the horse cars though the streets.[69] In fact, the epidemic was quite widespread.

Epizootic

In the late days of September 1872, an equine influenza attacked horses in Markham, Ontario. From there it spread as a panzootic along the rail lines, first entering the U.S. in Michigan and upstate New York. It then proceeded explosively to the west and south, so that it spread over the entire U.S., Mexico, the Caribbean, and Central America, affecting virtually every horse, mule, donkey, and carnival zebra, and spilling over to dogs and cats.[70] An avian outbreak that followed it, with more deadly effect on poultry, may or may not have been associated with the equine panzootic.

The mortality rate among horses was low, one to 5 percent, but more severe among mules and donkeys.[71] Animals were reported to be in "a stupid condition." The effect of the epizootic was particularly severe in urban areas, stopping passenger vehicles of all kinds, obliging doctors to walk to their patients, preventing undertakers from burying the dead for lack of horses to draw the hearses, and crippling firefighting, calling for help from citizens to pull the fire engines.[72] The crises, though severe, was relatively short-lived. Its lasting effect, however, was that in the various fields where horses served it hastened the search for an alternative to the horse, whose traditional dependability was put in question, despite the horse's devotion.

Cable Cars

Across the continent, in San Francisco, another scenario was unfolding. Application of a square-grid street pattern to this hilly site without regard to its contours had left some streets in the city with grades of over 20 percent. When mining engineer Andrew Smith Hallidie witnessed a struggling team being whipped to drive it up a steep San Francisco street, his thoughts went to the rope pulley system he had worked with for moving materials up from mines. Why not apply the continuous rope principle for moving mine loads to moving vehicles up the steep streets of the city?[73]

Variations of the idea had come before. Proposals earlier in the nineteenth century had envisaged moving vehicles along a fixed cable with winding devices on each vehicle or by having vehicles grasp a moving rope or chain. A cable-traction system for large-scale passenger movements had in fact operated in London since the 1840s. There the first car was attached to a hemp rope, later changed to a cable, paid out and redrawn in, with other cars picked up or set out at intermediate stations.[74] It had not come to America for lack of urban concentrations, which were just giving rise to the omnibus and horse car.

Hallidie's efforts in San Francisco, with the aid of other investors and civic leaders, were successful, and the first system of passenger vehicles gripping a continuous moving cable opened in 1876. It was an expensive, complicated system. A steam-powered engine house had to pull a long, continuous cable through a route of underground conduits topped by a slot through which a lever controlled by a gripman tightened a grip grasping the cable to move the vehicle and released the grip to slow and stop.

In 1880, C.B. Holmes, president of the Chicago City Railway, visited San Francisco and determined that the San Francisco system could run in Chicago. Replacing 1,000 horses and 200 stablemen, the Chicago cable car system opened in 1882, and, in the face of snow, cold, and traffic density, was operated with considerable success.[75] This set off a spurt of cable car system building in the larger American cities.

The cable car system was attractive mainly to large cities, whose dense populations could justify the large initial investment and the cost of keeping a cable moving continuously. It had particular advantage also to cities with steep grades on their streets, since, unlike horse cars, cable cars did not depend on surface traction in order to climb a hill.

The system was not simple. Pulleys had to be installed to carry the cable around corners, to level it at the top and bottom of hills, to raise or lower it when crossing a street with another cable, and to slow it down with reductions gears for critical crossings or steep grades. Gripmen had to let go of the grip when crossing higher cables at a cross street or approaching a "let-go curve" but not a "pull curve." Though a continuous examination of the cable at the engine house served to avoid cable imperfections, occasional loose wires could snag a car's grip and prevent it from stopping. The system still depended on horses to move the cars, which had no switching mechanisms, through the switches to their night time storage, in emergencies, and in the night time "owl runs," when the traffic did not warrant continuous cable operation.

Central to the system's operation was the wire cable. Introduced in British mines for underground haulage, wire cables were developed in America by John Roebling, who manufactured cables to replace the endless hemp hawsers used on Pennsylvania railroads. He went on to apply the cables to the building of the Brooklyn Bridge, which, quite appropriately, included a cable car rapid transit line as part of the planning process from the outset to avoid the heavy burden of a steam engine for moving passengers across the bridge.[76] Cable car companies did not have to invent their cables but simply order them from any of the several cable companies already in business. The cables ready for cable car use were the product of the new open hearth process of steel making developed around 1880.[77]

A typical endless cable was 1¼ to 1½ inches in diameter. It had a hemp core, included for flexibility, that was impregnated with tar as a waterproofing lubricant. This was surrounded by 96 steel wires wound into six strands of 16 wires each, with the wires wound to the left within each strand and the strands wound to the right around the core. Variations in cable structure had some advantages but were found to be difficult to splice.[78] Most cables for the systems were from 22,000 to 27,000 feet long, five miles being judged the maximum limit.[79] They would customarily stretch fifty to a hundred feet in the first weeks of service and more as the gripping and ungripping lengthened them further and narrowed the diameter. Regularly impregnated with hot tar and coated with linseed oil to prevent the tar from sticking to the grips, cables lasted from several months to perhaps two years, depending on the curvature of the line, precipitation, the severity of winters, gradients, speed, and traffic. The friction from the grip taking hold of the cable after a stop set an upper limit to the speed of the cable at fourteen miles an hour, beyond which the friction could set the cable afire.[80]

Depending on their length, the new cables weighed from 45,000 to 100,000 pounds. Wound in specially constructed massive wood and iron shipping reels, the cables were shipped on special flatcars and carried from railroad siding through city streets to the power house on huge wagons. The wagon in St. Louis was said to be the heaviest four-wheel wagon in the world. It was pulled by fifty-four horses, with at least ten riders.[81]

While the cables could be ordered from the catalogues of the several cable companies, the grips, with which the cars could grasp the cable to move and release it to stop, presented an engineering challenge. Several solutions were advanced, each based on a set of rollers which could be stopped to grip the cable and propel the car at the speed of the cable, or allowed to rotate to leave the car at rest while the cable passed through. The grips varied in that they controlled the rollers, with or without additional jaws, from the top, the side, or the bottom.[82] The intricacies of grip design led to a number of competing patents. The original patent holders combined into a trust. Despite court challenges, the trust was able to require new cable car systems to pay for licenses under the patents, which came to cover two-thirds of all cable car companies.

Control by the grip man in the grip car, which pulled trailer cars or carried some passengers as a combination car, was applied by means of a control lever or with wheels on a screw spindle extending through the floor of the car. There were advantages in the ease and assurance with which certain grips could drop and pick up the cable. Since in some situations the cable had to be dropped and picked up again after proceeding on momentum—for example when crossing a street with a higher cable—side and bottom grips had some advantage. Street signs were posted at such sites reading: LET GO or DROP ROPE.[83]

Some 60 percent of the huge investment that horse car companies had to make in converting to cable cars was the construction between the rails of cast iron and concrete conduits that accommodated the cable, sheaves and pulleys supporting it, a slot at the top through which the lever reached the grip, and a drain at the bottom for the rain, ice, or snow entering through the slot.[84] Excavation was four feet deep and three feet wide for the conduit with extending side bays every four or five feet for the yokes supporting the running tracks. Slots were generally ¾ inch wide to avoid cutting the rear calk on horseshoes or the wheels of the typical buggy.[85]

At the terminal at the end of the line, the cable ran around a horizontal wheel, or sheave, ten to twelve feet in diameter which turned the cable to go in the opposite direction and return to the power house.[86] To carry the cable horizontally within the conduit there were pulleys about every thirty or forty feet, twelve to twenty four inches in diameter, with a face three or four inches wide depressed in the center to hold the cable.[87] Additional pulleys served to depress or elevate the cable at the top and bottom of an incline or guide it around a curve.

The engine needed for a cable car system power house to pull the cable was already available by 1880, having been developed elsewhere. The stationary steam engines chosen ranged from two hundred to fifteen hundred horsepower, depending on the length of the cable, the number of curves and inclines, and the number of cars. They operated with large, heavy flywheels, eighteen to twenty five feet in diameter, whose momentum regulated the output as cars gripped and ungripped the cable and ran up and down grades.[88] The cable itself was wound around a driver and an idler taking up slack as cars gripped and ungripped.[89]

The boom in cable car system construction lasted for six year, from 1882 to 1888. Then the next energy system, electricity driving the trolley car, came onto the scene. It replaced cable cars and the remaining two thirds of horse cars on American city rails.

In all, there were fifty nine cable car street railways in the U.S., two rapid transit lines and one in-grounds hospital facility, totaling 360.6 miles in length, though not all operating at the same time. Twenty-nine lines were established because of extreme gradients. Forty lines, with 64 percent of the mileage, operated under license from the patent trust.[90]

Trolley Cars

Trolley cars came onto the streets representing the latest advance in electrical knowledge that had come in many steps over several centuries.

In classical Greece and Rome it was noted that when amber was rubbed with fur it acted as a magnet, attracting light objects, such as a feather, and gave off static electricity.

William Gilbert (1544–1603), by methodological experiments, showed that more than a dozen other substances did this as well: sulphur, glass, wax, crystals, and some gems. They too had attractive power when rubbed.[91]

Otto von Guerricke (1602–1686) formed an electric machine by pouring sulphur into a glass sphere, which he then broke when the sulphur cooled. An iron shaft was inserted into the sulphur sphere and was mounted between two wooden supports. When it was revolved, and a dry hand was applied to the sphere, it was electrified and attracted light objects such as paper, lint, and feathers. When the revolving sphere was rubbed in a dark room, light resulted, as well as sparks and a crackling sound.[92]

Around 1750, E.G. von Kleist devised a Leyden Jar, a glass jar or bottle with the outer surface covered with tinfoil and a wire or hair dipped into the jar half filled with water. Because it was capable of storing electricity, it increased the power of its discharge.[93]

Benjamin Franklin (1706–1790), by tapping the electricity of lightning during a thunderstorm with a key suspended from a kite, was able to compare it with the static electricity stored in a Leyden Jar and demonstrate that they were the same.[94]

Alessandro Volta (1745–1827), reacting to a proposal attributing to "animal electricity" the jerking legs of a frog touched by a scalpel, decided it was instead the interaction of two metals—the iron braces holding the legs and the copper scalpel—in the brine solution. He constructed a pile of discs of silver (later copper) and zinc separated by brine-soaked cloth or paper and found that it produced a continuous flow of electricity.[95]

With the continuous electric flow available, studies in the nature and measurement of electricity could proceed, notably by Andre Marie Ampere (1775–1836),[96] Karl Friedrick Gauss (1777–1853),[97] and George Simon Ohm (1787–1854).[98]

In 1827, Hans Christian Oersted (1777–1851) noted that a compass needle near a wire conducting electricity from a nearby voltaic pile swung strongly aside as though a magnet had moved close to it.[99] He concluded that an electric current generates a magnetic field circular to the flow of the electric current.[100]

Investigators could then produce powerful magnets by the flow of an electric current in a wire, but wondered why electricity could not be produced from magnetic forces.

Then, in 1831, Michael Faraday (1791–1867) moved a cylindrical bar magnet into the center of a coil of 220 feet of wire formed into a solenoid connected to a galvinometer, which measures electricity flow. When he lowered the magnet into the solenoid, the galvinometer needle moved. When he removed the magnet, the galvinometer moved in the opposite direction. He then placed a copper disc with wires connected to its axle and rim in the magnetic field running from pole to pole of the British Royal Society's great magnet. He turned the disc with a crank, deflecting the galvinometer needle and confirming that electricity was indeed produced. He concluded that it was the cutting of magnetic lines of force, that is, the relative motion of magnet and wire, that induced the generation of electrical current. Electricity had finally been produced from magnetism and the way was open for the generation of electricity by rotating a circuit, or armature, within the field of a magnet.[101]

This discovery was soon followed by the development of magneto-electric machines, or dynamos, putting into practice the generation of electricity by turning an armature within a magnetic field. By the 1870s, another discovery took place. This was the "reversibility of function." If a dynamo shaft was turned, it generated electricity, but if it was fed current its shaft would turn. The dynamo was turned into an electric motor.[102] This was to have a telling effect on the fate of the horse car.

Electricity could be generated centrally, transmitted by wire or by an insulated rail, and drawn upon by a vehicle moved by an electric motor, with the electricity returned through a circuit of a second wire, a rail, or through the ground. Werner Siemens ran a small electric locomotive, operating off an electrified third rail—that is, not either of the two running rails—and hauling passengers at the 1879 Berlin Industrial Exhibition.[103] Thomas Edison built an electric locomotive in 1880 using the rails as electric conductors, which could shock people if used on public streets, and was not put into general use.[104] John C. Henry built an electric rail line in Kansas City in 1884, keeping the electricity out of reach by stretching two copper wires above the tracks with two little wheels, or "trollers," running on top of them towed along by wires from the car below. It had trouble controlling the speed electrically, installed a cumbersome mechanical gear system, but went into bankruptcy, and was replaced by a cable car system.[105]

An attempt by Edward M. Bentley and Walter H. Knight to run an electric car line in Cleveland, in 1884, and later in Pittsburgh, was based on concealing the electric wires in a slotted conduit beneath the surface, as cable cars did, with a thin-bladed "plow" reaching down from the car to collect the current. It had endless troubles with the wooden conduit boards springing loose, the plow breaking off, and the springs holding the motor below the car breaking loose. The attempt was abandoned and horse cars took over, followed by cable cars.[106]

Greater success greeted British-born Leo Daft's three-mile line opened in 1885 in Baltimore, the first regularly operated electric car line in America. It operated with electric locomotives powered from a third rail, except at crossroads, where the engineer had to raise up the third rail contact wheel and erect a pole contacting a gas pipe overhead. To keep the cars from slowing down away from the powerhouse the voltage had to be raised to 120 volts, and difficulties arose with short circuits in the rain and electrocuted dogs, cats, and chickens, though not horses. This line, too, was turned back to horses. After an interval with electric locomotives on New York city elevated lines, Daft installed his electric car lines in several New Jersey and Connecticut cities, though with electrified cars rather than with separate locomotives.[107]

Another pioneer with some measure of success was Belgium-born Charles J. Van Depoele, whose electric cars carried the motor on an overhanging front platform and drew their current from a wire in a trough between the tracks. Launched with a tiny show car hauling visitors at the Chicago Industrial Exposition of 1883, Depoele's electric cars operated in four or five cities by 1886, sometimes with the use of trollers on a wire overhead and sometimes with a trolley. They ran on higher voltages and used the running rails, with sometimes open joints, as the return of the electric current, so that the current often found a better underground route via buried water and gas pipes that were electrically corroded and soon burst. The cars' overhanging front platforms proved too weak to support the heavy motors over the rough horse car tracks, and heavy sparking and the need for overhaul every few hours of service caused continuing problems.[108]

By the beginning of 1887 there were ten intermittently running electric car installations in the U.S., with about 60 miles of track, far less than the cable car totals, and a small fraction of the horse car lines, which still provided two-thirds of all street rail service.[109]

Onto this scene came Frank Julian Sprague (1857–1934), a mathematical genius, graduate of the U.S. Naval Academy, veteran of a year in Thomas Edison's workshop, and inventor of superior electric motors. Rather than depend on dynamos used reversibly, he designed electric motors afresh that had greatly improved performance. To drive a streetcar he used two gear-drive motors in one "truck" ingeniously mounted "wheelbarrow fashion," part supported around the axle and part spring-mounted on the car frame. They had flexible controls and "regenerative braking," that converted to a generator as it slowed the car, sending electricity back into the system.[110]

In May 1887, the Sprague Electric Railway and Motor Company signed a contract to provide Richmond, Virginia, in ninety days, a working twelve-mile street railway system with a steam and electric central station plant of 375-horsepower capacity, forty cars and eighty motors, thirty cars to be operating at one time, capable of mounting grades as steep as 8 percent. With the track laid by an independent contractor, though with resulting grades of up to 10 percent, and the wires strung above the route, testing proceeded, with redesigned double-reduction gears to handle the hills, and real mules sent out after dark to bring home cars that expired away from the car barn.

To reach the overhead wire, what finally worked, after forty trials, was a trailing inclined pole, freely pivoted, topped by a roller in contact with the wire, and pressed upward by springs, reversible at the end of the line, a suggestion by a draftsman named Eugene Pommer. With current returning through the rails, and probably also through the ground, Richmond telephones experienced hissing noises when cars passed, until the telephone company was persuaded to install wire returns on the phone circuits.

The system finally opened for regular service in February 1888, and reached forty cars in service in the spring. But the original operating syndicate had gone bankrupt. Sprague estimated that the company had spent $75,000 more than it was paid but that this was exceeded by the value of the technical experience and national reputation it had gained. This was soon evident. With a convincing demonstration for a delegation from Boston's West End Railroad, Sprague was engaged to electrify the West End Railroad, which had employed several thousand horses. This success was quite convincing. Soon more than 200 electrical streetcar systems were either in operation or under construction in the U.S., more than half equipped by Sprague and over 90 percent based on his patents, with Sprague lines under way also in Germany and Italy.[111]

Between 1888 and 1902 the conversion from horse car to trolley car was just about complete, with 97 percent of U.S. street car trackage electrified. Some 100,000 animals had powered the horse cars in 1886; in 1902 only 8,902 remained, pulling only 6 percent of the number of passengers they had pulled before. In 1902, only 67 of the 817 street car companies used horses.[112]

Some cable car construction continued into the 1890s, however, for extensions of existing systems and in Washington and New York, where overhead electric wires were prohibited.[113] In Washington, Congress prohibited overhead wires in town, that is, south of Boundary (Florida Avenue) and east of Georgetown, and required the replacement of horse cars. Car companies, consequently experimented with storage battery cars, compressed air cars, a surface contact system with long contact bars beneath the cars to pick up current from energized contact plates between the track, and an underground pneumatic tube propelling the cars on the principle of a screw.[114] In 1895 a cable car line was constructed and operated till 1899.[115]

By the end of the 1890s, however, a new system was adopted. In-town Washington street cars were powered electrically by a system of underground conduits, located between the tracks, adapted from a Budapest system designed by the Siemens-Halske German firm in 1899.[116] Suburban cars, operating with overhead trolley poles coming into town had to stop at a plow pit, to change from overhead operation inbound and the reverse outbound.[117] Some suburban lines had a double trolley system, two trolley poles rising from the car connecting to two overhead wires. The return current went through the second overhead line rather than through the rails, to prevent stray current from corroding underground pipes through electrolysis.[118]

New York, like Washington, did not permit overhead wires. It continued construction of cable car systems in the 1890s and in 1894 constructed a conduit electric car system similar to that to be constructed in Washington.[119] Brooklyn, across the East River, did not share Manhattan's aversion to overhead wires. It became a part of New York City in 1898 and became so identified with trolley cars that its baseball team became known as the Trolley Dodgers.[120]

Horsecars continued to operate longer in some locations. One new

Trolley car No. 265, Forty-second Street West at Queens Avenue, Minneapolis, with conductor Roy Harvey at the wheel (Library of Congress).

immigrant, arriving at New York's Battery Park on September 17, 1909, with no English and not knowing how to reach his sister's house, later recalled: "I at last discovered someone who understood me, and I was off via horsecar in the direction of the lower East Side."[121] The last horsecar system in New York City—the Belt Line System which ran from the Battery along the waterfront on both sides of the city to 59th Street—was finally replaced by electric cars in 1913, with several hundred horses sold.[122]

Ironically, the New York subway was built with the services of some 1,500 horses, the contractor's order for 500 horses in 1911 constituting the largest sale in the city to a single concern.[123]

Clearly, the age of horse-drawn urban public transport was drawing to an end.

Transporting Burden

In 1917, one observer, Charles Allan of Ross County, Ohio, would write to *The Breeder's Gazette*: "A comparatively limited number of horses is used for pleasure or transportation purposes other than transporting burden."[124] Horse-drawn people-transport—stagecoach, omnibus, horsecar, and buggy—were gone or fading. Now horses survived by hauling freight or services.

Outside the cities, cross-country wagons had already given way as the railroads covered the East Coast states and moved west. A Hollywood movie portrayed the mid–nineteenth century scene. Actor Wallace Beery's freight wagon company in Western Maryland is confronted by a new railway line brought in by actor Robert Taylor and has no choice but to gather its wagons, drivers and horses and move west.[125] Inside the cities, horse teams transporting burden found themselves in competition with trucks.

There were two fields in which they competed: in government services and in commercial services. Most prominent among government services were the fire departments. In New York City, the fire department announced in 1911 the purchase of 150 automobile fire engines and high-pressure hose wagons, with plans for another 750 over the next five years. Some 2,000 horses would be retired and sold.[126] It took longer in some cities. In 1923, Chicago city officials joined a banquet commemorating the passing of fire horses from the streets of the city as the fire equipment was completely motorized. "All friends of the horse," a commentator wrote, "will rejoice in his release from this hard and inhumane service."[127]

Postal service was also passing from the horse-drawn realm. In New York City, replacement of horse-drawn mail wagons serving Manhattan north of 42nd Street began in 1909 and concluded in the rest of Manhattan on September 1, 1913, when 85 horse-drawn mail wagons were replaced by 80 three-ton trucks and 20 two-ton trucks.[128]

This left the commercial competition between the horse teams and the trucks, which was to continue for some time. In this competition, the characteristics of urban commerce affected the roles trucks and horses were to play. At one extreme, waiting to load and unload meant long, inactive stopping times. At the other extreme, longer distances made speed a priority. The horse team's role centered on the short run.

One 1912 article in *The Breeder's Gazette* quoted one firm's manager explaining:

> Within a three-mile radius trucks cannot be used to advantage. We figure that our wheels turn only three hours daily. The rest of the time is consumed in waiting, loading or unloading. We could use motors only when the work would permit the wheels to turn six hours daily.

Citing the greater cost of trucks, a larger initial outlay, depreciation over five years, repairs, interest and insurance, he went on, "There is a big difference between having a $5,000 outfit delayed an hour, as compared with a $1,200 three-horse equipment."[129]

Beyond the three-mile or five-mile limit, however, the advantage lay increasingly with the truck, with a twenty-mile an hour speed compared with a six-mile an hour speed for the horse. Department stores found they could extend their customer base through delivery service to the suburbs using trucks rather than horses. Speed was important also for transporting perishables. Chicago's Swift & Company, which began using trucks early in 1909, found trucks indispensable for long hauls and for transporting perishable meats from stockyards to downtown in twenty minutes rather than the hour-and-a-half a team could consume on the journey.[130]

A 1917 report cast the emerging division of labor in a favorable light, commenting that

> long-hauls take the motor-trucks; the short-hauls require horses.... Horses are much more efficient at starting an overload, handling a load in soft alleys and around railway tracks and freight platforms and docks so that they retain a high esteem.... A new feature of the business is the longer life of big horses in cities now since they are relieved of the long trips and take shorter routes with more stopping time. Instead of lasting four or five years they are now remaining serviceable to ten years or more.[131]

In evidence of the short-haul versus long-haul division, *The Breeder's Gazette* could report in 1919 that

> in the older and more congested business sections of New York only about 38 percent of horses have been displaced by power trucks, while in Staten Island [where less congestion and longer distances are involved] the reduction has been nearly 60 percent.[132]

With time, the contrast between truck and horse-team functions grew more extreme. Trucks took on longer, intercity, trips, much to the surprise of railroad interests, who too long viewed them as local carriers serving each end of a railroad run.[133] With trucks delivering door-to-door service, the need for local pickup and delivery was reduced.

Horses, meanwhile, held on to those tasks requiring stop-and-go service, such as door-to-door milk delivery. The Flynn Dairy Company of Des Moines, Iowa, reported in 1925 that their horses were so well trained that they were able to teach a new man the route they traveled.[134]

Well into the 1930s ice wagons went from house to house, stopping so the iceman could cut off blocks of ice and carry them, in tongs, up to the icebox. Housewives placed signs in their windows, reading 15 cents or 25

Horse-drawn ice wagons, circa 1900. Photograph by Daniel Murray (Library of Congress).

cents, for example, so that the iceman would cut off the right-sized block of ice.[135] Junk wagons moved slowly through the neighborhoods with a jangling cowbell gaining people's attention. And for a long time, too, fruit and vegetable wagons passed slowly through neighborhoods and stationed themselves at strategic points so that housewives and the children they sent could do their daily shopping.

Even into the era of the musical radio commercials of the 1930s and early1940s the street wagon horse survived. His clippety-clop provided the rhythmic background for such songs as: "Here comes the milkman, hooray, hooray. He's bringing milk from Sheffield Farms, it's seal select grade A."[136] It lives in the memory of older inhabitants, along with the sight of the milkman, the iceman, the junkman, and the fruit and vegetable man, each with his own characteristic wagon pulled by a slow-moving horse.

Denial

Recognition of the effects of motor vehicles on the horse's future took several forms. One was denial. Some recalled the panic in the horse trade generated by the bicycle boom of the early 1890s, when it was thought that people would ride bicycles rather than horses to get to work. Writing in 1920, George E. Brown of Kane County, Illinois, wrote:

> ... advice to "go slow in horse breeding" is also premature. "History repeats itself." The same prediction was made in the panic of the early 90s. "Bicycles, autos and tractors will soon displace horses." Farmers all through the Middle West quit breeding, and sold good draft mares and geldings in Chicago at $80 to $100. When the panic was over and business in general revived, the same class of drafters were picked up wherever they could be found, and higher prices were paid for them than ever before. The same condition is bound to come again.[137]

As auto use grew there was the belief that this was the result of "the fabulous sums expended in advertising by manufacturers and dealers" of automobiles which "has held public attention and seemed to sway the judgment of men." The answer to this, defenders of the horse felt, lay in launching a publicity campaign educating people on the merits of the horse, "showing the economic advantage of the horse in local transportation in cities and on the farm; [and] To impress upon the public mind the value of the horse as a factor in the development and progress of our country."

For this purpose a national organization, The Horse Publicity Association of America, Inc., was established by an October 30–31, 1919 meeting at the Hotel Pennsylvania in New York. Represented on its board of directors were the many interests associated with the horse. These were listed as: the National Hay Association, National Grain Association, American Feed Manufacturers Association, Associated Manufacturers of Saddlery, Wholesale Saddlery Associations, National Saddlery Manufacturers Association, Master Horseshoers, Horseshoe Manufacturers Association, Horseshoe Nail Manufacturers, Farming and Livestock Interests, Horse Aid & Humane Association, Heavy Hardware Organizations, Horse Markets, Veterinary Interests, Wagon & Implement Manufacturers, Wire & Iron Interests, The American Association of Breeders & Importers of Belgians, The Shire Association, The Percheron Society of America, Truck & Transfer Companies, Cavalry Interests, and Thoroughbred & Racing Interests.[138] The Horse Publicity Association of America, centered in New York, was succeeded by the Horse Association of America, which met in Chicago.[139]

Supporters of the horse found hope in analyses that companies were using horses for delivery in congested downtown locations and motor vehicles for delivery in lighter-traffic outlying areas. Rumors of companies that had switched to motor vehicles and then abandoned them for the greater efficiency of horses raised hopes for a while until proven false. With increasing frequency, however, the use of horses by city services diminished. Between 1911 and 1921 the number of work horses in Chicago dropped from

80,354 to 37,582, leading one observer to conclude that the average number of horses displaced by a truck is three.[140]

At the founding convention of the organization for the promotion of horses, one speaker reflecting the role of horses in the World War, called for greater respect and recognition for this "loyal and patriotic animal." The convention called on the New York Secretary of State, attending the convention, to use road funds to build not only paved main highways for motor traffic but also a 12-foot unpaved pathway on one or both sides of each road to accommodate horse-drawn traffic.

But to no avail. Horses disappeared from city streets and highways and through auction sales moved to farms and other uses. For the millions of farmers across the country who bred horses and raised them to the three or four-year old working age, failure of horse prices to keep up with other prices, and the prospect of further declines in the future, discouraged the breeding of horses at previous levels. The average birth rate of horses, that is the percentage of the total population under one year old, was 8.02 percent in 1900 and 1910. As farmers bred fewer horses, the birth rate declined. Each year between 1922 and 1936 the shortfall in births below the 1900–1910 average rate was even greater than the total year-to-year decline in the horse population. Farmers remarked about the aging population of horses they were working. There was no upswing in the slaughter of horses. Rather the horses worked on, grew old, and were not replaced by newborn horses.

With time, a third explanation appeared for where the horses went; slower in coming, it gathered momentum. And that was slaughter for horsemeat. Historically, from Roman times, old horses were destined for rendering plants—"glue factories"—with hides a principal product, along with tallow for soap, and horsehair.[141] In continental Europe, though not in Great Britain, slaughter of horses for human consumption was common well before the World War. A 1918 report states:

> In France the people are now eating 2,000 donkeys and 300 horses a day. About 70,000 horses were eaten last year. Many of the horses slaughtered are wounded and otherwise crippled animals from the armies. There are many of these and a plentiful supply of horsemeat is maintained so that the meat shortage in France has been greatly relieved.[142]

Consumption of horsemeat was not widespread in the United States, however. Inquiring farmers could learn from the weekly *Breeder's Gazette* that isolated butchers operated on horsemeat in Portland, Oregon, and Cincinnati. On July 24, 1919, however, Congress passed a law providing for inspection and certification of horsemeat as "U.S. Inspected and Passed by the U.S. Department of Agriculture."[143] By 1930 136,000 horses were slaughtered under Federal inspection and in 1951 340,000.[144] This was to grow to greater proportions, and controversy, in later years, as noted below.

Fire Horse

For a brief, sixty-year interlude between introduction of the external combustion steam engine and the internal combustion automotive engine that replaced it, the fire horse was the face of firefighting. Charging through the streets with a smoking, clanging machine behind them, fire horses embodied the excitement and hope of warding off or controlling an impending disaster. How did this come about? To begin at the beginning…

After man discovered fire he discovered that it could be very destructive and that he would need help to put it out. This made fire a social issue in two ways. He needed others to help put out the flames and if his fire could not be controlled it could spread to destroy the property—and lives—of others.

For millennia man struggled with how to manage this social issue. In primitive society the village could all jump in to help put out a fire. In towns and cities, who would help? In ancient Rome, one man, Marcus Licinius Crassus, organized a team that ran to a fire but would not help until the owner agreed to pay Crassus. The emperor Augustus then organized such teams[145] but did not ask each fire-threatened owner to first pay. He financed the team, and a program of night firewatchers with a 4 percent tax on slave purchases.[146]

A millennium and a half later, one finds in the fifteenth and sixteenth centuries schemes for the organization of groups that agree to help fight fires in each others' houses but not in the houses of others, fire protection clubs. Boston, after its disastrous fire in 1711, had Mutual Fire Societies in the 1720s.[147] Benjamin Franklin saw these and the need they met when he was a boy. Later, in Philadelphia, he decided it would be better not to have a closed-membership club but a group of volunteers who would help all in the community. He organized the first American volunteer fire fighter brigade, the Union Fire Company, and volunteer firefighting brigades became an enduring American institution.[148]

Alongside the problem of fire-fighting organization was the issue of meeting the costs of failure: replacing the home. Meeting this risk, and sharing it with others, was the role played by insurance, in this case fire insurance. Maritime insurance came first, as an implicit increase of interest on loans financing maritime shipment. It involved forgiveness of the loan in the event of disaster, in accord with the Code of Hammurabi (1750BCE).

The insurance component was not separated from the loan until the fourteenth century, CE, in Genoa, when it emerged as an explicit independent transaction. The peril risk was thus separated from the credit risk.[149]

Insurance was implicit in the annual gifts to the Achaeminian monarchs in ancient Persia by their subjects, with the expectation of assistance should an unanticipated need arise. Another form of implicit insurance came with membership in a guild, whose resources would be expected to assist a member in the event of special need. When the right to such assistance came to be fixed in law, it became an instance of group insurance.[150] There were cases of groups other than guilds contributing to a common fund to meet individuals' unanticipated disasters, labeled "fire association," such as when a hundred households concluded the Hamburg Fire Contract of 1591.[151]

The earliest formal establishment of fire insurance came in 1681, following the disastrous London fire of 1666, in which 13,200 houses, 87 churches, several hospitals, libraries, a prison, and 10,000 boats and barges on the river had burned.[152] Dr. Nicholas Bardon, a doctor, economist, and wealthy investor, realized that much of his wealth was in property. Together with eleven associates, he established The Insurance Office for Houses at the Back of the Royal Exchange and insured brick and frame homes. Other fire insurance schemes, too, were established in the wake of the Great Fire.[153] They were of three kinds: mutual insurance, owned by the insured, private shareholder-owned insurance companies, and chartered insurance companies, later granted limited-liability status by law.[154]

To share the risks the insurance companies took on, they resorted to reinsurance with others who took on the responsibility of underwriting their risks, Edward Lloyd's tavern becoming the center of such underwriting activity.

To protect their interest in the houses they insured, the fire insurance companies organized their own fire-fighting brigades. They issued to each householder they insured a "fire insurance mark" to be posted on the front of the home. The insurers' fire brigade would fight the fire in the house with their mark but would let those without it burn. The mark was also meant to prevent fraudulent insurance claims for houses that burned down if they did not have the insurance company's mark posted.[155]

It took just fifty-five years for fire insurance, started in England, to be taken up in America. It occurred first in 1736, when the Friendly Society was founded in Charleston, South Carolina. It did not survive the 1740 fire that destroyed 300 houses.[156] This was followed most prominently by Benjamin Franklin in 1752 in Philadelphia, where he started the Philadelphia Contributorship for the Insurance of Houses from Loss by Fire. It did not found its own separate fire brigade, but contributed toward fire prevention and refused to insure houses it did not deem safe. Franklin had already established a network of volunteer fire brigades serving the community as a whole.

There followed in America fire insurance companies, reinsured by underwriters, but separate from fire brigades, which were manned by volunteers. In some smaller communities, as in colonial Boston, all citizens were called out and were expected to respond to fight a fire. Following Franklin's initiative in Philadelphia, the organization of separate volunteer groups prepared to fight fires became quite general in the century that followed. Fire insurance companies, and the underwriters who backed them, were concerned over their losses in sometimes extensive fires. They could appeal to the fire fighters to do a better job but it fell to the insurers to seek improved methods of cutting down on fire losses.

Essentially, from the beginning, the main means of fighting fire was with the application of water. A fire needs fuel, heat, and oxygen to burn. The heat to raise the temperature of the water to form steam is taken away from the fire. The greatly expanded space filled by the steam granules blocks the fire's access to oxygen, which is why water is effective.[157] The water to fight fires had come from nearby streams, lakes, or wells, from giant cauldrons stationed in the street in ancient Rome, from strategically placed cisterns, as in San Francisco, for example, and more recently from water pipe networks, usually below ground.[158]

In 1840 New York City this infrastructure was changing. Previously, to draw on the wooden water pipes buried four feet below ground since 1799 by the Manhattan Company, fire fighters would dig down, cut a hole in the pipe, draw their water, and close the hole with a wooden "fire plug" which future fire fighters might identify and remove as needed.[159] In 1817 New York fireman George Smith created the fire hydrant, which could open and close the connection to the underground water pipe by turning a nut at the top.[160] In 1841 water was brought to New York from the Croton Reservoir and distributed through new metal underground pipes.[161] In 1852, Dr. William F. Channing in Boston invented the fire alarm box system, using telegraph technology.[162]

How was the water to be applied to the fire? Previously the major method had been with leather buckets. As early as in American colonial days houses had been required to stock several buckets—on which they painted their names—and in the event of a fire the call rang out: "Throw out your buckets!"[163]

Improvements had been invented soon after the 1666 Great Fire in London. In 1672, in The Netherlands, Jan Van der Heyden and his son Nicolaas invented the leather fire hose, which had to be hand sewn. Fifty feet in length and connectible with brass fittings, hoses allowed the flow of water to be carried right up to and into a burning building. In 1807, James Sellers and Abraham Pennock of the Philadelphia Hose Company riveted leather strips together to make hoses that were nearly leak-proof and were strong enough to suction a large volume of water.[164]

A major improvement was the pump, which came to be the centerpiece of each fire brigade's operation. The most widely used pump was that invented by Richard Newsham in London in 1725, sold widely in Europe and ordered by many towns in the U.S. It consisted of a tub of water on wheels, to be filled up by a bucket brigade, two long handles to be raised and lowered to pump, a metal pipe which could be aimed at the fire or connected to the leather hose for either providing water or acting as suction, but not both at the same time. Operating the pump at sixty strokes a minute provided eighty gallons of water, but was exhausting for the twelve firemen, who could usually keep it up for a few minutes before being relieved, fifty strokes a minute being more doable. The larger pumps might take as many as forty people to operate.[165] A powerful effort could send a stream of water ninety feet into the sky and fire brigades competed in periodic contests to see who could send the stream higher.

When the source of water was far from the fire, a line of hoses and pumps might be organized. The first fire company arriving could connect a hose to the water source, pump water into its tank, and then run a hose to the next, until a line of engines connected by hoses would extend, sometimes for some distance, to get close to the fire. The firemen manning each engine would exert themselves to pump out water coming to them. Should they fail to keep up, their tank would overflow, their engine would be said to have been "washed," indicating that the pump, and the strength and stamina of its men were inferior to the pump and firemen on the engines feeding them. An engine never "washed" was considered a virgin, and one company took pride in their engine labeled "Old Maid."[166] Pump to pump cooperation was an important part of fire fighting. Around 1827, the New York fire chief reported seeing thirty pumpers in a line a mile and a half long extending from the water source to the fire scene.[167]

Pulling the pump to the site of the fire was the job of the firemen, who, depending on the distance and the terrain, could arrive at the fire exhausted, or perhaps too late, only to see the fire already out or the building burned down. Brigades competed to get to the fire early, monopolize the water source, and get paid by the homeowner or insurance company. At times this could lead to violence. In one instance, the mayor of a small town with two competing volunteer fire brigades locked up the firehouse with one brigade's pump to put a stop to the violence, leading the other brigade to take out its pump and hide it on a barn behind some hay.

Centered on the pump, the firehouse, the shared effort of pulling and pumping, the club-like camaraderie of each volunteer brigade became a way of life. It was to be threatened by technological change.

Steam

In 1840, the insurance underwriters in New York City, still recovering from the city's Great Fire of 1835, said to be the most destructive non-military fire since the 1666 London disaster, and concerned over the frequency and extent of fires over the 1839–1840 winter,[168] asked the insurance companies to find a better means of fighting fires.[169] The insurance companies approached Paul Rapsey Hodge, an ingenious mechanic. In London, in 1829, George Braithwaite assisted by John Ericsson, later noted for inventing the Monitor, had built the first steam fire-engine, which could throw 200 to 250 gallons of water a minute to the height of ninety feet. Though demonstrating its effectiveness, Braithwaite met bitter opposition in London, but built a few of the pumps for other jurisdictions, was particularly well received in Berlin, and built his last engine in 1833. Eight years later, in March 1841, in New York, Hodge completed the first steam fire engine built in America. It was self-propelled, 13½ feet long, weighed between seven and eight tons, and passed the test for certification by throwing a 1½-inch stream of water over the flag-staff in front of City Hall.[170]

But none of the volunteer fire brigades would agree to work with the steam fire engine. Opposition was bitter. The engine remained unused, in the possession of the insurance companies, until they were finally able to persuade Pearl Hose Co., No. 28, to take possession and use the engine. After a few months, however, the firemen returned the engine, saying it was too heavy and did not generate enough steam. Concerned that persistence in the face of the continued hostility of fire brigades could increase their losses rather than reduce them, the insurance companies withdrew the engine and sold it to a packing-box manufacturer for stationary use.

To the West, in Cincinnati, Ohio, a system of volunteer fire fighters using hand pumps had resulted in immense losses of property and scenes of disorder and violence. In 1851, thirteen fire companies fought each other while a mill they came to save burned down.[171] Sentiment grew for establishment of a paid fire department and a new means of fighting fire. In 1852, Moses Latta demonstrated before the City Council an experimental steam fire engine that could raise steam from cold water in four minutes and ten seconds from the time smoke rose out of the stack and could force water through 350 feet of hose to a distance of 130 feet. The Council was convinced and appropriated $5,000 for a working engine to be built. Volunteer fire brigade opposition was intense. Latta received anonymous threats, and there were fears his engine would be destroyed before the test. The test, however, was an overwhelming demonstration, as the engine exceeded anything that had been claimed. Not long after, a fire broke out at a great warehouse. The new engine, four mammoth grey horses pulling it at a gallop, smoke streaming from its stack and coals gleaming in its grates, arrived at the fire. It soon had four streams of water directed at the blaze when the cry went out: "The hose is cut!" In the melee that followed the citizens overpowered the volunteer firemen, the engine's streams continued, and the fire was put out, to widespread celebrity in the city and beyond. A fire department was established, Cincinnati became a center of steam fire engine production by the Latta Company and others that followed.[172]

Following the Cincinnati success of 1852, the manufacture of steam fire-engines blossomed as new builders arose in the Atlantic states, in Baltimore, Philadelphia, Pittsburgh, New York, Boston, and Manchester, New Hampshire. Writing in 1896, fireman William T. King could list eighty manufacturers who had built steam fire engines in America.[173]

Interesting was the case of the Ettinger & Edmond firm of Richmond, Virginia, chronologically the twentieth manufacturer, which built its first steam fire-engine in 1859 for St. Petersburg, Russia. It built another for Russia and three for the city of Richmond and had a contract for further deliveries to Russia, which had to be cancelled because of the U.S. Civil War. It resumed the building of steamers, built its last for Russia in 1877, and discontinued that branch of its business.[174]

Steam fire-engine building didn't reach west, to Chicago until 1875, chronologically the forty-fourth builder on the list. A Chicago Fire Department committee had visited Cincinnati in 1855 to investigate possible purchase, but the explosion of the Cincinnati engine on December 6, 1855, killing its engineer, discouraged purchase plans for several years.[175] In his 1896 book, King was able to provide for almost all of the engines built the manufacturer, the dimensions of the engine and the broiler, broiler design, the diameter and stroke of the steam cylinder and the pump cylinder or cylinders. Included also was the time each took to raise steam from cold water and to throw a stream for a given distance from a hose of fifty or a hundred feet. The engines' weights ranged from over 8,000 pounds for the largest to about 3,000 pounds for the smallest, which some manufacturers specified could be pulled by hand or by horses. Most manufacturers built piston, reciprocal, pumps; a few built rotary pumps. Some early models positioned the boiler horizontally, most vertically.

Some manufacturers had previously built hand-engines. Some built just a few, some several hundred. The four most successful manufacturers—Silsbury, Ahrens, Clapp & Jones, and Button—were consolidated in 1891 to form the American Fire-Engine Company,[176] which later became the American La France Company.[177] The durability of some of the engines was outstanding. One engine, manufactured by Hanneman & Co. in Boston in 1866, was designed with two separable pump cylinders. After many years of service, it was purchased from a junk dealer in 1895 by H.M. Young, who tried unsuccessfully to sell it to St. Charles, Illinois, which had no fire protection. When a large fire broke out in the town, the old engine was put to work. Suddenly, one cylinder head was blown off. The balance wheels for the two cylinders were then disconnected, and, as designed thirty years earlier, the remaining pump cylinder and steam cylinder were put into operation and saved the town.[178]

Reviewing the long history of steam fire engines, King stressed the need to put men in charge of the engines who were practical engineers with a knowledge of how to run and take care of the engines, appointed on the basis of real merit instead of political influence. He warned against using more steam than was required, from sixty to eighty pounds being adequate for fire duty. Interestingly, writing just before the advent of the internal combustion engine, he expected that just as the hand-engine had been replaced by the steam engine, it would be replaced in turn by the Holly system of direct pressure, or high gravity, water supply.[179]

Enter the Horses

With the onset of the steam fire engine era, horses were bought into the fire-fighting picture. Though some self-powered early steam fire engines could move, it was too slowly to get to a fire in time. In addition, there were speed limits on mechanical conveyances on the street but not for horses.

Some horses had previously been used for the fire service, one by a volunteer company in New York in 1832, when a yellow fever epidemic had thinned the firemen's ranks. Firefighters were reluctant at first to switch to horses, since they were expensive and had to be housed, fed, watered, groomed, exercised, and tidied up after, which could seem excessive in a place where fires were infrequent. But, firefighters pulling engines of 5,000 or 6,000 pounds through the mud were soon convinced that horses were necessary.[180] Soon routines were developed for a team of two, three or four horses to pull a steam fire engine through the streets at a gallop.

The question became how to pick or breed the best horses for the job, train them, house them, and hitch them up as quickly as possible. To find potential firehorses, authorities searched for horses that were fast, strong, agile, obedient, fearless, and able to stand calm and patient in difficult circumstances in all kinds of weather. In Portland, Oregon, Percheron-Morgan hybrids were bred that would have the power to pull the heavy engines through muddy streets and get them to the fire on time.[181]

Over the years, different pieces of fire-fighting equipment had been developed to meet the needs of higher buildings and additional, longer, hoses. Different size horses were found to be appropriate for the different vehicles. Detroit officials set standards calling for 1,400 pound horses to pull a steam fire-engine, 1,100 pound horses for a hose wagon, and 1,700 pound horses for a hook and ladder. While most fire departments trained their horses on the job, Detroit established a horse college, with all the accoutrements of a working fire station, as well as a racetrack. Horses graduating successfully were placed with Detroit fire stations, where they might work for four to ten years. In Philadelphia, one company gave their horses vacations, long before that tradition extended to its firefighter.

When the 1872 epizootic epidemic hit the horses of the U.S., the Boston fire-fighting forces were particularly hard hit. The Great Boston Fire of November 9, 1872, burned for sixteen hours, as the absence of four dead and twenty-two unfit horses, out of a force of seventy-five to ninety, meant firefighters and citizen volunteers had to pull the fire equipment manually, with disastrous results. There were fourteen fatalities, including eleven firefighters, besides the 776 buildings consumed in what was later labeled the Epizootic Fire.[182]

At first horses were stabled next door to the firehouses. This lost valuable time, however, when they had to be brought out to the firehouse and harnessed to the steam fire-engine. The solution adopted was to house the horses in the ground floor of the firehouse, in the rear, so they could be rapidly brought forward and harnessed, with the firemen living upstairs. Smelling the food being cooked upstairs, some horses climbed the stairs. The solution was spiral staircases and, thanks to 1870s Chicago fireman David Kenyon, poles for the firemen to slide down rapidly when the alarm sounded.[183]

Techniques for rapid harnessing advanced over the years. Harnesses were suspended by ropes from the ceiling to be automatically lowered over the waiting horses. In 1871, Charles A. Berry, a Massachusetts firefighter, invented a quick hitch so rapid and popular that he left firefighting to sell

Steam fire engine in front of Engine 15 firehouse at 2150 California Street, San Francisco, April 10, 1894. Photograph by W. Cathcart (Library of Congress).

it across the country.[184] Practice between fires added to the harnessing skills of the firemen and the alert readiness of the horses. In San Jose, California, the firemen descended, the horses moved into place, the harnesses were dropped and secured, and the engine left the fire house just thirteen seconds after the alarm was received, arriving at the fire six minutes after the alarm sounded.[185]

To prepare for sudden departure at any time, the steamer was kept warm with hot boiling water from a firehouse connection with a quick disconnect. With a fire banked down or ready for quick ignition, the kerosene-soaked kindling and small chunks of coal on the grate were lit as the horses were hitched. The engineer managing the fire let the steam into the pumps when the pressure reached about fifty-five pounds. So well rehearsed was the routine, that one New York engine company in 1910 was able to put water on the fire four blocks from the fire house just two minutes and 35 seconds after the alarm sounded.[186] A photograph of a major fire in November 1908, shows the steamer horses having been led away to shelter, and the horses connected to the ladder wagon covered with blankets to protect them from the chill.[187]

Steam fire engine drawn by three white horses and carrying three fire fighters rushing to fire, with crowds watching from street and windows. Between 1900 and 1920 (Library of Congress).

Regularly accompanying the horses on their fire-fighting duties were the Dalmatian dogs, that came to be known as firehouse dogs. Previously running alongside aristocrats' carriages as a status symbol in 1700s England, Dalmatians were adopted for firehouse use. At the sound of a fire alarm, the Dalmatians would bark inside the firehouse to wake the horses and outside the fire house to alert people to get out of the way. Running alongside the horses, they would protect them from other dogs or horses along the way, protect them from the crowd at the fire scene, calm them, and guard the firemen's belongings and equipment and the horses themselves.[188]

In some small towns both firemen and horses were volunteers, busy with other occupations between fires. Horses busy with other tasks might drop everything and head for the firehouse when the alarm sounded. An iceman away from his wagon at the sound of the alarm might find his ice wagon at the firehouse. In the years after the retirement of the steamers and their horses, old fire horses were known to go over or through the fences, when an alarm sounded, and be found at the firehouse waiting to be hitched.[189]

Exit the Horses

By the 1890s, the prospect of movement by internal combustion was becoming a reality. It was being introduced for small vehicles and was being taken up by tractor manufacturers, as described in the chapter on horses on the farm, below. Its application to fire engines, however, was more difficult. A fire engine had to have speed, absolute reliability, and the power to pump water as well as move the vehicle. It had to replace the steam engine as well as the horse. And, while the internal combustion engine might move the family car, and the fire chief's vehicles that were purchased, it had to be powerful enough to move the large, heavy engine.

The first gasoline-powered fire engine was built by the Merryweather Company in England in 1904. In the U.S., the first automotive fire engine was built in 1906 by the Watrous Engine Works in St. Paul, Minnesota, with one engine for movement and another, four-cylinder engine, powering a 350 gallon-per-minute pump. It used one engine for both in its 1907 model. Also in 1907, the Webb Fire Apparatus Company customized a touring car to carry a pump and ladders, the Seagram company of Cleveland, Ohio, built two engines, one a four-cylinder and one a six-cylinder, the Rapid Motor Vehicle Company, of Pontiac, Michigan, later forming part of General Motors, produced a two-cylinder chemical and hose wagon, with no pump,[190] and the America LaFrance Company produced a gasoline powered chemical wagon,[191] producing a pumper in 1910.[192] Beginning in 1911, Mack Trucks started producing fire engines, and in 1913 Ahrens-Fox, of Cincinnati, converted from steam fire engines to automotive.[193]

More powerful engines were produced in the following years and attracted customers among fire departments working with horse-drawn steam engines. In 1910 the New York Fire Department purchased a motor-driven hose wagon and a motor-propelled hose tower. Then, in 1911, the city acquired its first automotive fire engine, twenty-three feet long, with a 110-horsepower motor that could pump 700 gallons-a-minute at 125-pound pressure. It could go 30 to 40 miles an hour, compared to the horses' 15 to 18 miles an hour. At that point the Department had 1,550 fire horses in service. It announced two years later that it would purchase no more horses and would retire those still in service as soon as possible. The New York authorities found that it cost $85 a year for gas and oil for the new automotive rig compared with $660 for a team of horses pulling a similar rig.[194] The change also affected the firehouses. One New York firehouse, which had been built to accommodate horses and had three doors that opened automatically when the fire bell rang to allow the seventeen horses to charge out, was converted in 1912 to house the motorized engine and tower vehicle.[195]

Chicago took delivery of its first motorized fire engine in 1912, at a point when there were a total of six motorized engines in the country, and in 1923 placed its last horse-drawn fire engine out of service.[196] Portland, Oregon, bought its first motorized apparatus in 1911, having purchased an automobile for its chief in 1909, and retired its last fire horse and steam fire engine in 1920.[197]

The last New York horse-drawn steam fire engine responded to a call in 1922. In Brooklyn, on December 22, 1922, the borough president, the fire commissioner, the firefighters and other dignitaries assembled behind Borough Hall to pay final tribute to the fire horses. Assistant Fire Chief Smokey Joe Martin tapped out the final call on the fire alarm box. At the fire house the three-horse team was then hitched to the steam fire engine, came dashing down the street with a long blast on the steam whistle, and arrived at the back of Borough Hall. As the ceremony was about to start, Jiggs, the firehouse dog, ran circles around the engine, confused that no one was dragging the nozzle or hooking up to the hydrant. After the speeches, the ceremony ended with the placement of a flower wreath around each horse's neck and the posing for photographers. The horses were retired to either light duty or an upstate farm operated by the ASPCA and the horse-drawn steam engine was sent to a small town or village.[198]

The fire horse interlude had come to an end. In the end, the reluctance with which firefighters had accepted the horses into the fire service some sixty year earlier was turned into affection and respect for the horses' loyalty, effort, and dependability. There was a reluctance to exchange them for the gasoline-powered fire engines that might or might not be dependable. The affection for the horses was shared by the people on the street who had thrilled to their exciting galloping by. In New York City, on the west side of Manhattan at 100th Street and Riverside Drive, at the site of a monument "To the heroic dead of the fire department," a tablet honoring the fire horse was dedicated in May 1927. It reads: "This tablet is dedicated to the horses that shared in valor and devotion and with mighty speed bore on the rescue. Subscribed under the auspices of the American Society for the Prevention of Cruelty to Animals."[199]

Four

On the Farm

Even as horses faced difficulties and were replaced on the road and in the city, farm horses faced a different, more complex set of problems. This reflected, of course, the more complex nature of farming, but also their history over the previous half century.

To produce a crop it was necessary to cut and turn the earth so as to aerate the soil and dig out the weeds and roots of previous crops; break up the resulting clods and smooth over the soil to receive the seeds; scatter or enter the seeds into the earth; smooth over the soil again to cover them; remove the weeds that come up around or between the growing plants; then cut the grown plants, tie them in a bundle, transport them to a barn for storage or to a threshing floor where the grain can be shaken or beaten out of the cut plants, assembled, prepared for storage or shipment for milling, with the final product consumed on the farm or shipped to market.

Animals were inserted early into the routine of cereal farming in the Near East. Cattle plowed the fields, which were sown and opened to sheep, who buried the seeds under their hooves. Donkeys carried the sheaths to the threshing floor where three or four oxen stamped out the grain.[1]

Horses, however, came late to the farming scene. It was not until about the ninth century on the heavy-soil farms of northern Europe that breast and shoulder harnesses replaced the throat harnesses that had pressed against the horses' windpipes and had restricted their pulling to a 500-kilogram load. This was the limit set by the ancient code of Theodosius for the load of a horse-drawn chariot harnessed in the ancient fashion.[2] With the new harness, and the nailed horseshoes introduced about this time,[3] horses could begin to replace oxen, which, because of their high shoulders, could be harnessed more simply. Though slower and less agile, a pair of oxen could be placed on each side of a single shaft with a wooden crosspiece resting as a yoke across their shoulders.[4]

In the centuries that followed, as gunpowder removed the need for the large horse to carry the knight and his armor, the large armor-bearing stallion was released for work on the farm. Adoption of the three-field system of crop rotation, producing a surplus of oats that could be fed to horses, and the later improvement of grasses, resulted in a growing role for the large plow horse in northern Europe.[5]

With time, the large stallion plow horse took on star status on the British estate, as did the plowman working him. One horseman, John Grout, wrote:

> The horsemen were the big men on the farm. They kept in with each other and had secrets. They were a whispering lot....
> The head horseman was called the "lord"—and that's what he was, lord of the horses. That was me one day. I was lord of the horses. The place ran like clockwork. All the harnessing was done in strict order, first this, then that. The ploughing team left and returned to the stable yard according to the rank of the ploughman. If you happened to get back before someone senior to you, you just had to wait in the lane until he arrived. Then you could go, but not before.
> The horses were friends, and loved like men. Some men would do more for a horse than they would for a wife. The ploughmen talked softly to their teams all day long, and you could see the horses listening. Although the teams ploughed twenty yards apart, the men didn't talk much to each other, except sometimes they sang. Each man ploughed in his own fashion and with his own mark. It looked all the same if you didn't know about ploughing, but a farmer could walk on a field ploughed by different teams and tell which was ploughed by which. Sometimes he would pay a penny an acre extra for a perfect ploughing. Or he would make a deal with the ploughman—"free rent for good work." That would mean £5 a year. The men worked perfectly to get this, but they also worked perfectly because it was their work. It belonged to them. It was theirs.[6]

Little changed over the centuries, and American farmers at the time of the American Revolution were said to be using the same farming methods as their ancestors two thousand years before. They were still using crude wooden plows, pulled by oxen or horses to break up the soil, uproot weeds and let in more air and water. To break up the resulting clods and smooth out the seedbed, they used a wooden harrow with spikes pointing down. Seeds were sown by hand, and cultivation between the plants—uprooting weeds—was carried out by using the hoe. To cut the grain they used sickles, an arc shaped implement with a short handle, and for hay the longer handled scythe.[7] To separate the grain from the stalk on the threshing floor they used flails, jointed sticks with one part held by the thresher and the other part swung down forcefully against the outspread cereal stalks.[8]

Change came first in Great Britain during the eighteenth century, as the industrial revolution was getting under way. It was set off by Jethro Tull's 1702 invention of the seed drill, which sowed seeds in evenly spaced rows instead of the wasteful method of broadcasting by hand.[9] This made it possible to move from hoeing by hand to using horse-drawn hoes for cultivation between the evenly spaced rows. Setting the stage for eighteenth century British innovation was Jethro Tull's influential book, *Horse-Hoeing Husbandry*, published in 1733.[10] Scientific principles of manuring and crop rotation[11] were accompanied by innovation of a whole range of new implements: seed drills, plows, cultivators, and harvesting machines for which the horse provided the necessary motive power and agility.[12] Improvements in plowing, for example, included introduction of the all-metal plow, the wheeled plow, and the chilled and hardened self-sharpening steel plowshare whose better steel made it unnecessary to halt plowing operations to sharpen the plow.[13]

The invention of the new horse-drawn farm implements in Great Britain continued in the nineteenth century in the United States. This formed the basis for a horse-dependent American agricultural revolution in the second half of the century. In 1814 Jethro Wood patented an iron plow with interchangeable parts. This replaced the wooden plow American farmers had been using, as they overcame their fear that iron would poison the soil.[14] In 1837 John Deere demonstrated a steel plow he had made from a cast-off saw blade. By 1842 he was making 200 plows a year by hand and by 1857 producing 10,000 a year in a factory in Illinois, as the stronger, self-polishing plow made it possible to plow the rich, sticky, heavily-rooted, matted soil of the prairies of the Middle West.[15]

Metallurgical progress soon reached beyond the single plow blade that horses had been pulling for centuries. Several plows were connected to each other to form a gangplow cutting multiple furrows. And rather than walk behind the plow, a farmer could ride above it on a high sprung seat with room for one person, called a sulky as being anti-social. By the 1860s, many farmers were riding sulky gangplows, with larger teams of horses, farming more land faster than was possible with the single plow. Harnessed to their traditional task, the plow horses greatly increased farm productivity, saving many man-hours of labor farmers had previously expended.[16]

Metallurgical progress and the mechanization it made possible extended the role of horses to take on functions they had never done before, replacing manpower in tasks that were previously done by hand. In the 1840's William Pennock began the manufacture of horse-drawn grain drills in the United States. This led to replacement of the broadcast sowing of wheat in the Middle Atlantic States by the 1860's and in the prairie region in the 1870's.[17] Horse-drawn corn drills, which sowed fertilizer with the corn and covered it with soil at the same time, became popular at the same time. The regular rows of seeds made possible the horse-drawn straddle-row cultivator, which replaced the hand-held hoe used to uproot the weeds that emerged between the growing plants. To replace the hand-held scythe a horse-drawn mowing machine was invented in 1844,[18] and in 1865 Edward Haber invented the hay rake.[19]

The most significant horse-drawn invention of the 1830's to 1860's period was the mechanical reaper. It introduced horsepower replacing many hands at the critical point in the grain production process when quick work is necessary to save the crop from ruin. More than fifty different models of the reaper were developed between 1786 and 1831. Then, in 1834, Cyrus Hall McCormick patented his reaper. It substituted for the hand-held scythe and cradle a horse-drawn revolving reel that pressed the stalks against a fixed blade that cut them. By 1851, McCormick's factory in Chicago was producing a thousand reapers a year.[20]

In 1859, the Marsh harvester replaced the two men who had followed the reaper to bind the stalks into sheaves and delivered the stalks to a table to be bound. A wire tie binder was adopted by 1877 but farmers complained that livestock were eating pieces of metal. John F. Appleby then invented the twine binder, which stepped up the speed of harvesting and greatly increased the production of grain.[21]

The increased volume of grain production following introduction of the McCormick reaper in mid-nineteenth century added urgency to the need for an improved means of separating the grain from the stalks that had been harvested. To replace the no longer adequate method of beating the stalks with hand-held flails on the threshing floor, efforts to develop a mechanical threshing machine had long been under way. The earliest practical threshing machine, the "ground hog," was developed by a Scotsman, Andrew Merkle, in 1786. It treated the stalks with beaters, pegs on a rotating cylinder as they rubbed against a concave iron framework.[22] A few models reached the United States soon after 1800 but were easily broken and not easily repaired. Some unsuccessful American models were on the market in the 1820's, and by the 1830's, to meet the growing demand for small, inexpensive machines, over 700 models were being advertised. One thresher, which combined threshing, winnowing, and separating the grain from the chaff, was patented in 1837 and by the late 1840's was used in leading American wheat fields.[23]

To power the threshing machine, however, a source of rotary motion was necessary. This was a new challenge for horses, who powered other farm equipment with forward motion. One solution found was the treadmill, which "utilized the weight and energy of the animal by forcing it to walk uphill on a moving floor which activated the drums around which the endless floor-belt was wrapped."[24] Smaller treadmills had been used for lighter farmstead tasks, such as churning butter, operating washing machines, or

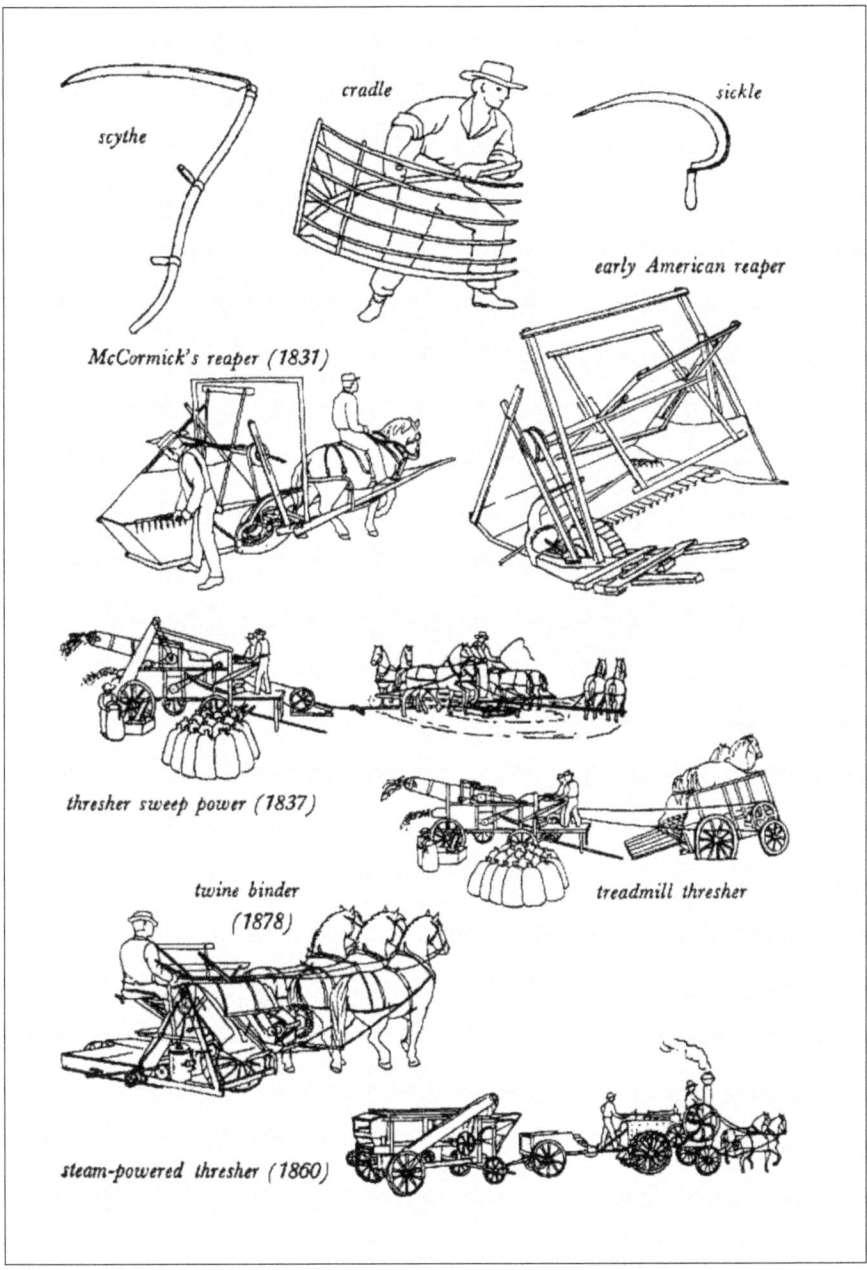

Array of nineteenth century harvest implements used by American farmers. From *Power to Produce, The Yearbook of Agriculture, 1960*, U.S. Department of Agriculture.

Gray & Sons Three Horse Tread Power. From Paul C. Johnson, *Farm Power in the Making of America*.

pumping water, and were operated using dogs, goats, sheep, cattle, and even children. To provide the rotary motion for the new threshing machines, more massive treadmills were constructed, some with room for three horses.[25]

As the demand for more power for the threshing machines grew, advances in metallurgy made possible the development of a more powerful piece of horse-drawn rotary action equipment. In 1847, Daniel Woodbury patented the sweep power, sometimes called the horsepower, the lever power, or the horse sweep. It consisted of a central hub from which there radiated several poles, at the end of which were hitched teams of horses or other draft animals that walked in a circle. Cast iron bevel gears made it possible for the horses' motion to turn the central shaft vertically and then to change the axis of rotation from vertical to horizontal, as the power was transmitted outward through a series of tumbling rods to the nearby threshing machine. There, additional gears converted the slow, measured turn of the sweep to the greater speed needed for the thresher.

With anywhere from only one or two spokes and a small hub in a staked down position to six or seven spokes radiating from an elaborate machine on a movable wagon, horse sweeps came to be an essential part of threshing machine operation. Horses had to step over the tumbling rods each time they passed that part of the circle. They had to respond to the pace set by the operator of the team, standing or sitting over the hub and trying to meet the needs of the threshing machine operator.[26]

To provide the power to drive the threshing machines, manufacturers of threshing machines found it necessary to offer also horse sweeps that could run them. A prime horse sweep manufacturer was the J.I. Case company, which built Woodbury Sweep Powers and, after modifications by W.W. Dingee, the Woodbury Power of the Dingee Pattern. Its sweep arms were each 12½ feet long and travelled in a circle 79 feet in circumference. Horses travelled around the circle at about 2¼ miles per hour. The tumbling rods were geared to 101 revolutions for each round of the horses, or 250 revolutions per minute, which was geared up to a far higher speed—1,000 rpm—for the threshing machine at the other end.[27] Most threshing machines were operated not by individual farmers but by threshing outfits, which arrived in the fall and moved from farm to farm. With the number

Horse sweep, from the Germans from Russia Heritage Collection, North Dakota State University Libraries.

of horses hitched to a sweep limited to twelve, or at most fourteen, each horse worked at full capacity. Farmers were called upon to add one or two teams to the threshing operation when the custom thresher arrived in the fall, but by this time the horses were usually worn out from the work of plowing, cultivating and harvesting. With the constant overload of pulling on the monotonous merry-go-round in the heat, dust and flies, threshing was sometimes called a horse-killing job. In addition, as the horses were constantly pulling on twist, with a constant side draft which forced the collar out at the top of the inside shoulder, sores frequently resulted.

Other requirements had to be met for the threshing operation. To maintain an even speed in the threshing cylinder, the horses had to walk steadily—neither too rapidly nor too slowly—or poor separation of the grain from the straw would result.

Outside the sweep machine, where the rotary motion was transmitted to the threshing machine by the set of tumbling rods fastened together with knuckle joints, the exposed moving parts at times caught on someone's clothing and caused serious injuries. Some states, as a result, passed laws requiring the tumbling rods and knuckle joints to be boxed in.

A growing problem with horse sweeps, however, came with the great increase in agricultural production beginning with the Civil War. Manufacturers met the demand by building machines that could thresh nine hundred bushels of grain a day rather than the three to four hundred bushels a day accommodated by threshing machines powered by horse sweeps or treadmills. This focused attention too on the lack of power coming from small, lightweight horses that predominated as breeders raised trotters, pacers, and coach horses rather than heavy draft horses.

Though the manufacture and use of horse sweeps continued to the end of the nineteenth century, with catalogue sales as late as the 1920's, another source of rotary power was needed to drive the threshing.[28]

Steam

Threshing machine manufacturers searching for a more powerful means than the twelve-horse sweep to drive their larger threshers had before them the example of steamboats plying the nation's rivers and railroad engines steaming across the country to join the Atlantic and Pacific coasts in 1869.

Steam propulsion had been some time in coming. In 1712, Thomas Newcomen directed steam—which expands to 1,300 times the space occupied by water when heated to 212 degrees Fahrenheit—into a cylinder to drive a piston, much as gunpowder had driven a cannon ball out of the barrel of a cannon. In 1769 James Watt, a Scottish instrument maker, had added a second cylinder to eliminate cooling delays and a connecting rod to convert the piston's reciprocal action to rotary action.[29] Using the rotary motion of Watt's steam engine, England's Richard Trevithick developed a steam carriage travelling on rails at ten miles an hour in 1804. In 1807 American Robert Fulton's Clermont steamed up the Hudson River at five miles an hour. By 1820, seventy-five steamboats were moving people and cargoes up and down the Mississippi River,[30] and by 1851 nearly 600 steamboats travelled the rivers of the U.S. interior.[31]

While the railroad and steamboat served the expansion of farming, bringing in supplies and taking crops to market, steam engines found no direct application on the farms until taken up by the manufacturers of threshing machines. Then, one by one, manufacturers invented steam engines to sell along with their threshing machines. George Frick, with a reputation as a mechanical genius, began building grain threshers in the 1840's and built his first steam engine in 1850.[32] The brothers Meinrad and John Rumely took first prize in the threshing competition at the U.S. Fair in Chicago in 1859 and in 1861 added steam engines to their line.[33] John Increase Case, who went on to become the largest manufacturer of threshers in the world, built his company's first steam engine in 1869.[34]

The first steam engines for use with threshers were set on wheeled platforms. They were hauled from place to place by teams of horses and used only for belt power. Then, in the 1870's, 1876 in the case of the Case company, the steam power was geared to also drive the wagon's wheels, so that it became self propelled and was referred to as a steam traction engine. But no steering mechanism was used, so that the traction engine was hitched to a yoke of horses for steering. By 1886, the Case Company added a steering device to its steam traction engine. Though horses were no longer needed to haul or steer the engine, however, the spectacle of a fire and steam-bearing machine advancing down a road was frightening to passing horses. A team of horses was therefore hitched to the front of the advancing engine to reassure and calm the horses it encountered.[35]

Thus, over the years that steam engines powered America's threshing machines, the demand for accompanying horses continued. Horses were also busily engaged in hauling fuel and water to the steam engines during the day. In South Dakota, for example, an average day's threshing with a twenty-five horsepower steam engine required four tank loads of water. Sometimes water was not available close by. In North Dakota and Saskatchewan, water haulers were sometimes obliged to haul water from ten miles away.[36]

During the second half of the nineteenth century the role of the horse on the farm had greatly expanded. One invention after another had made tasks formerly done by people the function of a horse-drawn machine. One result was the increase in the number of horses on American farms, from 6.8 million in 1867 to 17.9 million in 1900.[37] Another result was the contribution to increased farm production during the American agricultural revolution. Other factors too contributed to increased production, including the larger area under cultivation, better methods of cultivation, the use of fertilizers, better seeds and crop rotation. Of crucial importance, however, was the introduction of horse-drawn equipment at a time when labor was scarce and land abundant.[38]

Progress had indeed been striking. What had taken fifty to sixty man-hours of labor to produce 20 bushels on an acre of wheat in 1825 took only eight to ten man-hours in 1890. In use in 1825 was a walking plow, a bundle of brush to harrow, hand broadcasting of seed, harvesting by sickle, and threshing by flail. By 1890, there was in use a gangplow, a harrow, a binder, a thresher, wagons and horses.[39]

By 1890, however, as a chronology of United States agriculture concluded, "most of the basic potentialities of agricultural machinery dependent on animal power had been discovered."[40]

Tractors

Though over the decades leading to 1890 horses took on new tasks they had not done before, this was to change. In the 1890's the power of the steam traction engine began to be applied not only to propel itself but to pull a plow through the ground. Up until that time, the horse and the steam engine were replacing human labor. With steam engine plowing, however, steam took on a function that had for a thousand years been the function of the horse.

Plowing was central to the farmer's need for horses. One large-scale farmer complained in mid-nineteenth century England that he needed seventy horses for his plowing but only fifteen for the rest of the year. Tellingly, the British Parliament had offered a prize of £500 for whoever could invent a workable steam plow; but there were no successful claimants. Any steam engines with enough power to cut furrows through the ground were simply too heavy. As one expert noted, they just sank into the ground.

One British solution advance in mid-nineteenth century was the "steam tackle." A steam engine stationed at the edge of a field pulled a reversible plow by cable from one end of the field to the other. Patented by

John Fowler in England in 1852, some 1,000 such rigs were made and soon sold, but only two reportedly in the United States, where the larger size of farms made the cable haul impractical.[41]

Over the years that followed, as thresher-powering engines flourished, marked improvements were made in the mobile steam engines: better balance, higher piston speed with shorter strokes, compound cylinder action, and valves with closer tolerances, increasing the average horsepower from 10 in 1875 to around 40 in 1910. By the 1890s traction engine manufacturers were ready to produce and sell steam plows.[42] But weight remained a problem, with five hundred to seven hundred pounds of iron and steel required for every horsepower delivered at the crossbar and at least thirty pounds of water per horsepower hour.[43]

Two approaches were taken to solve the problem of weight by spreading it over a larger area. One was to make the drive wheels bigger and broader, as much as twenty feet wide in the open country of the Great Plains and Far West. The other was to move the engine on tracks, and was employed by the California manufacturers Daniel Best and Benjamin Holt, predecessors of the Caterpillar Company. Their engine had two wood-covered drive wheels with a separate clutch for each track, which could be engaged and disengaged so as to pivot the machine sharply to steer.[44]

The biggest plow engines, burning coal and pulling 10 to 20 bottoms, that is plows, went to the semi-arid wheat plains of the West, while the smaller or moderate size ones went to the East and Middle West. The Geiser Manufacturing Company's Peerless steam plow was introduced in 1889 and the company was second only to the J.I. Case Company in the number of engines turned out during the steam plow era. Plow-hauling steam engines gained momentum through the 1890s, so that by 1900 thirty firms were building 5,000 large engines a year in the U.S. and Canada.[45]

Even as the steam plow was moving to replace the horse, however, another source of power was waiting in the wings, preparing to move onstage and replace the steam plow. This was the internal combustion engine. While in a steam engine steam from an externally heated boiler enters the cylinder and moves the piston, in an internal combustion engine a combustible mixture is fed into the cylinder and ignited with a spark so that the piston is moved by the combustion of fuel within the cylinder itself.[46] A German inventor, Nikolaus August Otto, produced the first working internal combustion engine in 1867, and another German, Gottlieb Daimler, developed the gasoline engine, complete with a carburetor to mix gasoline and air to form an explosive mixture, in 1892.[47]

Experimental gas propelled engines came out during the 1890s, as progress was delayed by the slow development of petroleum fuels and lubricating oils and by the Otto Company of Philadelphia's patent protection, which did not expire until 1890.[48]

Construction of the first self-propelled gas tractors in the U.S. is attributed to the Charter Gas Engine Company, which put its single-cylinder engine on a Rumely steam tractor chassis in 1889. A workable machine was built by John Froelich of Iowa in 1892 and experimental machines by the Case Company in 1895 and the McCormick Company in 1894.[49] The Hart-Parr Company established the first exclusively gas tractor engine factory in Charles City, Iowa, in 1901[50] and its sales, manager, W.H. Williams, is credited with coining the word "tractor" in 1906 to describe the gas-traction engine.[51]

From 1900 to 1920 there was great competition between external combustion (steam) and internal combustion (gas) engines, both in transportation and agriculture.[52] Initially, successful gas tractors were slow to develop, however, as manufacturers simply mounted their gas engine on steam engine frames and wheels. Early gas tractors, consequently, were even larger than their steam engine predecessors, as they had two massive cylinders, large radiators, flywheels, and 50 to 100 or more gallons of water used for cooling.[53] The huge, cumbersome and expensive early gas tractors had to be suited also for belt pulley work, to power threshing machines, corn shellers, feed grinders and other belt-driven equipment.[54]

By 1910, the more than 70,000 steam tractors reported on U.S. farms still supplied practically all the power for farm belt pulley work.[55] This proved to be the peak of steam engine dominance of the market, however, as almost all old-line steam engine builders switched to gas tractors and farmers demanded smaller, lighter tractors.[56]

A few manufacturers convinced of the superiority of steam tractors continued to promote them. A.D. Baker, for example, brought out a lightweight steam tractor with auto guide steering, automatic stoker, enclosed crankcase and gear train, and increased boiler pressure, as late as 1925. But by 1920, the age of steam in agriculture was about over.[57]

Competition among gas tractor manufacturers was great, however, for, as a 1916 handbook on Successful Farming estimated, "the power required annually to plow the farm land of the United States exceeded that used in the operation of all the mills and factories in the country."[58] By 1919 over 150 manufacturers were offering some 200 different models of farm tractors.[59]

Onto this scene in 1917 came Henry Ford, who had in 1908 changed the automobile economy with his mass-produced, assembly line Model T Ford and now did the same thing in the tractor economy. He brought out the Fordson, an inexpensive, lightweight, smaller gas tractor to take on the plowing and harrowing of American farms. The Fordson soon took over the majority of the country's farm tractor market. Competitors dropped out or merged and by 1923 the Fordson's market share reached 76 percent of gas tractor sales in the U.S.[60]

But the Fordson could not perform all farm operations. It could plow the furrows and break up the clumps by harrowing to prepare for the seeding. But it could not take on the necessary cultivating that followed, digging out the weeds between the rows as the plants came up. In 1924, the International Harvester Company brought out the Farmall tractor, which could also cultivate. Its tricycle design had its front wheels close together to fit between the two rows of plants and its rear wheels wide apart on a raised frame that let them ride outside the two surrounding rows. Its belt pulley powered stationary equipment and its power takeoff ran pulled equipment. The Farmall tractor soon outdrew the Fordson, which in 1928 ceased manufacturing in the U.S. and moved production to Ireland. By 1929, the Farmall's market share reached 60 percent of all U.S. tractor sales.[61] Other row crop tractors followed in the U.S. market. The Oliver Company, for example, brought out a row crop tractor when it learned that the Ford Corporation was not planning to do so.[62]

Over the following decades tractor variations were introduced that took on other farm functions, to accommodate orchards, cotton farms, and others. The distance between the wheels on both front and back axles could be varied on some tractors, and some row crop tractors could cover more than two rows. By 1933, pneumatic, air-filled rubber tires were offered by nine tractor makers, replacing the studded metal wheels that had previously carried tractors through the dirt.[63] Some manufacturers increased tractor speeds so they could travel over the roads.

Following about ten years behind car engines in efficiency, tractors progressed from kerosene and distillates, to high-compression gasoline, diesel, starters, power steering, enclosed cabs, heaters, and lights.[64] In 1939, the hydraulically controlled integral three-point hitch, invented by Harry Ferguson and produced jointly with Henry Ford, was introduced. It permitted farmers to lift the trailing implements as they moved from row to row and field to field and to vary the depth at which they operated.[65]

Farm Workers

There were 6.4 million farms in the United States in 1910, with 12.7 million farm workers (ten years or older),[66] 20 million farm horses, and 4.2 million mules.[67] Onto this scene came the long-awaited practical gasoline tractor. Though it was eventually to eliminate most roles for farm horses, its most significant effect, a 1933 analysis concluded, was the reduction in labor requirements per unit of crop production.[68] Indeed, surveying American farmers soon after the introduction of gas tractors, the Department of Agriculture found that chiefly responsible for early efforts for the adoption of tractors was a desire by farmers to reduce the labor requirements in farm operation in the face of the high cost of man labor and the unreliability of transient help.[69] Labor scarcity, in fact, had set off the previous century's agricultural revolution when the Civil War took a million men off northern farms and obliged those remaining on the farms to adopt labor-saving technical changes. World War I, in which American men were drafted and sent overseas, played a similar role in spurring labor-saving technical change, but this time in the adoption of farm tractors.

Many of the men the army took from the farms did not return to the farms. As the popular song ran: "How ya gonna keep 'em down on the farm after they've seen Paree?"[70] Of those that did go back, many bought farms at peak prices but were caught by the deflation and agricultural depression that followed.[71] In addition, the massive road-building program undertaken by the Federal Government during the war to help bring supplies to the East Coast stimulated the trucking industry and the building of further all-weather roads. This reduced the isolation of farms and made it easier for other workers to leave. Industries and cities absorbed the departing farm manpower. Then, in the 1920s, the Congress passed the immigration bills which cut off much of the manpower that had fed labor needs over the previous decades.[72]

While prices received by farmers had doubled between 1910 and 1920, farm wage rates had outpaced them, increasing by 150 percent.[73] Scarce labor and elevated wage rates led to the replacement of horses with mechanically driven tractors applying far greater power to move a greater load and finish in a shorter time. One horsepower was defined as the power that could be exerted by the average 1,200-pound horse. The average weight of horses on farms in 1918 was 1,203 pounds, of mules 956 pounds. In contrast, the 246,000 tractors counted in the 1920 census averaged 20 horsepower each.[74]

The appeal of the manpower-saving advantages of farm tractors can be seen in a 1920 advertisement by the Case tractor company. "Keep The Boy In School," it read:

> With the help of the Case Kerosene Tractor it is possible for one man to do more work in a given time, than a good man and an industrious boy, together, working with horses.... Your boy can get his schooling without interruption, and the Spring work will not suffer by his absence.[75]

Tractor use did in fact reduce the need for manpower. Horse-drawn technology had reduced the man-hours of labor producing one acre of wheat from 57.7 in 1830 to 8.8 in 1896. Tractor and motor truck use reduced it further to 3.3 man-hours in 1930.[76] The reaper and thresher had reduced the labor-intensive harvesting burden earlier and the tractor's belt function reduced it further. The greatest use of the tractor's power, however, was for plowing, and while the power of the tractor was most necessary for plowing, and its belt functions for threshing, its replacement of horses would depend on what other functions horses performed to keep the farm operating through the annual agricultural cycle.

Farm Horses' Functions

What did the horses do on the farm before the advent of the tractor? A 1919 Department of Agriculture study of three representative farms showed that, as expected, preparation of the soil for planting—by disking, plowing, and harrowing—played an essential role—18 to 32 percent of all hours—with a lesser role for cultivating during growth and reaping and threshing when the crop matured. Most striking, however, was the large portion of horses' total activities devoted to hauling: about half of horses' time—46, 54, and 56 percent—on all three types of farms. This included road hauling, manure hauling, and other on-the-farm hauling.[77] See Appendix Table 2.

The prominence of horses' hauling duties helps explain farmers' early acquisition of motor trucks. A survey of corn belt farmers who had motor trucks in 1920 found that only 50 percent of them had tractors but 95 percent already had automobiles. The primary advantage they found in using trucks lay in saving time, since trucks required only one-third the time to take a trip that wagons did. They used their trucks primarily for road hauling, seldom on the farm, since trucks could not often obtain traction in the fields. On average, farmers with trucks lived farther away from their markets than farmers without trucks. They continued to use horses for some road hauling because of poor roads and for 8.4 weeks a year when mud, snow, ice, or frost made horses preferable. Three-fourths of the truck owners reported that the truck reduced the expense for hired help. For the reporting group as a whole the number of working animals was reduced by 1.2 head per truck. The reduction came mostly on larger farms, as those with only three or four horses, which could be used as a team, seldom disposed of any when they purchased a truck.[78]

Trucks on farms reached 900,000 by 1930, about the same level as tractors. Ahead of both tractor and truck acquisition, however, were farmers' purchases of automobiles. Farmers' automobiles reached 2 million by 1920 and 4 million by 1940. This was facilitated by the building of all-weather roads and necessitated by the farmers' need to overcome their physical dispersion. Their early experience with motorcars made it easier for farmers to take on the mechanical tasks involved in operating a tractor, a complete departure from working with horses.

Another feature of farm horses' work that emerged from the three-farm survey of 1919 was the extreme seasonality of farm work. "All but a few operations," it pointed out, "are carried on for only a few days or, at most, a few weeks a year."[79] The resulting short seasons of use of any specialized equipment imposed severe limitations on investment of capital, for tractors, for example.[80] It also had an effect on the efficient use of farm horses. Horses usually worked more in the spring and summer than in the fall and winter. A U.S. Department of Agriculture study in the mid–1920s found that horses worked about one-third the work days during spring and summer, about one-fourth the work days during the fall, and one-tenth the work days in winter.[81]

Clearly, the farms were supporting horses that were idle in the months between the greatest need for them. Feeding work animals through the winter months had always been a problem. An account of medieval England, for example, reported that: "The expense of feeding animals through the winter months means that many are slaughtered at Martinmas (November 11)."[82] The cost of maintaining horses on American farms through the idle months affected the attractiveness of tractors, which could reduce the number of horses needed during the peak months of plowing. The average annual cost of keeping horses, studied in 1920 and 1921, included bedding, chores, depreciation, interest, stabling, harness costs, shoeing, and veterinary care, was offset in part by the credit for manure. The total cost of one year's maintenance exceeded the cost of a newly purchased horse.[83]

The prescribed approach to reducing the horses' off-peak idleness was to minimize the number of horses needed for the peak duties. Tractors could not completely replace peak-hour needs for horses, however, since at times several functions had to be carried out at the same time. A team of horses could be split to perform separate concurrent functions, but a tractor could not.

By 1933 it could be concluded that "with a tractor available for heavy drawbar work and a truck for hauling, the use of work animals on some farms is largely confined to light drawbar work."[84] By 1946, tractors had taken over 82 percent of plowing and 85 percent of disking.[85]

As the number of horses declined, the Department of Agriculture's maintenance of separate statistics for horses and mules was discontinued, so that only combined numbers for horses and mules were available. These showed that over the half-century between 1910 and 1960, and particularly after 1915, as the number of tractors grew the number of horses and mules declined. In the aggregate, a 1948 study had shown, 3.9 work animals were displaced by each farm tractor in the 1920 to 1947 period.[86]

The Supply of Farm Horses

As the demand for farm horses declined under the impact of tractors and trucks, the supply of horses also varied, as the result of several factors. The six million small farmers who had to decide whether to breed new colts were influenced by expectations of future demand as reflected primarily in the ongoing price of horses. A farmer had to look ahead to a pregnancy period of 340 days, plus or minus 15 days,[87] the only 60 percent chance that mares bred would produce a live foal,[88] and the two or three additional years of growth before the colt could be sold or put to work. There was a three or four year delay, therefore, between the farmer's breeding decision based on market price and the shortfall or addition in the supply of horses. Adding to this lag was another factor that produced a longer price and production cycle for horses and mules than for other livestock.

As pointed out by the *Department of Agriculture 1933 Yearbook* analysis comparing horse and mule production during the 1890 to 1930 period with production of all cattle, milk cows, sheep and lambs, and hogs, the horse and mule cycle was much longer "because numbers of work animals are not decreased over short periods of time by increased slaughter, as is the case with meat animals, but they tend to live out their natural lives, which average about 15 years for horses and about 20 years for mules."[89]

The long cycle of horse prices and population is effectively illustrated for the 1871–1919 years by an analysis prepared by W.S. Dunn, of Schoharie, New York, appearing in the September 1921, *Breeders' Gazette*.[90] Dunn divided the period into cycles, with regular up and down movements of American horse prices. Following a firm price period reflecting the depleted horse population of the Civil War, oversupply caused prices to drop between 1871 and 1879. Prices then rose for five years, remaining steady for five more, but plunging for eight years beginning in 1889. This reflected oversupply in the wake of previous high prices and demand reduced by the coming of bicycles, which threatened to do away with the pleasure horse and carriage. By 1897 the resulting low prices had led farmers to stop producing colts, so that around 1900, when the Boer War called for a large number of American horses, prices rose steadily until 1911. Then a decline set in, affected by the rise of automobiles, but was interrupted by the heavy demand generated by the First World War. Recognizing the pattern of cycles, Dunn wrote, meant that 1921 marked the "threshold of another period of oversupply and a growing demand that should have been anticipated but which apparently, as in the past, was not."[91]

But this time the increase in demand did not come. Looking back from the *1933 Department of Agriculture Yearbook*, C.L. Harlen, C.A. Burmeister, and G.B. Thorne wrote:

> By 1920, the demand for horses and mules for nonagricultural uses almost disappeared, and there was no market for surplus work animals. Horse and mule prices dropped sharply in 1921, along with prices of other commodities, but continued to decline in the following years after other prices improved.[92]

The period 1920–1929, in fact, was characterized largely by farm depression and urban prosperity.[93] The supply of horses continued to decline. The number of farm horses under one year declined every year of the 1920s. It went from 1.2 million in 1920 to .4 million in 1932.[94] The decline in total farm horses was slowed, however, by the dropping off in the previously significant movement of older animals from farming to non-farming uses, the demand for horses for nonagricultural uses having almost disappeared. Alongside the decline in the number of farm horses, from 20 million in 1920 to 12.7 million in 1932, therefore, there came a distinct aging in the population of horses working on the farms.[95]

By 1933, "because of the high average age of all working stock and because of the depletion in the number of suitable breeding stock," the *1933 Agricultural Yearbook* concluded, colt raising was below a replacement basis.[96] Given the average age of horses of 15 years, a birth rate of 6.66 percent would be necessary to maintain a stationary horse population, 5 percent for an average lifespan of 20 years. But the birth rate measured by the percent of horses under 1-year-old in the total horse population declined from 6.06 percent in 1920 to 3.53 percent in 1929.

Then came the Depression. Farmers were forced to reduce cash expenditures of all kinds. Tractor purchases declined from 137,000 in 1929 to 25,000 in 1933.[97] Expenditures for fuel and mechanical repairs also had to be reduced. Farmers decreased the use of mechanical power and increased the use of work stock. Though the price of horses initially declined, the decline was less than that for other farm products.[98] Then, beginning in 1933, the price of horses rose and the birth rate of horses climbed from the 3.26 percent in 1932 to a 6.42 peak in 1938, remaining over 5 percent through 1942. The price of horses reached a peak of $79.80 in 1943 (see Appendix Table 10). Tractor purchases picked up after 1933, reaching 297,000 in 1941 before declining as a result of the World War II war effort.

The aging of the horse population is reflected in a 1942 study. It found that of the horses working on farms at that time 30.5 percent were over 15 years old. Those 16 to 20 years old represented a survival rate of 47 percent of their 1922–1926 crops of colts. Those 20 to 25 years old represented a survival rate of only 17.3 percent of their 1917–1921 colt crops. The 6.1 percent of those working who were over the age of 25 represented only 5.1 percent of their 1910–1916 colt crops (see Appendix Table 7).

Work was distributed unevenly between the age groups of working animals. The most hours were worked by the 6 to 10 year olds: 970 hours a year. All those 5 to 15 years old worked over 900 hours a year, while those under 3 or 25 years and older worked only half as many hours—475 for those under 3 and 420 for those 25 and older (see Appendix Table 8).

A 1942 study of farm tractors and horses and mules 3 years old and over found an average of 1.27 tractors and 3.8 work animals on each farm. Comparing the cropland worked, it concluded that 4.4 animals were displaced by each farm tractor (see Appendix Table 9).

By 1950, the population of U.S. farm horses had declined to 5.4 million, down from its 1915 peak of 21.4 million. As noted, in 1950 the U.S. Government stopped publishing separate statistics for the farm horse population, and instead provided the numbers for horses and mules combined. That total, which stood at 7.0 million in 1951, declined to 3.0 million in 1960. A figure of 2.2 million was provided for 1969 and footnoted as horses and ponies.[99]

The *1960 Yearbook of the Department of Agriculture*, entitled *Power to Produce*, recalled:

> The concept of farming without horses, which swept the country after the First World War, was derided, denounced, and resisted by many who solemnly predicted various evils that would befall agriculture and the Nation in the wake of mechanical power instead of animal power on American farms.

By 1960, however, it would conclude that cars, trucks, tractors, electricity, and services provided from off the farm, had taken over the many farm tasks that horses had provided in 1920. In addition, the farm population had declined steadily, with an interruption during the Depression, since its peak in 1915; so that the amount of power equipment per farm worker had nearly quadrupled between 1940 and 1960.[100]

Effects

This shift away from horses brought profound changes to the countryside. The *1975 Yearbook of Agriculture* could declare that "there has been more change in farming in the past 40 years than in the previous 4,000."[101]

With the new mechanical power, farmers could handle more acreage. So they expanded, buying land from their neighbors, many of whom moved to the cities. By 1974, the average farm size in the U.S. was double that of 1940: 385 acres compared with 174 acres.[102]

With fewer horses, if any, many of the chores children had carried out were no longer necessary, and they could not take on mechanical tasks, which required adult skills. As a result, large families were no longer needed, and the birth rate among farm families went down. From its 1910 level of 32 million, the farm population had shrunk to 9.3 million in 1974,[103] or by 70 percent, the farm horse population having shrunk by 90 percent.[104]

Inevitably, the effects reached well beyond the farms. On the one hand, the draining of personnel from the farms provided workers for the nation's expanding industries.[105] On the other hand, however, it resulted in the emptying out of the nation's small towns. No longer needed for the goods and services a larger farm population would require, small towns themselves were losing people to the cities. Their populations declined. Their younger workers migrated to the cities, leaving an older population that aged much as the farm horse population had. Towns' tax revenues declined, making it difficult to support services and maintain infrastructure. Typical small towns were reduced to a few stores, with empty store fronts that once housed the drug store, pool hall, hardware store, doctor's office, a barbershop, and a couple of implement stores.[106]

With the improved mobility cars now provided, people could travel to nearby larger towns for their shopping, as they increasingly did for high schools, churches, and medical care. Some small towns turned into bedroom communities for commutable-distance cities. But the national structure of widespread small towns serving surrounding farms was thinned out and faded or disappeared in some cases. Like mining towns that vanished with the exhaustion of a mine, many small towns turned into ghost towns or meager skeletons of their former selves.

The horse-drawn inventions built by farmers and blacksmiths in eighteenth century Great Britain and nineteenth century America were now greatly magnified and drawn by huge fossil-fueled mechanical engines. The horseless agriculture debated in the post–World War I years had now arrived and a partially depopulated rural landscape surrounded it.[107]

Five

On the Range

In the West, where ranchers raised livestock as farmers elsewhere raised crops,[1] horses were playing a diminished but continuing role: herding cattle, whose origins lay in ancient times and other lands. From ancient times communities had kept cattle grazing in pastures where crops could not be raised. But horses were not always involved even when large numbers of cattle were raised. So, where did horse-led cattle raising come from?

The late cultural geographer Terry G. Jordan traced the origins of American cattle raising to the Old World fringe of the Atlantic. Pressed westward by the advance of farming and settlement, more profitable users of land than grazing, the range cattle herders found themselves facing the end of available land but in a position to profit from the discovery of the New World. There the cattle culture could be transplanted to North and South America early in the colonial era. "Four regions exported their particular methods of cattle ranching across the Atlantic—the British highlands, Extremadura in Western Spain, Andalusia in southern Spain, and tropical West Africa."[2]

Only in Andalusia, however, did horses play an important cattle herding role. There, uncastrated, semi-feral cattle grazed unsupervised over extensive salt marshes until mounted herders moved them in late autumn to adjacent woodland and brush to avoid the winter floods.[3] In the Extremadura meseta, the castrated cattle grazed in enclosed, partitioned pastures, carefully tended by boys and old men.[4]

In Highland Britain, families moved with their castrated cattle in the spring to the hills above the "acrewall" marking the border of tillable land, returning in the late autumn after the harvest, and the cattle entered fenced pens and pastures. In the hills, the docile cattle, sometimes hobbled to restrict their movement, were tended by the elderly, women, or children. Horses were not used for herd control, that role being filled by herding dogs, with any bulls within the docile herd managed by the bulldog breeds British herders had developed.[5]

In West Africa, in areas between the tsetse fly infested area to the south and the Sahara to the north, cattle raising flourished. The nomadic Fulani venerated their Zebu cattle and followed them by season to sources of water and pasture. Subject to meticulous care and protection, the cattle were returned each evening to the camp pen. They were tended during the day by pedestrian herders using long staffs, cattle calls, thrown stones and hand signals to keep them away from crops. Unlike the Fulani, the cattle-keeping Taureg and Maures (Moors) left their cattle largely unsupervised. All, however, though skilled horsemen, used their horses for military, ceremonial, or transport purposes, and not for cattle control.[6]

Emigrants from the cattle-raising zones of the Old World, Jordan posits, were in a position to carry their distinctive herding systems to the cattle frontier in America, first in the West Indies, to which Columbus brought cattle and four mares[7] on his second voyage, and then with a profound impact on Spanish, French and British colonies.[8] On the four large islands of Hispaniola, Jamaica, Cuba, and Puerto Rico, bearers of the four European cattle-raising traditions brought together a confluence of cultures which coalesced in a diversity of herding techniques suitable for the various American settings.[9]

From the West Indies the Spanish colonists brought cattle raising to Florida, then west to Mexico. It was in Mexico, and its northern expansion in Texas and California, that the extensive-territory raising of cattle, with the dominant role of the horse and horseman was to develop and thrive. Escaping horses from even the earliest colonists had run wild and provided the Indians with mounts to hunt buffalo, changing their way of life for several centuries. Turmoil in the war for Texan independence in the 1830s resulted in abandoned ranches releasing hordes of longhorn cattle into West Texas where they multiplied into the millions. Onto this scene in the 1860s came the temptation of the demand for meat in the growing population centers of the northeast. With Indians retreating and the buffalo being decimated, the path to market, and the new railroad leading to it was opening up in the 1860s. The new railroads carried in hundreds of hunters between 1870 and 1880 and shipped out thousands of buffalo hides. By 1880 the southern region buffalo was gone and five years later the northern region buffalo as well.[10]

To meet the demand for meat in the northeast, and the profits to be gained, Texans rounded up the wild grazing cattle in the west and enough wild horses—mustangs—to ride herd over them. They then set off on the months-long cattle drive to the railheads to the north. At first they faced the opposition of farmers, in Sidalia, Missouri,[11] who didn't want cattle trampling their land. So they moved west ahead of the farmers and reached the new railheads as the railroad built westward, to Abilene, Dodge City, and Ellsworth.

While it lasted, from 1865 to about 1885, the long drive north from Texas was probably the most dramatic episode of American cattle history. Preparation began in January each year with the "cow hunt," usually about six weeks, for the capture of longhorns running wild in West Texas and the horses, mustangs, to be used in capturing and herding them. To keep up with the longhorns, capable of running for two days without eating or sleeping, the cowboys had to have fresh mounts brought to them, since mustangs could keep up the pace for only about three hours. The herds were then driven to southern Texas, where they were branded and prepared for the drive north.[12]

A typical herd heading north consisted of three thousand cattle, eighteen men, a hundred mustangs, and two four-mule teams to haul the chuck wagon carrying the bedding and biscuit flour.[13] Setting off on the three-month, six-hundred-mile trek from around San Antonio to Kansas in March or April, when prairie grass was lush, the herds traveled about fifteen miles a day. About a hundred herds set off each year, and were usually spaced from twenty to fifty miles apart on the trail. During the drive, a wrangler kept the unused mustangs some distance from the cattle and brought fresh mounts to the cowboys every four hours. He kept the horses at night in a "remuda," a makeshift pen in which the horses were encircled with a rope tied to posts.[14] Reportedly, "trained cow ponies had great respect for ropes, and the best ones would stand in position through a long session at the chuck wagon if their riders merely dropped the bridle reins on the ground in front of the horses' feet."[15]

At the end of the drive, at the railroad yards at Abilene, Caldwell, Dodge City, Wichita or Ellsworth, the cattle were loaded on railroad cars for shipment to the packinghouses north and east. The mustangs were exhausted.

> With their bones beginning to show, their bodies ached from saddle sores and sore hooves.[16] ... They had worked two shifts of four hours every day since the spring, and had survived on wild grasses with no corn or other feed. Drained of energy and strength beyond recovery, their useful life ... used up in four months ... they might be butchered or released into the wild to compete with healthy mustangs, cougars and wolves.[17]

Over the twenty years of the Long Drive, some five million longhorns reached Kansas, so that virtually all of the cattle in West Texas had been caught and trailed north. By one account, nearly a million longhorns died on the trail, 800,000 mustangs, and a thousand cowboys.[18]

Not all longhorns driven north were loaded on rail cars for the trip east, however. Some continued north and were sold to ranchers in Nebraska, Wyoming, Montana, and the Dakotas,[19] to be crossed with Hereford and angus cattle,[20] brought west by British ranchers whose origins lay in South Carolina.[21] But while the milder winters allowed the cattle in the south to graze uninterrupted all year, winters did not permit this in the north. Blizzards in 1885–1887—the Great Blizzard of January 1887 howling for three days and depositing snow as high as a cowboy's shoulder[22]—wiped out cattle and whole ranches in the north, and changed the scene to winter feeding and use of forage.[23] At the same time, as farming moved west, the unfenced open range upon which ranchers could graze their cattle gave way to fenced-in ranching. Barbed wire, invented in 1873, and homesteading farmers moving west, brought the open range system of ranching to an end.[24]

Barbed Wire

Barbed wire was invented to meet the needs of the farmers, who moved west to the plains and found no materials with which to build fences that could keep the animals out of their fields. There were no trees for wood to build fences, and no stones they could pile up, as in New England. They tried ditches and sod wall, that eroded, and hedges, which were slow to grow, took space, cast shadows, and harbored vermin, and smooth wire, which eroded, drooped, and couldn't stand up to the strength of the longhorn cattle.

So clear was the need for effective fencing, and intense the search for a solution, particularly after the 1862 Homestead Act, that between 1866 and 1868 alone the U.S. Patent Office issued 365 fence patents. Much of the invention activity came in Illinois, and particularly in DeKalb, Illinois, a farming community that was a stopover point for travelers moving west to the cattle country. Inspired by a wire design exhibited at the 1873 DeKalb County fair, a number of farmers began experimenting with designs they thought could do better.

Joseph F. Glidden, responding to his wife Lucinda's appeal for a means of keeping the farm animals out of her garden, used the coffee mill in his kitchen to twist and loop short strands of wire into barbs. He then stretched a long wire strand through the loop in the barb and intertwined another long strand to keep them both in place. It worked. His wife thus pleased, he applied for a patent and began producing it for others.

Not far off in DeKalb County, Jacob Haish, who was also inspired by the County Fair exhibit and thought he could do better, twisted a short piece of wire into an "S," rather than a loop, to be held between two intertwined strands. He submitted his patent application two months after Glidden's, but received his patent ten months before Glidden received his. After years of legal battles, embattled advocacy on the field, a "free wire" movement advocating unlicensed wire fencing and justifying patent violation, the U.S. Supreme Court on December 15, 1880, ruled in favor of the Glidden patent and Haish began paying royalties to the Glidden company.

On the land, meanwhile, the barbed wire fencing was having a profound effect. Stimulating the establishment of farms farther and farther west, it disrupted buffalo movement, Indian hunting trails, and the cattle trails from Texas to the railroads. For years a tug-of-war continued between farmers fencing their land, some fraudulently over land not yet theirs, and ranchers cutting the fences to preserve their right to move their cattle through the Open Range. In the end, legislators made wire-cutting a felony, assigned police to enforce it, and authorized fencing bordering roads with intervening gate openings, in one case every third of a mile. Cattlemen shifted their operations to fenced ranches and became major users of barbed wire.[25]

But cattle needed more grazing land than most fenced ranches could include. Though in Texas and California Spanish land grants laid the foundation for some extensive ranches, in the rest of the west the U.S. Government policy of granting limited, 160–acre homesteads, set out originally in the Homestead Act of 1862, could provide for farming but not for the needs of cattle ranching. This led to ranchers leasing grazing rights on government lands—public forests and public parks—with ensuing tensions over allocations, grazing fees, grazing practices, and environmental effects.[26]

In the conduct of cattle raising in the largest ranches in the south as well as in the more modest lands in the north, horses played a critical role. To play this role, a horse had to be trained to perform particular functions very different from those of a plow horse, a carriage-pulling horse, or a riding horse. These required quickness and agility as well as strength. Not every horse could meet these requirements and become a cow horse, a cutting horse, performing functions perfected by the Mexican, Texan, and Californian cattle workers in a tradition traced back to Spain. Because large herds of cattle were left to graze untended for all seasons, they had to be rounded up, singled out for identification from other groups, and branded, usually in the spring, and rounded up again in the fall, for possible dispatch to market.

The cowboy, or vaquero, threw the lariat, a rope with a large loop at the end, around the cattle's neck or leg, and wound the end of the rope around his saddle horn, or pommel. He needed the horse to hold steady as the cowboy jumped off the horse and tied up, or threw down the cow in preparation for branding or to keep it from straying.[27] Approaching a cow in the herd and separating it out required the horse to move with great agility, stopping and turning sharply more quickly than ordinary horses so as to counter the cow's evasive movements.[28] Long training by the cowboy was necessary to prepare a horse to perform these maneuvers.[29] The cowboy, too, had to be skillful in carrying out these maneuvers. A how-to book by experienced cowboy Fay E. Ward detailed even with what fingers to hold the rein.[30]

With the transition from unfenced open range to fenced ranches, the cowboy and his horse had additional duties:

> The ordinary cowboy's job consisted of picking up cattle and horses that wandered away from the herds and needed feeding, of putting out salt, greasing the windmills and repairing them, classifying the cattle, separating the cows and the calves, moving the cattle to good summer pastures, branding the cattle in early and midsummer, cutting out the yearling steers and two-year-old heifers, seeing that the bulls had access to the cows for breeding purposes, and putting up and repairing fences ... [besides] the two roundups, one in the spring and another in the fall.[31]

Meanwhile, ranchers, over the years, were studying how to improve their stock, crossing their cattle with new breeds and searching the world for exotic breeds they could bring into the country overcoming regulations designed to prevent the spread of foot and mouth disease. To the original Longhorn and Hereford, ranchers were able to add Angus, Limousin, Simmental, Charolais, Beefmaster, Gelbvieh, Red Angus, Shorthorn, Saler, Saint Gertrudis and Chianina.[32] The search for bigger and better breeds brought in a Chianina bull six feet tall and weighing 4,000 pounds, but the largest cattle proved too large for the packinghouses to handle.[33]

The demand for horses on cattle ranches was to change, however, with the introduction of mechanical power to the ranch. This was less the result of tractor purchases than the acquisition of ranch pickup trucks. A study of commercial family-operated cattle ranches in the southwest United States found that less than a third of the operators owned tractors in 1950, three-fourths already owned pickups in 1945, all owned pickups in 1950, and more than half owned two pickups in 1954.[34] The effect of pickup trucks on the demand for horses was quite pronounced. By 1959 there were 281 percent as many pickup trucks on the ranches as in the 1940–44 period but only 47 percent as many horses as in the 1940–44 period. Horses worked only 60 percent as many hours in 1959 as in the base period, while ranch pickup trucks drove 348 percent as many miles as in the base period.[35]

Though light trucks had been available before World War II, wartime development of vehicles capable of moving over all types of terrain made the postwar ranch pickup far more attractive. Ranchers began using them for distributing winter food to cattle out in the field, for moving supplies to operations away from ranch headquarters, and for "riding fences" to see to repairs in some cases. With the availability of the cattle trailer beginning in the 1960s, the pickup became even more useful. Now horses could be moved rapidly by pickup and cattle trailer, unloaded at distant pastures, and employed in the roundup and other work with the herd. Cattle sighted with some malady out in the field could be transported aboard the cattle trailer back to headquarters for treatment. Cattle ready for sale could also be transported by cattle trailer to the nearest auction, where sellers' and buyers' trailers filled the parking lot.[36]

Even as the ranch pickup and cattle trailer absorbed some of the horses' functions, another development changed the face of the cattle industry and reduced the need for cattle-herding horses. This was the cattle feedlot. Cattle had historically been moved closer to market where they could be fattened up before slaughter. With the expanded agricultural production that followed the use of tractors, the widespread use of petrochemical fertilizers after World War II, and the utilization of lands previously devoted to growing feed for horses, grains became available at low enough prices and could feed and fatten cattle far more rapidly than grazing at pasture.[37]

Beginning in the 1950s, cattle were taken from the ranch at a younger and younger age to be gathered in more compact fenced lots and fed a combination feed of corn, other grains, growth hormones, antibiotics, and other nutritional requirements. By the end of the twentieth century, most cattle were raised in cow and calf ranches, nursed by the mother for six to eight months, weaned, and sent to a stocking or backgrounding facility.[38] There they were prepared for trough or "bunk" feeding and transported to the feedlot for fattening to over a thousand pounds, for dispatch finally to the slaughter facility. With the accelerated weight gain from the grain nutrition, cattle now reached full weight, ready for slaughter, at eighteen to twenty months, compared to the four or five years necessary earlier in the century, before the feedlot regime.[39]

Feedlots were of varied design. They ranged from fenced-in open-air football field-sized lots with or without windbreaks, to far smaller roofed-over enclosures.[40] With the larger open-air pens, some role, though a far-limited one, remained for the horse, as mounted "pen riders" moved among the cattle in each pen looking for any ill cattle needing attention.[41]

While some of the 30,000 feedlots were enormous, handling as many as 100,000 cattle at the same time, the cow-calf end of the cattle-raising industry, of some 650,000, consisted of mostly smaller, "lifestyle," ranches and huge commercial ranches. In 2011, two-thirds of cattle ranches operated with less than 50 head and accounted for 11.6 percent of the total inventory of cattle. Most small, life-style ranchers worked off the ranch, less than half listed their primary occupations as farming, and 77 percent derived less than 25 percent of their income from farming. The largest operations, with over 1,000 head of cattle, though only 1.2 percent of all ranches, accounted for 35 percent of total inventory. Among feedlots, too, operations were concentrated at the top. The top 10 percent of feedlots, with over 4,000-head capacity, accounted for about 80 percent of all cattle sold.[42] Concentration was even greater among meatpacking firms, with the four largest meatpackers accounting for 79 percent of steer and heifer slaughter in 2005.[43]

It was on the ranches of all sizes that horses continued to carry out their cattle-tending functions. With the cattle population for a given volume of slaughter reduced from five years to eighteen to twenty months, however, there were fewer cattle in the fields and fewer horses needed to tend to them. Now sharing some of the horses' functions too was the SUV, the sports utility vehicle, able to "ride fences" with greater facility than the pickup and in some cases approach the cattle herds. Most cowboys continued to prefer horses for their cattle work, however, as SUVs disturbed the cattle's calm and could not maneuver to cut a cow from the herd or allow the cowboy to lasso the cattle. In some ranches cattle dogs have been trained to help move cattle, as they did historically in the British Highlands and throughout the ages with sheep.[44]

Though the cow horse has not lost his function, feedlots have reduced the scope of his operations, and SUVs, pickups, and cattle trailers have taken over some of the duties he previously performed in cattle-tending, calling attention to the diminished role working horses play on the American scene.

Six

Recreation

But a funny thing happened on the way to extinction. The same flood of technological advances that had eliminated, one-by-one, each of the horses' work functions, now released so much of the people's time for leisure that "horses stopped being beasts of burden in this country and became mostly recreational partners and companions."[1] While the number of farm and cattle ranch horses had dwindled drastically, the country's new appetite for recreation brought the number of horses in dude ranches, rodeos, horse shows, and suburban recreation barns to a national total of ten million by the end of the new century's first decade, with 40 percent in pleasure riding and another thirty in showing.[2]

Dude Ranch

An early intrusion of recreational users into the workhorse's world came with the arrival of paying guests at the cattle ranches in the west. In 1882, Bert Rumsey, of Buffalo, New York, signed a guest register at the Eaton's Custer Trail cattle ranch in Medora, North Dakota, and paid $10 a week for a ranch experience. The practice soon spread to other ranches, and when railroads were extended into the area and started issuing promotional material, "dude ranch wagons" began to pick up guests at the nearest train station. The Burlington Northern and Union Pacific railroads were promoters of dude travel, sending out brochures filled with photos, graphics, and directions to lure travelers out west.

As the number of automobiles increased, a greater flow of guests arrived in their own cars and the number of dude ranches grew. In 1926, ranch proprietors accepting guests met in Bozeman, Montana, and formed the Dude Ranchers Association. Association rules eventually provided that guests should stay at least a week, ranchers would not solicit business from the road, riding would be the main activity, and ranchers would not sell

Dudes returning from a morning ride across the range. Quarter Circle U Ranch, Birney, Montana, August 1941. Photograph by Marion Post Wolcott (Library of Congress).

alcoholic beverages. These guidelines remain in the expanded realm of dude ranches today.³

With the expansion of leisure following World War II, dude ranches were joined by other recreational uses of horses, the impetus coming from two directions. From the west came the image of the cowboy, roping cattle and bronco busting. From across the Atlantic came the image of English riding, in hunting, polo, steeplechase jumping, and dressage.

The western, cowboy, story was spread even before the cattle culture faded, as dime novels and other popular literature glamorized and romanticized the cowboy life. Beginning in the 1880s, touring wild-west shows, most prominently that of Buffalo Bill Cody, brought demonstrations of cattle roping, bronco-busting, trick riding, and sharpshooting to audiences in other parts of the United States and even to Europe. Buffalo Bill presented Indian chief Sitting Bull and sharpshooter Annie Oakley and staged Indian raids on wagon trains to thrill audiences. Soon other traveling wild-west shows were launched as well. When the popularity of the wild-west show subsided, one component—cowboys roping cattle and riding bucking broncos—survived, more attractive because it pitted cowboys competing with each other rather than simply participating in a demonstration.⁴ The early rodeos of cowboy competition emerging from the wild-west shows joined the many informal neighborhood contests among cowboys in celebration of holidays and other occasions. Their origin lay in the practices of the Mexican cowboys in California and the spontaneous competition between trail groups bringing their cattle to the railheads and relaxing after the long drive.[5] From both sources the popularity of rodeos grew, with a new influence from another source, which added to the popularity of the western story.

Movies

This was the advent of motion pictures—the movies. Growing out of Thomas Edison's invention soon after the turn of the century, the movies were short and silent and in need of action to keep their images lively.[6] This meant western movies, with horses and cowboys, which presented to a nation-wide audience an appealingly romanticized part of American history. Western movies came to dominate the movie screen through the silent Twenties. Then, with the coming of sound, B-Westerns provided the second feature as the double-feature practice was adopted during the 1930s Depression. The double-feature practice waned, however, in the Fifties.[7]

Writing in 1967, Anthony Amaral reported that about one thousand horses were stabled around Hollywood for motion picture work. They were classified, like human actors, by the functions they performed. About half were extras. They carried the posses for westerns and troopers for cavalry pictures, pulled wagons and buggies, and provided atmosphere for particular scenes. They had to be gentle, since the human extras playing posse men and cavalrymen might never have ridden before.

A second category were the stunt horses, trained to fall on command, leap from a cliff, or gallop steadily alongside a moving train or stagecoach while their rider leaped from the saddle. In another category were specialty horses, with a particular routine, a natural deformity, like a swayback, or a characteristic bucking style. One favorite specialty horse was Steele, who at various times carried John Wayne, Robert Taylor, Joel McCrea, and Randolph Scott.

The final category of movie horses was the star horse, with exceptional personality, beauty, talent, and enough intelligence to understand what a plot required. Some star horses became quite famous. Studios received fan mail requesting their photographs and some went on individual celebrity tours. Like human stars, star movie horses had doubles and stand-ins. Doubles did the rough-and-tumble routines, and stand-ins held the star's position on the set as lights and cameras were adjusted.[8]

Famous movie horses were identified with their famous riders. The Lone Ranger had Silver, Tonto had Scout, Gene Autry had Champion, Dale Evans had Buttermilk, Roy Rogers had Trigger, Tom Mix had Tony, Hopalong Cassidy had Topper, John Wayne had Duke, Andy Devine had Joker, and Jimmy Stewart had Pie.[9]

Rodeos

With horses and movie stars telling the cowboy story, there came a wider consciousness of western culture as a part of American history. This blossomed in the time of expanding American leisure in the great growth of rodeos, western horse shows, and dude ranches. By the end of the twentieth century, rodeo organizers ranged from national and regional professional associations—with close to 300 events a year—to the National Intercollegiate Rodeo Association, the National High School Rodeo Association, the American Junior Rodeo Association, the National Little Britches Rodeo Association, with around 220 sanctioned rodeos in 15 different states for children 5 to 18, the National Pro Senior Rodeo Association for contestants 40 and older, with over 75 rodeos in the U.S. and Canada, the Women's Professional Rodeo Association,[10] the Professional Bull Riders Association,[11] the National Cutting Horse Association,[12] the Military Rodeo Cowboys Association, the National Police Rodeo Association, the National Firefighters Rodeo Association, several prison inmate rodeo programs,[13] and the International Gay Rodeo Association.[14]

Unlike professional athletes in other sports, though rodeo cowboys compete for money they are not part of a team. Rodeo is an individual sport. Rodeo cowboys and cowgirls choose where they want to enter, cover their own travel costs, and those of their horse if they are in a timed event, pay the entry fees, and have no guarantee that they will win and recover their costs.[15] Entry into the professional finals is based on a scoring system, with one point for every dollar of prize money won.[16]

The standard events in most rodeos, are bareback riding, saddle-bronc riding, bull riding, tie-down roping, team roping, steer wrestling, ladies barrel racing, and in most rodeos steer roping.[17]

Rodeo horses are of two sorts: bucking horses provided in groups by stock contractors, and individual horses for cowboys' roping events. As half the score of a bucking event measures the performance of the horse, stock contractors—about seventy of whom serve the professional rodeo association—go to great lengths to collect hard-to-ride bucking horses. Formerly, they found their bucking horses among feral horses on the open range, from difficult horses brought to them by other horse owners, and from bucking stock auctions at which buyers watched animals buck and bid for them. As the supply became scarce in the 1950s, however, a Montana stock contractor, Ernest Tooke, reasoned that since others were breeding horses for gentleness, it should be possible to breed horses selectively for their bucking qualities. He succeeded, and now virtually all professional rodeo association stock contractors breed bucking horses and some breed bucking bulls as well.[18]

Stock contractors, having bred or purchased a young bucking horse, may take two years to evaluate it, send the two-year old to a high school or college rodeo, and wait until it is five years old before taking it to a professional rodeo.[19] Since a bucking horse may be ridden only once or twice in a rodeo, one stock contractor, Harry Vold, noted: "These animals work only a minute and a half each year."[20] Carried to the rodeo on large transport trucks, the bucking horses may then be grouped in pens for consistency, to assure each contestant an equal chance of winning on most every horse.[21] Cowboys draw bucking horses in a lottery-like arrangement before each rodeo and hope to stay on for eight seconds.

Horses that score highly in bucking events may gain considerable celebrity, bringing their stock contractor a bonus to participate in a particular rodeo. Outstanding horses may be voted bucking horse of the year by cowboys in the professional finals and may even gain all-time hall of fame honors.

One characteristic, however, distinguishes bucking horses from all other recreation horses. Back on the ranch, between rodeo appearances bucking horses are placed in open fields, away from human contact, which would "spoil" them and take away "that independence, that sense of freedom."[22] Other recreation horses, in contrast, are in intimate contact with humans, who care for them, train with them, and participate with them in either organized competition or the simple pleasure of riding.

Rodeo cowboys provide their own individual horses for timed events involving the roping or wrestling with cattle. Rodeo cowboys' horses may be initially trained by trainers or by the cowboys themselves, but once they begin to participate in events they train very closely with the cowboy who rides them. They travel with the cowboy, either continuously with full-time rodeo cowboys, or for weekend events with weekend cowboys, sometimes called weekend warriors, in which case they can spend the in-between time in their own paddock or pasture. To cut down travel time for weekend-rodeo-cowboys, the country has been divided into regions by the Professional Rodeo Cowboys Association, with separate regional rodeos in each.[23]

Rodeo horses specialize in particular timed events, each of which involves particular behavior by the horse, complementing the actions by the cowboy. For steer wrestling, the cowboy drops from his horse, grabs the steer by the horns and wrestles it to the ground. The cowboy's horse must bring him alongside the steer while the hazer, on another horse, keeps the steer from straying.[24]

For tie-down roping, previously called calf roping, the mounted cowboy gives a calf weighing about 250 pounds a head start, chases it, ropes it, dismounts while the rope is tied fast to his saddle, throws the calf on its side, ties any three of its legs, and remounts. The record is 6.5 seconds. The cowboy's horse must pursue the calf, skid to a stop, and hold the rope taut after the lassoing.[25]

For team roping, one cowboy, the header, ropes the steer around the horns or neck, dismounts, and turns the steer to the left so that the second cowboy, the heeler, can rope both of the steer's hind legs. Time is counted when both cowboys' ropes are taut and their horses face each other. The header's horse must pursue the steer, skid to a stop, hold the rope taut after the lassoing, and keep it taut until the heeler has lassoed the steer's hind legs. The heeler's horse must get him into position and back up, facing the steer's hind legs, while holding the rope taut after the lassoing.[26]

In barrel racing, primarily a women's rodeo event, the mounted cowgirl runs a cloverleaf pattern around three barrels set up in a triangle. A horse's speed and agility determines how fast it can complete the pattern without knocking over any of the barrels.[27]

In events sponsored by the National Cutting Horse Association, a mounted cowboy separates, or cuts, a steer from a small group of cattle and, dashing from side to side, prevents the steer from rejoining the herd. The high skill of expert cutting horses has attracted wealthy urban riders to the sport, in one case paying $460,000 for a cutting horse stallion.[28]

The specialization of horses for each event is evident in the sales advertisements for rodeo horses. They list saddle broncs, bareback broncs, heel horses, head horses, tie-down roping horses, steer wrestling horses, hazing horses, and barrel racing horses.[29]

Each of these rodeo horses, other than the saddle broncs and bareback broncs, provided by stock contractors, lives the life of a rodeo partner. They share in the training, the travel to the rodeo, the outcome of the events, and the trip home or directly to the next rodeo with the successful or less successful cowboy partner.

How equal is this partnership? The comments of one successful rodeo cowboy, world champion calf-roper Fred Whitfield, may be indicative. "A good horse is 80–90 percent of a winning run," says Whitfield, who was reported to have the fastest hands in the world when tying a calf. "If you don't have a good horse, you don't win. I don't care how fast you can tie a calf."[30]

Poet and ex-rodeo cowboy Paul Zarzyski writes nostalgically of driving all night between rodeos with his barrel-racing wife and ground tying the sorrel at 3 A.M. with water and grass at some sagebrush wayside while they took their sleeping bag break.[31]

For the rodeo cowboy and his rodeo partner horse, it was clearly a life of sharing.

Horse Shows

The cowboy tradition was to influence also the rising wave of horse shows accommodating the leisure-fed volume of horse ownership in America. The western tradition shared the horse-show movement with the English fox-hunting tradition, with its fence-jumping history and more formal attire.

Both western and English horse shows shared many features. Both had an event in which horses alone were judged and another in which riders were judged. In their event, horses were judged for conformation to a physical ideal, gait, and manners. In their event, riders were judged for control of the horse, as well as the horse's gait and grooming. Beyond these two events, and the level, smooth riding events, English and western shows had particular, characteristic, performance events. They were based in English shows on jumping over fences, with style in the ring, and, in time, apart from style, in more extensive arrangements. The western shows' particular performance events centered on ranch practices: cutting a steer out of a herd, maneuvering a steer in a determined pattern, or cutting a few marked steer out of a herd and moving them into a pen. In addition, both English and western shows included an event calling on the horse to perform complicated, perhaps dance-like, moves, forward, backwards, sideways, in small circles, and in spins. In English shows this was dressage, descended from a long European military tradition. In western shows this was reining, which concluded with a sliding stop from a full gallop.

English shows utilized a flat English saddle, rather than the deep-seat, high cantle western saddle. English riders used both hands and closed reins; western riders loose reins held in one hand. Approximating English hunters' dress, English show riders wore boots, britches or jodhpurs, a shirt with a tie or stock, a jacket, and a hard cap or derby. Western show riders wore a long-sleeved shirt, tie, denim jeans, belt, boots, and a wide brimmed cowboy hat or helmet.

So prevalent did horse shows become, it could be stated that: "During the summer months, one can probably find a horse show every weekend to watch that is a reasonable drive" anywhere in the U.S.[32] Commenting on the popularity of horse shows, one participant explained: "As long as there are horses, there'll be horse shows. It's like racing; people want to beat someone else."[33] And while younger horse riders, another expert explained, go to horse shows to compete, older riders go to show, since it is their hobby.[34]

Shows were organized by breed organizations (the American Quarter Horse Association, for example, had 2,284 horse shows in the U.S. in 2010[35]), by type of event (cutting horses), or by more general organizations, such as the National Equestrian Federation, or the Intercollegiate Equestrian Federation. A 2004 survey identified 4,865 organizations running horse shows.[36] All depended on meticulous rules for conduct and judging, and awarded ribbons or cash. At the lower end of the spectrum were unrated local schooling shows, often run by local training barns to give starting riders needed experience. Winners in rated lower level shows could enter regional and national championship competitions. Respondents to a 2010 survey said, on average, that they expected to participate in five shows the following year.[37]

Like rodeo horses, other than bucking horses, both western and English show horses underwent considerable training for the events in which they were to perform. Articles in horse journals recounted in detail the training techniques particular experts had found useful,[38] as did more extensive anthologies of various experts' experiences.[39]

Organizations sponsoring horse shows recognized the importance of experience and maturity in horses' performance. American Quarter Horse Association rules called for amateur halter divisions to have individual classes for yearlings, 2-year-olds, 3-year-olds, and 4-year-olds and older.[40] U.S. Equitation Federation jumper events were held separately for 5-year-old horses, 6-year-olds, and 7 and 8-year-olds, with higher obstacles in each case.[41] For world championship jumping events horses had to be 9-years-old or older.

Most horse show riders were amateurs. The American Quarter Horse Association counted amongst its 300,000 members fewer than a thousand professionals.[42] Horse show professionals could count on far less prize money than in rodeos or horse racing. Their money could come from riding lessons, training fees, stud fees for successful horses, resales, or sale of offspring.[43] A 2005 study found that most horse show professionals' revenue came from horse sales, boarding and training, in addition to purses and fees, which were only one-sixth the average level of racing purses and fees per horse.[44]

A horse show professional's routine was not an easy one. As one working horsewoman, Carol Shepherd, reported:

> For shows that are twenty to thirty miles away it means getting up at 4:30 A.M., being at the barn at 5 A.M., packing trunks and equipment, leaving at 6 A.M., getting to the show around 8 or 8:30, doing some schooling and showing. Then it's arrive back at the stable anywhere from 9 P.M. to midnight, unpacking, checking over the horses, and then home to bed.[45]

Professionals performed a key function in bringing new entrants into the world of recreational horses and horse shows. Participants were dependent on trainers for help in buying a horse, riding lessons, grooming lessons, guidance on choosing a horse show, on what to wear to a horse show, and, not infrequently, for help in selling the horse after the rider went off to college. Riders might spend a brief few minutes in the show ring but hours in and around the training barn.

Professionals who operated training barns faced a sizeable challenge, since each stable had to operate as a business. One training barn owner wrote:

> You must diversify to be successful: you must offer year-round riding lessons, perhaps a summer day camp, a polo league, horse shows, a tack shop.... A stable is a big financial investment, since it generally must be near a highly populated area.... The cost of your land is high, the cost of horses is high, you have employees' wages to pay, and you have to make the entire operation show a profit.[46]

Not only horse show participants depended on training barns. The barns provided also for the noncompeting recreational riders. A 2005 study found that while about 30 percent of horse owners were involved in horse shows, 42.4 percent were involved in noncompetitive recreation.[47] A 2010 survey of respondents over 18 years of age who owned, leased, or managed at least one horse, found that 59.4 percent were pleasure riders and only 35.2 percent were competitive riders.[48]

Feminization

The most striking feature of the shift in horse use to recreation, outside of the rodeos, was the feminization of horse ownership and ridership. A collection of writings by horsewomen in a volume entitled *Of Women and Horses* offers interesting insights into this development.

Mary Wanless wrote that over the past century horses have shifted from being utilitarian beasts of burden and transport to take on social roles as family members, dealing with female "significant others" rather than the mostly male riders and handlers. The economic and social changes that followed World War II brought so many more women into contact with horses that the idea of *horsey women* came to be glamorized in film and became a part of public awareness. It gave women the confidence to rally against the male-dominated psychoanalytical perspective.[49]

This transformation was borne out by the numbers. By 2009, a survey of respondents over 18 years of age who owned, leased, or managed at least one horse found that 88.8 percent were female.[50]

Another contributor, Mary Midkiff, found sound reasons for female domination of equine recreation and sports activities, from backyard horse keeping and training through Olympic competition. She cited the horse as the equalizer in making equine sports one of the rare sports where women can compete on equal terms with men. It offsets the disparities in strength between men and women and in fact brings emphasis to qualities in which women excel: finesses, touch, and understanding.[51]

Since women lack upper body strength, another rider, Frankie Chesler, pointed out they succeed in communicating with their horses by the use of greater finesse.[52]

Whatever the explanation, women's predominance in equine competition is most evident. Examination of a list of 1995 to 2012 Equitation Finals winners, for example, shows that 80 percent were female.[53]

Highlighting the increased female participation in equine affairs are the frequent media reports bringing examples to public attention. At one end of the age spectrum was the story of New York area schoolgirls' weekend airline migration to the training and show jumping marathon held over twelve weekends at the Palm Beach Winter Equestrian Festival allowing the girls to escape the cold practice barns and arenas during the winter.[54]

Toward the more mature end of the spectrum is the case of Linda Rice, 51, the first female horse trainer to top the standings at a major racetrack. Having worked twenty years at Belmont Park, she has joined other women in a horse-owning syndicate, restricted to women, which purchases and races thoroughbred mares at the high end of the racehorse price range.[55]

Away from the limelight, out on the trail or pasture, in the world the majority of horses inhabit, women play a different role, varying widely in the nature and frequency of their involvement.

Demographer Emily R. Kilby wrote that while one woman kept a recreational horse in the trailer, went to trail rides, overnight camping, and special training clinics regularly, another, with half a dozen horses at her home, might be too busy to squeeze in more than an occasional ride to a neighbor several times a month. Their recreational time with a horse might range from focusing on care to pamper a horse, to roughing it on the trail, from a Zen-like search for perfection in a dressage maneuver to gaining inner peace volunteering in a therapeutic riding program. There were horse-focused opportunities for everyone: solitary trail rides for the reclusive, joining opportunities in the myriad equestrian organizations for socializers. A surprising number, in fact, concentrate on caring for their horses twice a day, forking manure and moving heavy hay bales, and focusing on ailments and injuries throughout the year, leaving little time for actually riding the horse. When surveyed on how they make use of their horse, they respond "Just for pleasure."[56]

Psychologist Delphi M. Toth wrote about the involvement with horses by adult professional women, whose job may be filled with loose ends, obstacles, unsolved problems, slow progress and waiting for appreciation. In contrast, grooming a dirty horse, mucking a stall and cleaning tack, with no requests or demands, can bring the joy of completing a real though simple job in the quiet environment of a barn that can be relaxing and calming. While pumping hay and water may be physically equivalent to a gym or spa workout, it can be more emotionally soothing and gratifying.[57]

As for the younger generation, Dr. Toth wrote that for a girl encountering the hypercritical world of adolescence and high school, the tiny clique with her horse offers unconditional and noncritical acceptance.[58]

Typical was the case of Roxana Robinson, writing in the collection entitled *What My Mother Gave Me*. She grew up horse-crazy, she wrote, reading every horse book she could find, including *National Velvet, Silver Snaffles, A Pony for Jean, The Ten Pound Pony, The Horse of Hurricane Hill,* and *Tam the Untamed*. Each usually began with a young girl longing for a horse and finished with her owning one. She herself concluded that the greatest gift her mother gave her was a horse that, in retrospect, was "at the center of that romantic passage in my life, when she was my partner in the wild, dangerous, and beautiful ride across adolescence."[59]

Clearly, feminization of ownership and the horse's recreational role, have brought the horse a new function in human society.

Seven

Racing

In the long history of American horses losing each of their work functions—at war, on the road, in the city, on the farm, and on the range—and their resurgence as a recreational partner, one of the horses' roles remained unchanged: racing.

As an historian of thoroughbred racing in America, William H. P. Robertson, wrote:

> An original colonist who happened to have gone Rip Van Winkle one better, and slept for 300 years, undoubtedly would be mystified by the mechanical gadgets and elaborate procedures should he by chance awaken at a modern American race course, but so far as the basic action is concerned, he would catch on right away: the horse which gets there first is the winner.[1]

Already on the scene in colonial days, American horse racing was derived from Great Britain's thoroughbred racing, which was based on the descendants of three Arabian stallions: the Darby Arabian, the Godolphin Barb, and the Byerly Turk, imported to Great Britain between 1690 and 1730, with descendants entered in the General Stud Book from 1791. Their American descendants were entered in the American Stud Book from 1897.[2]

Thoroughbreds imported into America launched the several American horse racing breeds: From Eclipse descended the thoroughbreds[3]; from Janus, foaled in 1746 and arrived in America in the 1750s,[4] and Sir Archy, foaled in 1805,[5] descended the quarter horses; and from Hambletonian, foaled in 1849,[6] descended the standardbred harness racing line. Fox hunting gave rise to the steeplechasing line. Arabian racing's stud book begins with the mare Nejde and stallion Obeyran, imported in 1893.[7]

American thoroughbred racing established itself in the northern colonies, with a racetrack in New York as early as 1675.[8] Quarter horse racing arose first in Virginia and North Carolina, where quarter-mile paths, often through a town's main street, favored the breed with a burst of speed that could carry it through a dash.[9] Harness racing, centered in upper New York state, bred pacers and trotters that could pull the sulky for a mile in three minutes and qualify as standardbreds. Pacers race with legs on the same side of their body moving in unison, trotters with diagonal legs moving in unison. Harness racers raced on separate, dedicated tracks since the wheeled vehicles could not share the differently contoured thoroughbred tracks.[10]

Steeplechasers, following the British tradition, began in Ireland with about a four-mile run across country from steeple to steeple. Some American steeplechase racers brought portable obstacles, 52 inches high, to thoroughbred tracks and ran two or three miles. Others, particularly since 1970, run in the country, from three to four miles with fences up to five feet high. Most steeplechase meets are run by non-profit organizations, with the profits for charitable causes.[11]

Thoroughbred racing, the predominant, but clearly not the only American horse racing form, engaged mainly two-and three-year olds racing counterclockwise around flat oval tracks mainly for one-and-a-quarter miles but sometimes for as little as five-eighths of a mile or as much as two miles.

While the soul of horse racing is competition, it took on changing forms. Early on, it consisted of challenges, one horse owner challenging another, with the outcome determined by a series of heats rather than by a single run. Every horse owner with a fast horse thought it could beat other horses. It was said of one horse that "he was just fast enough to lose money."[12] The years of challenge matches, highlighted by North-South rivalry, stretched through the middle of the nineteenth century. In 1845, the South's Peytona met and defeated the North's Fashion in a $10,000 challenge run before a crowd estimated at 70,000 to 100,000 in New York.[13]

By the late nineteenth century, however, racing went from a private challenge between wealthy owners to a public spectacle. As the number of tracks grew, each track competed to attract the best horses by offering greater purses, which led to one winning horse's owner finding that the check for the prize money bounced.[14] Tracks came to feature widespread gambling, with bookmakers at each track. Soon, however, intense anti-gambling sentiment brought legislation outlawing the quoting of odds, soliciting bets, and recording bets in a fixed place. Anti-gambling legislation closed racing in New York in 1911 and horse owners moved south, with some tracks expanded and some new tracks opened in Maryland, in Havre de Grace, for example. Some 1,500 American horses reportedly went to Europe, along with jockeys and trainers.[15] Of the 314 tracks operating in the United States in 1890, only about 25 survived the anti-gambling legislation.[16]

In Kentucky in 1908, however, when the Louisville mayor started to enforce a law against bookmaking as Churchill Downs was about to open, the Court of Appeals ruled that, while bookmaking was illegal under the anti-gambling law, pool selling, in the form of pari-mutuel betting, was not.[17] In pari-mutuel betting, all wagers are put into a common pool and those who bet on the winning horses share the total amount bet minus a percentage, perhaps 14 to 25 percent for racing purses, track management, and state or local taxes.[18] In time, other states accepted pari-mutuel betting as an acceptable horse racing activity, and tracks were reopened. Racing returned to New York in 1913.[19] The Twenties was racing's Golden Age, before the Depression, and smaller purses, came on in the Thirties.[20]

To attract people to the stands in the Nineteen Thirties, tracks introduced the Daily Double, in which bettors picked the winners in two consecutive races. This was the first "exotic" wager, in that it involved a win by more than one horse.[21] Previously, winning bets were those on the horse that finished first (win), first or second (place), or first, second or third (show). The daily double was a bet on which horses would finish first in two consecutive races, originally the first two races, to induce fans to come to the track before the start of the first race. With time, all manner of exotic wagers were developed: the exacta (choosing the first two finishers in exact order), the trifecta (selecting the first three finishers in exact order), the superfecta (selecting the first four finishers in exact order), and the quenelle (selecting the first and second finishers without regard to order).[22] Other exotic wagers were based on selecting the winners of three, four, five, or six consecutive races, or a combination, such as the first, second and third horses in two races, known as the Twin Trifecta.[23]

From the beginning, to make each horse race competitive, separate races were organized for horses of equal quality. Starting at the bottom are Maiden Races, for horses that have not yet won. Then come Claiming Races, in which horses can be bought before the race for delivery after the race, the winnings, if any, going to the original owner. Next are Allowance Races, for horses meeting certain conditions, such as non-winners in one, two, three, or four races, with carrying weights assigned accordingly. Above that are Handicap Races, in which weights are assigned according to the racing secretary's evaluation of each horse's racing ability. Finally, there are the Stakes Races, which require owners to put up a stake, or fee. A special stakes race is the Futurity, for which owners put in their stakes far in advance, even as the horse is foaled, and at specified intervals thereafter.[24] Stakes Races are graded by the quality of the horses and the size of the purse and reach all the way up to the Triple Crown Races—the Kentucky Derby, Preakness, and Belmont Stakes—and the Breeders' Cup Classic.[25]

Organized quarter horse racing, begun in the 1940s and held at about a hundred tracks, has its own triple crown, consisting of the Kansas Futurity, held in June, the Rainbow Futurity, held in July, and the All-American Futurity, held on Labor Day, all at Ruidoso Downs, New Mexico.[26] Steeplechasing's triple crown comprises the Grand National, the Temple Gwathmey, and the Colonial Cup.[27] Harness racing has its Trotting Triple Crown consisting of the Hambletonian, the Yonkers Trot, and the Kentucky Futurity, and its Pacing Triple Crown, comprising the Little Brown Jug, the Cane Pace, and the Messenger Stakes.[28]

Within individual races, in order to equalize each horse's chance of winning, greater or lesser carrying weights may be assigned to different horses, depending on their winning records, age, gender, or apprentice jockey. Each five pounds of added weight is considered by some estimates to cost a length at the finish line of a one-mile race.[29]

To guide those betting on each race, detailed information on the history of each horse—its owner, trainer, breeder, jockey, color, sex, breeding, the weight it will carry, and its record of starts, firsts, seconds, thirds, earnings, and speed rating[30]—is provided in the *Daily Racing Form*, whose intense study makes dedicated, and some would say addicted, students of the sport of some gamblers.

At-the-track gambling has faced a major challenge in recent years. Simulcast gambling, authorized by the Interstate Horse Racing Act of 1978,[31] and accounting for as much as 90 percent of all betting by 2009,[32] allowed gamblers to wager on races in real time away from the track. While the tracks and purses shared in the take, it was smaller, perhaps by half,[33] of that in on-track betting. This cut down the number of people coming to the track, which was already reduced by other forms of entertainment such as television and by the attraction of football and other spectator sports. The volume of gambling on the horses was affected also by other new forms of betting, notably the new state lotteries offering millions of dollars to the winners. The main competition came from casinos, which had begun in tribal casinos and river boats but had moved closer to population centers and resulted in what was called a nation-wide explosion of gambling. By 2013 the number of thoroughbred races was down 19 percent from a decade before, the wagering "handle" down 30 percent. Racetracks with at least one thoroughbred race totaled 100, compared with 111 in 1991, and a number of racetracks were closed, selling their land for housing developments and office parks.[34]

Faced with reduced attendance and lower pari-mutuel profits, and sometimes with patrons attracted to casino horse tracks in neighboring states, tracks pressed their legislatures, and in some cases citizens voting in state-wide referendums, for casinos to be placed at their tracks and for a share of profits from slots establishments to be authorized elsewhere in the state. The percentage of slots revenue—7 percent in Maryland, for example—permitted the tracks to offer larger purses, attracting better horses and larger attendance.

Besides dwindling attendance and reduced gambling revenues, horse tracks were facing other issues. In the late twentieth century, horse racing fell victim to the same temptation of drug use as other big-money sports, as pharmaceutical advances came up with medications that, aside from their curative value, could give the athlete a competitive edge. This was the result of several factors. Competition increased and larger sums were involved. Pharmaceutical research developed many new drugs affecting both human and equine health. Divided jurisdiction resulted in different regulations in different states, as each state's racing commission, which had succeeded track organizations and jockey clubs in controlling the sport,[35] issued its own regulations. Horses racing in different states could find their regular drugs, legal in their home state, illegal where they now happened to race. Complicating all regulations was the testing authorities' difficulty of detecting new drugs as they were developed. Testing methods advanced from saliva, to urine, to blood, with increasing sophistication.

By 2013, about 95 percent of racehorses were receiving furosemide, also called Lasix or Salix, before and during the day of the race. A diuretic, first approved for race-day in the 1970s, it reduced a horse's water retention by 10, 20, or 30 pounds, and was applied to prevent exercise-induced pulmonary hemorrhaging (EIPH), that is, bleeding in the horse's lungs resulting from a high level of exercise and exertion.[36] Another drug legal in some states but not in others was Butazolidan (phenylbutazone), an analgesic that counteracted the pain a horse might feel and permitted it to race in that condition.

The uneven advance of drug use and its regulation is reflected in the case of Dancer's Image, which won the Kentucky Derby in 1968 but was disqualified three days later when Butazolidan was detected in the post-race urine sample. The colt's owner appealed the Kentucky State Racing Commission's approval of the disqualification ruling, won initially in the Franklin Circuit Court but lost when that decision was appealed to the Kentucky Court of Appeals. Failing his further appeal, after five years of court battles and $250,000 in legal fees, the owner gave up the fight. Within a year, however in March 1974, the Kentucky Racing Commission legalized Butazolidan.[37] In 2010, the Association of International Racing Commissioners voted to lower the permitted threshold of phenylbutazone from 5 to 2 micrograms per milliliter of plasma or serum.[38]

The principle of who was to be held responsible for illegal medication of a horse was established at the Saratoga, New York, racetrack in 1931, when a drug—reportedly Choral—was administered to a filly, Ladana, that had to be scratched, that is, withdrawn from the race. Though he had not been involved, the trainer was suspended, establishing the principle of a trainer's responsibility for a horse's condition regardless of the acts of third parties.[39] The Ladana precedent was followed in a 1945 case when the money-leading trainer had his license revoked for a year when his horse was administered an ephedrine nasal spray by mistake, accident, or misunderstanding.[40]

In 2008, Eight Belles, a filly, finished second in the Kentucky Derby but broke both front ankles as she crossed the finish lines, and had to be euthanized. This followed the 2006 incident in which undefeated Derby winner Barbaro broke his right hind leg in the Preakness Stakes.[41] The strong public reaction brought the Jockey Club, in charge of thoroughbred standards throughout the nation, to appoint a Thoroughbred Safety Committee which found that the 2008 Derby winner, Big Brown, had been getting Winstrol, a steroid, on the fifteenth of every month. The Committee brought in a number of recommendations: a ban on the use of anabolic steroids (now in effect in most racing states), better drug regulations, prerace inspection by an official veterinarian, establishing an equine injury data base, limiting horseshoes with raised front edges (called toe grabs), using softer, shock-absorbing, whips (two inches shorter and with the part that touches the horse's skin longer and with more padding[42]), testing the racetracks' dirt, grass, and synthetic surfaces, and improving track surfaces. Widespread discussion, including congressional hearings, raised the possibility of a central, national, drug testing organization. In 2013, eight mid–Atlantic states agreed on a set of rules. It restricted to twenty four the list of equine medications allowed to treat injury or illness of horses, established when they could be administered—up to four hours before post time—by a third-party veterinarian in some cases, and required use of accredited testing laboratories.[43]

Action was hastened by distressing reports of widespread horse racing deaths, reportedly greater among horses in claiming races than in horses in higher grade races.[44] While some attributed the deaths to drug use, which others contested, American racing deaths were reported to be at a rate greater than in countries where drug use was severely restricted.[45] The Jockey Club reported to Congress that there were 2.04 deaths per 1,000 starts at 73 U.S. and Canadian tracks between November 2008, and October 2009.[46] This compared with less than one breakdown for every 2,000 starts in overseas jurisdictions that did not allow raceday injections of performance-enhancing drugs,[47] and one per 5,692 starters in Hong Kong, with perhaps the most restrictive medication rules in the world.[48]

The breakdown rate and the apparent need for medications called attention to the condition and training of America's racehorses, particularly its thoroughbreds. While breeding from stock registered in the Jockey Club's American Stud Book makes a horse a thoroughbred, it takes many stages of development to make it a race horse. These steps were laid out in detail by T.A. Landers in his *Insider's Guide to Horseracing*.[49]

Training racehorses

As a foal, or suckling, before it is weaned from its dam at five or six months, the horse is familiarized with being led, being groomed, and having its feet handled and cleaned.[50] Placed in a stall in a training barn, the weanling is tied to the stall wall and taught to stand quietly. It is daily turned out into a separate paddock, according to its sex, where it plays, grazes, and develops mentally and physically.[51] As a yearling, following the January 1 after its birth year, it is introduced to a saddle, bridle, and rider, usually at a special farm or training center. Training begins in the stall, where the horse is trained to walk in a circle in both directions by the handler, first without a saddle and then with a saddle. Then, as the horse keeps walking in a circle, the rider lies belly down on the horse to accustom it to his weight and then mounts it in the saddle. Outside the stall, the horse with the rider is led around the aisle of the barn, jogs with other horses, leading up to a mile, and is taught to back up and stand quietly with a rider. Taken out to the paddock, the horse learns to jog in a figure-eight pattern, and then pick up the pace to a canter.[52]

Next comes the training track, in some cases with a starting gate through which the horse walks on the way to the track, and learns to run on the inside, outside, and in between horses, as it would in an actual race.[53]

As a two-year-old, the horse is shipped to racetracks for conditioning and race training, to develop its speed, stamina, and ability to break from a starting gate. To gain the approval of an official starter, allowing it to race in any racetrack in the country, the horse "must be able to stand quietly inside the starting gate; back out of the gate in the event that there is a problem at the start of a race; alertly break from the gate, first alone and then with company; and alertly break from the gate with company at the sound of a ringing bell."[54] Before entering a race, the horse's identity must be verified by the racetrack's official identifier, who is aided by the tattoo of the horse's Jockey Club registration number under its upper lip and by the Jockey Club foal certificate.[55]

Moved to a track at which it will race, the horse is stabled at the track, exercised each morning, and put through workouts around the track whose timing may be listed in the *Daily Racing Form* when it races. The horse is examined by the track veterinarian before a race to see if it is fit, though treatment with some medications, such as phenylbutazone, may tend to mask pain and cover up lameness, interfering with the evaluation.[56]

Reflecting the thoroughbred racehorses' breeding and training regime, more than two-thirds of each year's foal crop has reached the starting gate. A study of the thoroughbred foal crops of 1989 through 2001, by Dr. Larry Bramlage, president of the American College of Veterinary Surgeons, found that the probability of racing rose from 65.8 percent for the foal crop of 1989 to 72.5 percent for the foal crop of 2001.[57] Decisions as to when a horse should race are made by its trainer, though he may have to accede to requests by the owner or the track management seeking to fill the minimum requirements for a particular race.[58] How frequently the horse runs may depend on various elements. In 2010, the average starts per year for a thoroughbred racehorse in the U.S. was 6.1. This was down from 11.3 in 1960, 10.1 in 1973, and 7.9 in 1990.[59] Standardbred horses, in harness racing, might start 35 to 40 races a year, sometimes starting as often as once a week, compared to once every three to six weeks for thoroughbreds.[60]

As T. A. Landers has written, each racehorse faces "those ever-present obstacles found in every racehorse's career, including physical infirmities, poor track conditions, unfavorable post position, unfavorable distance, unfavorable pace, poor start, high weight impost, faulty equipment, and poor jockey decision."[61] While each racehorse strives to reach the finish line and go on to a life after racing, the racing industry itself strives to survive in a world in which technological advances in mass communication have nurtured competing forms of gambling and entertainment and pharmaceutical progress has given birth to tempting new drugs that racing competition makes it hard to resist.

What came after a horse's racing career? Where did "retiring" thoroughbred racehorses go? Some went to prison to help with the Jockey Club's program of vocational training in equine care for inmates at rural correctional facilities begun in 1984.[62] One example, reported in the *Washington Post* in 2013, was the James River Work Center, a prison farm in Central Virginia. There,

> On 100 acres, outlined by razor wire and patrolled by guards, eight inmates and 22 retired thoroughbred racehorses coexist in the Greener Pastures program. For now, each man's life is defined by crime and a countdown toward freedom; each horse was bred and trained to thunder around a track, before age or health or cost made them irrelevant.

Inside Barn 4 "a wall lists the names of 35 horses adopted as pleasure horses since the program began."[63]

Some retiring thoroughbred race horses went to stud farms, though this route was restricted to racehorses with outstanding running records and had been reduced to 1,700 stallions in 2013, less than half the number twenty years earlier.[64] Some entered steeplechase racing, where, though the jockeys were heavier than level-race jockeys, the horses were all thoroughbreds, many of them geldings, and mostly veterans of level track racing.[65] Some retrained as rodeo horses, though the quicker quarter horses more readily took on the cutting and lasso holding duties, both at the rodeo and at the ranch. Some went into horse shows, many, with training, excelling at dressage. Some were retrained for ranch work and trail riding.[66] Some went into police work. There their height allowed their riders to observe a greater field, their commanding bulk and stature facilitated crowd control, their stately presence brought dignity to ceremonial occasions, and their slim profile and stepping locomotion allowed riders to enter terrain unavailable to wider, wheeled, vehicles.

Budgetary constraints in recent years, however, have led to the reduction or elimination of mounted police units in many jurisdictions. Some thoroughbreds, with no further prospect of sustaining the considerable cost of maintenance, including veterinarian charges, went to early slaughter. A visit to Mexican slaughter houses identified a number of thoroughbreds among the horses being processed.[67]

Most thoroughbred racehorses, fortunately, went on to private owners, used mostly—70 percent according to a 2005 survey—for pleasure riding.[68] A small number took on a career as therapeutic horses, with a non-threatening, friendly presence providing therapy for a wide spectrum of clients ranging from special needs children to blind adults. A growing number of thoroughbred racehorses, meanwhile, were recruited for the increasingly popular sport of polo.

Eight

Polo

Polo comes with a history different from that of other popular participation equine sports. As the fastest of all contact sports, with close human-horse cooperation that used several horses in a single game and was played on the largest field of any sport, polo's requirements—multiple horses and immense playing grounds—restricted it initially to the wealthy few. It was The Sport of Kings. Arriving it the U.S. with these elite beginnings, could it survive to serve the wider population in the era of expanded popular recreation in the second half of the twentieth century? Examination of polo's long history—the longest of any sport—provides the background for this question.

Polo's origin, the subject of various conflicting legends, is traced back to the sixth century BCE in Persia, to which it may have come from central Asian tribes who originally hunted and ate horses but eventually domesticated them and used them in battle. Polo was played in Persia even before the victories of Darius the Great (521–485 BCE) who with his cavalry established the Achaemenid dynasty. Accounts of royal polo tournaments and encounters are to be found in Persian poetry and history. They tell of fourth century CE Emperor Sapour II, who learned to play polo when he was only seven years old, and of sixth century CE Emperor Khosrov II Parvig and his beautiful consort Shirin and the matches between the emperor and his courtiers against Shirin and her ladies in waiting.

Beginning in the seventh century CE, with the conquest of the Iranian Empire by the Arabs, the game spread to the west, as far as Egypt, and to the east to China with the polo-playing Iranian nobilities who sought refuge in Chinese courts after the Arab invasion. The game enjoyed a prominent place in Islamic court life, with Haroon-al-Rashid, the first Abbasid Caliph to play, and in China, where it enjoyed the enthusiastic support of Ming-Hung, the Radiant Emperor. The polo stick became a prominent motif in Chinese royal coats of arms and in Islamic heraldry.

Moslem conquerors took the game with them to India, where it was played by the Moslem rulers and by the local kings and princes. Near the bazaar in Lahore there is the statue of the thirteenth century king Sultan Qutabuddin Aibak, who died in a fall from his horse in a polo match.

When Chengiz Khan and his mounted followers came down from the north and captured Asia Minor, either they already knew the game or learned it from the Iranians. One of his descendants, Timurlane, reportedly ordered his cavalry to play polo with the heads of their captives. When his follower, Baber, in the sixteenth century founded the Mughal Empire, polo was even played at night by torchlight. When the capital was moved to Esfahan, the city was redesigned around a vast central square which was a 500-yard long, 150-yard wide royal polo ground, with stone goal posts eight yards apart at its ends.

For over twenty centuries polo was the favorite game of the royal courts, played by kings, queens, nobility, and mounted warriors. It was something of a national sport from Egypt to Japan, where it had reached from China. With the collapse of the empires and their court life, the game retreated to remote villages, where it was preserved.[1]

India

Onto this scene in mid-nineteenth century, came British tea or indigo planters to the tiny northeastern Indian state of Manipur. Inhabiting Manipur were a rare breed of ponies, descendants of wild horses and one of the five indigenous horse breeds of India. Smaller than other breeds, they excelled in speed and stamina, and could survive harsh weather conditions. Semi-wild, the ponies were allowed by their owners to roam the Manipur wetlands, their natural habitat. As Manipur was surrounded by Myanmar to the east, China to the north, and the Indian states of Nagaland and Assam, it was often involved in battles. It was with the help of the ponies that Manipur defended its territory, won battles, and conquered land. According to Manipur legend, Lord Marjing, chieftain of the Chenglei tribe, introduced the game of Sagol Kangjei, the predecessor of modern polo around the first century. When there was no war, Manipuris used the ponies to play Sagol Kangjei.

The ponies are revered in Manipur society. At the temple of Lord Marjing, outside the capital, Imphal, a statue of the main deity, Iboudhou Marjing, the god of the horses, sits on a winged pony surrounded by small marble ponies. Having been there for centuries, the temple welcomes many devotees every day, and thousands on Manipuri New Year's day, who pray that they can be blessed with prosperity, good health, and virility.

In the mid-nineteenth century, British planters and army officers watched with fascination the horsemanship of the Manipuri riders and the speed and endurance of the ponies as they played Sagol Kangjei.[2] They decided to try the game as well. Lieutenant, later General, Joseph Ford Sherer and Captain Robert Stewart of the Army's Sylhet Light Infantry witnessed play around 1859, adapted the traditional Sagol Kangjei into modern polo, and organized the Silchar polo club. In 1860, the Calcutta Polo Club was organized. A captain in the British forces in India, the 10th Hussars, witnessed a match early in 1866 and organized a team made up of fellow officers.[3] Before the end of 1866, informal matches were held between other British cavalry units stationed in India, and soon polo clubs proliferated throughout the subcontinent.

England

Troops returning from India introduced the sport in Malta in 1868, the year the Malta Polo Club was formed, and *The Field* magazine reported on the game. In England, Edward "Chicken" Hartopp of the 10th Hussars stationed in Aldeshot read the account of the game and organized play with his fellow officers. The first regular polo game in England was played on a field at Hounslow Heath. It matched the 10th Hussars against the 9th Lancers, with eight on each side and almost no rules, the Hussars winning by three goals to two. The first set of rules of the game was formulated by an Irishman, Captain John Watson, of the British Cavalry's 13th Hussars, in India in the 1870s.[4] The sport expanded rapidly in England, with games at Richmond Park and the Hurlingham Club in Fulham attended by over 10,000 spectators, and spread beyond the military to universities, the nobility, and royalty.[5]

In 1874 the first British rules were created by the Hurlingham Club, which went on to become the governing body of British polo. It limited the number of players to five and formulated the offside rule, which prevented an attacking player from hitting the ball unless there was an opponent between himself and the goal, a rule that slowed the game, was not adopted in subsequent U.S. rules, and was repealed in British and Indian rules in 1910.[6]

America

Introduction of polo into the United States is attributed to James Gordon Bennett, noted sportsman publisher of the *New York Herald*, who witnessed the game in Europe. He played polo in the southern French town of Pau, a British wintering resort where British sports included rugby, steeplechasing, and fox hunting, as well as polo. Returning to New York with great enthusiasm for polo, Bennett commissioned a friend, Hermann Oelrichs, American agent for the North German Lloyd shipping line, who was going to Europe, to bring back polo mallets, balls and shirts and, reportedly, a set of the Hurlingham Club's rules. At a gathering of friends for dinner at Bennett's home in 1876 the decision was taken to bring polo to the United States. One member of the group, Harry Blasson, was sent to Texas with instructions to purchase mustangs he judged suitable for polo. On his return with twenty ponies, he was charged with putting them in good form.

Undertaking construction of an outdoor field, the group began practicing indoors at Dickel's Riding Academy, a large wooden structure located at the northeast corner of East 39th Street and 5th Avenue in New York City.[7] With completion of the field, stables, and a clubhouse north of Jerome Park near Fordham Station, activity moved outdoors. In March 1876, the Westchester Polo Club was created by Bennett and fourteen friends. The first game took place in Jerome Park, with a saddle as the prize. Attire included buckskin or cord riding britches and blue and cardinal or blue and orange jerseys. Success soon followed and the team decided to move its headquarters to the more fashionable Newport, Rhode Island, with jersey colors changed to yellow. The result was confusion of the Westchester Polo Club, persisting in Newport, with a subsequent polo club in Westchester County, New York, which had to be named the Country Club in Westchester.

Part of the polo group remaining in New York formed the Manhattan Polo Association, with August Belmont as president, on a field between 110th and 112th streets from 5th to 6th avenues. There the first game was played in the spring of 1880, with the formal opening to the public September 25, 1880, for the fall season. Westchester club members formed both sides in the game, some in blue and some in red. Intervals between goals were termed bouts, the first lasting 20 minutes, others between 1 1/2 to 13 minutes. Two hundred spectators were in attendance and the brass band played between bouts. The blues won 4 to 2.

As the Manhattan Polo Association closed, the Brighton Polo Association opened in Long Branch, New Jersey. In mid–1879, some 10,000 spectators watched a game between players from the Westchester Club and the Queens County Hunt Club at the Prospect Park Parade Grounds, in Brooklyn. The first formal match between clubs saw the Westchester Polo Club face off against the Buffalo Country Club in Newport in 1879, with Westchester winning. The return match was held in Buffalo the following year using Buffalo rules. It was sixty minutes before the first goal was scored, by Buffalo, which won the game with fresh ponies, as the Westchester ponies were exhausted. Also notable were the cigar-shaped mallet heads, invented in Buffalo, contrasting with Westchester's square-shaped English mallet head.

In Texas, retired British army officers played polo in Grayson County, near Dallas, with reports of an early polo club in Denison. In San Antonio the Texas Polo Club introduced polo in a July 1883, match with twenty minute periods and ten minute intervals. This was followed by a match a few days later between Texas cowboys and Englishmen. The Texas club issued a challenge to Bennett's New York club, but en route the Texas team was accommodated at the local racetrack in New Orleans, became involved in racetrack action, and had to sell their ponies to cover their losses and go home.

Further west, in California, several polo playing episodes ensued, some abortive attempts to found a polo club, others for paucity of Englishmen, and others surviving with British rules, using 30-inch planks at the sidelines, following the British offside rule, and at times with only three players on each side.

Back in Newport, play followed British rules. Games had no time limit, ending with the winning of two goals out of three, or three out of five. After each goal the ball was placed at the center of the field and a player chosen by each captain charged for it. With no period time limits, mounts could be changed only after a goal was scored or after a knock-in of balls that went over the side or end lines. The burden on ponies was quite severe. Soon, departing from the British rules, the hooking of mallets was abolished, the off-side rule was dropped, and the backstroke was eliminated. This made for a faster game, and outstanding individual play rather than team play.[8]

International Play

The first U.S. participation in international polo competition came in 1886. In that year, as the result of discussions during a visit to the Hurlingham club by Westchester player Nathaniel Griswold Lorillard, tobacco fortune heir, a game between Hurlingham and Westchester teams was arranged. Coming to Newport across the Atlantic with their fifteen ponies, all four of the Hurlingham team were military, a marked contrast to the American team. At the start of the first of the two matches, the captain of the Hurlingham team, John Henry Watson, who is credited with inventing the backhand stroke, held up the start. He insisted that the referee, who, along with the two umpires, was mounted, as was the American custom, should instead stand on a platform at the edge of the ground, or the British team would refuse to play. The referee, S. Howland Robbins, Jr., was put on a small stand for the first match, but refused to referee the second match. The issue of reconciling rules differences was to persist for coming close to a century and a half.

In the game itself, though the Americans quickly scored the first goal, it became evident that sparkling individual play by Americans could not match the coordinated team play of the British. John Watson's powerful backhand strokes made it clear too that the Americans' banning the backhand stroke was folly and would have to go. In the end, Hurlingham won the first game ten goals to four and the second fourteen to two. To mark the contest, The Westchester Cup, manufactured by Tiffany with 396.3 ounces of silver, was created, changing hands between the victorious teams for well over a century.[9]

The Americans took to heart the lessons of the 1886 match, practicing the backhand and greater team coordination. They failed to win the second meeting in 1902 at England's Hurlingham club, which thus retained the Westchester trophy. The Americans' at the time legal defensive tactic of holding off attack by hitting the ball behind their own back line so they could resume play by their own "hit-out," brought a quick change in the Hurlingham rules. Thereafter, a defending team hitting the ball behind their own back line constituted a safety, initially costing a quarter point off their score, but after a later rule change giving the attacking team a free hit from 60 yards out against the undefended goal.[10]

The 1909 cup challenge, played in England, was a different story. The U.S. team carried the name of the Meadow Brook Club, of Long Island. The task of putting together the team and the string of ponies was undertaken by the team captain, Harry Payne Whitney. He believed that it would be preferable to play with long passes, hard riding and ready switching of positions rather than by moving the ball forward in short passes, in a positional strategy. For this he needed faster ponies.[11] He recruited the best players in America and commissioned purchasing agents in California, England, Ireland, Texas and elsewhere to look for the best ponies.

The pony string assembled was spectacular. From California came Cottontail, a bay gelding considered by some the best pony in the history of the game. From England were purchased Cobnut, a chestnut mare, and Greyling, a chestnut gelding. Purchased by Whitney in Ireland were Balada, a bay mare, and Cinders, a grey mare. From Ireland, La Souris, a grey mare, and Little Mary, a bay mare, were purchased by others and loaned to the team, as was Cinderella, a black mare. Whitney also bought other Irish-bred mares: Solitaire, a brown mare awarded the prize for best polo pony in Dublin, and Ballin a Hone, a blazed-face chestnut mare. Ralla, the biggest and most powerful of the 1909 string, was a chestnut mare. An Argentine pony, Mallard, a bay gelding not considered fast enough for American polo, was hailed as a marvel at Hurlingham. A Whitney–owned Texas pony was Conover. Finally, after Whitney wired for extra ponies, Mohawk Chief, an American black gelding, arrived on loan in time for the second match.

The American team, with a combination of speed, long hitting, and ready interchange of places, won both matches, 9–5 and 8–2. The trophy was presented to Whitney by Lord Frederick Roberts, who had made polo helmets compulsory when serving as commander-in-chief in India. Recognizing the contribution of the celebrity ponies they had used—saddling 18 out of the string of 28—the American team presented to Lawrence J. Fitzpatrick, who was in charge of the ponies and kept them in perfect trim also later for the 1911 and 1913 cup matches, a silver cup inscribed: In appreciation of his care and conditioning of the ponies for the international match.[12]

Three English-American contests followed, in 1911, 1913, and 1914, all played at the Meadow Brook club. The Americans won the first two, the first with the 1909 crew and the core of the 1909 pony string, the British the third, returning the Westchester Cup to England.[13]

U.S. Polo Developments

Back home in the U.S., a great deal had been happening on the polo scene. In June 1890 seven polo clubs decided they needed some means of coordinating their activities and promoting the sport and formed the Polo Association. A major step in this direction had already been taken two years before by Henry Lloyd Herbert, who established the concept of individual handicaps and had handicapped 42 players. The Polo Association, for which Mr. Herbert was to be chairman for thirty years, from 1890 to 1921, took on the task of operating the handicap system and assigning handicaps to all players.[14]

The objective of the handicap system was to evenly match teams in a game on the basis of the sum of the individuals' handicaps. Games would be set up for low, medium and high handicap totals, and teams could enter if their totals fell within the numerical range. Within each range, should one team's total be greater than its opponent's, the opponent would start out with an additional goal already on the scoreboard. Games in which goals were not bestowed on the team with the lower handicap total, with zero on the scoreboard for both teams, were termed flat out. Though Herbert had built his handicap assignment with a maximum of five, the Association's handicaps ran from minus two to ten, with ten the best.

The terminology that came to be assigned to the handicaps unfortunately became a source of confusion to persons unfamiliar with the system. The handicap numbers were called goals, leading some to misunderstand that a game in which the total on each side was twenty, for example, meant that twenty goals were expected to be scored, and that a player called a three-goal player was expected to score three goals. Aside from the tendency for misunderstanding, however, it was quite helpful to indicate that a twenty goal game would present a higher level of play than a ten goal game, regardless of the number of goals that might eventually be scored in each.

To carry out the responsibility of assigning appropriate handicaps to each registered player, the Association, later renamed the United States Polo Association (USPA), received recommendations from each member club's delegate to the Association, as well as from regional and central authorities, and issued revised handicaps twice a year. Handicaps of foreign players were assigned by their national polo authorities.

Besides assigning handicaps and arranging for annual tournaments, the Association's principal responsibility was to establish rules, which were revised and issued regularly as needed. Thus, under the rules, the dimensions of an outdoor polo field were set at 300 yards in length and 160 yards in width if low sideboards were used, but up to 200 yards in width if no sideboards but only delimiting white lines were used. Eight-yard wide goals with ten-foot high goalposts were centered at each end, with the ball passing between the posts, at any height, whether hit by mallet or kicked by a horse of either team counting as a goal.

Players on horseback held reins in their left hand and in their right hand a flexible mallet 49 to 53 inches long with a cigar-shaped hardwood head at its end. They tried to hit the four-ounce white plastic ball, three and a quarter inch in diameter, originally of willow root, with the flat side of the mallet head into the goal.

Play extended for six seven-and-a-half minute periods, called chukkers, with three-minute intervals between chukkers and a five-minute interval at the half. If the score was tied at the end, a sudden-death chukker was added. A player's uniform consisted of white breeches, brown boots, knee guards, a protective helmet with a chinstrap, and a team jersey. Play began with the four mounted players on each team lined up facing each other at midfield and the referee bowling the ball between the two lines. This was repeated when a goal was scored and the team changed ends.[15]

Unlike other sports, polo players wore on their jersey a number indicating their position on the field. Number One's position was closest to the other team's goal. Number Two was not far behind him, both of them considered forwards. Number Four, the Back, played in front of his own team's goal, while Number Three, who was often the captain, ranged ahead of Number Four, initiates attacks by driving the ball forward.[16]

Techniques of Play

A player began by positioning the strap around his wrist, the mallet resting against the palm, held firmly by the index, middle, and ring fingers. The mallet was held in a vertical position, both at rest and at the beginning of a stroke. To hit, the player's body was in a standing position, rising from the stirrups with the seat clear of the saddle. The basic strokes were the off-side forehand (the off-side being the right side), the off-side back hand, the near-side forehand, the near-side back hand, the off-side neck stroke, the near-side neck stroke, tail strokes, push strokes, and between the legs strokes.[17]

The first aim of the rules on play was clearly safety. With horses charging across the field at perhaps 35 miles an hour, guiding or restricting their movement was clearly essential. The basic principle established for this purpose was the line of the ball and the right of way. A player hitting the ball and following its trajectory on his right had the right of way, which no other player could cross, except so far ahead as not to be involved. Following it on his right or offside, in contrast to his left or nearside, was important because players were required to hit the ball with their right hand, holding their reins in their left. Except for left-handed players who could be registered up to 1974 but not thereafter, all had to hold the mallet in their right hand. Making polo a contact sport, players could interfere with a player and his horse playing along his right of way by jostling or bumping him in what was called a ride-off. To do this a player had to ride alongside or approach at a low angle at a comparable speed and nudge the horse and rider at the shoulder.

A player could use his mallet to hook or obstruct another player's mallet swing but only at the lower part of the swing and not reaching over or under the horse. Interfering with the right of way, hooking a mallet illegally, or riding in a manner endangering safety constituted a foul. This resulted in a penalty: a free hit for the other team from 30 or 60 yards out or at half field, defended or not defended depending on the severity of the foul. A free hit from 60 yards out was the penalty for a safety, that is, the defending team hitting the ball over its own back line. Before the rule changes in 1910 a foul subtracted a half point from the team's score, a safety a quarter point.

This explains the fractional scores listed for some early games before the rule change.[18] Calling the foul would be one of the two umpires riding on opposite sides along the long length of the field. Were they to disagree it was the task of the third man, the referee, to make the decision.

Arena Polo

To overcome space or weather limitations, polo was played in a smaller venue, as arena polo, sometime called indoor polo. In contrast to the grass polo's 300 by 160 yards dimensions, an arena field would vary from 300 by 150 feet to as little as 75 by 50 feet, with a 10 by 15 foot goalpost area recessed in the arena wall. Played indoors or outdoors on dirt or sand in a four-foot high enclosure, it used regular polo mallets but an inflated white, leather ball somewhat smaller than a soccer ball. In arena polo, there were three players on each side, rather than four, and four seven-minute chukkers rather than six or eight. Sides were changed after each chukker rather than after each goal.

Arena polo was the reigning model in collegiate and scholastic play, in cities, and quite popularly in clubs.[19] Arena polo clubs were organized in 1915 in New York City as the Indoor Polo Association. It merged in 1955 with the U.S. Polo Association, which issued separate handicaps for regular and arena play.[20] Arena advocates pointed out that players had less of the long distances to cover, passes did not have to go several hundred yards, and there was close interaction between the teams. For spectators, the action was close at hand, and the players' faces were clearly seen. Indoor college games were enjoyed by several thousand spectators.[21]

The Ponies

Changing with time was the permitted size of the players' ponies. Originally, the Hurlingham Club rules of 1875 permitted ponies of only 14 hands (56 inches) or smaller from the withers to the ground.[22] Following one upward adjustment, all limitation on the height of the mounts was completely gone. Though still referred to as ponies, above the pony definition of 14 hands two inches, the horses bearing polo players generally came to over 15 hands. With the inclusion of thoroughbreds, retired racehorses in many cases, horses of over 16 hands were seen in the games.

Play required horses with special qualities: ability to reach bursts of speed of up to 35 or 40 miles an hour, "stop on a dime," turn 180 degrees and speedily accelerate back to the gallop. Polo horses, it has been observed, must be like triathletes, running fast like racehorses, stopping, pivoting, and starting again like cutting horses, and yet keeping calm like trail horses.[23] Stamina was of great importance.[24] Though some substitution could occur at goal or foul interruption, the seven or seven-and-a-half minutes of each period, or chukker, involved intense, non-stop activity for a period longer than that on the racetrack or the usual five-minute duration of a steeplechase contest.

The search for the best ponies therefore ranged far and wide, and top players often undertook to breed their own ponies. Efforts by Harry Payne Whitney assembling the American team's pony celebrities for the 1909 contest with England is described above. Such efforts continued. Preparing for its participation in the Cup of Americas contest in Argentina in 1932, the American team shipped twenty mounts. These included, as to breeding, thirteen from Argentina, three from the United States, two from Chile, one Australian, and one English.[25] Breeding of the horses over the years involved Thoroughbreds, Quarter horses, Morgans, Arabians, the Argentine Criollos, as well as Apaloosas, Palaminos, Pintos, and crossbreeds.[26]

Efforts to breed the progeny of champions ran into difficulties not prevalent in other equine sports. Most polo ponies were mares. Their best performing years were between the ages of five and twenty, which were also their best breeding years. Taking time out for an eleven-month gestation period was therefore a problem. One solution followed since 1986 in Argentina has been embryo transfer. Fertilized eggs are taken from the top mares and implanted in recipient, surrogate mares. Top mares may thus have multiple offsprings in a year without being taken out of the playing string. The procedure was not recognized by Thoroughbred racing associations concerned over protecting the integrity of the breed.

One such breeding farm, La Picaza, outside Buenos Aires, Argentine, buys embryos from top breeders and players, leases recipient mares that are implanted with the embryos and keeps them on the farm until the foals are born and weaned at about six months old. The foals are raised carefully on the farm and go on to polo careers. One played two years in the Argentine Open, where, by one estimate 50 percent of the ponies are from embryo transfers. Some instances have been cited of daughters, mothers, and grandmothers playing in the same polo match.[27]

An American facility following the same Argentine embryo transfer procedure, the New Bridge Embryo Center, was opened in Aiken, South Carolina. It had a managing partner experienced in breeding horses the traditional way and the help of two Argentine veterinarians who were associated with La Irenita Embriones, a world-renowned breeding operation.

The New Bridge Embryo Center was planning to hold embryo sales, modeled on an Argentine event, at the time of U.S. Polo Association Gold Cup Championships held in Aiken.[28]

Still "far out" but already under way in Argentina since 2010 was the cloning of successful polo ponies. Following the technique used to clone Dolly the Sheep in 1961, Adolfo Cambiaso, recognized as the world's best polo player, worked with Crestview Genetics, a Texas firm, to have eight of his ponies cloned. Use of clones in competition has reportedly been approved by various polo governing bodies, and, though it had not yet been tested in a match, a three-month-old clone of Mr. Cambiaso's Cuartelera sold for $800,000 at auction in Buenos Aires.[29]

Pressure to ensure an adequate supply of ponies reflected the number of ponies needed for a player in each game. In less advanced play, ponies, by regulation, could serve at most in two chukkers and required at least one chukker's rest. Players would ride at least three ponies in the course of a six-chukker match and in high-goal polo some might arrive with ten horses apiece.[30] Rapid turnover in the use of horses had gone even further in high-goal English polo. Guards Polo Club manager Antony Fanshawe complained that whereas they used to play one horse for an entire chukker when he played, they had come to use a horse for only two minutes, playing three horses a chukker. Forcing top players to pass, and to use only one horse per chukker, he believed would speed up the game and return greater importance to the individual pony.[31]

Widening Polo Participation

Aside from the polo strings of top players, access to the sport for less wealthy hopefuls seeking to play was limited by the requirement of several ponies for each individual, especially in the early years. Progress in overcoming this limitation came from some polo clubs that offered to lend or lease ponies to players for their games. The Piping Rock Club in Locust Valley, Long Island, founded in 1909 and joining the Polo Association in 1912, pioneered the practice of purchasing ponies and renting them to players with no polo string or a depleted string. This proved successful with newcomers and players with low handicaps.[32]

One important channel providing access to polo play was the universities. Polo was played at Harvard in 1885, Princeton and Yale in 1903, the Pennsylvania Military Academy in 1915, Cornell in 1919 and at the Virginia Military Academy in 1921.[33] In the West, the University of Oklahoma started polo in 1919, Oregon State University in 1920, when it played Stanford and

Utah universities, and the University of Arizona at Tucson in 1922. Others playing in the early 1920s were the New Mexico Military Institute, and Texas A & M. By 1930 they were joined by the University of Missouri and by 1938 by the University of Southern California.[34] Players enjoying polo at the university were likely to join or found polo clubs in the years following graduation.

To regularize intercollegiate polo in the East, the Intercollegiate Polo Association was formed in 1925, including also the U.S. Military Academy and Norwich University.[35] The early experience with intercollegiate polo was to lay the basis for collegiate and scholastic participation in the sport's country-wide expansion of the late twentieth century. Easier entry to the sport was facilitated by college or school polo teams that provided the ponies. The Michigan State Polo Club explained that in the intercollegiate contests each team brought a string of six or seven ponies to the game and both teams rode each other's horses to make the playing equal.[36]

A second channel that served to embrace and promote polo in the U.S. since its earliest days was the Army. The first regular regimental polo club was formed in 1892 by officers of U.S. 4th Cavalry stationed in Walla Walla, Washington, with little in the way of opponents, however. Army polo got its full start in 1896 in Fort Riley, Kansas, which was to gain prominence as a center for polo over much of the next century. By 1897, civilian polo teams from Kansas City and St. Louis had already arrived and played there.

Polo started at West Point in 1900, the Army Polo Association joining the Polo Association in 1902, and West Point, as noted, helping to form the Intercollegiate Polo Association in 1925. An Army Championship, a weeklong event, was held in Washington in 1912, with the 11th Cavalry, from Fort Myer, the 5th Field Artillery, of Washington, the 6th Field Artillery and West Point participating. The team winning the Army Championship then entered the competition for the Overture Cup in Rhode Island, at Narragansett Pier, where the best civilian players were to be found, and reached the finals.[37] High level polo continued in the Army, interrupted of course by U.S. entry into World War I in April 1917.

At the close of the war, when international polo resumed with competition at the 1920 Olympics in Ostende, Belgium, the Army was called upon to enter a team from its personnel serving post–World-War-One occupation duty in the Rhineland. Travelling to England for preliminary action, the team succeeded in taking the Novices' Cup at the Ranelagh Club. At the Olympics, the team won the bronze medal, an achievement that added considerable weight to the Army Polo Committee's efforts to make polo an integral part of officers' training.[38]

The decade that followed has been called the golden age of military polo in the U.S.[39] An Army team entered the U.S. Open Championship in 1921, 1927, and 1928, and the Junior Championship in 1922, and six more times before 1932. Military teams won the U.S.P.A. National Twelve Goal Championship and the Twelve Goal Inter-Circuit Championship fourteen times between 1925 and 1938, and West Point cadets won the 1931 and 1937 Eastern Intercollegiate Championship. Army teams experienced also international play: against a British Army team in 1923 and 1925, in Mexico in 1924 and 1926, and in Argentina in 1930.

Throughout the period, polo gained appreciation as an important contribution to military readiness. Major George S. Patton, a veteran of World War I and captain of the Army polo team that won the 1922 Junior Championship, put it quite frankly in a 1923 *Cavalry Journal* article. He wrote that polo presented the closest thing to armed combat in presenting exciting circumstances in which the participant must practice restraint yet make immediate decisions.[40] General Lucian K. Truscott, chosen by General Eisenhower to head Special Forces training in part because of his outstanding abilities in polo, wrote that the hard-riding intensity of polo was similar to combat and that it resulted in improving officers' quality of command.[41] Across the country Army teams were playing in Montana, Kansas, Nebraska, Arizona, and Washington, as were two cavalry regiments in the Philippines.[42] Polo continued to attract athletic, aggressive-type officers, benefitting in physical and mental toughness through the 1930s until organized play was discontinued with the coming of World War II.[43]

The Army was also playing a wider role. Horses were provided to Reserve Officers' Training Corps (ROTC) units, which served to sustain polo activities in a number of colleges. Some club and college polo teams that found their playing fields disappearing as a result of development were accommodated at Army facilities. Government provision of ROTC horses, in fact, had made possible the establishment of polo at Princeton at the beginning of the twentieth century. It was a key in the 1920s to the inauguration of polo at the University of Arizona and the University of Oklahoma, which joined with others—Stanford, the University of Missouri, the University of Utah, the University of Southern California and the New Mexico Military Institute—in competing for the Southwestern Intercollegiate Championship organized in 1923.[44] Army players flourished during the interwar years, comprising 1,276 of the total of 2,889 U.S. Polo Association playing members.[45]

Polo matches attracted a great deal of attention in the interwar years, with 20,000 spectators at the U.S. Open Championship, 35,000 at the U.S.-England Westchester Cup match at Long Island's Meadow Brook Club, the dominant club of the era, and 10,000 at the Princeton-Yale contest for the intercollegiate title.[46] The spotlight was to be shared with international caliber teams from Argentina, which had advanced to match and rival U.S. and English polo levels. The Argentines shone in the 1926 Open Championship and in the Argentine–U.S. Cup of the Americas series begun in 1928.

Competition was coming also from the American West, sending teams that succeeded in some of the national tournaments in the East. With international competition damped down by the international Depression, a domestic two-out-of-three East-West domestic series was arranged in 1933, pitting the best teams that could be assembled in each section of the country. Set in the middle of the country at the Onwentsia Polo Club, north of Chicago, the contest went to three games, with 15,000 at the first game, and 25,000 at the third, which was won by the West. Unfortunately, the games were marked by exceedingly rough play, with an historic high of fouls and injuries, resulting in a subsequent rule change that when two players were together the third one had to give the right of way.[47]

Across the country, clubs struggled to survive the Depression. The Carranor Hunt and Polo Club, affiliated with the USPA since 1922, went dormant in 1932, was revived briefly in 1940, but did not survive the war. The Cincinnati Polo Club, organized in 1924, closed in 1929.[48] By the time the war brought to a close the Depression era, the number of civilian USPA players had declined from 1,600 to 750. Registered military USPA players peaked at 1,432 in 1940, as cavalry gave way to mechanization. USPA tournament play was suspended between 1942 and 1945.

Rebuilding at the war's end, some clubs found their fields being taken over by suburban growth, The Meadow Brook Club flourished until 1953, when urbanization cut a swath through its polo grounds, leading some commentators to fear that Robert Moses' development plans might destroy polo on Long Island.[49] New clubs opened and efforts were made to encourage newcomers to the game. Thus, in Kansas and Oklahoma the Northwestern Circuit Invitational Four-Goal Handicap Tournament was created. Players could not use more than three ponies and could not have a handicap of more than one.[50]

Riding the wave of the late twentieth century leisure time expansion, which increased other horse-borne recreational activities, the popularization of polo playing took off. The number of USPA-affiliated clubs grew from 55 in 1950, to 88 in 1960, 112 in 1970, 147 in 1975, 212 in 1990 and 223 in 2009. The number of registered players rose from 1,230 in 1975 to 3,037 in 2000.[51] Tournament and international competition revived, and across the world polo was played in about 80 countries.

Polo Pony Training

In the U.S. and Argentina new training procedures had evolved. Argentine breeder Carlos Reyes Terrabusi explained that the first step was hugging the horse during its first twelve hours of life, imprinting a friendly impression so that it lost its fear of humans.[52] The training routine at an Argentine facility, the Don Pepe Polo Farm, after the hugging, began with the polo horse running free for three years, developing its bones and muscles. At about three, the horses were introduced to the saddle and halter, working with the gaucho for six to eight months, learning to relate to people. Using a pole to which the horse's halter was attached, the palenquear, the gaucho accustomed the horse to human touch by touching the horse on the neck, flanks, rump, and legs until it did not flinch. When the gaucho's work was completed, the horse was ridden for a week or two to relax and condition it, and put out to grass for two to three months.

It was then returned and training began, focusing on changing legs and stopping. For four to five months it was ridden once or twice a day, and then put out to grass again for two months. The horse was then introduced to the stick (mallet) and ball, riding in the morning and working with the stick and ball in the afternoon, when it was a little tired. This was followed by another two months out to grass, after which the horse was introduced to polo. Together with other horses that were new and not accustomed to the game, the horse would play in slow chukkers, learning the game, for a year. The horse was then ready to play.[53]

Horses were trained to respond to the leg and weight cues of their riders for movement forward, sideways or stopping, and to reins held in one hand. Mallet and ball became familiar to them, often by their presence in their stall. The horses were trained to maneuver in ever-decreasing circles, so that they were comfortable with turns and figure eights, and would learn to switch leads and maintain balance. They learned to stop with their back feet drawn up under them so they could immediately go left, right, or straight ahead. Entering polo play at about five, the horses continued to twelve and well beyond, even into their twenties in some cases. Chosen for their sudden bursts of speed, agility, and maneuverability, they had to have the stamina to continue for the seven minutes of a chukker. An important, indispensable, quality was temperament, the ability to stay calm and in control at 35-mile-an-hour speed, with other horses nudging or bumping them, mallets swinging past their heada, and the white polo ball speeding past at up to a hundred miles an hour.[54] When they were ready to play, ponies had their manes "hogged" or clipped and their tails plaited up before a match so as to avoid entangling the mallet.

The early polo ponies were thirteen hand and two inches in height, under the early Polo Association rules fourteen hands and two inches, but following a 1919 regulation subject to no height limitations. They would range to over 16 hands but preferences centered around 15 hands or 15 hands and 2 inches as more convenient for handy mallet size and player mallet reach to the ground. The predominant breed in U.S. polo ponies was Thoroughbred, with Arabian, and Quarter horse and Western Range horse blood. Increasingly, since 1930, Argentine Criollo horses' contributions were particularly prized.[55]

Typically, the horses' teeth were checked twice a year, they were wormed ever six weeks, and vaccinated for tetanus. In season they were shod every six weeks and their hind shoes had studs put in to prevent slipping. Depending on climate, they may have had their shoes removed and been turned out to herd in the fall for a vacation that might last for nine months in some areas before being brought back in early spring.[56]

Not unusually, horses would come to polo after having completed their other careers, most notably thoroughbred racing horses, sometimes referred to as off-the-track-thoroughbreds (OTTBs) or horses from a ranch. Owners might see a way to get out of locked up equity by having their horses retrained for polo. Coming onto the polo scene at perhaps four years of age, racehorses underwent a year or two of training by outfits specializing in this function, frequently operated by former polo players. The horses then began their polo career at five or six, with a speed that might let them succeed.[57]

Recognized as being responsible for 70 to 80 percent of a polo team's success, polo ponies attracted outsize sales prices, and on occasion recognition on the field. The polo string assembled for the U.S. team's participation in the 1909 Westchester Cup contest, it will be recalled, achieved great celebrity. Cottontail, in fact, was put forth as the greatest pony in the sport. More recently, beginning in 1965, an award, the Willis Hartman Award, was bestowed upon the best playing pony in each year's U.S. Open Tournament. The solid silver image of a pony was manufactured by Garrard & Company of London, the royal jewelers. It went to Lovely Sage in 1965, to other ponies in subsequent years, and to reside in the Polo Museum, in Florida.[58] In other matches, without the award, ponies were honored with the designation "best playing pony."

Health

On Sunday, April 19, 2009, as spectators awaited the start of the first match of the semifinal rounds of the U.S. Open Championship in Wellington, Florida, fifteen ponies preparing to compete in the first match staggered out of their trailers and collapsed onto the grass. Veterinarians rushed over to help, but within an hour all fifteen were dead. Overnight another six ponies that had been kept in the same Lechuga Caracas team's trailers were dead as well. The death of twenty-one horses in one day was a shock to the wide polo and equine sports community, and speculation as to its cause was rife. The match was cancelled, an exhibition game played in its place. The Lechuga team, though offered ponies by other teams, chose not to compete, and the semifinals were played later in the week.

On Thursday of that week, Francki Pharmacy, an Ocala, Florida, compounding pharmacy serving human and veterinary patients with no history of complaints, announced that the strength of one ingredient it had included in the medication ordered by the veterinarian was incorrect. The necropsy performed on six of the dead horses concluded that they had died of selenium toxicosis. Just prior to the onset of their illness the horses had received an intravenous injection of a "vitamin/mineral" supplement containing toxic levels of selenium.[59] It emerged that before polo matches the Lechuga Caracas team horses were routinely given doses of a Biodyl-type supplement, a mixture of vitamin B-12, selenium, and other minerals. Produced by the Merial pharmaceutical company, Biodyl, though not approved by the U.S. Food and Drug Administration, was widely used in Europe and Latin America to treat horses' and other animals' muscle fatigue and exhaustion.[60]

The Lechuga Caracas team, owned by affluent Venezuelan businessman Victor Vargas, was made up of mostly Argentine horses and players, and traveled the greater part of the year.[61]

A year after the April 2009, tragedy, three horses from each of the four semifinal teams at the 2010 U.S. Open, and two from the two finalist teams at the USPA President' Cup were tested for drugs. On the recommendation of the USPA Polo Pony Welfare Committee, the USPA Board of Governors had unanimously voted to apply random blood and/or urine testing. Agreement to the testing had become a requirement of membership spelled out in USPA rules. Samples were taken after the match, before a horse left the game area.[62] The rules of the USPA listed permitted drugs, restricted use drugs, therapeutic drug use, emergency treatment exceptions, prohibited drugs and substances, the veterinarian's responsibilities, others' responsibilities, and testing procedures and protocol, including transfer of samples to the U.S. Equestrian Federation (USEF) testing laboratory.[63]

Over the years, reflecting polo's status as the fastest-moving and most exhausting equine sport, medical interest in the effect of polo on the health of the ponies was the focus of a number of studies. A 1999 study continuously monitored the heart rate of six low-goal polo ponies before, during, and after a typical chukker of competition. Measured against the ponies' maximum heart rate previously determined in field and treadmill exercises, the study found that the heart rates during the chukker were above 90 percent of the maximum heart rate 17 percent of the time, between 75 and 90 percent of the maximum heart rate 39 percent of the time, and below 75 percent of the maximum 44 percent of the time. As a result of the uneven calls on ponies' efforts during play, with occasional bursts of speed and abrupt stopping, the study concluded that low-goal polo placed moderate to high stress on ponies' cardiovascular system.[64]

A 2011 study clinically examined twelve "high-goal" polo horses that played one chukker a day for four days, with data collected each day at rest before the chukker, immediately after the chukker, and 30 minutes after the chukker. It found that the exercise caused changes typical of a mixed aerobic/anaerobic metabolic pathway prevailing in the sport and that they returned to the reference range by 30 minutes after the exercise.[65]

Attention focused also on the nature and frequency of injuries to polo horses. A British study published in 2015 surveyed eighty-four polo players owning a total of 815 ponies. Overall, 10.6 percent of the ponies were reported to have sustained injuries requiring veterinary treatment during the previous season, a rate not dissimilar with the rate for the British general horse population. The highest single risk reported by most owners was of tendon injuries, a lower risk requiring veterinary attention being cuts and stud wounds, and, lower still, splints. Hard ground was characterized as the most important risk factor for polo injury, followed by sticks and balls, poor pony fitness, speed and nature of the game, and poor bandaging. Mitigating against injury were owners bandaging ponies' legs during or after training, besides bandaging during games. To cool tendons, owners checked and hosed legs after exercise and used clay coolants.[66]

These findings on the prevalence of tendon injuries were in line with those of a 1943 study of polo ponies. It found that the most common polo pony injuries were tendon damage on the lower part of the leg, which was most susceptible to swinging mallets, particularly in the use of neck shots instead of back shots, and to tangling feet and collision with the sideboards. Furthermore, it was pointed out that though the horses might be trained to turn by shifting their weight to the rear and pivoting on their hind feet, circumstances might occur in which both the weight and pivoting might be on the forefeet, resulting in torn ligaments, sprains and strains.[67]

Critical to the protection of ponies' legs from both kinds of injuries, therefore, were properly applied leg bandages, which support the tendons and protect the leg from external harm. One expert's bandaging instructions called for starting at the knee, spiraling the bandage down till reaching the fetlock, where it was wrapped a second time, then spiraling back up to the starting point at the knee and fastening the two ends with the Velcro. The wrap, it was stressed, should not hamper free movement of the knee joint above or the fetlock below and should not be so tight as to restrict blood flow or movement of the tendons, yet still provide adequate support.[68] Poor bandaging, it may be recalled, was one risk factor for pony injuries mentioned by respondents in the 2015 British study of polo pony injuries cited above.

To analyze the nature, frequency, and severity of injuries to polo players, Argentine researchers enlisted the cooperation of thirty-four high-goal players, average handicap 8.5 and average age 27, to register all injuries resulting in missed games or practice sessions during the 1996 season, and to recall also their previous injuries. Injuries were classified as minor if causing absences for less than seven days, moderate if seven to thirty days, and major if more than thirty days. The 34 riders sustained nine injuries during the ten-week study, and reported they had incurred 55 injuries previously. Of the total of 64 injuries reported, 10 were minor, 13 were moderate, and 41 were major. As regards parts of the body injured, 39 percent occurred in the arms, 30 percent in the legs, 19 percent in the head, 5 percent in the back, and 4 percent in the face. Some 39 percent of injuries involved fracture, most resulting from a fall from the horse.

While the calculated injury rate was 7.8 per 1,000 game-hours played, not as great as in some other sports, the severity of polo injuries was greater, including fractures and facial lacerations. The study concluded that doctors experienced in serious trauma management should be present at all games, and that helmets with face protectors should be worn.[69]

A U.S. study, covering the 1987–2000 period, indicated that low or medium goal polo players could expect an injury requiring a physician's attention for every 100 hours of play. One third of players injured had two or more injuries during the same six-month season, and 11 percent of the injuries were concussions.[70]

A 2010 survey of 84 British polo players' injuries dealt with an older, more recreational group, mean age 41.7 years, mean handicap 0, restricted to horse owners so as to combine it with the pony injury study mentioned above. Players were asked about falls and injuries requiring hospital visits during the previous season. Fifty-eight percent of the players reported falls during the previous season, 17.3 percent reported injuries requiring hospital visits, and 56.8 percent reported they were bruised regularly.

Relating the risks of falls to a number of personal factors, and controlling for height, weight, and riding experience, it was found that female riders were half as likely to fall as males, possibly because they may have been better riders, had better balance, or were more risk-averse. Players seeking to improve their handicaps were eight times more likely to fall as others. Examining other risk factors, it appeared that riders with more days of pre-season pony exercise were more likely to avoid falling.

By this time helmets were compulsory in British polo, but almost half of the players, in choosing a helmet, considered appearance more important than safety. As to the presence of a doctor at a game, most gave it a low priority, though a number voiced support for having paramedics and an ambulance in attendance.[71]

The Scene in 2016

With its long history of play by the wealthy through its first century in America, sustained by players in the Army and universities and spectator events, how would the sport fare in the more recent era of expanded leisure and wider horse-borne recreation?

Curiously, it went in two directions. At the top, in high-skill play, it went to a format of wealthy patrons engaging paid professionals, mainly from Argentina, to fill out their team. Why Argentina? Polo was introduced in Argentina by British settlers and grew rapidly in the welcoming environment of the cattle-raising pampas and horse breeding. It grew as a popular, rather than elitist, sport, with thousands of active players, crowds of over 30,000 at major matches, and live TV feeding the national obsession. As a result, the standard of polo play in Argentina came to be considered the highest in the world, with nine of the ten top players in world ranking being Argentine. Players who play as amateurs in the main Argentine spring polo season, from late September to early December, go abroad to play as professionals for patrons in the highest level polo in Europe and the U.S., earning money to support their year-round polo operations.[72] Their advent was noted in England soon after World War II, when, using a term mentioned in Burma military polo days in the 1930s, Argentine players in England's Cowdray Park Gold Cup were referred to as "hired assassins." In the U.S., every Open Championship winning team since 1997 included at least one Argentine in its lineup.[73]

The evolving style of play in high-goal polo has not been without criticism, particularly of the uneven composition of teams with one patron and three high-goal professionals.[74] Criticism of the conduct of the game, which has given rise to the All Pro Polo League, came in a 2009 essay by Javier Tanoira entitled "Reflections on Argentine Polo." He argued that possession of the ball and the generation of fouls, rather than active play has resulted in the great frequency of whistle blowing that has reduced the contest to penalty shoot-outs. He proposes several changes. To speed the game, instead of umpire throw-ins, at midfield after a goal or at the sidelines after a ball goes out of bounds, he would follow the practice on some other sports that give possession to the scored upon team at the goal line and at the sideline to the team that did not hit it out. Different values would be assigned to penalty goals and to goals hit through the mouth of the goal posts at a gallop.

Perhaps most important, only one horse per chukker would be allowed and patrons and sponsors would be restricted to supporting teams or tournaments, rather than participating as a team member. An injured player or horse would have to leave the field, the team playing on without them, unless a reserve player replaces the injured player, but would have to use the injured player's horse. To demonstrate the proposed rules, a series of tournaments was planned for the U.S. and other countries in the spring of 2016.[75]

At the grass roots level in the U.S., 80 percent of men and 99 percent of women were playing with outdoor handicaps of one or less, and polo had experienced a broad expansion. The number of clubs grew from 47 in 1946[76] to 296 in 2015. From 1980 to 2015, while the number of clubs doubled, the number of players tripled to 5,267.[77] More than 35 colleges offered polo as a varsity or club sport.[78] Arena polo handicaps were a little higher; 75 percent of men and 97 percent of women had handicaps at one or less. Handicaps specifically for women's polo were somewhat higher, with 67 percent at one or less. Of affiliated USPA members, that is, those from abroad, 49 percent had outdoor handicaps of one or less.[79]

Typically, at the neighborhood polo club, in horse country where neighbors kept horses for a variety of recreational purposes, twenty or thirty members, bringing their own horses or leasing horses from the club or the farm across the road, would have a couple of practice sessions during the week and hold matches on the weekend, the larger matches played usually on Sunday afternoon.

The Polo Training Foundation, founded in 1967, concentrated on training at polo summer camps, promoting intercollegiate and interscholastic play, and training umpires, in close cooperation with the USPA.[80] To further promote club play, the USPA adopted a policy of providing professionally trained umpires free to clubs for low-goal polo.[81] On the calendar for a typical month—April 2016, for example—40 tournaments across the country would be listed. For the month, of the dozen specifying the level of play, three listed team handicaps of four, five were at levels of six to eight, two at twelve, and one at twenty-twenty-six.[82]

One factor in the polo expansion has been the growing participation of women. By 2015, 36 percent of USPA membership was female, and among student members 54 percent were female. Rare among athletics, polo is a co-ed sport. Men and women can play on the same team, besides the matches restricted to women. The U.S. Women's Polo Association was founded in 1934 on the west coast. The U.S. Women's Open, inaugurated in 1990, had over sixty women competing at several levels by 2015, and the Women's Championship was founded in 2005. The USPA Girls' National Interscholastic Championship, with 30 teams competing, marked its twenty-fifth anniversary in 2016. The Women's National Intercollegiate Katydid Farms Trophy had 32 women's college teams competing, compared with just three when it was originated in 1976.[83] In 2014, the women's handicap, specific to women's tournaments, was introduced, besides the regular handicap for co-ed games.[84]

In the world of equine recreation, the prospects for further polo expansion may be quite favorable. Its excitement, particularly for the competitive, is addictive. Perhaps indicative is the story of a boy in a horse-centered family. He confided that he found his time in the hunter/jumper barn to which he had been sent as exciting as being in a sewing circle. He was then given a few polo lessons and was hooked.[85]

Nine

Unwanted Horses

When a 2009–2010 survey asked people over eighteen who owned, managed, or leased horses what they thought were the chief issues facing the American equine industry, the most frequent response—63 percent—was what to do with unwanted horses. This was followed by the cost of horsekeeping, the loss of trails and riding areas, owners who don't understand horses, and not having the option of slaughter.[1]

The unwanted horses issue reflected a number of influences. Some say overbreeding in an earlier boom period. Others could point to the declining uses for horses, others to the expense of horses' maintenance outside the previously available farm or range. The situation became more obviously critical in the years of recession following 2008, when the reduced economic situation of many horse owners made retention of horses a newly burdensome expense. Calling attention to the crisis were instances of abandoned horses and the discovery of hungry horses suffering from neglect. In a sense, the longer-term structural unemployment of horses was now supplemented by cyclical unemployment, as effective demand for the horses was reduced by depressed income of horse owners.

One horse rescue organization listed the reasons for abandonment and neglect of horses it had encountered:

> ... death of an owner, owners becoming too old to care for themselves, let alone a large animal, loss of interest of a young person on the way to college or a career, an assessment that the horse is no longer "useful," and lack of knowledge of how to care for an older horse.[2]

An additional cause of horse abandonment came directly from the recession in the economy beginning in 2008–2009. Foreclosure of mortgages caused many families to leave their homes and move to facilities where keeping a horse was no longer possible.[3] While rescue operations increased, to cope with abandoned or neglected horses, they remained inadequate. A 2009 survey found that 63 percent of equine rescue facilities were at or near full capacity and on average were turning down 38 percent of horses brought to them.[4]

Greater attention, therefore, focused on horse slaughter, particularly for human consumption in Europe and the Far East, which had increased over the late decades of the twentieth century. United States Department of Agriculture inspection and certification of horse slaughter had its origin in the Congressional law of July 24, 1919, which had provided for inspection and certification of horsemeat as "U.S. Inspected and Passed by the U.S. Department of Agriculture" and had appropriated $100,000 to carry out the work during that fiscal year.[5] In 2007, however, increasing sentiment against horse slaughter, reflecting, no doubt, the horse's new role as a recreation companion, led Congress to discontinue the appropriations. The result was the greatly increased shipment of horses for slaughter in Mexico and Canada, from where the frozen product was shipped for consumption in Europe or the Far East.

The consequences of the ban were unexpected and untoward, however, as even the transport of horses to slaughter, in this case to Mexico and Canada, could no longer be inspected by the Department of Agriculture, as they previously had been, and transport conditions were reported to have deteriorated. A study by Congress's General Accountability Office in 2011 concluded that the effect of the ban on Department of Agriculture inspections had been negative on balance.[6] Congress thereafter returned to appropriating funds for the inspection in 2011,[7] but withdrew them again in 2014. Controversy over horse slaughter for human consumption continued in the interim as state and local legislatures banned the reestablishment of slaughterhouses, with ensuing litigation.[8]

A complication arose also at the European, horse-consuming end, where European Community legislators banned the sale of horse meat containing the residue of particular drugs. This rendered problematic the slaughter for European consumption, of American racehorses, the great majority of which had been treated with drugs. The question was clouded by the 2012 discovery in Europe of horsemeat contained in advertised beef products, leading to highly publicized investigations as to their origin.[9] In the U.S., horse medication practices, legal changes, and shifting attitudes made the horse slaughter for human consumption a continuing concern.

Wild Horses

Closely related to the question of slaughter was the fate of the wild horses roaming the American West. Over the five centuries since Columbus brought horses to the new world and their descendants were carried into Mexico and Florida, escaped and abandoned horses have roamed free in parts of the North American continent. Multiplying in freedom to seemingly inexhaustible numbers—with estimates in the millions—they were drawn down to meet succeeding demands. They staffed the cattle drives of the 1860s and 1870s, the cattle ranches of the century that followed, the farms of people moving west, and the sudden demands from abroad for the Boer War and the First World War. Through the first half of the twentieth century the wild horses and burros of the West "were considered wildlife of sorts, fair game for public taking for taming, selling for pet food or slaughter, or killing to reduce grazing competition for domestic stock."[10]

In 1932, Congress passed the Taylor Grazing Act to improve rangeland conditions and regulate grazing on the public lands. It created the Department of Interior's Grazing Service, which merged with the General Land Office to form the Bureau of Land Management (the BLM) in 1946.[11] The Grazing Service, and it successor BLM, issued grazing permits, with nominal fees, for use of the land and followed the mandate to improve grazing lands. Eight-man advisory boards were created for each of fifty-two western grazing districts, elected in secret ballots by ranchers holding permits in the area.

One director of the Grazing Service in 1939 declared: "A wild horse consumes forage needed for domestic livestock, brings in no return, and serves no useful purpose." The Service then facilitated "range clearance" by allowing permit holders to poison water holes, shoot the wild horses, or otherwise slaughter them.[12] Permits were issued for the removal of wild horses, with the destination in most cases the slaughterhouses preparing food for pets, chickens, and zoo animals.[13] Roundups were conducted by aircraft accompanied by cowboys and trucks on the ground. While some private persons would separate a horse from the herd and train it for private use, the overwhelming majority were collected by what were called mustangers, who took horses off BLM-managed rangelands for returns of six cents a pound on the hoof paid at rendering plants and slaughter houses. Between 1946 and 1950 over 100,000 abandoned and unclaimed horses were removed from BLM lands in Nevada alone, with branded horses returned to their owners, and the rest sold by those conducting the operation as compensation for their work.[14]

Onto this scene came Velma Johnston, a polio-surviving woman going from her small ranch to her work as an executive secretary to a real estate and insurance executive in Reno, Nevada. Driving her 26-mile commute one spring morning in 1950, she saw a livestock truck coming from the wild horse area with blood dripping onto the road. Deciding it was her duty to alert the driver in case he didn't know, she followed the truck onto the parking lot of a stockyard. There she peered through a gap in the slats in the back of the truck and saw a horrendous tableau of mutilated horses, some barely alive. A colt, or what was left of him, lay trampled, his bone crushed and coat blood-soaked. Other horses had bloody stumps instead of legs, others with hooves torn off and hides shredded by buckshot, a stallion with head bowed, blood seeping from empty eye sockets.

When she asked the driver where the horses came from and why they were in such terrible shape, he replied that they were "run in by plane out there." "No use in crying your eyes out over a bunch of useless mustangs," he said, "They'll all be dead soon anyway."[15]

Shaken, she investigated what legal recourse there was to stop such operations. She found there was none. As a result, when she and her husband, Charlie, learned some time later that there was a collection enclosure of rounded-up wild horses near their ranch, they drove out to it and liberated the horses. Similar information reached them of other collection enclosures and they were able to free other wild horses.

Then, in 1952, they learned that a hearing was to be held in Virginia City, Story County, for county approval of a BLM permit for the aircraft roundup and removal of about five hundred horses, and that an opposing petition with 147 signatures had been collected. Attending the hearing, when no one else would speak in opposition, Velma Johnston stepped forward. She asked the BLM representative supporting the permit as a means of saving government money why government-owned horses on government land, which would bring about $3,000 at the slaughterhouse or rendering plant, were being given as a gift to these two pilots. Were they relatives or special friends? She asked.

The county commissioners voted against the permit and ten days later the county outlawed airborne pursuit of wild horses in the county. This had limited effect, however, as it applied to state-held land and not to BLM land, with its own jurisdiction.[16]

The story of the Virginia City hearing and of Velma's other efforts for the mustangs appeared in local papers and was picked up by other papers. Then a feature story appeared in the 1957 Christmas issue of the *Reader's Digest*, which brought the plight of the wild horse to national and international attention.[17]

Grown-ups and children wrote to Congress, Velma was called to testify before the House Judiciary Committee, and in 1959 Congress passed a law banning the roundup of wild horses with aircraft and motor vehicles. As Velma Johnston had been called, disparagingly, Wild Horse Annie by a BLM official, that name stuck and the 1959 law was referred to as the Wild Horse Annie law.[18]

The law, however, did not result in effective enforcement. Ranchers could release a few of their own, branded horses, to run with a wild herd, round up the herd with plane and truck, and claim it was their own horses they were rounding up with attendant wild horses. Attempts to bring enforcement cases and set an example failed in court.[19]

Sentiment built for the cause of the wild horses. Then, in 1966, a prominent children's book author, Marguerite Henry, came to stay with Annie and wrote her story, though fictionalized, in a children's book called *Mustang, Wild Spirit of the West*. This drew even wider attention to the issue of defending the mustangs, Annie spoke to children's groups, and Congress was inundated with children's letters.[20]

In 1971, Congress passed the Wild Free-Roaming Horse and Burro Act reading:

> Be it enacted by the Senate and House of Representatives of the United States of America in Congress assembled, That Congress finds and declares that wild free-roaming horses and burros are living symbols of the historic and pioneer spirit of the West; that they contribute to the diversity of life forms within the Nation and enrich the lives of the American people; and that these horses and burros are fast disappearing from the American scene. It is the policy of Congress that free wild-roaming horses and burros shall be protected from capture, branding, harassment, or death, and to accomplish this they are to be considered, in the area where presently found, as an integral part of the natural system of the public lands.[21]

Ironically, the law, as amended in 1975, 1978, 1996, and 2004, assigned responsibility for the horses and burros on public lands to the Department of Interior Bureau of Land Management, which had long pressed for the removal of wild horses and burros from government lands. This was to be applied, however, only to the lands where the wild horses and burros were presently found. This applied also to Public Forest lands, with responsibility assigned to the Department of Agriculture Forest Service.

The delineation of wild horse territory, as distinct from grazing lands, was to prove a matter of contention in the following years. Wild horse advocates pointed out in 2014 that the original wild horse territory of 53.8 million acres had shrunk to 31.6 million acres, and the BLM cited particular reasons for each reduction.[22]

The law facilitated the removal of excess horses and burros that posed a threat to their own habitat and other rangeland resources. With Federal protections and a lack of natural predators, wild horse and burro herds can double every four years. To avoid the overpopulation that could cause soil erosion, sedimentation of streams, and damage to wildlife habitat, the BLM established for each Herd Management Area (HMA) an Appropriate Management Level (AML) which it sought to maintain by "gathers" of the animals every few years. Conducted more recently by helicopters, the animals were herded into dead-end traps from which they were sent to short-term holding areas where they were prepared for adoption, long-term pastures, returned back into the herd, or sold in some cases.

In 1971 there were 17,300 wild horses and 8,045 burros in the BLM areas in ten Western states. By 2014 there were 33,780 horses and 6,825 burros, a total nearly 14,000 more than the West-wide Appropriate Management Level of 26,677. As a result of the "gathers" there were 14,163 horses and 1,066 burros in corrals for short-term holding, pending adoption, and 32,965 horses in long-term pastures, maintained by contract ranches, for a combined total of 48,194, compared with the BLM holding capacity of 52,138. Strikingly, there were more horses in long-term holding pastures than still roaming, casting doubt on the sustainability of the program.

The 1971 law authorized the transfer of title of ownership of adopted horses to individuals after one year, so long as the animal had received humane care and treatment during the year. Between 1971 and 2013 the BLM had adopted out 230,000 horses and burros. The adoption rate was influenced by economic conditions, of course. Adoptions in Fiscal Year 2013, at 2,671, were less than half the 5,701 adopted in Fiscal 2005.

In 2012, 10,350 wild horses and burros were "gathered." Of highest priority for removal from the herd were wild horses four years old or younger, which made up half the herd, since they were more appealing to the public for adoption. The lowest priority for removal were animals five- to ten-years old, since they were in their prime reproductive years and were not as appealing to the public for adoption. A higher priority was assigned to removing animals eleven- to nineteen-years old, since the BLM had the authority to sell animals over ten-years old and, if not sold, they would spend less time in long-term pastures, which would reduce costs. Animals twenty years or older were returned to the herds since they would adapt with greater difficulty to living in captivity or handling the stress of transportation.

To identify the horses and burros gathered from the range, the BLM applied a freezemark to the left side of the neck indicating U.S. ownership, year of birth, and registration number that incorporated the state and herd from which the animal was removed. Performed usually at the short-term holding facility as vaccination and worming was done, freeze branding involved application of an iron, cooled with liquid nitrogen, for eight to twelve seconds. This destroyed the color follicle so that the hair at the brand site, grown back in about three months, would contain no color pigment and appear white. Mares receiving fertility control vaccines were usually freeze marked with an identifying brand on their left croup.[23]

To promote the adoption of wild horses, the BLM initiated a number of programs. Beginning in 2000 it joined with prison authorities in seven states to have inmates train and gentle wild horses for public adoption. Several thousand horses were trained and adopted and recidivism among inmates who trained horses was about half the level of recidivism of inmates who had not been in the program. Calculations of costs in 2013 compared $2,100 for training and adoption with $46,252 for the lifetime cost of an un-adopted mustang, or a saving of over $40,000 a horse. The largest number of adoptions by agencies came from the U.S. Border Patrol.

In 2007 the BLM launched a Trainer Incentives Program under which trainers prepared horses for adoption, beginning with three- and four-year old Nevada geldings in 2007, mares and mustangs from other states in 2008, yearlings in 2009, and five- and six-year olds in 2010.

Under a youth program begun in 2008, youths had about 140 days to gentle and train a previously "untouched" mustang yearling for halter breaking, trailer loading, picking up feet, and leading through obstacles and maneuvers. Competition at the end of the training period took place in Fort Worth, Texas, for a $50,000 purse and other prizes.

In the most ambitious of mustang promotion events, trainers and adopters could select their choice at one of seven adoption auctions around the country and after 120 days compete in classes and divisions of their choice in the Mustang Million. Preparing 3.5-minute free style performances with music and choreography, they competed for $200,000 and a 2014 Ram truck. The event brought widespread attention to the adoption program, and stimulated the number of wild horse and burro adoptions.[24]

To carry out its mission on a more scientific basis, the BLM asked the National Academy of Sciences to study its operations and make recommendations for improvement. The National Academy concluded, in its report issued June 5, 2013, that the BLM's "current practice of removing free-ranging horses from public lands promotes a high population growth rate, and maintaining them in long-term holding facilities is both economically unsustainable and incongruent with public expectations." To manage horse populations without periodic removals, the report stated, would require widespread and consistent application of fertility controls. It recommended porcine zona pellucida (PZP) and GonaCon for mares and chemical vasectomies for stallions, a method that had proved effective with wild horses on Assateague Island, on the Atlantic coast. The report stressed also improved counting, suggesting that previous BLM undercounting could range from 10 to 50 percent.[25]

The BLM had been applying population control measures, though apparently on a more limited scale. The sex ratios of herds had been adjusted, with more males than females. Besides the gelding of stallions, females had been darted with pelletized PZP during the three to four month period prior to foaling, effective for 22 months. By 2013 the BLM had administered pelletized PZP to more than 4,562 mares on 80 of its 179 herd management areas, but significant decreases in population growth were not apparent.[26] In March 2014, the BLM invited submissions of research proposals for new, innovative techniques of contraception and sterilization from veterinarians, scientists, universities, pharmaceutical companies and other researchers.[27]

Not all wild horses were on government lands. The Agriculture Department's 2002 agricultural census counted 115,464 horses on 12,174 properties on Indian reservations, though this may have been approximate since reservation horses were often owned as communal property and large herds were managed as range animals.[28] Since reservation lands were outside the legal reach of U.S. Government authorities, they did not have in place the institutions, programs, and facilities available on government lands. In the Navajo Indian territory, facing years of unrelenting drought, uncontrolled wild horses were a serious problem. One feral horse would consume five gallons of water and 18 pounds of forage a day, often the water and food a family had bought for itself and its cattle. To avoid the overgrazing of the land and attendant erosion and stream blockage, Navajo authorities had carried out periodic roundups of wild horses, for which horse slaughter had been an important outlet, which was now threatened by Congressional action on its continuation.

Interestingly, in 2012, when two non–Indian celebrities—actor Robert Redford and former New Mexico governor Bill Richardson—sponsored an ad opposing the reopening of horse slaughter, and saying they were standing with Native American leaders to whom horse slaughter violated tribal cultural values, the president of the Navajo Nation released a letter supporting horse slaughter. Wild and feral horses were growing in number, he said, and were costing the Navajo $200,000 a year in damages to property and range. Also supporting slaughter was the National Congress of American Indians, citing hillsides and valleys denuded by overgrazing by feral and wild horses, which throughout the West were nearly everywhere you look.[29] Following extended negotiations, however, and outspoken Navajo tribe members' declarations against horse slaughter as a violation of Navajo religion and traditional values, Navajo leaders reversed themselves, ordered the temporary suspension of roundups for slaughter on the reservation, and agreed to a program to be supported by animal welfare groups for the more orderly and humane management of wild and feral horses on Indian lands, with attention to adoption and contraception.[30]

Far from the Western lands of the BLM and Forest Service and their Indian neighbors, on seven areas of the barrier islands and outer banks of the Atlantic Coast from Georgia to Maryland, wild horses, some pony-sized, roamed on mostly National Park Service land. Management varied from government agencies to a volunteer fire department, to local horse-preservation foundations.[31] On Ocracoke Island, North Carolina, the horses were cared for by the Ocracoke Boy Scouts in the 1950s and then by the National Park Service, the herd later dwindling to seventeen horses fed twice a day and subject to veterinary care.[32]

Some supporters maintained the horses were descendants of Spanish horses abandoned by the failed de Ayllon colony of the 1520s on what was to become the Carolinas, or of horses released from the British flagship, the Tiger, beached in 1585, or of horses that swam ashore from other shipwrecks.[33] Elsewhere, farmers had left their horses on the islands and outer banks for their safety and protection from predators and taxation.

Management of the herds, which range from seventeen to close to two hundred, presents a sharp contrast. On Assateague Island, a fence separates horses on the Maryland and Virginia portions of the island. Maryland horses are treated with periodic contraceptive inoculations and chemical geldings. Virginia horses, managed by the Chincoteague Volunteer Fire Department are rounded up on the last Wednesday in July and swim across the Assateague Channel to Chincoteague Island. There some of the foals are auctioned off before the rest of the herd swims back to Assateague Island.[34] Concern for some of the smaller herds further south is that they may become inbred and not sustained genetically, requiring controlled importation of mares or stallions from elsewhere.

Concern centers also on interaction with visiting tourists. On Assateague Island visitors are prohibited from approaching closer than ten feet from horses, under penalty of fine. Further south some prohibitions specify thirty feet or fifty feet. Defenders of the wild ponies, which are generally about twelve hands tall, contend also with questions of damage to the environment, given the size of the herd, and to sharing the space in some cases with other wildlife—in bird sanctuaries and sea turtle nesting areas.

Defense of the horses comes also from those dependent on the tourist trade. As a supporter in one coastal town concerned for its tourist trade lamented: All we have is the lighthouse and the horses.

Opposed, tolerated, or defended, remnants of America's wild horses on the outer banks and barrier islands have survived, with the continent and its five-century history of horses behind them, facing the wide Atlantic, across which the Spanish had brought their horses to conquer the New

World and a million American horses had been shipped back to fight the war in the Old World.

Mountain Warfare

Then, from across the world, a striking anachronism was brought to the attention of the American people. Half a century after the U.S. Army had closed the book on battlefield horses, an episode in Afghanistan in October-November 2001 reopened the book. Reacting to the 9–11 suicide attack on the New York World Trade Center directed by Al Quaida headquarters in Afghanistan protected by the country's Taliban government, the U.S. dispatched a team of twelve special forces soldiers to Afghanistan. Their task was to direct American bombing missions in support of the several Northern Alliance guerrilla groups fighting the Taliban forces.[35]

Flown by helicopter over the high mountain border from Tajikistan, the team found the group they joined moved on horses through mountain terrain inaccessible by any other means but by foot. They were assigned six horses, shaggy, deep-chested, short-legged animals bred for mountain walking. This left half the team behind for logistic support at the base. Of the six who rode off on the horses, three had ridden before but two of them only as children in summer camp.[36] The team found the small wooden saddles, made up of three boards hinged together and covered by goatskin, painful but they persevered.[37] The horses, accustomed to the terrain, on one occasion climbed a three-foot path carved into the side of a mountain. When one horse stumbled and the U.S. soldier toppled off, he fortunately landed on a lower ledge only a few feet down rather than falling the hundreds of feet to the valley.

The Americans' aid proved most valuable. Operating much like the forward artillery observers of previous wars, they radioed the GPS locations of Taliban targets to pilots overhead who programmed and launched smart bombs directed to enemy positions. At one point, a line of Northern Alliance horsemen charged the enemy line in a twenty-first century cavalry charge that, surprisingly, succeeded with the aid of the smart bombs hitting the enemy position.[38] One part of the team rode off separately into the mountains with Afghan assistance, set themselves up on high vantage points, and for days directed smart bombs to keep Taliban forces from advancing through a strategic pass.

The success of the combined U.S. Special Forces and Northern Alliance attacks pried the Taliban from a strategic town and helped clear a wide area the Taliban had controlled. A second U.S. Special Forces team, attached to another Northern Alliance group, was assigned just eight horses to carry out its operations and was also effective.

The success of the small Special Forces teams gained wide attention in the U.S. and was celebrated in a book entitled *Horse Soldiers*. The book made clear, however, that though the Special Forces were trained in various skills and tactics, they had no preparation in the use of horses in warfare, as no such training was being offered in the U.S. military at the time. In fact, such training had not been offered for decades.[39]

Mountain warfare training associated with cold weather training had been undertaken by the U.S. Army in World War II, reacting to the lessons of Finland's resistance to Russia with white-clad ski troops in the 1939 Russo-Finnish war.[40] The mountain training proved effective for American forces in their operations in Sicily and the Apennines.[41] Cold weather training for Marines going to Korea was undertaken beginning in 1951 at the Pickel Meadow Marine Camp in the Toiyabe National Forest in northern California. The camp was deactivated and reactivated over the following decades, used to prepare for the annual NATO winter training exercises in Norway in the 1980s, and, with the end of the Cold War, broadened its operations to cover the full spectrum of mountain warfare.

This covered an assault climber's course, animal packing course, engineer course, and communication course. Training was broadened to cover personnel of all branches of the U.S. armed forces, as well as participants from other nations. The focus was on combat in complex, compartmentalized mountain terrain.[42]

Besides the mule-packing course given since the 1980s, in 2011, responding to requests from Special Forces soldiers, the Center undertook horsemanship training, the only such course in the U.S. military. To carry this out, it was necessary to acquire appropriate horses. Instructors found, however, that horses trained in equestrian sports, such as dressage and jumping, were too specialized for the military needs. Over time, American horses had been bred to be more athletic, making it more difficult to find well-rounded horses. Most horses used in the course, as a result were former mustangs, trained by inmates in the Northern Nevada Correctional Center.[43]

Trainers foresaw a continuing need for mounted mountain warfare training, as small-scale, surreptitious mobility on terrain inaccessible to internal-combustion vehicles remains a part of unconventional warfare.

Like the need for animal transport over the broken terrain of the last few miles to the front in World War I, where railroads and trucks could not go, there reappeared the need for mounted movement in the mountain terrain inaccessible to technologically advanced ground vehicles.

Conclusion

The horses are gone: from the road, the farm, the range, and the military. Their presence, their departure, the technology that affected them and their resurgence in new careers form an important chapter in American history. It is a story that had to be told, and this book has attempted to tell it.

The book details how over a century and a half, a succession of new technologies moved American horses out of one field after another. Previously, when the horse was the sole or primary source of mobile energy, advances in technology had strengthened the horses' abilities and expanded the tasks they could perform. Early on, horseshoes and the better harness had won for the horse a thousand-year career in agriculture. More recently, the series of nineteenth century inventions made the horse the star of the American agricultural revolution. On the road, the spoked wheel, smoother pavements, street rails, and stronger, lighter carriages had helped the horse carry more people with less effort.

The book points out that with the onset of the twentieth century, new technologies drawing on new sources of energy either eliminated the horses' jobs or took them over themselves. Rather than depending on the metabolism that gave the horse energy, vehicles moving people or freight came to depend on various forms of combustion. The steam engine had turned thermal energy into mechanical energy, which, a century later, could turn a generator of electrical energy that could be transmitted by wire or rail over long distances to an electric motor providing mechanical energy where it was needed. Then came the internal combustion engine, whose mechanical energy took from the horse the distinction it had enjoyed over the centuries as the sole, or primary, source of mobile energy.

Facilitating it all, the book explains, were the remarkable improvements in metallurgy, making possible the revolutionary farm implements of the nineteenth century, the better carriages and street rails, the cable cars, the overwhelming advances in armaments, and the internal combustion engines that swept the horses from the road, the farm, and the battlefield.

How important was the horses' contribution to the American economy? It is difficult to measure. One example: as horses were ceding their function to steam and tractors, the power of horses pulling the plow was reported to have exceeded the power exerted in all the country's mines and factories. There are other examples. Without horses there could have been no Wild West, no cattle industry, no horse-and-buggy doctor, no stream of new farm implements revolutionizing American agriculture after the Civil War, no early inter-city travel, and no early urban commuting

How important to the economy was the impact of the horses' departure? It may be difficult to gage from this distance but it was not difficult for the people who lost their livelihood as a result. For, not only the horses' jobs were gone. Gone too were the jobs of all those involved with the horse economy: the teamsters, the hostlers, or grooms, the horseshoers, blacksmiths, wheelwrights, carriage painters, draymen, livery men, makers of saddles, of harnesses, whips, blankets and other horse clothing, manure transporters, and rendering workers. Gone too were the jobs of the farmers in the belt of farms around each city, growing the forage to feed the city horses, and the hay and grain dealers transporting the forage to market in the city. It was a major adjustment.

Clearly, both the horses' contribution and the impact of their departure merit careful consideration as a part of the history of the American experience.

The story is also a self-contained case study of change that can be viewed in historical perspective. Since change is ongoing even in our own day—digitalization, globalization, and climate—there are lessons in this story on how change takes place and its intended and unintended consequences.

From all of these viewpoints, it is a story that needed to be told.

Appendix (Tables 1–10)

Table 1—Approximate Labor Requirements for Major Operations in the Production of 1 Acre of Wheat (20 Bushels)[1]

HAND METHODS, ABOUT 1830					
Operation	Equipment Used	Operators	Power		Man Labor
			Horses[2]	Tractors[3]	
		Number	Number	Number	Hours
Plowing	Walking plow	1	2	....	6.7
Sowing	Sack	1	....	....	1.2
Harrowing and covering seed	Brush	1	2	....	2.5
Reaping, binding, and shocking	Sickles[4]	2	....	....	20.0
Hauling bundles to barn	Wagon	2	2	....	4.0
Threshing and stacking straw	Flail and forks	1	....	....	13.3
Winnowing	Shovel, sheet, and measure	3	....	....	10.0
Total					57.7
MACHINE METHODS IN CENTRAL WINTER-WHEAT BELT, 1896					
Operation	Equipment Used	Operators	Power		Man Labor
			Horses[2]	Tractors[3]	
		Number	Number	Number	Hours
Plowing	2-bottom gang plow	1	4	....	2.0
Sowing	Broadcast seeder	2	2	....	.2
Harrowing and covering seed	Section harrow	1	4	....	.3
Harvesting	Binder	1	3	....	.7
Shocking		2	....	....	1.3
Hauling bundles to thresher	Wagons	12	16	....	2.0
Threshing and stacking straw	Thresher and forks	7	....	1	1.0
Hauling water and fuel	Wagons and barrels	1	2	....	.2
Hauling wheat to granary	Wagons	1	4	....	.9
Unloading at granary	Shovels	1	....	....	.2
Total					8.8
MACHINE MEHODS IN GREAT PLAINS AREA, 1930					
Plowing	3-bottom gang plow	1	....	1	1.0
Disking	10-foot tandem disk	1	....	1	.3
Harrowing	6-section harrow	1	....	1	.1
Drilling	Two 10-foot drills	2	....	1	.3
Harvesting and threshing	12-foot combine	2	....	1	.8
Hauling to granary or elevator	Motor trucks	2	....	....	.8
Total					3.3

Table 1 cont.
1. Figures for 1830 and 1896 based on U.S. Department of Commerce and Labor, *Thirteenth Annual Report of the Commissioner of Labor, Hand and Machine Labor*, vol. 2, 1899, General Table, 427–1604; those for 1930 based on R.S. Washburn, *Cost of Producing Winter Wheat in Central Great Plains Region of the United States*, U.S. Dept. of Agricultural Bulletin, 1924, 1198; and L.A. Reynoldson, R.S. Kifer, J.H. Martin, and W.R. Humphries, *The Combined Harvester-Thresher in the Great Plains*, U.S. Dept. of Agr. Tech. Bul. 70, 1928; and estimates.
2. Oxen used in 1830.
3. Steam tractor used in 1896; 3-plow gas tractor used in 1930.
4. With cradle, approximately 10 man-hours required per acre for reaping, binding, and shocking.

Source: *Power and Machinery in Agriculture*, U.S. Department of Agricultural Miscellaneous Publication No. 157, Washington, D.C., April 1933. 2–3.

Table 2—Distribution of Horse Labor by Operation (in Percentages)

	WISCONSIN DAIRY FARM	ILLINOIS CORN & HOG FARM	IOWA GRAIN & STOCK FARM
Total	100	100	100
Road Hauling	13	20	26
Farm Hauling	35	22	21
Hauling Manure	8	4	9
Potatoes	1	1	1
Cutting Grain	2	1	2
Cultivating Corn	6	11	12
Raking & Tedding	1	1	1
Mowing		1	4
Planting Corn	1	2	1
Sowing Small Grain	1	1	3
Rolling	1	4	
Harrowing	5	4	6
Plowing	11	16	3
Disking	8	12	8
Breaking & Raking Stalks			1
Cultivating Tobacco	2		
Cutting Corn	2		2
Planting Tobacco	1		

Source: Oscar A. Juve, "The Horse Power Problem on the Farm," *Yearbook of Agriculture 1919*, U.S. Department of Agriculture, 1919. 486–493.

Table 3—Average Annual Cost of Keeping Horses in Corn Belt, and Relative Importance of Various Items, 1921 (279 Farms, 1,975 Horses)[1]

Item	Cost per Horse	Percent of Total Cost
Feed and Bedding[2]	$63.88	60.2
Chores	11.88	11.2
Depreciation	6.70	6.3
Interest	7.37	6.9
Stabling	7.28	6.9
Harness costs	4.78	4.5
Shoeing	1.90	1.8
Miscellaneous	2.29	2.2
Total gross cost	106.08	100.0
Credit for manure	6.87	....
Net cost	99.21	....

1. United States Department of Agriculture Farmers' Bulletin No. 1298, "Cost of using Horses on Corn Belt Farms," p. 3.
2. The item of bedding is included with feed, because on many farms straw and stover were used both as feed and bedding, and owing to the fact that refuse from the mangers was used for bedding, it was contrary to actual practice to attempt to make bedding a separate item.

Source: *Horses, Mules, and Motor Vehicles*, U.S. Department of Agriculture Bulletin No. 5 (Washington, D.C.: U.S. Department of Agriculture, 1925), 29.

Table 4—Cost of Keeping Work Animals in Different Areas for the Year Ended October 31, 1920[1]

Area	Number of Farms	Average Number of Work Animals per Farm	Cost per Head							Manure Credit	Net Cost per Head
			Feed	Shoeing	Veterinary	Chores	Interest	Harness	Depreciation	Total		
Madison County, Ohio	34	8.1	$135.96	$3.05	$0.58	$15.43	$9.57	$5.43	$3.36	$173.38	$15.00	$158.38
Seneca County, Ohio	34	5.0	160.25	3.75	.66	22.58	9.02	5.21	4.64	206.11	15.00	191.11
Madison County, Ind.	42	5.4	135.56	3.13	1.19	16.52	7.87	4.87	1.20	170.34	15.00	155.34
Montgomery County, Ind.	56	6.0	123.10	2.23	1.04	16.47	8.49	3.52	13.68	168.53	15.00	153.53
Livingston County, Ill.	60	8.4	128.78	1.27	1.69	14.07	8.86	5.10	6.72	166.49	15.00	151.49
Knox County, Ill.	60	7.0	135.13	1.41	1.03	14.65	8.08	4.97	12.09	177.36	15.00	162.36
Total, average	286	6.5	133.04	2.16	1.13	15.83	8.62	4.82	7.79	173.99	15.00	158.99

1. United States Department of Agriculture Bulletin No. 997, "the Cost and Utilization of Power on Farms where Tractors are Owned," p. 40.

Source: *Horses, Mules, and Motor Vehicles*, U.S. Department of Agriculture Bulletin No. 5 (Washington, D.C.: U.S. Department of Agriculture), 29.

Table 5—Horses and Mules: Number on Farms, by Classes, United States, January 1, 1920–1952

YEAR	HORSES				MULES			
	ALL HORSES	2 YEARS AND OVER	1-2 YEARS	UNDER 1 YEAR	ALL MULES	2 YEARS AND OVER	1-2 YEARS	UNDER 1 YEAR
	Thousands	Thousands	Thousands	Thousands	Thousands	Thousands	Thousands	Thousands
1920	20,291	17,512	1,362	1,217	5,651	4,874	338	389
1921	19,369	17,280	1,108	981	5,768	5,008	362	338
1922	18,764	17,056	892	816	5,824	5,215	316	293
1923	18,125	16,684	740	701	5,893	5,366	273	254
1924	17,378	16,119	636	623	5,907	5,459	228	220
1925	16,651	15,522	563	566	5,918	5,516	209	193
1926	16,083	14,964	557	562	5,903	5,527	188	188
1927	15,388	14,296	544	548	5,804	5,469	177	158
1928	14,792	13,740	530	522	5,656	5,380	146	130
1929	14,234	13,227	504	503	5,510	5,287	123	100
1930	13,742	12,772	475	495	5,382	5,209	94	79
1931	13,195	12,253	489	453	5,273	5,122	82	69
1932	12,664	11,797	454	413	5,148	5,025	72	51
1933	12,291	11,461	414	416	5,046	4,943	54	49
1934	12,052	11,141	416	495	4,945	4,843	51	51
1935	11,861	10,761	490	610	4,822	4,712	52	58
1936	11,598	10,338	605	655	4,628	4,501	54	73
1937	11,342	10,016	642	684	4,460	4,314	62	84
1938	10,995	9,609	680	706	4,250	4,081	69	100
1939	10,629	9,310	685	634	4,163	3,963	86	114
1940	10,444	9,200	623	621	4,034	3,800	101	133
1941	10,193	9,000	602	591	3,911	3,651	120	140
1942	9,873	8,810	560	503	3,782	3,536	116	130
1943	9,605	8,718	485	402	3,626	3,399	115	112
1944	9,192	8,444	384	364	3,421	3,224	99	98
1945	8,715	8,059	343	313	3,235	3,057	91	87
1946	8,081	7,547	290	244	3,027	2,887	75	65
1947	7,340	6,897	231	212	2,789	2,681	58	50
1948	6,704	6,311	201	192	2,575	2,489	46	40
1949	6,096	5,738	182	176	2,402	2,336	36	30
1950	5,548	5,233	164	151	2,233	2,182	29	22
1951	4,993	4,724	140	129	2,074	2,039	20	15
1952[1]	4,370	4,136	124	110	1,923	1,894	17	12

1. Preliminary.

Source: U.S. Department of Agriculture, *Agricultural Statistics*, 1952.459.

Table 6—Horses and Mules: Numbers on Farms, and Value, United States, January 1, 1867–1952[1]

YEAR	HORSES			MULES		
	NUMBER	FARM VALUE		NUMBER	FARM VALUE	
		PER HEAD	TOTAL		PER HEAD	TOTAL
	Thousands	Dollars	1,000 Dollars	Thousands	Dollars	1,000 dollars
1867	6,820	57.56	392,534	1,000	67.73	67,727
1868	7,051	52.54	370,469	1,057	50.70	59,932
1869	7,304	60.48	441,724	1,130	78.57	88,788
1870	7,633	66.99	511,332	1,245	89.71	111,689
1871	8,054	70.02	563,933	1,305	91.47	119,372
1872	8,441	66.54	561,692	1,360	86.02	116,983
1873	8,767	65.52	574,399	1,419	83.49	118,473
1874	9,055	64.12	580,610	1,485	80.26	119,187
1875	9,333	60.10	560,880	1,548	71.64	110,902
1876	9,606	56.48	542,531	1,608	65.51	105,338
1877	9,910	55.11	546,127	1,674	63.18	105,761
1878	10,230	55.38	566,525	1,746	62.61	109,310
1879	10,574	51.55	545,134	1,816	57.06	103,626
1880	10,903	53.74	585,910	1,878	61.74	115,951
1881	11,187	57.91	647,847	1,912	68.84	131,630
1882	11,444	58.75	672,354	1,928	71.64	138,223
1883	11,794	69.92	824,580	1,975	77.79	153,626
1884	12,215	73.80	901,434	2,047	83.53	170,984
1885	12,700	72.94	926,398	2,102	81.88	172,112
1886	13,276	70.62	937,602	2,162	78.96	170,712
1887	13,821	71.59	989,480	2,213	78.39	173,467
1888	14,490	72.03	1,043,687	2,260	79.06	178,666
1889	15,064	72.39	1,090,454	2,295	78.95	181,191
1890	15,732	69.27	1,089,794	2,322	77.61	180,210
1891	16,329	67.19	1,097,153	2,377	76.93	182,854
1892	16,846	64.56	1,087,578	2,459	74.31	182,737
1893	17,289	60.72	1,049,718	2,550	69.18	176,405
1894	17,709	46.63	825,855	2,632	60.65	159,635
1895	17,849	35.57	634,921	2,708	47.23	127,899
1896	17,876	32.34	578,165	2,782	44.08	122,632
1897	17,803	30.92	550,435	2,836	40.49	114,841
1898	17,698	33.35	590,304	2,918	42.31	123,461
1899	17,728	36.61	648,977	3,012	43.52	131,081
1900	17,856	43.56	777,843	3,139	51.46	161,524
1901	17,955	53.03	952,084	3,190	63.47	202,480
1902	17,968	58.52	1,051,452	3,264	67.23	219,427
1903	18,121	62.27	1,128,470	3,353	71.73	240,524
1904	18,331	67.59	1,238,957	3,465	78.02	270,351
1905	18,491	69.73	1,289,291	3,586	87.06	312,188
1906	18,806	79.77	1,500,114	3,680	97.75	359,719
1907	19,090	92.85	1,772,596	3,814	111.46	425,112
1908	19,444	92.76	1,803,687	3,949	107.81	425,732
1909	19,731	95.13	1,876,920	4,085	108.20	442,014
1910	19,972	107.70	2,150,950	4,239	119.98	508,599
1911	20,418	111.11	2,268,677	4,429	125.73	556,865
1912	20,726	105.58	2,188,308	4,551	120.33	547,625

(cont.)

Appendix (Table 6, continued)

YEAR	HORSES			MULES		
	NUMBER	FARM VALUE		NUMBER	FARM VALUE	
		PER HEAD	TOTAL		PER HEAD	TOTAL
	Thousands	*Dollars*	*1,000 Dollars*	*Thousands*	*Dollars*	*1,000 dollars*
1913	21,008	110.58	2,323,083	4,683	124.10	581,161
1914	21,308	109.27	2,328,261	4,870	123.47	601,282
1915	21,431	103.23	2,212,399	5,062	112.19	567,891
1916	21,334	101.45	2,164,360	5,200	113.78	591,658
1917	21,306	102.64	2,186,809	5,353	118.45	634,073
1918	21,238	103.97	2,208,056	5,485	128.97	707,381
1919	20,922	97.94	2,049,051	5,568	135.58	754,927
1920	20,091	96.45	1,937,859	5,651	148.29	837,990
1921	19,369	84.48	1,636,297	5,768	117.37	676,975
1922	18,764	71.01	1,332,508	5,824	88.99	518,300
1923	18,125	70.49	1,277,649	5,893	86.87	511,919
1924	17,378	65.39	1,136,311	5,907	85.89	507,345
1925	16,651	64.28	1,070,336	5,918	82.91	490,688
1926	16,083	65.31	1,050,367	5,903	81.51	481,153
1927	15,388	63.73	980,645	5,804	74.51	432,434
1928	14,792	66.71	986,783	5,656	79.84	451,550
1929	14,234	69.68	991,869	5,510	82.45	454,300
1930[2]	*13,384*	....	....	*5,354*	....	....
1930	13,742	69.98	961,664	5,382	83.93	451,725
1931	13,195	60.64	800,198	5,273	69.23	365,049
1932	12,664	53.48	677,211	5,148	60.70	312,494
1933	12,291	54.12	665,178	5,046	60.42	304,895
1934	12,052	66.88	805,994	4,945	82.42	407,566
1935[2]	*11,858*	....	....	*4,818*	....	....
1935	11,861	77.05	913,870	4,822	99.34	478,998
1936	11,598	96.73	1,121,851	4,628	120.63	558,253
1937	11,342	99.14	1,124,405	4,460	130.25	580,911
1938	10,995	90.89	999,365	4,250	123.39	524,409
1939	10,629	84.32	896,201	4,163	118.58	493,654
1940[2]	*10,087*	....	....	*3,845*	....	....
1940	10,444	77.30	807,611	4,034	116.00	466,798
1941	10,193	68.20	695,216	3,911	107.00	419,013
1942	9,873	64.70	638,296	3,782	107.00	405,980
1943	9,605	79.80	766,384	3,626	127.00	462,201
1944	9,192	78.60	722,782	3,421	143.00	490,371
1945[2]	*8,499*	....	....	*3,130*	....	....
1945	8,715	64.90	565,363	3,235	134.00	433,776
1946	8,081	57.50	464,453	3.027	133.00	403,000
1947	7,340	59.30	435,405	2,789	141.00	392,197
1948	6,704	55.70	373,663	2,575	133.00	341,764
1949	6,096	52.50	320,184	2,402	116.00	279,635
1950[2]	*5,402*	....	....	*2,202*	....	....
1950	5,548	46.00	255,385	2,233	99.10	221,298
1951	4,993	43.50	217,116	2,074	81.60	169,270
1952[3]	4,370	45.80	199,958	1,923	72.80	139,008

1. Including colts.
2. Italic figures are from the census. Census dates: Apr. 1, 1930; Jan. 1, 1935; Apr. 1, 1940; Jan. 1, 1945; Apr. 1, 1950.
3. Preliminary.

Source: U.S. Department of Agriculture, *Agricultural Statistics* 1952. Washington, D.C., 455–456.

Table 7—Estimated Age Distribution of Horses and Mules on Farms and Number of Animals Remaining per 100 Colts Raised, United States, Jan. 1, 1943

AGE. JAN. 1, 1943 (YEARS)	HORSES AND MULES ON FARMS JAN. 1, 1943		TOTAL COLT CROP FROM WHICH ANIMALS OF SPECIFIED AGE WERE DERIVED[1]	HORSES AND MULES ON FARMS JAN. 1, 1943, PER 100 COLTS RAISED
	Thousands	*Percent*	*Thousands*	*Number*
Less than 3	1,846	13.8	1,882	98.0
3-5	2,181	16.3	2,306	94.5
6-10	2,890	21.6	3,175	91.0
11-15	2,382	17.8	2,815	84.6
16-20	1,886	14.1	4,013	47.0
21-25	1,378	10.3	7,971	17.3
Over 25	816	6.1	15,987	5.1

1. Animals less than 3 years of age include the colt crops of 1940-42 inclusive; the 3-5 year group includes the 1937-39 colt crops; the 6-10 year group the 1932-36 colt crops; the 11-15 year group the 1927-31 colt crops; the 16-20 year group the 1922-26 colt crops; the 21-25 year group the 1917-21 colt crops, and the group over 25 years of age the 1910-1916 colt crops. Few animals now alive were foaled prior to 1910.

Table 8—Influence of Age on Annual Use of Work Animals, by State Groups, 1942

STATE GROUP[1]	AVERAGE TIME WORKED IN 1942 BY ANIMALS OF SPECIFIED AGE								
	ALL WORK ANIMALS	3 YRS OLD	4 YRS OLD	5 YRS OLD	6–10 YRS OLD	11–15 YRS OLD	16–20 YRS OLD	21–25 YRS OLD	25 YRS AND OVER
	Hours	Hours	Hours	Hours	Hours	Hours	Hours	Hours	Hours
Northeast	950	460	930	1,025	1,090	980	920	710	495
Corn Belt	765	390	660	820	900	860	735	580	415
Lake States	860	360	700	990	1,015	930	750	645	465
Great Plains	685	290	560	740	830	760	700	480	245
Appalachian	910	375	855	1,030	990	960	865	755	345
Southeast	1,100	835	1,145	1,135	1,190	1,145	1,025	890	670
Delta	1,050	745	1,050	1,135	1,135	1,080	1,000	925	630
Oklahoma-Texas	765	550	810	820	850	790	710	580	530
Mountain	685	460	685	780	810	685	610	555	210
Pacific	565	210	475	530	745	615	540	465	215
United States	835	475	750	900	970	910	785	640	420

1. Northeast includes Maine, New Hampshire, Vermont, Massachusetts, Rhode Island, Connecticut, New York, New Jersey, Pennsylvania, Delaware, and Maryland. Corn Belt includes Ohio, Indiana, Illinois, Iowa, and Missouri. Lake States includes Michigan, Wisconsin, and Minnesota. Great Plains includes North Dakota, South Dakota, Nebraska, and Kansas. Appalachian includes West Virginia, Kentucky, and Tennessee. Southeast includes Virginia, North Carolina, South Carolina, Georgia, Florida, and Alabama. Delta includes Mississippi, Arkansas, and Louisiana. Mountain includes Montana, Idaho, Wyoming, Colorado, New Mexico, Arizona, Utah, and Nevada. Pacific includes Washington, Oregon, and California.

Source: U.S. Department of Agriculture, *Agricultural Statistics* 1944. 439.

Table 9—Size of Farms and Area of Cropland Harvested in 1942, Number of Farm Tractors and Horses and Mules 3 Years Old and Over, by Specified Farm Types and State Groups

STATE GROUP[1]	TOTAL NUMBER OF REPORTS FOR:		TRACTOR FARMS REPORTING WORK STOCK					HORSE AND/OR MULE FARMS			
	TRACTOR FARMS	HORSE FARMS	SIZE OF FARM IN 1942	CROPLAND HARVESTED PER FARM IN 1942	TRACTORS PER FARM, JAN. 1, 1943	WORK ANIMALS PER FARM, JAN. 1, 1943	ANIMALS DISPLACED PER FARM TRACTOR[2]	SIZE OF FARM IN 1942	CROPLAND HARVESTED PER FARM, 1942	WORK ANIMALS PER FARM, JAN. 1, 1943	CROPLAND HARVESTED PER HEAD OF WORK STOCK
			Acres	Acres	Number	Number	Number	Acres	Acres	Number	Acres
Northeast	1,120	748	197	98	1.20	2.7	1.8	127	50	2.5	20.0
Corn Belt	2,676	1,071	237	152	1.25	3.1	3.4	152	68	3.3	20.6
Lake States	1,441	657	219	132	1.19	3.1	2.3	139	68	3.0	22.7
Great Plains	1,752	357	755	340	1.33	4.4	5.3	481	149	5.0	29.8
Appalachian	379	1,206	292	113	1.09	3.8	2.2	158	51	2.8	18.2
Southeast	528	1,454	381	143	1.18	4.1	2.1	145	53	2.4	21.7
Delta	214	903	600	309	1.80	10.5	5.8	130	49	3.1	15.8
Oklahoma-Texas	542	486	894	294	1.31	3.8	8.6	187	72	3.7	19.5
Mountain	698	412	1,709	265	1.28	5.5	7.3	753	96	5.4	17.8
Pacific	672	412	920	297	1.43	3.8	10.6	270	55	3.5	15.7
United States	10,022	7,706	522	202	1.27	3.8	4.4	139	63	3.2	19.7

1. Northeast includes Maine, New Hampshire, Vermont, Massachusetts, Rhode Island, Connecticut, New York, New Jersey, Pennsylvania, Delaware, and Maryland. Corn Belt includes Ohio, Indiana, Illinois, Iowa, and Missouri. Lake States includes Michigan, Wisconsin, and Minnesota. Great Plains includes North Dakota, South Dakota, Nebraska, and Kansas. Appalachian includes West Virginia, Kentucky, and Tennessee. Southeast includes Virginia, North Carolina, South Carolina, Georgia, Florida, and Alabama. Delta includes Mississippi, Arkansas, and Louisiana. Mountain includes Montana, Idaho, Wyoming, Colorado, New Mexico, Arizona, Utah, and Nevada. Pacific includes Washington, Oregon, and California.

2. It was assumed that, if there were no tractors, the number of work stock needed in each State group would be the same per 100 acres of cropland as for horse farm. From the calculated number of needed work stock on tractor farms, the actual number of work stock on tractor farms was deducted and this figure, divided by the average number of tractors, gives the work animals displaced per tractor. Bureau of Agricultural Economics

Source: U.S. Department of Agriculture, Agricultural Statistics 1944.438.

Table 10—U.S. Farm Horses, Percent Under One Year Old and Price per Head, 1900–1955

Year	Price per Head in Dollars	Percent Under One Year Old	Year	Price per Head in Dollars	Percent Under One Year Old
1900	43.56	7.19	1928	66.71	3.53
1901	53.03		1929	69.68	3.53
1902	58.52		1930	69.98	3.60
1903	62.27		1931	60.64	3.43
1904	67.59		1932	53.48	3.26
1905	69.73		1933	54.12	3.39
1906	79.77		1934	66.88	4.11
1907	92.85		1935	77.05	5.14
1908	92.76		1936	96.73	5.65
1909	95.13		1937	99.14	6.03
1910	107.70	8.73	1938	90.89	6.42
1911	111.11		1939	84.32	5.96
1912	105.58		1940	77.30	5.94
1913	110.58		1941	68.20	5.80
1914	109.27		1942	64.70	5.09
1915	103.23		1943	79.80	4.19
1916	101.45		1944	78.60	3.96
1917	102.64		1945	64.90	3.59
1918	103.97		1946	57.50	3.02
1919	97.94		1947	59.30	2.89
1920	96.45	6.06	1948	55.70	2.86
1921	84.48	5.06	1949	52.50	2.89
1922	71.01	4.35	1950	46.00	2.72
1923	70.49	3.87	1951	43.50	2.58
1924	65.39	3.58	1952	45.80	2.52
1925	64.28	3.40	1953		2.66
1926	65.31	3.49	1954		2.71
1927	63.73	3.56	1955		2.80

Data based on Tables 5 and 6.

Chapter Notes

Introduction

1. Clay McShane, and Joel A. Tarr, *The Horse in the City, Living Machines in the Nineteenth Century* (Baltimore: The Johns Hopkins Press, 2007), 17.
2. *Ibid.*, 137.
3. *Ibid.*, 82.
4. *Ibid.*, 31–34; Thomas J. Campanella, *Cities from the Sky, an Aerial Portrait of America* (New York: Princeton Architectural, 2001) 45; *Hagstrom's Atlas and Official Postal Guide of the City of New York Five Boroughs*, 5th ed. (New York: Hagstrom Company, 1947), 24.
5. Kate Ascher, *The Works, Anatomy of a City* (New York: Penguin, 2005), 285.
6. Clarke F. Ansly, ed., "Pony Express," in *The Columbia Encyclopedia, in One Volume* (Morningside Heights, NY: Columbia University Press, 1942).
7. McShane and Tarr, *Horse in the City*, 169.
8. Ansly, "Automobile and Internal Combustion Engine" in *Columbia Encyclopedia*.

Chapter One

1. The American Battle Monuments Commission, *A Guide to the American Battle Fields in Europe* (Washington, D.C.: United States Government Printing Office, 1927), 1–2.
2. *The Breeder's Gazette: A Weekly Publication Devoted to the Interests of Live-Stock Breeders*, April 11, 1912, 892.
3. William Harding Carter, "The Story of the Horse, the Development of Man's Companion in War Camp, on Farm, in the Marts of Trade, and in the Field of Sport," in *The National Geographic Magazine*, 44, No. 5 (1923): 553.
4. W. S. Dunn, "Causes and Effects," *Breeder's Gazette*, September 1921, 372.
5. *Breeder's Gazette*, November 12, 1914. 832.
6. J.M. Brereton, *The Horse in War* (New York: Arco, 1976), 118.
7. *Breeder's Gazette*, October 23, 1919, 854.
8. United States Department of Agriculture *Yearbook 1920* (Washington: Government Printing Office, 1921). 701–717, Table 229.
9. Irving Parmeter, "The Horse in War Today and Yesterday," *Current History*, June 1928, 451.
10. *Breeder's Gazette*, August 20, 1914, 314.
11. *Breeder's Gazette*, October 22, 1914, 692.
12. John S. Cooper, "American Horses in the European War," *Breeder's Gazette*, December 16, 1915, 1112, 1140, 1142.
13. J'Nell L. Pate, *Livestock Legacy, the Fort Worth Stockyards, 1887–1987* (College Station, TX: Texas A & M University Press, 1988), 99.
14. Bureau of Agricultural Economics, "Horses, Mules, and Motor Vehicles," *United States Department of Agriculture Statistical Bulletin No. 5* (Washington, D.C.: Government Printing Office, January 1925) 21–22, Table 28.
15. *Ibid.*, 25–26, Table 30.
16. *Breeder's Gazette*, February 7, 1918.
17. *New York Times*, June 12, 1915, 6:7.
18. *Ibid.*, December 18, 1915, I: 3, December 9, 1915, II, 5:2.
19. *Ibid.*, November 11, 1914, 1:2.
20. *Ibid.*, March 15, 1916, 3:2, 5.
21. Parmeter, "Horse in War," 451.
22. Robert Koenig, *The Fourth Horseman: One Man's Secret Mission to Wage the Great War in America* (New York: Public Affairs/Perseus Books Group, 2006), 21–35, 70, 71, 74, 81, 84, 96, 97, 99, 100, 107, 109, 113, 114, 116, 148, 164, 168, 173, 264, 283–286.
23. W.J. Ratigan, "Taking Horses to War," *Breeder's Gazette*, August 5, 1915, 196.
24. Lyn Macdonald, *1914* (London: Guild Publishing Company, 1987) 63.
25. "Britain's Horses for the War," *Breeder's Gazette*, January 9, 1919. 66.
26. David E. Buckingham, "The U.S. Army Against the Allies in Buying Its Animals," *Journal of the American Veterinary Medical Asso-

ciation, February 1917, Washington, D.C., 3, No. 6, 698–699.

27. *New York Times*, April 6, 1917, 1.

28. Christina Schaefer, *The Great War, a Guide to the Service Records of All the World's Fighting Men and Volunteers* (Baltimore: Genealogical, 1998), 47, 53, 65.

29. *New York Times*, April 29, 1917. 1.

30. Christina Schaefer, *A Guide to the Service Records*, 123, 126.

31. *Report of the Quartermaster General to the Secretary of War, Fiscal Year 1917* (Washington D.C.: Government Printing Office, 1917), 90, https://catalog.hathitrust.org/Record/008607233; George H. Conn, "Buying Horses and Mules for the Army," *Breeder's Gazette*, February 28, 1918, 428.

32. Conn, "Buying Horses and Mules," 428–429.

33. John S. Fair, "The Supply of Animals for the Army," lecture, Quartermaster Reserve Corps, Washington, D.C., July 3, 1917 (Washington D.C.: Government Printing Office, 1917), 7.

34. *Report of the Quartermaster General to the Secretary of War, Fiscal Year 1916* (Washington D.C.: Government Printing Office, 1916), 62, https://catalog.hathitrust.org/Record/008607233; Fair, "The Supply of Animals," 6.

35. *Report of the Quartermaster General, U.S. Army, to the Secretary of War, 1919* (Washington D.C.: Government Printing Office, 1920), 44–46, https://catalog.hathitrust.org/Record/002138437.

36. Conn, "Buying Horses and Mules," 428.

37. "Army Horse Business," *Breeder's Gazette*, February 7, 1918, 258.

38. *Regulations Issued by the Quartermaster General Governing the Purchase and Inspection of Animals for the Army* (Washington D.C.: Government Printing Office, 1917), 2, 8.

39. *Annual Report of the Quartermaster General, Fiscal Year 1915* (Washington D.C.: Government Printing Office, 1915), 62, https://catalog.hathitrust.org/Record/008607233.

40. Wayne Dinsmore, "Army Horse and Mule Requirements," *Breeder's Gazette*, May 3, 1917. 924.

41. W. S. Anderson, "Selling Army Horses Directly," *Breeder's Gazette*, May 24, 1917, 1071.

42. "Government Attitude Towards Horse Buying," *Breeder's Gazette*, August 16, 1917, 211.

43. Conn, "Buying Horses and Mules," 428–429.

44. Fair, "The Supply of Animals," 30–31.

45. "New Horse Buying Policy," *Breeder's Gazette*, November 22, 1917, 937.

46. Anderson, "Selling Army Horses Directly," *Breeder's Gazette*, December 27, 1917, 1267.

47. Conn, "Buying Horses and Mules," *Breeder's Gazette*, February 28, 1918, 429.

48. *Report of the Quartermaster General, 1919*, 44.

49. Wayne Dinsmore, "Military Exports of Horses and Mules," *Breeder's Gazette*, April 25, 1918, 865.

50. "Army Conservation of Fertility," *Breeder's Gazette*, May 16, 1918, 1037.

51. Allan T. Heninger, *Present Sabres: A Popular History of the United States Horse Cavalry* (Tucson: Excalibur, 2002), 121.

52. John J. Pershing, "Final Report to the Secretary of War," Paris, September 1, 1919, in *United States Army in the World War, 1917-1919: Reports of the Commander-In-Chief, AEF, Staff Sections and Services* (Washington, D.C.: Center of Military History, United States Army, 1991), Vol. 12, 17, http://www.history.army.mil/html/books/023/23-18/.

53. Charles H. Grasty, "Allies See Victory Only in Defeat of U-Boats, and Look to America for Utmost Efforts," *New York Times*, March 17, 1918.

54. Charles H. Grasty, "U-Boat Sinkings Cut to 62,000 Tons in a Week," *New York Times*, September 24, 1917.

55. "Gain 100,000 Tons a Month in Ships," *New York Times*, July 31, 1918.

56. Pershing, "Final Report to the Secretary of War," 71.

57. *Ibid.*, 24.

58. Maurice F. De Barneville, "The Remount Service in the A.E.F.," *The Cavalry Journal*, 30, No. 123 (1921): 137.

59. *New York Times*, June 28, 1917.

60. John J. Pershing, *My Experience in the World War* (New York: Frederick A. Stokes, 1931), Vol. 1, 91–92.

61. *Ibid.*, Vol. 2, 58; De Barneville, "Remount Service," 138.

62. Pershing, *My Experience in the World War*, Vol. 2, 130; De Barneville, "The Remount Service," 138.

63. *Report of the Quartermaster-General, 1919*, 45.

64. Pershing, *My Experience in the World War*, Vol. 2, 58.

65. De Barneville, "Remount Service," 138.

66. Pershing, *My Experience in the World War*, Vol. 2, 130.

67. Pershing, *My Experience in the World War*, Vol. 2, 131; Pershing, "Final Report to the Secretary of War," 184; De Barneville, "Remount Service," 138.

68. De Barneville, "Remount Service," 138. Pershing, *My Experience in the World War*, Vol. 2, 169–170.

69. Pershing, "Final Report to the Secretary of War," 184.
70. *United States Army in the World War, 1917–1919,* Vol. 12, 105, 110, 186–187.
71. Pershing, "Final Report to the Secretary of War," 184–185; De Barneville, "The Remount Service," 138–139.
72. Pershing, "Final Report to the Secretary of War," 185.
73. *Ibid.*

Chapter Two

1. "Work Done by 1,500,000 Horses in France During the War," *Scientific American,* No. 2250, February 15, 1919, 105.
2. John Keegan, *An Illustrated History of the First World War* (New York: Alfred A. Knopf, 2001), 68.
3. Arthur Cotterell, *Chariot: From Chariot to Tank. the Astounding Rise and Fall of the World's First War Machine* (Woodstock, NY: Overlook, 2005), 39–70.
4. J. Edward Chamberlin, *Horse: How the Horse Has Shaped Civilizations* (Blue Ridge, NY: United Tribes Media, 2006), 171.
5. *The Photographic History of the Civil War. Complete and Unabridged. Volume 2: The Cavalry; Decisive Battles* (Secaucus, NJ: Blue and Grey Press, 1987). 9, 38.
6. Lyn Macdonald, *Somme* (London: Michael Joseph, 1983), 110.
7. Joseph Jobe, ed., *Guns: An Illustrated History of Artillery* (New York: Crescent Books, 1974), 161.
8. *Ibid.,* 104.
9. Chamberlin, *Horse,* 172–175; John Ellis, *Cavalry: The History of Mounted Warfare* (Barnsley, UK: Pen & Sword, 2004), 144.
10. Jobe, *Guns,* 176.
11. Theo F. Rodenbough, "Cavalry of the Civil War: Its Evolution and Influence" in *Photographic History of the Civil War,* Vol. 2, 34.
12. Michael J. Varhola, *Everyday Life During the Civil War: A Guide for Writers, Students and Historians.* (Cincinnati, OH: Writer's Digest, 1999), 138.
13. Philip J. Haythornthwaite, *A Photohistory of World War One* (London: Arms and Armour, 1995), photo No. 65, 1917.
14. George C. Marshall, *Memoirs of My Services in the World War, 1917–1918,* ed. James L. Collins, Jr. (Boston: Houghton Mifflin Company, 1976), 183–184.
15. Heniger, *Present Sabers,* 129.
16. Chauncey Baker, "Baker Board Report" in *United States Army in the World War, 1917–1919: Organization of the American Expeditionary Force* (Washington, D.C.: Center of Military History, United States Army, 1988). Vol. 1, 81.
17. Macdonald, *1914,* 83–90.
18. F. Stansbury Haydon, *Aeronautics in the Union and Confederate Armies: With a Survey of Military Aeronautics Prior to 1861* (Cranbury, NJ: Scholar's Bookshelf, 2006), 195.
19. John Christopher, *Balloons at War, Gasbags, Flying Bombs & Cold War Secrets* (Stroud, UK: Tempus, 2005), 65.
20. Neil Hanson, *Unknown Soldiers. the Story of the Missing in the First World War* (New York: Alfred A. Knopf, 2006), 70.
21. John Buchan, *A History of the First World War,* ed. Victor Neuburg (Moffat, UK: Lochar, 1991), 43–44, 77.
22. Nicholas Watkins, *The Western Front from the Air* (Stroud, UK: Sutton, 2000), 20.
23. Ernst Volbehr, *Das Gesicht Der Westfront. Ein Kriegsdocument Und Erinnerungbuch* (Potsdam: Athenaion, 1932).
24. Buchan, *History of the First World War,* 42.
25. John Terraine, *To Win a War: 1918 the Year of Victory* (Garden City, NY: Doubleday, 1981), 34.
26. Terraine, *To Win a War,* 24.
27. Haythornthwaite, *Photohistory of World War One,* photo No. 22, 1917.
28. Terraine, *To Win a War,* 169–171.
29. *Ibid.,* 171.
30. Lyn Macdonald, *1915: The Death of Innocence,* New York: Henry Holt, 1994), 78.
31. Anthony Livesey, *The Historical Atlas of World War I* (New York: Henry Holt, 1994), 15.
32. Pershing, "Final Report to the Secretary of War," Vol. 12, 19.
33. Baker, "Baker Board Report," Vol. 1, 60.
34. Pershing, "Final Report to the Secretary of War," Vol. 12, 51.
35. *Ibid.,* 19.
36. *Ibid.,* 56–57.
37. George M. Rommel (speech recorded in *Minutes of the Organization Meeting of the Horse Publicity Association of America* held at the Pennsylvania Hotel, New York, October 30–31, 1919, New York: Harris & Stacy Stenographic Reporters), 214.
38. R.C. Craven, "The Red Star and the War Horse," *Breeder's Gazette,* July 18, 1918, 82.
39. [Ray A. Edwards], *Over There: The Story of America's First Great Overseas Crusade,* by Frank Freidel (Short Hills, NJ: Burford Books, 1964), 127.
40. Marshall, *Memoirs of My Services,* 85–86.
41. *Breeder's Gazette,* May 16, 1918, 1035.
42. Marshall, *Memoirs of My Services,* 85.
43. "General Orders: No. 66" in *The United*

States Army in the World War, 1917–1919: General Orders, GHQ, AEF (Washington, D.C.: Center of Military History, United States Army, 1992), Vol. 16, 300, http://www.history.army.mil/html/books/023/23-22/.

44. Paul Fussell, *The Great War and Modern Memory* (London: Oxford University Press, 1977), 41, 81, 125.

45. Marshall, *Memoirs of My Services*, 113.

46. Baker, "Baker Board Report," Vol. 1, 57.

47. "Bulletin No. 9," *The United States Army in the World War, 1917–1919: Bulletins, GHQ, AEF* (Washington, D.C.: Center of Military History, United States Army, 1992), Vol. 17, 11–12, http://www.history.army.mil/html/books/023/23-23/index.html.

48. Pershing, "Final Report to the Secretary of War," Vol. 12, 206–207.

49. George H. Allen, et al., *The Great War, Fifth Volume: The Triumph of Democracy* (Philadelphia: George Barrie's Sons, 1921), 31–35.

50. Edward N. Wentworth, "Artillery Horse Routine," *Breeder's Gazette*, October 4, 1917, 554.

51. "Four-Footed Experts in War," *Literary Digest*, 1, No. 5 (1915): 213.

52. Spencer C. Tucker, *The Great War, 1914–1918* (Bloomington, IN: Indiana University Press, 1998), 38.

53. *Photographic History of the Civil War. Volume 2*, 216–217.

54. Baker, "Baker Board Report," Vol. 1, 62.

55. Baker, "Baker Board Report," Vol. 1, 87.

56. Freidel, *Over There*, 125.

57. Tucker, *The Great War*, 62.

58. *Ibid.*, 128.

59. Albert Palazzo, *Seeking Victory on the Western Front: The British Army and Chemical Warfare in World War I* (Lincoln, NE: University of Nebraska Press, 2002), 152.

60. Haythornthwaite, *Photohistory of World War One*, photo No. 10, 1917.

61. Buchan, *History of the First World War*, 45.

62. *Photographic History of the Civil War. Volume 2*, 162.

63. Terraine, *To Win a War*, 71.

64. Allen et al., *The Great War, Fifth Volume*, 37.

65. Samuel L. A. Marshall, and Edmund O. Stillman, *The American Heritage History of World War I*, eds. Alvin M. Josephy, Jr., and Joseph L. Gardner (New York: American Heritage, 1964), 232.

66. *Ibid.*, 231.

67. *The Great War, Fifth Volume*, op. cit. 276.

68. Bill Yenne, *Tommy Gun: How General Thompson's Submachine Gun Wrote History* (New York: Thomas Dunne Books, 2009), 29, 44.

69. Allen et al., *The Great War, Fifth Volume*, 47.

70. Marshall and Stillman, *American Heritage History of World War I*, 269.

71. Terraine, *To Win a War*, 24–25.

72. Alexander Woolcott, "The Tanks," in *The Command Is Forward: Tales of the A.E.F. Battlefields as They Appeared in the Stars and Stripes* (New York: Century, 1919), 158.

73. Bernard Fitzsimons, ed., *Tanks & Weapons of World War I* (New York: Beekman House, 1973), 109–121.

74. Allen et al., *The Great War, Fifth Volume*, 319–320.

75. *Ibid.*, 509.

76. *Ibid.*, 36.

77. Fitzimmons, *Tanks & Weapons of World War I*, 88.

78. Terraine, *To Win a War*, 24.

79. Fitzimmons, *Tanks & Weapons of World War I*, 94.

80. Allen et al., *The Great War, Fifth Volume*, 36.

81. Fitzimmons, *Tanks & Weapons of World War I*, 109–121.

82. Dale E. Wilson, *Treat 'Em Rough! The Birth of American Armor, 1917–20* (Novato, CA: Presidio, 1990), 75–82.

83. Marshall, *Memoirs of My Services*, 183.

84. Wilson, *Treat 'Em Rough!* 214–218.

85. Larry H. Addington, *The Patterns of War Since the Eighteenth Century*, 2nd ed. (Bloomington, IN: Indiana University Press, 1994), 5–6, 39.

86. "General Orders: No. 34," *United States Army in the World War, 1917–1919*, Vol. 16, 233.

87. Chamberlin, *Horse*, 27.

88. "General Orders: No. 65," *United States Army in the World War, 1917–1919*, Vol. 16, 297.

89. Pershing, *My Experience in the World War*, Vol. 2, 130.

90. De Barneville, "Remount Service," 139.

91. *United States Army in the World War, 1917–1919*, Vol. 12, 189.

92. Marshall, *Memoirs*, op. cit. 53.

93. "Bulletin No. 93," *United States Army in the World War, 1917–1919*, Vol. 17, 135–136.

94. "General Order No. 34," *United States Army in the World War, 1917–1919*, Vol. 16, 235; "Bulletin No. 55," *United States Army in the World War, 1917–1919*, Vol. 17, 84–86.

95. "Bulletin No. 66," *United States Army in the World War, 1917–1919*, Vol. 17, 101–102; "Bulletin No. 5," *United States Army in the World War, 1917–1919*, Vol. 17, 162.

96. *Breeder's Gazette*, February 7, 1918, 258.

97. *Ibid.*, April 3, 1919, 786.

98. *Ibid.*, February 7, 1918, 258.

99. *Ibid.*, August 22, 1918, 267; George H. Conn, "Auxiliary Remount Depots of the Army," Camp Greene, NC.

100. Ratigan, "Taking Horses to War," 196.

Notes—Chapter Two

101. "Bulletin No. 8," United *States Army in the World War, 1917–1919*, Vol. 17, 35–37.
102. "Remounts," *United States Army in the World War, 1917–1919*, Vol. 12. 188.
103. "The Indispensable War Horse," *Breeder's Gazette*, December 8, 1917, 1036.
104. E.H. Townsend, *Punch or the London Charivari*, February 9, 1916, 111, fig.
105. "Bulletin No. 104," *United States Army in the World War, 1917–1919*, Vol. 17, 146.
106. *Ibid.*, 154.
107. *United States Army in the World War, 1917–1919*, Vol. 12, 188–189.
108. *United States Army in the World War, 1917–1919*, Vol. 12, 189.
109. Alfred Gradenwitz, "A Horses' Hospital: Work of the German Army Veterinary Surgeons," *Scientific American*, 114, No. 5 (1916): 126.
110. Brereton, *The Horse in War*, 132.
111. *Breeder's Gazette*, January 31, 1918, 205.
112. *Ibid.*, July 18, 1918, 82.
113. Koenig, *The Fourth Horseman*, 296.
114. "Work of the Blue Cross on the Battle Front," *Literary Digest*, 55, No. 20 (1917): 84.
115. *Ibid.*, "The Horse's Gallant Part in the War," 59, no.8 (1918): 44.
116. *Ibid.*, "Work of the Blue Cross on the Battle Front," 55, No. 20 (1917): 82, 84, 86.
117. R.C. Craven, "The Red Star and the War Horse," *Breeder's Gazette*, July 18, 1918, 82–83.
118. *Ibid.*, 83.
119. *Ibid.*, "The Red Star," August 30, 1917, 283.
120. *Ibid.*, "The Indispensable War Horse," December 6, 1917, 1036.
121. *Ibid.*, "The Red Star," August 30, 1917, 283.
122. Brereton, *The Horse in War*, 132.
123. Juliet Clutton-Brock, *Horse Power: A History of the Horse and Donkey in Human Society* (Cambridge, MA: Harvard University Press, 1992), 164.
124. *United States Army in the World War, 1917–1919*, Vol. 16, 78–80, 382–384. 396–398.
125. De Barneville, "Remount Service," 130.
126. *The United States Army in the World War, 1917–1919: Organization of the American Expeditionary Forces* (Washington, D.C.: Center of Military History, United States Army, 1992), Vol. 1, 324, table 109.
127. *Breeder's Gazette*, January 31, 1918, 205.
128. Freidel, *Over There*, 194.
129. *United States Army in the World War, 1917–1919*, Vol. 12. 188.
130. *United States Army in the World War, 1917–1919*, Vol. 17, 46, 149.
131. De Barneville, "Remount Service," 136.
132. Rommel, *Minutes of the Organization Meeting of the Horse Publicity*, 214.
133. Gradenwitz, "A Horses' Hospital," 126, 132.
134. *Ibid.*, 68, 80–81.
135. *Ibid.*, 159–160.
136. *Ibid.*, 111.
137. *Ibid.*, 260.
138. *Ibid.*, 371.
139. *Ibid.*, 231–232.
140. *Ibid.*, 232.
141. *Ibid.*, 234–235.
142. Pershing, *My Experience in the World War*, Vol. 2, 141.
143. Freidel, *Over There*, 144–145.
144. Osborne De Varila, *The First Shot for Liberty, the Story of an American Who Went Over with the First Expeditionary Force and Served His Country at the Front* (Philadelphia: John C. Winston, 1918, 50–51.
145. Terraine, *To Win a War*, 181.
146. Marshall, *Memoirs of My Services*, 77–78.
147. Freidel, *Over There*, 106.
148. Marshall, *Memoirs of My Services*, 192.
149. Marshall, *Memoirs of My Services*, 182.
150. *My Experience in the World War*, Vol. 2, 380.
151. Woolcott, "The Final Smash," in *The Command Is Forward*, 179.
152. *United States Army in the World War, 1917–1919*, Vol. 12, 185, 191.
153. *Ibid.*, 190.
154. Brereton, *The Horse in War*, 126–127.
155. *United States Army in the World War, 1917–1919*, Vol. 12, 190–191.
156. Koenig, *The Fourth Horseman*, 293–294.
157. *Breeder's Gazette*, January 9, 1919, 66.
158. "Bulletin No. 33: Quarantine Regulations for Private Mounts to Be Returned to the United States," *United States Army in the World War, 1917–1919*, Vol. 17, 253–255.
159. *United States Army in the World War, 1917–1919*, Vol. 12, 190–191; De Barneville, "Remount Service," 142–143.
160. *Breeder's Gazette*, January 9, 1919, 66.
161. *Ibid.*
162. *Ibid.*, January 23, 1919, 169.
163. *Report of the Quartermaster General, 1919*, 48.
164. *Report of the Quartermaster General, U.S. Army, to the Secretary of War, 1920* (Washington D.C.: Government Printing Office, 1920), 50, https://catalog.hathitrust.org/Record/002138537.
165. *Report of the Quartermaster General, 1919*, 47–48.
166. *Ibid.*
167. *Report of the Quartermaster General, 1920*, 55.
168. *Ibid.*, 57.

169. *Report of the Quartermaster General, 1919*, 45.
170. *United States Army in the World War, 1917-1919*, Vol. 12, 185.
171. *Report of the Quartermaster General, 1920*, 55, 57.
172. George E. Wentworth, "Losses of Army Horses," *Breeder's Gazette*, April 3, 1919, 786.
173. *Breeder's Gazette*, February 12, 1920, 385; Anna L. Waller, "Horses and Mules and National Defense" (Fort Lee, VA: Office of the Quartermaster General, 1958), 45, http://www.qmfound.com/horse.htm.
174. Waller, *Horses and Mules and National Defense*, 5, 8, 31.
175. *Ibid.*, 10, 16, 19.
176. *Ibid.*, 24, 27.
177. Emmett M. Essin, *Shavetails & Bell Sharps: The History of the U.S. Army Mule* (Lincoln, NE: University of Nebraska Press, 1997), 166-167.
178. *Ibid.*, p. 167.
179. *Ibid.*, 162.
180. *Ibid.*, 177.
181. *Ibid.*, 180-181.
182. Warren Unna, "'Last Roundup' Comes for Theater Animals: Horses and Mules Played Key Role in Combat Action," *India-Burma Theater Roundup*, 4, No. 27, March 14, 1946, http://www.cbi-theater.com/roundup/roundup0314 46.html.
183. Waller, Horses and Mules and National Defense, 31.
184. Norbert Ehrenfreund, communication to the author, October 15, 2012.

Chapter Three

1. M.G. Lay, *Ways of the World: A History of the World's Roads and of the Vehicles That Used Them* (New Brunswick, NJ: Rutgers University Press, 1992), 28; Pierre Paul Grasse, *Larousse Encyclopedia of the Animal World* (New York: Larousse, 1975), 557.
2. Lay, *Ways of the World*, 28.
3. Arthur Cottrell, *Chariot: From Chariot to Tank, the Astounding Rise and Fall of the World's First War Machine* (Woodstock, NY: Overlook Press, 2005), 41-46.
4. *Ibid.*, 296.
5. Lay, *Ways of the World*, 29.
6. *Ibid.*, 145.
7. *Ibid.*, 146.
8. *Ibid.*, 137.
9. *Ibid.*, 55-56.
10. *Ibid.*, 69-70.
11. *Ibid.*, 74-75.
12. *Ibid.*, 77.
13. *Ibid.*, 77.
14. *Ibid.*, 81.
15. *Ibid.*, 77.
16. *Ibid.*, 242.
17. *Ibid.*, 209.
18. *Ibid.*, 214-215.
19. *Ibid.*, 216.
20. *Ibid.*, 217-218.
21. *Ibid.*, 219.
22. *Ibid.*, 231.
23. *Ibid.*, 217.
24. *Ibid.*, 203.
25. *Ibid.*, 85.
26. *Ibid.*, 87.
27. *Ibid.*, 224.
28. *Ibid.*, 225.
29. *Ibid.*, 227.
30. *Ibid.*, 228.
31. *Ibid.*, 89.
32. *Ibid.*, 29, 32.
33. *Ibid.*, 33.
34. *Ibid.*, 34.
35. *Ibid.*, 39.
36. June Kinoshita, and Nicholas Palevsky, *Gateway to Japan*, rev. ed. (Tokyo: Kodansha International, 1992), 54.
37. Hope Ryden, *America's Last Wild Horses, the Classic Study of the Mustangs—Their Pivotal Role in the History of the West, Their Return to the Wild, and the Ongoing Efforts to Preserve Them* (Guilford, CT: Lyons Press, 2005), 135.
38. Lay, *Ways of the World*, 121-126.
39. *Ibid.*, 124-126.
40. *Ibid.*, 128.
41. *Ibid.*, 129.
42. Henry Charles Moore, *Omnibuses and Cabs: Their Origin and History* (London: Chapman & Hall, 1902), Part I, Chapter III, 3; II, 6; VI, 4, https://archive.org/details/omnibuses cabsthe00mooruoft.
43. *Ibid.*, Part I, Chapter XI, 6.
44. Charles Leehrsen, *Crazy Good: The True Story of Dan Patch, the Most Famous Horse in America* (New York: Simon & Schuster, 2008), 9.
45. *Ibid.*
46. *Ibid.*, 7.
47. The following account is based on Richard Weingroff, "The Rambler Sidebar: Bicycles and Automobiles in Central Park," Highway History Website, Federal Highway Administration, https://www.fhwa.dot.gov/..../stone.cp.pdf, Washington, 2010, 24 pages.
48. *Ibid.*, 23.
49. James J. Flink, *America Adopts the Automobile, 1895-1910* (Cambridge, Massachusetts, and London: MIT Press, 1970), 166.
50. Laws of Maryland, Chapter 518, Section 4, Approved April 12, 1904, 901.
51. Rector R. Seal, Maryland Automobile

History 1900 to 1942 (Chicago, IL: Adams Press, 1985). 162.

52. Laws of Maryland, Chapter 449, Section 138, Approved April 3, 1906, 819.

53. *Breeder's Gazette*, August 16, 1911, signed Manhattan, 250.

54. *Breeder's Gazette*, November 6, 1913, 882.

55. *Breeder's Gazette*, November 20, 1913, signed Manhattan, 992.

56. *Breeder's Gazette*, October 2, 1913, signed Manhattan, 621.

57. Seal, Maryland Automobile History, op. cit. 164.

58. Stephen B. Goddard, *Getting There, the Epic Struggle Between Road and Rail in the American Century* (New York: Basic Books, A Division of HarperCollins Publishers, 1994) 63,104, opposite 192. Communication from Mark Charney, February 8, 2010.

59. Organization Meeting of the Horse Publicity Association of America, op. cit. 3–4.

60. *New York Times*, May 2, 2007, A20.

61. Associated Press, "Horses' Future Uncertain If NYC Carriage Rides End," February 10, 2014, http://www.bostonherald.com/news_opinion/national/northeast/2014/02/horses_future_uncertain_if_nyc_carriage_rides_end.

62. *New York Times*, January 19, 2014, 26.

63. *New York Times*, April 18, 2014, A20.

64. *Columbia Encyclopedia*, New York, 1942, 1675.

65. Larry Caldwell, and Michael Buehler, "Picturing a Networked Nation: Abraham Bradley's Landmark U.S. Postal Maps," in *Portolan*, No. 77, Spring 2010. (Washington, D.C: Journal of the Washington Map Society), 7.

66. Clay McShane, and Joel A. Tarr, *The Horse in the City*, op. cit., 58–59.

67. LeRoy O. King, Jr, *100 Years of Capital Traction, the Story of Streetcars in the Nation's Capital* (Dallas, TX: Taylor Publishing, 1989), 3.

68. Goddard, *Getting There*, op. cit., 65–66.

69. *Ibid.*, 15; McShane and Tarr, *The Horse in the City*, op. cit.,169; and Jonathan V. Levin, "Peru in the Gauano Age," in *The Export Economies, Their Pattern of Development in Historical Perspective* (Cambridge, MA: Harvard University Press, 1960) 116.

70. David M. Morens, and Jeffrey K. Taubenberger, "An Avian Outbreak Associated with Panzootic Equine Influenza In 1872: An Early Example of Highly Pathogenic Avian Influenza?" *Influenza and Other Respiratory Viruses* 2010:4, 373–377.

71. Thomas G. Murnane, "James Law, America's First Veterinary Epidemiologist and the Equine Influenza Epizootic of 1872," presented to the 2008 Annual Meeting of the American Veterinary Medical History Society in New Orleans, LA, July 21, 2008. Long Riders Guild Academic Foundation. Accessed 4/5/16. http://www.lrgaf.org/medical/jameslaw-murnane.htn.

72. Jean Howerton Coady (Louisville) Courier-Journal, "The 1972 Epizootic," January 8, 1977, Editorial Viewpoints, *Journal of the American Veterinary Medical Association,* April 1, 1977, Vol. 170, Issue 7, 668.

73. George W. Hilton, *The Cable Car in America*, Revised Edition (Stanford: Stanford University Press, 1997), 21.

74. *Ibid.*, 14.
75. *Ibid.*, 27–31.
76. *Ibid.*, 14, 32.
77. *Ibid.*, 14.
78. *Ibid.*, 77.
79. *Ibid.*, 79.
80. *Ibid.*, 82.
81. *Ibid.*, 85.
82. *Ibid.*, 51.
83. *Ibid.*, 65.
84. *Ibid.*, 99–100.
85. *Ibid.*, 105.
86. *Ibid.*, 106.
87. *Ibid.*, 107.
88. *Ibid.*, 131–133.
89. *Ibid.*, 137.
90. *Ibid.*, 48.

91. Bern Dibner, *The Founding Fathers of Electrical Science* (Norwalk, CT: Burndy, 1954), 7–10.

92. *Ibid.*, 11–14.

93. Bern Dibner, *Alessandro Volta and the Electric Battery* (New York: Franklin Watts, 1964), 14–15.

94. *Founding Fathers*, op. cit., 17–18.

95. *Founding Fathers*, op. cit., 21–22. ; Volta, op. cit., 64–68.

96. *Founding Fathers*, op. cit., 23.
97. *Founding Fathers*, op. cit., 31.
98. *Founding Fathers*, op. cit., 27.

99. Bern Dibner, *Oersted and the Discovery of Electromagnetism* (Norwalk, CT: Burnby Library, 1961), 16.

100. Oersted, op. cit., 29.

101. *Founding Fathers*, op. cit., 37–38.

102. Frank Rowsome, *Trolley Car Treasury* (New York: Bonanza Books, 1956), 67.

103. *Trolley*, op. cit., 67.
104. *Trolley*, op. cit., 70.
105. *Trolley*, op. cit., 71.
106. *Trolley*, op. cit., 71–72; *Cable Car*, op. cit., 17.
107. *Trolley*, op. cit., 72–78.
108. *Trolley*, op. cit., 77–80.
109. *Trolley*, op. cit., 80.
110. *Trolley*, op. cit., 83–84.
111. *Trolley*, op. cit., 81–89.

112. *Trolley*, op. cit., 17; *The Horse in the City*, op. cit., 172.
113. *Cable Car*, op. cit. 299, 301, 309, 443, and 447.
114. King, *Capital Transit*, op. cit. 19, 27–28, 37.
115. *Ibid.*, 34–35.
116. *Ibid.*, 32.
117. *Ibid.*, 28.
118. *Ibid.*, 35.
119. *Ibid.*, 32.
120. *Cable Car*, op. cit., 361.
121. Louis Waldman, "Lessons in Labor Relations," reprinted from *Labor Lawyer* (New York: E.P. Dutton, 1944), 19–38, in *Autobiographies of American Jews*, compiled with an introduction by Harold U. Ribalow. (Philadelphia: Jewish Publication Society of America, 1968), 334.
122. *Breeder's Gazette*, February 5, 1913, 331.
123. *Breeder's Gazette*, August 8, 1911, 209.
124. *Breeder's Gazette*, June 21, 1917, 1,241.
125. *Stand Up and Fight*, Hollywood, 1939.
126. *Breeder's Gazette*, September 13, 1911, 436.
127. *Breeder's Gazette*, February 15, 1923, 221.
128. *Breeder's Gazette*, September 10, 1913, signed by Manhattan, 457.
129. *Breeder's Gazette*, December 18, 1912, "Motor Trucks Supplementing but Not Supplanting Draft Horses, the Experience of Leading Firms in Chicago and New York," signed Manhattan, 1,334.
130. *Breeder's Gazette*, July 31, 1912, 178 and 1,366.
131. *Breeder's Gazette*, August 2, 1917, 144.
132. *Breeder's Gazette*, October 23, 1919, 854.
133. Goddard, *Getting There*, op. cit., 92.
134. *Breeder's Gazette*, March 12, 1925, 286.
135. Personal communication from Milton Rutstein, April 24, 2010.
136. Personal recollection.
137. *Breeder's Gazette*, April 1, 1920, 935.
138. Organization Meeting of the Horse Publicity Association of America. op. cit., 2, 4, 228, 229.
139. *Breeder's Gazette*, December 16, 1926, 715.
140. *Breeder's Gazette*, May 12, 1921, George E. Wentworth, Cook County, IL, 880.
141. Frank Burnham, *Rendering: The Invisible Industry* (Fallbrook, CA: Aero Publishers, 1998), 9.
142. *Breeder's Gazette*, October 3, 1918, 540.
143. *Breeder's Gazette*, September 25, 1919, 598.
144. Bureau of Agricultural Economics, U.S. Department of Agriculture, *Agricultural Statistics 1952* (Washington, D.C.: 1952), 454.
145. Mitch O'Brian, "How Fire Stations Evolved," *Fire Find*, 2009, accessed 3/16/2016, http://fire-find.com/history-of-fire-stations/.
146. Michael lXYZ, "History of Firefighting," *Thread*, accessed 4/13/2016, http://www.firehouse.com/forums/t126027/.
147. Dennis Smith, *Dennis Smith's History of Firefighting in America, 300 Years of Courage* (New York: Dial Press, 1978), 11.
148. Smith, *History*, 12.
149. David Buckham, Jason Wahl, and Stuart Rose, *Executive's Guide to Solvency II* (Cary, NC: SAS Institute, 2010), 1–4.
150. Andrew Beattie, "The History of Insurance," *Investopedia*, accessed 4/12/2016, http://www.investopedia.com/articles/08/history-of-insurance.asp.
151. "A Brief History of Insurance," *RandMark40*, http://www.randmark40.com/index.php?option=com_content&view=article&id=33.
152. Joy Masoff, *Fire* (New York: Scholastic, 1998), 40.
153. Barry Klein, "The World's First Insurance Company," https://www.irmi.com/articles/expert-commentary/the-worlds-first-insurance-company, accessed 4/12/2016.
154. Alison C. Kay, "The Origins of Fire Insurance (& 'Lusty Able Body'd Firemen')," the *Victorian Vestibule* blog, March 11, 2011, http://www.alisonkay.com/historyjunkey/fire-insurance/, accessed 4/12/2016.
155. *Ibid.*
156. Smith, *History*, 13.
157. Niedner, "What Is Water's Contribution in Putting Out Fires?" October 9, 2013. http:www.niedner.com/en/blog/water-contribution-in-firefighting, accessed 4/14/2016.
158. "Water Supply Systems," *Fire Department*, http://sf-fire.org/water-supply systems.html, accessed 4/14/2016.
159. "The History of the Water Mains in New York City," accessed 4/14/2016, http://www.nyc.gov/html/dep/html/drinking_water/history.shtml.
160. "History and Usage of Fire Hydrants," accessed 4/13/2016, http://www.usd116.org/ums/apple/service/department/history/hydrants.html.
161. *History of the Water Mains in New York City*, op. cit.
162. "A Fire Pro-History of Fire Fighting," accessed 4/13/2016, http://afirepro.com/history.html.
163. Smith, *History*, 4.
164. Smith, *History*, 30. "The History of Water Hoose, Hoase, Hause, or Hose?" *Fire History*, http://firehistory.weebly.com/the-history-of-hoose-hoase-hause-or-hose.html, accessed 2/14/2016.
165. Margaret Simpson, curator, "Horse-

Drawn Fire Engines," (Sydney, Australia: Powerhouse Museum), accessed 2/14/2016, http://www.powerhousemuseum.com/collection/database/?irn=207677.
166. Smith, *History*, 40.
167. History of Water Hoose, op. cit.
168. Smith, *History*, 41.
169. William T. King, *History of the American Steam Engine* (Mineola, NY: Dover, 1896, 2001), 4.
170. *Ibid.*, 5.
171. Hans Halberstadt, *The American Fire Engine* (Osceola, WI: Motorbooks International), 1993, 44.
172. King, *Steam Engine*, 13–17.
173. King, *Steam Engine*, v, vi.
174. King, *Steam Engine*, 69–70.
175. Chicago Fire Department, "History of the Chicago Fire Department," Rev. 6/10/2004, 4. http://www.cityofchicago.org/content/dam/city/depts/cfd/general/PDFs/HistoryOfTheChicagoFireDepartment_1.pdf; King, *Steam Engine*, 17.
176. King, *Steam Engine*, 136.
177. Halberstadt, *American Fire Engine*, 88, 98–99.
178. King, *Steam Engine*, 101–102.
179. King, *Steam Engine*, viii, 148.
180. Smith, *History*, 61.
181. Smith, *History*, 55.
182. "A History of Horses in the Fire Service," *Fire History*, http://firehistory.Weebly.com/a-history-of-horses-in-the-fire-service.html, accessed 4/13/2016.
183. "Why Did Fire Stations Have Spiral Staircases?" *Firefighting History & Traditions-My Firefighter Nation*, http://my.firefighternation.com./group/firefightingmyths, accessed 2/14/2016.
184. A History of Horses, op. cit.
185. Smith, *History*, 61.
186. Smith, *History*, 51.
187. Smith, *History*, 53.
188. Remy Melina, "Why Are Dalmatians the Official Firehouse Dogs?" *Live Science*, May 19, 2011, http://www.livescience.com/33293-dalmatians-official-firehouse-dogs. html, accessed 2/15/2016.
189. "The Horses," http://www.engine3.org/Horses.html.
190. "Lamar No. 1, 1907–2007," City of Lamar, Colorado, Rapid Fire Truck, http://www.ci.lamar.co.us/index.asp?SEC=B45FE11F-D587-48CO-B6BD.
191. "American Lafrance Fire Engine Company, Manufacturers of First Automobile Combination Chemical Engine and Hose Car," *Cambridge Tribune*, January 27, 1923, http://cambridge.dlconsulting.com/cgi-bin/cambridge?a=d&d=Tribune19230127-01.2.117&sr.

192. Halberstadt, *American Fire Engine*, 68–69.
193. Daniel Patrascu, May 29, 2009, http://www.autoevolution.com/news/fire-truck-history-7249html, accessed 4/13/2016.
194. Halberstadt, *American Fire Engine*, 65.
195. "1922: Waterboy, Danny Beg, and the Last Horse-Driven Engine of the New York Fire Department," posted January 24, 2015, http://hatchingcatnyc.com/2015/01/24/last-horse-driven-engine-of -new... accessed 2/15/2016.
196. Chicago Fire Department, History, 12, From Past to Present, 3.
197. Trudy Flores, Sarah Griffith, "Horse-Drawn Fire-Engine, 1913," *The Oregon History Project*, 2002, https://oregonhistoryproject.org/articles/historical-records/horse-drawn-fire-engine-1913/#.WIeLUNBN38s.
198. "1922: Waterboy," op. cit.
199. Photograph by Mark E. Nerenberg.

Chapter Four

1. Jean-Claude Debeir, and Jean-Paul Deleage, and Daniel Hemery, *In the Servitude of Power: Energy and Civilization Through the Ages.* (London and New Jersey: Zed Books, 1986, 1991 [translation]), 25.
2. *Ibid.*, 35.
3. Lynn White, Jr., *Medieval Technology and Social Change* (London: Oxford University Press, 1969), 57, 64–65.
4. *Animal Power, Land and Water Transportation*, Vol. 6 (Danbury, CT: Grolier Educational, 2000), 5.
5. Juliet Clutton-Brock, *Horse Power: A History of the Horse and Donkey in Human Societies* (Cambridge, MA: Harvard University Press, 1992), 154–156; Jan Darnley-Smith, and Elwyn Hartley Edwards, *Horses, Their Role in the History of Man*, based on the original screenplay (London: Power Willow Books, 1987), 162; and *Medieval Technology*, 74.
6. Ronald Blyth, "Akenfield: Portrait of an English Village," in *The Book of Horses*, edited by Fred Urquhart (New York: William Morrow, 1981), 25.
7. *Medieval Technology*, op. cit., 155.
8. *Water and Pasture, Volume 4: Traditional Agriculture, Farming, Food & Biotechnology*, in *Inventions and Inventors* (Danbury, CT: Grolier Educational, 2000), 5–12; and "A Brief Chronology of American Agricultural History," compiled by Dorothy C. Goodwin, under the direction of Paul H. Johnstone, in *Farmers in a Changing World: The Yearbook of Agriculture, 1940.* (Washington, D.C.: U.S. Government Printing Office, 1940), Appendix, 1184.

9. D.J. Smith, *Discovering Horse Drawn Farm Machinery* (Aylesbury, Bucks, UK: Shire, 1979), 91.
10. *Inventions and Inventors, Volume 4*, op. cit., 8.
11. G.O. Sayles, *The Medieval Foundations of England* (Philadelphia: University of Pennsylvania Press, 1950), 120.
12. Smith, *Discovering Horse Drawn Farm Machinery*, op. cit., 3.
13. *Ibid.*, 6–7.
14. Everett E. Edwards, "American Agriculture: The First 300 Years," in *Farmers in a Changing World, The Yearbook of Agriculture*, United States Department of Agriculture (Washington, D.C.: U.S. Government Printing Office, 1940), 229.
15. *Ibid.*
16. Goodwin, *Chronology of American Agricultural History*, op. cit., 1190.
17. Edwards, *The First 300 Years*, op. cit., 229.
18. Goodwin, *Chronology of American Agricultural History*, op. cit., 1188.
19. C.H. Wendel, *Encyclopedia of American Farm Tractors* (Osceola, WI: Motorbooks International, 1992), 146.
20. Edwards, *The First 300 Years*, op. cit., 229.
21. Smith, *Discovering Horse Drawn Farm Machinery*, op. cit.,77; Wendel, *Encyclopedia of American Farm Tractors*, op. cit., 153.; Columbia Encyclopedia, op. cit., 1482; and Goodwin, *Chronology of American Agricultural History*, op. cit. 1190, 1191.
22. Smith, *Discovering Horse Drawn Farm Machinery*, op. cit., 70–71.
23. Edwards, *The First 300 Years*, op. cit., 230.
24. Paul C. Johnson, *Farm Power in the Making of America* (Des Moines, IA: Wallace-Homestead, 1978). 16.
25. *Ibid.*
26. Johnson, *Farm Power*, op. cit., 16–17.
27. C. H. Wendel, *150 Years of J.I. Case* (Sarasota, FL: Crestline, 1991), 214–216.
28. Reynold M. Wik, *Steam Power on the American Farm* (Philadelphia: University of Pennsylvania Press, 1953), 24–27.
29. The Columbia Encyclopedia, 1,683.
30. Robert T. Smith, "The Father of Waters," in *Water Trails West, The Western Writers of America* (New York: Avon Books, 1979), 28.
31. Edwards, *The First 300 Years*, op. cit., 216.
32. Wendel, *Encyclopedia of American Farm Tractors*, op. cit., 120.
33. *Ibid.*
34. *Ibid.*, 8.
35. *Ibid.*, 60.
35. Wik, *Steam Power on the American Farm*, op. cit., 78.
36. *Ibid.*, 118.
37. *Agricultural Statistics, 1952*, 455–456.
38. Edwards, *The First 300 Years*, op. cit., 228–230.
39. *Yearbook of Agriculture*, 1940, op. cit., 1,186, 1,192.
40. Goodwin, *Chronology of American Agricultural History*, op. cit., 1,192.
41. Johnson, *Farm Power in the Making of America*, op. cit., 41.
42. *Ibid.*, 62.
43. Wik, *Steam Power on the American Farm*, op. cit., 200.
44. Johnson, *Farm Power in the Making of America*, op. cit., 60.
45. *Ibid.*, 55, 60.
46. *Inventions and Inventors, Volume 10: Power and Energy* (Danbury, CT: Grolier Educational, 2000), 35.
47. *Ibid.*, 36.
48. Johnson, *Farm Power in the Making of America*, op. cit., 76–78.
49. *Ibid.*, 84.
50. *Ibid.*, 74.
51. Ralph W. Sanders, *Vintage Farm Tractors* (Stillwater, NM: Voyageur Press, 1997), 27; and Wendel, *Encyclopedia of American Tractors*, op. cit., 133.
52. Kenneth K. Barnes, and James H. Anderson, "If You Enjoy Eating, Thank the Machine," in *That We May Eat, the 1975 Yearbook of Agriculture* (Washington, D.C.: U.S. Department of Agriculture, 1975), 212.
53. Johnson, *Farm Power in the Making of America*, op. cit., 76–82.
54. Sanders, *Vintage Farm Tractors*, op. cit., 18.
55. Wik, *Steam Power on the American Farm*, op. cit., 109; and A.P. Brodell, and J. A. Ewing, *Use of Tractor Power, Animal Power, and Hand Methods in Crop Production*, Bureau of Agricultural Economics (Washington, D.C.: U.S. Department of Agriculture, 1948), 3.
56. Wendel, *Encyclopedia of American Tractors*, op. cit., 31, 38.
57. *Ibid.*, 38.
58. Frank D. Gardner, *Traditional American Farming Techniques* (Guilford, CT: Lyons Press, 2001), originally published in 1916 as L.T. Myers, *Successful Farming*, 67, 716.
59. Wendel, *Encyclopedia of American Tractors*, op. cit., 34.
60. Sanders, *Vintage Farm Tractors*, op. cit. 19.
61. *Ibid.*, 20–21.
62. *Ibid.*
63. *Ibid.*, 22.
64. *Ibid.*, 23.
65. *Ibid.*, 97–98.
66. W.M. Hurst, and L.M. Church, *Power*

and Machinery in Agriculture (Washington, D.C.: U.S. Department of Agriculture, Miscellaneous Publications No. 157, April, 1933). 8.
67. *Agricultural Statistics, 1952,* 455.
68. Hurst and Church, *Power and Machinery in Agriculture,* op. cit., 2.
69. *Ibid.,* 2.
70. Words by Sam M. Lewis, and Joe Young, Music by Walter Donaldson (New York: Waterson, Berlin & Snyder Co., Music Publishing, 1919).
71. A.B. Genung, "Agriculture in the World War Period," *Farmers in a Changing World, the Yearbook of Agriculture 1940* (Washington, D.C.: U.S. Department of Agriculture, 1940), 293–294.
72. Harold E. Pinches, "Revolution in Agriculture," in *Power to Produce, the Yearbook of Agriculture, 1960.* (Washington, D.C: U.S. Department of Agriculture, 1960), 1–7.
73. Brodell and Ewing, *Use of Tractor Power,* op. cit., 2.
74. Hurst and Church, *Power and Machinery in Agriculture,* op. cit., 11–12.
75. Sanders, *Vintage Farm Tractors,* op. cit., title page 5.
76. Hurst and Church, *Power and Machinery in Agriculture,* op. cit., 3.
77. *U.S. Department of Agriculture Yearbook, 1919,* 486–493.
78. H. R. Tolley, and L.M. Church, *Corn-Belt Farmers' Experience with Motor Trucks: A Study of 831 Reports from Farmers Who Own Motor Trucks* (Washington, D.C.: U.S. Department of Agriculture Bulletin No. 931, February 25, 1921), 11–13, 28, 31.
79. *U.S. Department of Agriculture Yearbook, 1960,* 3.
80. *Idem.*
81. *U.S. Department of Agriculture Yearbook, 1926,* 787.
82. *The Time Traveler's Guide to Medieval England: A Handbook for Visitors to the Fourteenth Century* (New York: Simon & Schuster, 2008), 169.
83. *Horses, Mules, and Motor Vehicles* (Washington, D.C.: U.S. Department of Agriculture Statistical Bulletin No. 5, January, 1925), 29.
84. Hurst and Church, *Power and Machinery in Agriculture,* op. cit., 22.
85. A.P. Brodell, and J.A. Ewing, *Use of Tractor Power,* op. cit., 8, and cover.
86. *Ibid.,* 7.
87. M. Horace Hayes, FRCVS, *Veterinary Notes for Horse Owners,* 18th Edition (New York: Simon & Schuster, 2002), 405.
88. Robert G. Lawrence, and James M. Downes, *Costs and Returns of Maryland's Standardbred Breeders,* (College Park: University of Maryland Agricultural Experiment Station, Eastern Shore Research Farms, MPS 963, July, 1981), 49.
89. C.L. Harlan, C.A. Burmeister, and G.B. Thorne, *Department of Agriculture Yearbook of 1933,* 220.
90. *Breeders' Gazette,* September, 1921, 372.
91. *Idem.*
92. Harlan, Burmeister, op. cit.
93. O.E. Baker, and Conrad Taeuber, "The Rural People," *The Yearbook of Agriculture, 1940,* 842.
94. Bureau of Agricultural Economics, 1952, 459
95. *Idem.*
96. *Ibid.,* 221.
97. *Agricultural Statistics, 1952,* Table 649.
98. Bureau of Agricultural Economics, *The Agricultural Outlook for 1933* (Washington, D.C.: The Department of Agriculture, Miscellaneous Publication No. 156, February, 1933), 30.
99. *Historical Statistics of the United States, Colonial Times to 1970, Part 1, Bicentennial Edition,* Washington, D.C.: U.S. Department of Commerce, 519–520.
100. Pinches, Revolution in Agriculture, op. cit., 7–8.
101. Joe M. Bohlen, Ronald C. Powers, and John A. Wallize, "Main Street Pokes Along While Urban Areas Bloom," in *That We May Eat, the Yearbook of Agriculture, 1975* (Washington, D.C.: The Department of Agriculture, 1975), 61.
102. *Ibid.,* 59.
103. *Ibid.,* 56.
104. *Historical Statistics of the U.S.,* op. cit. 519–520.
105. *Yearbook of Agriculture, 1960,* 7.
106. *Ibid.,* 56.
107. *Ibid.,* 55–64.

Chapter Five

1. John R. Erickson, *The Modern Cowboy,* Second Edition (Denton: University of North Texas Press, 2004), 155–156.
2. Terry G. Jordan, *North American Cattle-Ranching Frontiers, Origins, Diffusion, and Differentiation* (Albuquerque: University of New Mexico Press, 1993), ix.
3. *Ibid.,* 23.
4. *Ibid.,* 39; Charles Julian Bishko, "The Peninsular Background of Latin American Cattle Ranching," *Hispanic American Historical Review,* 32:4 (1952), 491–515; and Donald Chavez y Gilbert, *Cowboys—Vaqueros, Origins of the First American Cowboys,* self-published, 8–39.
5. Jordan, *North American Cattle-Ranching Frontiers,* op. cit., 47–50.

6. *Ibid.*, 60–63.
7. William H.P. Robertson, *The History of Thoroughbred Racing in America* (New York: Bonanza Books, 1964), 81.
8. Jordan, North American Cattle-Ranching Frontiers, op. cit. 64.
9. *Ibid.*, 65.
10. Bradley Smith, The *Horse in the West*, A Gemini Smith Book (New York: Leon Amiel, Publisher, 1969). 23.
11. John T. Schlebecker, *Cattle Raising in the Plains, 1900–1961* (Lincoln, NE: University of Nebraska Press, 1963). 5.
12. Jerry Stanley, *Cowboys and Longhorns, a Portrait of the Long Drive* (New York: Crown Publishers, 2003), 10, 21, 25; and Dee Brown, *The American West* (New York: Charles Scribner's Sons, 1994), 41–77.
13. Smith, *The Horse In The West*, op. cit., 21.
14. Stanley, *Cowboys and Longhorns*, op. cit., 32–34, 40, 46.
15. Brown, *The American West*, op. cit., 67.
16. Stanley, *Cowboys and Longhorns*, op. cit., 49.
17. *Ibid.*, 66.
18. *Ibid.*, 69–70.
19. *Ibid.*, 71.
20. *Ibid.*, 74; Erickson, *The Modern Cowboys*, op. cit., 91; and Christy Steele, *Cattle Ranching in the American West* (Milwaukee: World Almanac Library, 2005).
21. Jordan, *North American Cattle-Ranching Frontiers*, op. cit., 170–207.
22. John Williams Malone, *An Album of the American Cowboy* (New York: Franklin Watts, Inc., 1971), 79.
23. Schlebecker, Cattle Raising in the Plains, op. cit. 7. Paul F. Starrs, Let *the Cowboy Ride, Cattle Ranching in the American West* (Baltimore: The Johns Hopkins Press, 1998), 7.
24. *Ibid.*, 43.
25. Joanne S. Liu, *Barbed Wire, the Fence That Changed the West.* (Missoula, MT: Mountain Press Publishing Company, 2009), 27–31, 34–39, 42–43, 51, 60, 67, 70.
26. Starrs, Let The Cowboy Ride, op. cit., 38–81. and Martin Vavra "Livestock Grazing and Wildlife: Developing Compatibilities," *Rangeland Ecology & Management*, March, 2005. Vol. 58, 128–134.
27. Erickson, *The Modern Cowboy*, op. cit., 76–88.
28. Malone, *An Album of the American Cowboy*, op. cit., 13.
29. Fay E. Ward, *The Cowboy at Work, About His Job and How He Does It* (New York: Hastings House Publishers, 1958, 1976), 122–142.
30. *Ibid.*, 120–121.
31. Smith, *The Horse In The West*, op. cit., 23.
32. Sherm Ewing, *The Ranch, a Modern History of the North American Cattle Industry* (Missoula, MT: Mountain Press, 1995), 71, 254.
33. *Ibid.*, 260.
34. James R. Gray, and Wylie D. Goodsell, *Cattle Ranches, Organization, Costs, and Returns, Southwest Nonmigratory Grazing Areas, 1940–59*, Farm Economic Division, Economic Research Service, U.S. Department of Agriculture, in cooperation with Agricultural Experiment Station, New Mexico State University, Agricultural Economic Report No.1, 22.
35. *Ibid.*, 10, 23, 24.
36. Erickson, *The Modern Cowboy*, op. cit., 70–75, 179, 180.
37. Schlebecker, *Cattle Raising in the Plains*, op. cit., 93; and Michael Pollen, "Power Steer," *New York Times Magazine*, March 31, 2002, 5.
38. William D. McBride, and Kenneth Mathews, Jr., *The Diverse Structure and Organization of U.S. Beef Cow-Calf Farms*, Economic Research Service, Economic Information Bulletin Number 73, U.S. Department of Agriculture, March 2011.
39. Pollen, *Power Steer*, op. cit., 2–3.
40. Joseph P. Harner III, and James P. Murphy, *Planning Cattle Feedlots*, Department of Biological and Agricultural Engineering, Kansas State University, August, 1998, 1–8; and *Beef Feedlot System Manual* (Ames, IA: Iowa Beef Center, Iowa State University, undated), 1–27.
41. Erickson, *The Modern Cowboy*, op. cit. 182–184; and Pollen, *Power Steer*, op. cit., 6.
42. *Overview of U.S. Livestock and Aquaculture Production in 2011*, Tables 2, 5; *Statistics on Major Commodities*, National Agricultural Statistics Service, U.S. Department of Agriculture; and *The 2007 Survey of Agriculture*.
43. James M. MacDonald, and William D. McBride, *The Transformation of U.S. Livestock Agriculture: Scale, Efficiency, and Risks*, Economic Research Service, Economic Information Bulletin Number 43, U.S. Department of Agriculture, January, 2009, 25; and Alan Barkema, Mark Drabenstott, and Nancy Novack, "The New U.S. Meat Industry," *Federal Reserve Bank of Kansas City Economic Review*, Second Quarter, 2001, 33–56.
44. Erickson, *The Modern Cowboy*, op. cit., 36–37, 53, 54; and David Bowser, "Canine Cowboys Prove Helpful," *Feedlot Magazine Online*, Vol. 7, no. 1, January/February, 1999, 1–3; and Jennifer Denison, "The Canine Crew," *Western Horseman*, August, 2012. 69–73.

Chapter Six

1. Emily R. Kilby, "Demographics of the U.S. Equine Population," in *The State of the Animals IV*, 2007. New York, 175.

2. The American Horse Council, "Most Comprehensive Survey Ever Reveals a Nearly $40 Billion Impact on the U.S. Economy," June 28, 2005, 5.
3. Elizabeth Clair Flood, *Old Time Dude Ranches Out West* (Salt Lake City: Gibbs-Smith, 1995), 8, 9, 12, 14, 36, 94.
4. Joel H. Bernstein, *Wild Ride, the History and Lore of Rodeo* (Layton, UT: Gibbs-Smith, 2007), 77.
5. Mary Lou Lecompte, "The Hispanic Influence on the History of Rodeo, 1823–1922," *Journal of Sports History*, Vol. 12, No. 1, Spring, 1985, 21–38.
6. Bernstein, Wild Ride, op. cit., 76.
7. Phil Hardy, *The Encyclopedia of Western Movies* (Minneapolis, MN: Woodbury Press, 1984), xv, 188.
8. Anthony Amaral, *Movie Horses, Their Treatment and Training* (New York: The Bobbs-Merrill Company, Inc., 1967), 23–41.
9. http://www.wildwestweb.net/horses.html.
10. Bernstein, *Wild Ride*, op. cit., 71, 148–154.
11. Wayne S. Wooden, and Gavin Ehringer, *Rodeo in America: Wranglers, Roughstock & Paydirt* (Lawrence: University Press of Kansas, 1996), 237–238.
12. Kevin Helliker, "Rodeo Drive: Rich Urban Cowboys on Fine Horses Best Ranch Hands," *Wall Street Journal*, December 16, 2010.
13. Wooden and Ehringer, *Rodeo in America*, op. cit., 217–218.
14. Postal address: P.O. Box 460504, Aurora, Colorado 80046.
15. Bernstein, *Wild Ride*, op. cit., 131.
16. Ibid., 137.
17. Ibid., 158.
18. Wooden and Ehringer, *Rodeo in America*, op. cit., 116–118.
19. Ibid., 121.
20. Ibid., 128.
21. Ibid., 124.
22. Ibid., 125.
23. Les Sellnow, "Rodeo Horses," Helpful Info, Friends of Rodeo, www.thehorse.com, January 2002, 2.
24. Bernstein, *Wild Ride*, op. cit., 159.
25. Ibid., 161–162.
26. Ibid., 160.
27. Ibid., 167.
28. Helliker, *Rodeo Drive*, op. cit.
29. http://www.prorodeohorses.com/cgi-bin/PRHclassifieds.cgi?
30. Sellnow, *Rodeo Horses*, op. cit., 2.
31. Paul Zarzyski, "Good Horse Keeping," in *Horsepeople, Writers and Artists on the Horses They Love*, Michael J. Rosen, ed. (New York: Artisan, 2002), 98.
32. "Equitation Explained, Medalmaclay.Com" 2008, http:/www.medalmaclay.com/explained/, sponsored by Bigeq.com, 5.
33. Harlan C. Abbey, "Billy Dickerson: Out of the Ring and into the Ribbons," in *Horses and Horse Shows* (South Brunswick and New York: A.S. Barnes, 1980), 103.
34. Abbey, quoting Paul Oswald, "Common Mistakes Seen in the Show Ring," in *Horses and Horse Shows*, op. cit., 191.
35. American Quarter Horse Association Fact Sheet.
36. American Horse Council Study, June 25, 2005, op. cit., Table A-1.
37. American Horse Publications Study, 2010.
38. Kate Bradley, "Total Trust, Texas Horseman Mozaun Mckibben Has Found a Method to Teach Horses Extended Gaits Quickly and with Confidence," *Western Horseman*, August, 2013, 25–28.
39. Harlan C. Abbey, *Horses and Horse Shows* (South Brunswick and New York: A.S. Barnes, 1980).
40. American Quarter Horse Association Rule Book, 2012. Rule SHW 117.2.
41. *U.S. Equitation Federation Rule Book, 2013*, 15–16, JP116.
42. American Quarter Horse Association Fact Sheet, 2011.
43. Abbey, *Horses and Horse Shows*, op. cit., 90, 122, 129.
44. American Horse Council 2005 Study, Table 17.
45. Abbey, "Your Riding Future: Amateur or Professional," in *Horses and Horse Shows*, op. cit., 249.
46. Abbey, quoting Jack Frohm, "Your Riding Future: Colleges of Equestrian Knowledge," in *Horses and Horse Shows*, op. cit., 264.
47. *American Horse Publications 2005 Study*, June 25, 2005.
48. *American Horse Publications 2010 Study*.
49. Mary Wanless, "Living Your Love," in *Of Women and Horses* (Irvine, CA: Bow Tie Press, 2000), 50.
50. *American Horse Publications Survey*, conducted from October 15, 2009, through January 31, 2010.
51. Mary Midkiffe, "An Intuitive Edge," in *Of Women and Horses*, op. cit., 82–83.
52. Frankie Chesler, "Kindness, Patience, Friendship, and Time for Play," in *Of Women and Horses*, op. cit. 76.
53. Medalmaclay.com/eqresults/36.html.
54. Holly Peterson, "A Chance to Soar. for Young Equestrians Commuting to Florida on Weekends Is a Commitment and a Goal," *New York Times*, March 26, 2015, D1, 8, 9.
55. Julie Satow, "A Socialite Met a Horse Trainer, and a Rare Horse Partnership Was Born," *New York Times*, May 31, 2015, 25.

56. Kilby, *Demographics of the U.S. Equine Population*, op. cit., 194.
57. Dr. Delphi M. Toth, PhD, "The Psychology of Women and Horses," in *Of Women and Horses*, op. cit., 34.
58. *Idem.*
59. Roxana Robinson, "Heart's Desire," in *What My Mother Gave Me, Thirty-One Women on the Gifts That Mattered Most*, Elizabeth Benedict, ed. (Chapel Hill, NC: Algonquin Books, 2013), 1–10.

Chapter Seven

1. Robertson, History of Thoroughbred Racing, op. cit., 7.
2. "Horse Racing, Bloodlines and Studbooks," *Encyclopædia Britannica*, britannica.com, updated January 22, 2014.
3. Robertson, *History of Thoroughbred Racing*, op. cit., 50.
4. Robert Moorman Denhardt, *The Quarter Running Horse* (Norman: University of Oklahoma Press, 1979), 20.
5. *Ibid.*, 95.
6. *Harness the Excitement: Your Guide to the Sport of Harness Racing* (Columbus, OH: U.S. Trotting Association, undated), 14.
7. "Introduction of Arabian Horses to North America," *Arabian Horse History and Heritage*, Arabian Horse Association, www.arabianhorses.org/education/education_history_intro.asp, March 20, 2014.
8. Robertson, *History of Thoroughbred Racing*, op. cit., 7.
9. Denhardt, *The Quarter Running Horse*, op. cit., 77–114.
10. *Harness The Excitement*, op. cit. 14–15.
11. National Steeple Chase Museum, "The History of Steeplechasing," 2014. http://www.steeplechasemuseum.org/site/page/history.
12. Denhardt, *The Quarter Running Horse*, op. cit., 46.
13. Robertson, *History of Thoroughbred Racing*, op. cit. 64.
14. *Ibid.*
15. "History of Steeplechasing," op. cit.
16. "The State of Racing," in "Horse Racing," *Encyclopædia Britannica*, brittanica.com, updated January 22, 2014.
17. Robertson, *History of Thoroughbred Racing*, op. cit., 200.
18. "Horse Racing History," winningponies.com, 2013.
19. Robertson, *History of Thoroughbred Racing*, op. cit., 213.
20. *Ibid.*, 283.
21. "Innovation for 'Double' Tickets," *Wikipedia*, quoting *Montreal Gazette*, May 20, 1932, 19.
22. *Harness The Excitement*, op. cit., 22.
23. Louisiana Racing Commission, *Rules*, Chapter 112, 2013.
24. Robertson, *History of Thoroughbred Racing*, op. cit., 138.
25. Cindy Pierson Delay, "Understanding the Types and Classes of Horse Races," in About.com, "Horse Racing," 2013; and T.A. Landers, *Insider's Guide to Horseracing* (Yardley, PA: Westholme, 2005), 117–121.
26. "Quarter-Horse Racing," *Encyclopædia Britannica*, http:/www.britannica.com/EB checked/topic 486381/quarter horse-racing.
27. National Steeplechase Association, "History," http://www.nationalsteeplechase.com/chasing//history. 2010–2014.
28. *Harness The Excitement*, op. cit., 7.
29. Robertson, *History of Thoroughbred Racing*, op. cit., 428.
30. Jim Bolus, *The Insider's Pocket Guide to Horse Racing* (Dallas, TX: Taylor, 1990).
31. Joe Drape, "As Concerns Over Drugs Mount, the Jockey Club Says It Will Pay for Testing," *New York Times*, August 12, 2013, D4.
32. Gregory A. Hall, "Eight Belles' Death at Derby Spurred Safety Reforms," *Courier-Journal*, May 2, 2009.
33. Louisiana Racing Commission Rules, op. cit., paragraph 12014.
34. *The Wall Street Journal*, May 3–4, 2014, A3.
35. Robertson, *History of Thoroughbred Racing*, op. cit., 261.
36. Joe Drape, "Study Raises Questions About Antibleeding Drug," *New York Times*, December 16, 2013. B18.
37. Steve Haskin, "The History of Drugs in America," Bloodhorse.com, July 1, 2012, 1.
38. Ed Kane, "RCI Rules on Reducing Phenylbutazone Threshold," *DVM Newsmagazine*, December 1, 2010.
39. Robertson, *History of Thoroughbred Racing*, op. cit., 288–289.
40. *Ibid.*, 376–377.
41. T.D. Thornton, "For Horses' Safety He Thinks Outside the Hocks," *Boston Globe*, April 29, 2009.
42. Marcus Hersh, "Giving Softer Whips a Crack," *Daily Racing Form*, November 19, 2009.
43. Joe Drape, "Eight States Approve Medication Standards," *New York Times*, March 13, 2013, B13.
44. "Death and Disarray at America's Racetracks," *New York Times*, March 25, 2012.
45. Joe Drape, "Eight States Approve Medication Standards," op. cit.
46. Jeff Barker, "Congressional Study Looks at Drug Abuse, Injuries in Horse Racing, Na-

tional Governing Body Discussed for Sport," *The Baltimore Sun*, May 17, 2010.

47. Sid Gustafson, in the Rail, "Essay: Medication Continues to Stifle America's Triple Crown Hopes," *New York Times Racing Blog*, June 11, 2013.

48. Joe Drape, "Medication Is Cited in Horse Racing's Decline in U.S.," *New York Times*, June 14, 2011. B12.

49. Landers, *Insider's Guide to Horseracing*, op. cit., 24–32.

50. *Ibid.*, 25.

51. *Ibid.*, 26.

52. *Ibid.*, 30.

53. *Ibid.*, 30.

54. *Ibid.*, 32.

55. *Ibid.*, 34.

56. Matt Hegarty, "Official Calls for U.S. to Ban Lasix in Stakes," *Daily Racing Form*, August 23, 2009.

57. "Data Debunking Myths Gets Buried," *Daily Racing Form*, August 22, 2008.

58. Landers, *Insider's Guide to Horseracing*, op. cit., 37.

59. Matt Hegarty, "Official Calls for U.S. to Ban Lasix in Stakes," op. cit.; "Round Table Focuses on Medication Issues," *Thoroughbred Daily News*, August 24, 2009; and "Driving Sustainable Growth for Thoroughbred Racing and Breeding," Selected Exhibits, August, 2011, 16.

60. "Horse Racing Fantasy. Simple Answers to Common Questions," *About Horses in General*, http//www.horseracegame.com/communitycontent/stories/horseracing/28-09-2008.

61. Landers, *Insider's Guide to Horseracing*, op. cit., 2.

62. "Joint Announcement by the Thoroughbred Charities of America, the Thoroughbred Retirement Foundation, and the Jockey Club," *Thoroughbred Daily News*, November 12, 2008; and *New York Times*, December 27, 2009, WK 11.

63. Kent Babb, "Unlikely Companions," *The Washington Post*, August 18, 2013, D1, D7.

64. Annual Jockey Club Release of Report of Mares Bred Statistics, 2008–2013.

65. The Charlotte Steeplechase Association, Inc, "What Is a Steeplechase?" http://www.quenscup.org/about-the-chase/about-steeplechasing/what, February 2, 2014.

66. Katie Frank, "Learning to Downshift," *Western Horseman*, January, 2015, 70–76.

67. PETA "Overbreeding and Slaughter," https://www.peta.org/issues/animals-in-entertainment/horse-racing-2/horse-racing-industry-cruelty/overbreeding-and-slaughter.

68. The Horse Council, "Number of Horses by Breed and Activity, in Most Comprehensive Horse Study Ever Reveals a Nearly $40 Billion Impact on the U.S. Economy," June 28, 2005, Table 6; and Dr. C. Gill Stowe, consultant, *2009–2010 American Horse Publications Equine Industry Survey*, 2010.

Chapter Eight

1. Shapour Suren-Pahlav, "History of Chogan (Polo)," *Sport in Iran*, Iran Chamber Society, February 18, 2016, www.iranchamber.com/sport/chogan/chogan_history.php.

2. Anbarasan Ethirajan, "Concern Over Dwindling Number of Rare Indian Ponies," *BBC News*, July 13, 2015, www.bbc.com/news/world-asia-india-33308422.

3. Richard C. Latham, "Polo," *Encyclopædia Britannica*, www.britannica.com/sports/polo, accessed 2/19/2016; "History of the Equestrian Sport of Polo," SportPOLO corporation, 2013, http://sportspolo.com/History/default.hta.

4. "History of Equestrian Sport," op. cit.

5. Latham, Polo, op. cit.

6. Horace A. Laffaye, *The Polo Encyclopedia* (Jefferson, NC: McFarland, 2004), 177, 276.

7. Horace A. Laffaye, *Polo in the United States: A History* (Jefferson, NC: McFarland, 2011), 7–11.

8. *Ibid.*, 14–19.

9. *Ibid.*, 21, 23.

10. *Ibid.*, 62.

11. Frank Milburn, *Polo, the Emperor of Games* (New York: Alfred A. Knopf, 1994), 59–60.

12. Laffaye, *Polo History*, 65.

13. *Ibid.*, 66–69.

14. *Ibid.*, 51–52.

15. William C. Steinkraus, and M. A. Stoneridge, "Polo," in *The Horse in Sport*, foreword by H.R.H. Prince Philip, Duke of Edinburgh (New York: Stewart, Tabori & Chang, 1987), 154–177.

16. Steven D. Price, and Charles Kauffman, *The Polo Primer: A Guide for Players and Spectators* (New York: Stephen Greene Press, 1989), 70.

17. *Ibid.*, 30–50.

18. Laffaye, *Polo Encyclopedia*, 128, 330.

19. Blogger, "Types of Polo: Grass, Arena, Snow and Beach Polo," Polo101.com, February 8, 2010, http://www.polo101.com/about-polo-the-game/types-of-polo-gras.

20. Peter J. Rizzo, "G.C. Shermans, Father and Son Volunteered Much of Their Time to the Sport," *Yesteryears, Polo Players' Edition*, March, 2016, 60–63.

21. Frank Milburn, *Polo*, op. cit., 164.

22. Price and Kauffman, *Primer*, 2.

23. "Trial and Error, Breeders Look for the Best Formulas for Creating Top Ponies," *This

Month In Polo: Players' Edition, http://www.poloplayersedition.com/new/art0306.html.
24. Price and Kauffman, *Primer*, 20.
25. Laffaye, *Polo History*, 126.
26. Price and Kauffman, *Primer*, 20.
27. "Trial and Error," op. cit.
28. Sarah Eakin, "Embryo Center Imports Argentine Expertise," *The Month in Polo: Players' Edition*, http://www.poloplayersedition.com/new/art0306.html.
29. "Cloning Ponies: How Technology Could Transform an Ancient Sport," *The Economist*, Buenos Aires, from the print edition, January 5, 2013, http://www.economist.com/news/business/21569054-how-technology-c.
30. Alex Webbe, "All About Polo Ponies," *About Polo Horses*, Blogger, January 19, 2010, http://polo101.com./about_polo/202.html.
31. Gareth A. Davies, "Guards Polo Club Manager Believes the Top Professionals Should Be Forced to Pass to Speed Up the Game—And That Means Less Ponies," August 18, 2015. http://www.telegraph.co.uk/sport/othersports/polo/11809598/Modern-b.
32. Laffaye, *Polo History*, 102–103.
33. *Ibid.*, 27, 163–166.
34. *Ibid.*, 170–171.
35. *Ibid.*, 163.
36. Michigan State Polo Club, "Go Green! Go White! Go Polo. About the Team," http://www.msu.edu/ msupolo/.
37. Laffaye, *Polo History*, 174.
38. *Ibid.*, 73.
39. *Ibid.*, 174.
40. Bob Seals, "U.S. Army Captures World Polo Title," *Military History Online*, http://www.militaryhistoryonline.com/20thcentury/articles/polo in usarmy, published online 12/29/2013.
41. Lucian K. Truscott, *The Twilight of the U.S. Cavalry, Life in the Old Army, 1917–1942* (Lawrence: University of Kansas Press, 1987), xiv–xv, cited in Bob Seal, "U.S. Army Captures Title."
42. Laffaye, *Polo History*, 174.
43. Bob Seal, "U.S. Army Captures Title."
44. Laffaye, *Polo History*, 170.
45. WKP
46. Laffaye, *Polo History*, 113.
47. *Ibid.*, 145–147.
48. *Ibid.*, 96.
49. *Ibid.*, 43, 185.
50. *Ibid.*, 190.
51. *Ibid.*, 242, 264, 310.
52. "Trial and Error," op. cit.
53. "Training Polo Horses in Argentina," http://www.argentinapolo.com/gustavohorsetraining.html.
54. "El Caballo De Polo—The History of the Argentine Polo Horse," Camino Real Polo Country Club, San Vicente, Argentina, http://www.caminorealpolo.com/all-about-polo-ponies-what-is-polo-uk-argentina.html; and Terry Conway, "Polo Ponies: Hardest Working Athletes in Equine World," http://terryconway.net/cms/index.php?option=com_content&view=article&id=83:polo-ponies-hardest-working-athletes-in-equine-world&catid=14:racingcolumns&Itemid=10, accessed 3/7/2016.
55. Alex Webbe, "Why Are They Called Polo Ponies?" in Blogger, "15 Questions You've Always Wanted to Ask About Polo," January 26, 2011, http://www.polo101.com/faq/15-questions-you-alwaysnted-t-ask-about-polo.
56. "Polo Horses in Graffham," *BBC*, Domesday Reloaded, http://www.bbc.co.uk/history/domesday/dblock/GB-492000-117000/page/18; and "What Breed Is a Polo Pony?" http://www.sportpolo.com/polo_pony/default.htm; and Amy Pengra, "Polo Ponies: Horsing Around the Field, Luchese Bootmaker," https://www.lucchese.com/polo/article/polo-ponies-horsing-around-the-field/, accessed 3/7/2016.
57. "Engineered for Players," Thoroughbred Polo Ponies, Ltd., http://www.thoroughbredpoloponies.com/aboutus.html.
58. Laffaye, *Polo History*, 232.
59. B. Dista, G. Maldonado, H. Reid, B. Puschner, J. Maxwell, A. Agasan, L. Humphreys, T. Holt, "Acute Selenium Toxicosis in Polo Ponies," *J Vet Diagn Invest*, 2011 May; 23(3): 623–8, Doi: 10.1177/1040638711404142.
60. Katie Thomas, "Polo Ponies Were Given Incorrect Medication," *New York Times*, April 23, 2009, B11.
61. Brian Skoloff, "21 Polo Horses Die at Florida Match," *Huffpost Green*, http://www.huffingtonpost.com2009/04/20/21-polo-horses-die-at-florida-match; and Jim Kavanaugh, *CNN*, "Polo Ponies Are Pampered, Beloved, Hard-Trained Athletes," cnn.com.http://www.cnn.com/2009/U.S./04/21/polo.horses/index.html?eref=ib_us; and Tim Padget, "The Dead Ponies and Their Millionaire Owner," *TIME*, April 23, 2009, http://content.time.com/time/nation/article/0,8599,1893280,00.html.
62. Stephanie Fellenstein, "Drug Tests Begin for Polo Ponies," *Dvm360 Magazine*, June 1, 2010. http://veterinarynews.dvm360.com/drug-tests-begin-polo-ponies.
63. United States Polo Association, "Equine Drugs and Medications Rules of the United States Polo Association, 2015," 40–47.
64. D.J. Marlin, J.C. Allen, "Cardiovascular demands of competition on low-goal (non-elite) polo ponies," *Equine Vet. J.*, Sep. 31, 1999 (5) 378–82.
65. Rosanna Zobba et al., "Physical, Hematological, and Biochemical Responses to Acute Intense Exercise in Polo Horses," *Journal of Equine Veterinary Science*, September 2011 31:9, 542–548.

66. C.M. Innes, and K.L. Morgan, "Polo Pony Injuries: Player-Owner Reported Risks. Perception, Mitigation and Risk Factors," *Equine Veterinary Journal*, School of Veterinary Science and Department of Musculoskeletal Biology, Institute of Ageing and Chronic Disease (University of Liverpool, UK, 2015), 422–427.
67. G.E. Van Tuyl, W.J. Bonelli, "Polo Ponies," *Iowa State Veterinarian* 6:2, Article 8, available at http://lib.dr.iastate_veterinarian/vol6/iss2/8.
68. Don Harvey Pedrick, "It's a Wrap!" *Polo Players' Edition* magazine, September, 2003, Victoria Polo Club Page, http://carriagehousebandb.ca/wrap/html.
69. Matis Costa-Paz, Luis Aponte-Tinao, and D. Luis Muscolo, "Injuries to Polo Riders: A Prospective Evaluation," *British Journal of Sports Medicine*, 1999, 33:329–332.
70. Gwen Rizzo, "Life Wish, Player Moves Forward After Serious Injury," Polo, *Players' Edition*, April, 2016, 37.
71. C.M. Innes, and K.L. Morgan, "Falls and Injuries to Polo Players: Risk Perception, Mitigation and Risk Factors," *Sports Medicine-Open*, 2015, 1:2, https://sportsmedicine-open.springeropen.com/articles/10.1186/s40798-014-0002-8.
72. Diego Jemio, "Argentina's Love Affair with Polo," *BBC News*, February 26, 2015, http://www.bbc/news/business-31602941.
73. Horace A. Laffaye, *The Evolution of Polo* (Jefferson, NC: McFarland, 2009), 202, 213.
74. Ibid., 224–230.
75. Chris Ashton, "Into the Future: Reclaiming the Golden Era of Global Polo," Polo, *Players' Edition*, April, 2016, 14–15, 58–59.
76. Ibid., 206, 211.
77. Data provided by the U.S. Polo Association.
78. "Uspa News," *Polo, Players" Edition*, April, 2016. 6.
79. *USPA Annual Report, 2015*. 54.
80. PTF, Polo Training Foundation, "The Future of Polo in America," www.polotraining.org/about/history.html.
81. Karl Hilberg, "Ethics in Our Sports," *Polo, Players' Edition*, April 2016. 57.
82. Calendar, *Polo, Players' Edition*, April, 1916. 64.
83. "Uspa News, from Ceo Duncan Huyler," *Polo, Players' Edition*, March, 2016, 6.
84. "USPA Celebrates the 30th National Girls and Women in Sports Day," *News and Events*, February 2, 2016, https://uspolo.org/news-and-events/I/uspa-celebrates-the-30th-annual-n.
85. Rizzo, *Life Wish*, op cit., 32.

Chapter Nine

1. 2009–2010 American Horse Publications Equine Industry Survey, op. cit.
2. Equamore Foundation, 2014, www.equamore.org/portfolio/dancer/.
3. Claudia Nunez, "Horses Abandoned in Foreclosure Crises," translated by Elena Shore, *La Opinion* (San Francisco, CA: New America Media, March 31, 2011).
4. American Veterinary Medical Association, "Unwanted Horses and Horse Slaughter (FAQ)," 2013, 10.
5. *Breeder's Gazette*, September 25, 1919, 598.
6. United States Government Accountability Office, "Horse Welfare, Action Needed to Address Unintended Consequences from Cessation of Domestic Slaughter," Report to Congressional Committees, June, 2011.
7. *New York Times*, August 3, 2013, 2.
8. *The Wall Street Journal*, January 18, 2014, A4.
9. *New York Times*, February 9, 2013, A7; February 15, 2013, A6; February 20, 2013, B1, B2; and March 10, 2013, 1, 14.
10. Kilby, *Demographics of the U.S. Equine Population*, op. cit., 178.
11. BLM, Wyoming, Field Affairs Casper, "The Taylor Grazing Act," www.blm.gov/wy/st/en/field_0ffices/Casper/range/taylor.1.btml, accessed June 19, 2014.
12. David Cruise, and Alison Griffiths, *Wild Horse Annie and the Last of the Mustangs: The Life of Velma Johnston* (New York: Scribner, 2010), 58–59.
13. International Society for the Protection of Mustangs and Burros (ISPMB), "A Bit of History, BLM and Land Management," accessed June 19, 2014.
14. Cruise & Griffiths, *Wild Horse Annie*, op. cit., 59–60, quoting Dr. T. L McKnight., "Feral Livestock in America," in *University of California Publications in Geography*, Vol. 16, University of California Press, 1964.
15. Cruise, & Griffiths, *Wild Horse Annie.*, op. cit., 43–44.
16. Ibid., 73–79.
17. Ibid., 105–106.
18. Ibid., 131–137.
19. Ibid., 207.
20. Marguerite Henry, *Mustang, Wild Spirit of the West* (New York: Simon & Schuster, 1966).
21. Public Law, 92–195, December 15, 1971.
22. U.S. Department of the Interior, Bureau of Land Management, "Wild Horse and Burros Quick Facts," http://www.blm.gov/wo/st/em/prog/whbprogram/history_and_facts/quick_facts.html. Updated as of April 22, 2014.

23. "BLM Freezemarks," in "Wild Horse Education," May 11, 2014, http://wildhorseeducation.org/blm-freezemark/.accessed May 11, 20; U.S. Department of the Interior, Bureau of Land Management. "Using Freeze Marks," BLM: Wild Horses and Burros: Adoption Program: Freeze Marks, https://www.blm.gov/wo/st/en/prog/whbprogram/adoption_program/freezemarks.html, accessed May 11, 2014; Also "Operating Instructions for L & H Freeze Branders," http://www.lhbrandingirons.com/Feeeze/Instructions.html, accessed May 11, 2014.

24. Website of the Bureau of Land Management, U.S. Department of the Interior, updated April 22, 2014.

25. National Academy of Sciences, Office of News and Public Information, Washington, D.C., Press release, June 5, 2013.

26. U.S. Department of Interior, Bureau of Land Management, Rangeland and Herd Management, Wild Horse and Burro Program, Webpage, May, 2014. And U.S. Department of Interior, Bureau of Land Management, National Wild Horse and Burro Advisory Board Meeting Minutes, September 9–13, 2013.

27. Bureau of Land Management News Room, press release, March 11, 2013.

28. Kilby, *Demographics of the U.S. Equine Population*, op. cit., 179.

29. *New York Times*, August 11, 2013, 1, 16.

30. *New York Times*, October 8, 2013, A11; also *ABC News*, "Tribe, Robert Redford Group Ok Wild Horses Plan," http://abcnews.go.com/Entertainment/wire story/tribe-robert-redford-group-ok-wild-horses-plan, accessed May 11, 2014.

31. Sheridan Alexander, "Where to See Wild Horses and Ponies of the Southeast, Maryland, Virginia, North Carolina and Georgia Travel," at http://gosoutheast.about.com/od/beachesllakesrivers/tp/southeastus_in, accessed, 2014.

32. Sheridan Alexander, "Ocracoke Island Horses—Descendants of the Wild Horses of the Past," *About.Com*, http://gosoutheast.about.com/od/beachlakesrivers/a/ocracoke_ponies.htm, accessed May 30, 2014.

33. Carolyn Mason, "Shakleford Horses Timeline: History on Hooves: The Horses of Shakleford Banks, Their Role in the Culture and History of Eastern North Carolina," November 17, 1997. http://www.shaklefordhorses.org/timeline.htm, accessed May 30, 2014.

34. Assateague Wild Ponies—Assateague Island National Seashore. http://www.assateagueisland.com/wildlife/pony.htm, accessed May 23, 2014.

35. Doug Stanton, *Horse Soldiers: The Extraordinary Story of a Band of U.S. Soldiers Who Rode to Victory in Afghanistan* (New York: Scribner, 2009).

36. *Ibid.*, 124.

37. *Ibid.*, 125, 136.

38. *Ibid.*, 152.

39. *Ibid.*, 124.

40. Thomas P. Govan, Capt., "The Army Ground Forces: Training for Mountain and Winter Warfare," Study No. 23, 1946, http://www.history.army.mil/books/agf/agf23.htm, 3.

41. *Ibid.*, 9, 12.

42. Marine Corps Mountain Warfare Training Center, History, U.S. Marine Corps. http://www.29palms.marines.mil/mcmwtc/About/History aspx.

43. Jacj Gruber, "New Horsepower for War Zones: Special Forces Saddle Up: U.S. Special Forces and Marines Train to Be Combat Ready on Horseback at the United States Marine Mountain Warfare Training Center (Mwtc) Near Bridgeport, Calif.," *USA Today*, June 22, 2014.

Bibliography

Abbey, Harlan C. "Billy Dickerson: Out of the Ring and into the Ribbons," in *Horses and Horse Shows*. South Brunswick and New York: A.S. Barnes & Co., 1980.

Abbey, Harlan C. *Horses and Horse Shows* South Brunswick and New York: A.S. Barnes & Co., 1980.

Abbey, Harlan C. "Your Riding Future: Amateur or Professional," in *Horses and Horse Shows*.

ABC News. "Tribe, Robert Redford Group Ok Wild Horses Plan." http://abcnews.go.com/entertainment/wirestory/tribe-robert-redford-group-ok-wild-horses-plan

Addington, Larry H. *The Patterns of War Since the Eighteenth Century*, 2nd ed. Bloomington: Indiana University Press, 1994.

Alexander, Sheridan. "Ocracoke Island Horses—Descendants of the Wild Horses of the Past." About.com, Southeast US Travel, http://gosoutheast.about.com/od/beachlakesrivers/a/ocracoke_ponies.htm.

Alexander, Sheridan. "Where to See Wild Horses and Ponies of the Southeast, Maryland, Virginia, North Carolina and Georgia Travel," at http://gosoutheast.about.com/od/beachesllakesrivers/tp/southeastus_in.

Allen, George H, et al. *The Great War, Fifth Volume: The Triumph of Democracy*. Philadelphia: George Barrie's Sons, 1921.

Amaral, Anthony. *Movie Horses, Their Treatment and Training*. New York: Bobbs-Merrill, 1967.

The American Battle Monuments Commission. *A Guide to the American Battle Fields in Europe*. Washington, D.C.: United States Government Printing Office, 1927.

American Horse Council. "Most Comprehensive Survey Ever Reveals a Nearly $40 Billion Impact on the U.S. Economy." June 28, 2005.

American Horse Publications Study, 2005.

American Horse Publications Study, 2010.

American Horse Publications Survey. Conducted October 15, 2009, through January 31, 2010.

"American Lafrance Fire Engine Company, Manufacturers of First Automobile Combination Chemical Engine and Hose Car." *Cambridge Tribune*, January 27, 1923. http://cambridge.dlconsulting.com/cgi-bin/cambridge?a=d&d=Tribune19230127-01.2.117.

American Quarter Horse Association Fact Sheet, 2011.

American Quarter Horse Association Rule Book, 2012.

American Veterinary Medical Association. "Unwanted Horses and Horse Slaughter (FAQ)," 2013. 10.

Anderson, W.S. "Selling Army Horses Directly," *Breeder's Gazette*, May 24, 1917, 1071.

Anderson, W.S. "Selling Army Horses Directly," *Breeder's Gazette*, December 27, 1917, 1267.

Ansly Clarke F., ed. "Pony Express," in *The Columbia Encyclopedia, in One Volume*, Morningside Heights, NY: Columbia University Press. 1942.

Arabian Horse Association. "Introduction of Arabian Horses to North America." *Arabian Horse History and Heritage*. www.arabianhorses.org/education/education_history_intro.asp, March 20, 2014.

"Army Conservation of Fertility." *Breeder's Gazette*, May 16, 1918. 1037.

"Army Horse Business." *Breeder's Gazette*, February 7, 1918. 258.

Ascher, Kate. *The Works: Anatomy of a City*. New York: Penguin, 2005. 285.

Ashton, Chris. "Into the Future. Reclaiming the Golden Era of Global Polo." *Polo Players' Edition*, April, 2016.

Assateague Wild Ponies—Assateague Island National Seashore. http://www.assateagueisland.com/wildlife/pony.htm.

Associated Press. "Horses' Future Uncertain If NYC Carriage Rides End," February 10, 2014.

217

http://www.bostonherald.com/news_opinion/national/northeast/2014/02/horses_future_uncertain_if_nyc_carriage_rides_end.
"Automobile and Internal Combustion Engine" in *Columbia Encyclopedia*.
Babb, Kent. "Unlikely Companions." *The Washington Post*, August 18, 2013.
Baker, Chauncey. "Baker Board Report" in *United States Army in the World War, 1917-1919: Organization of the American Expeditionary Force*. Washington, D.C.: Center of Military History, United States Army, 1988. vol. 1, 81.
Baker, O.E., and Conrad Taeuber. "The Rural People." *The Yearbook of Agriculture, 1940*.
Barkema, Alan, Mark Drabenstott, and Nancy Novack. "The New U.S. Meat Industry." *Federal Reserve Bank of Kansas City Economic Review*, Second Quarter, 2001.
Barker, Jeff. "Congressional Study Looks at Drug Abuse, Injuries in Horse Racing, National Governing Body Discussed for Sport." *The Baltimore Sun*, May 17, 2010.
Barnes, Kenneth K., and James H. Anderson. "If You Enjoy Eating, Thank the Machine," in *That We May Eat, the 1975 Yearbook of Agriculture*. Washington, D.C.: U.S. Department of Agriculture, 1975.
BBC—Domesday Reloaded. "Polo Horses in Graffham." http://www.bbc.co.uk/history/domesday/dblock/GB-492000-117000/page/18.
Beattie, Andrew. "The History of Insurance," *Investopedia*. http://www.investopedia.com/articles/08/history-of-insurance.asp.
Bernstein, Joel H. *Wild Ride, the History and Lore of Rodeo*. Layton, UT: Gibbs-Smith, 2007.
Bishko, Charles Julian. "The Peninsular Background of Latin American Cattle Ranching." *Hispanic American Historical Review*, 32:4 (1952), 491–515.
"BLM Freezemarks," in "Wild Horse Education." May 11, 2014.http://wildhorseeducation.org/blm-freezemark.
Blogger, "Types of Polo: Grass, Arena, Snow and Beach Polo." Polo101.com, February 8, 2010, http://www.polo101.com/about-polo/polo-the-game/types-of-polo-grass-arena-snow-and-beach-polo.html.
Blyth, Ronald. "Akenfield: Portrait of an English Village," in *The Book of Horses*. Edited by Fred Urquhart. New York: William Morrow, 1981. 25–26.
Bohlen, Joe M., Ronald C. Powers, and John A. Wallize. "Main Street Pokes Along While Urban Areas Bloom." *That We May Eat, the Yearbook of Agriculture, 1975*. Washington, D.C.: The Department of Agriculture, 1975.
Bolus, Jim. *The Insider's Pocket Guide to Horse Racing*. Dallas, TX: Taylor, 1990.
Bowser, David. "Canine Cowboys Prove Helpful." *Feedlot Magazine Online*, vol. 7, no.1, January/February, 1999.
Bradley, Kate. "Total Trust, Texas Horseman Mozaun Mckibben Has Found a Method to Teach Horses Extended Gaits Quickly and with Confidence." *Western Horseman*, August, 2013. 25–28.
The Breeder's Gazette: A Weekly Publication Devoted to the Interests of Live-Stock Breeders, April 11, 1912.
Brereton, J.M. *The Horse in War*. New York: Arco, 1976.
"A Brief History of Insurance." *RandMark40*, http://www.randmark40.com/index.php?option=com_content&view=article&id=33.
"Britain's Horses for the War," *Breeder's Gazette*, January 9, 1919. 66.
Brodell, A.P., and J. A. Ewing. *Use of Tractor Power, Animal Power, and Hand Methods in Crop Production*. Bureau of Agricultural Economics. Washington, D.C.: U.S. Department of Agriculture, 1948.
Brown, Dee. *The American West*. New York: Charles Scribner's Sons, 1994.
Buchan, John. *A History of the First World War*. Ed.,Victor Neuburg. Moffat, UK: Lochar, 1991.
Buckham, David, Jason Wahl, and Stuart Rose. *Executive's Guide to Solvency I.*, Cary, NC: SAS Institute, 2010).
Buckingham, David E. "The Us Army Against the Allies in Buying Its Animals." *Journal of the American Veterinary Medical Association*, February 1917, Washington, D.C., 3, no. 6. 698–699.
"Bulletin No. 5." *United States Army in the World War, 1917-1919*, vol. 17. 162.
"Bulletin No. 9." *United States Army in the World War, 1917-1919: Bulletins, GHQ, AEF*. Washington, D.C.: Center of Military History, United States Army, 1992, vol. 17, 11–12, http://www.history.army.mil/html/books/023/23-23/index.html.
"Bulletin No. 33: Quarantine Regulations for Private Mounts to Be Returned to the United States." *United States Army in the World War, 1917-1919*, vol. 17. 253–255.
"Bulletin No. 55." *United States Army in the World War, 1917-1919*, vol. 17. 84–86.
"Bulletin No. 66." *United States Army in the World War, 1917-1919*, vol. 17. 101–102.
"Bulletin No. 93." *United States Army in the World War, 1917-1919*, vol. 17. 135–136, 235.
Bureau of Agricultural Economics. "Horses, Mules, and Motor Vehicles." *United States*

Bibliography

Department of Agriculture Statistical Bulletin No. 5. Washington, D.C.: Government Printing Office, January 1925.

Bureau of Agricultural Economics. U.S. Department of Agriculture, *The Agricultural Outlook for 1933*, Miscellaneous Publication No. 156, Washington, D.C., February, 1933.

Bureau of Agricultural Economics. U.S. Department of Agriculture. *Agricultural Statistics, 1952*.Washington, D.C., 1952.

Bureau of Land Management News Room. Press release. March 11, 2013.

Bureau of Land Management Website. U.S. Department of the Interior, updated April 22, 2014.

Bureau of Land Management, Wyoming, Field Affairs Casper. "The Taylor Grazing Act." https://www.blm.gov/wy/st/en/field_offices/Casper/range/taylor.1.html.

Burnham, Frank. *Rendering, the Invisible Industry*. Fallbrook, CA: Aero Publishers, 1998.

Caldwell, Larry and Michael Buehler. "Picturing a Networked Nation: Abraham Bradley's Landmark U.S. Postal Maps," in *Portolan*, No.77, Spring 2010. Washington, D.C.: Journal of the Washington Map Society. 7.

Camino Real Polo Country Club, San Vicente, Argentina. "El Caballo De Polo—The History of the Argentine Polo Horse." http://www.caminorealpolo.com/all-about-polo-ponies-whatpolo.

Campanella, Thomas J. *Cities from the Sky, an Aerial Portrait of America*. New York: Princeton Architectural, 2001. 45.

Carter, William Harding. "The Story of the Horse, the Development of Man's Companion in War Camp, on Farm, in the Marts of Trade, and in the Field of Sport." *The National Geographic Magazine*, 44, no. 5 (1923). 553.

Center of Military History. United States Army. *The United States Army in the World War, 1917–1919: Organization of the American Expeditionary Forces*. Washington, D.C.: 1992. Vol. 1.

Chamberlin, J. Edward. *Horse: How the Horse Has Shaped Civilizations*. Blue Ridge, NY: United Tribes Media, 2006.

The Charlotte Steeplechase Association. "What Is a Steeplechase?" http://www.queenscup.org/about-the-chase/about-steeplechasing/what. February 2, 2014.

Charney, Mark. Communication. February 8, 2010.

Chavez y Gilbert, Donald. *Cowboys—Vaqueros, Origins of the First American Cowboys*. Self-published, n.d.

Chesler, Frankie. "Kindness, Patience, Friendship, and Time for Play." *Of Women and Horses*. Irvine, CA: Bow Tie Press, 2000.

Chicago Fire Department. "History of the Chicago Fire Department," Rev. 6/10/2004.

Christopher, John. *Balloons at War, Gasbags, Flying Bombs & Cold War Secrets*. Stroud, UK: Tempus, 2005.

"Cloning Ponies: How Technology Could Transform an Ancient Sport." *The Economist*, January 5, 2013. http://www.economist.com/news/business/21569054-how-technology-could-transform-ancient-sport-cloney-ponies.

Clutton-Brock, Juliet. *Horse Power, a History of the Horse and Donkey in Human Societies*. Cambridge, MA: Harvard University Press, 1992.

Coady, Jean Howerton. (Louisville) *Courier-Journal*. "The 1972 Epizootic." January 8, 1977.

Columbia Encyclopedia. New York, 1942. 1675.

Conn, George H. "Auxiliary Remount Depots of the Army." Camp Greene, NC. *Breeder's Gazette*, August 22, 1918. 267.

Conn, George H. "Buying Horses and Mules for the Army." *Breeder's Gazette*, February 28, 1918. 428.

Conway, Terry. "Polo Ponies: Hardest Working Athletes in Equine World." http://terryconway.net/cms/index.php?option=com_content&view=article&id=83:polo-ponies-hardest-working-athletes-in-equine-world&catid=14:racing-columns&Itemid=10.

Cooper, John S. "American Horses in the European War." *Breeder's Gazette*, December 16, 1915, 1112, 1140, 1142.

Costa-Paz, Matis, Luis Aponte-Tinao, and D. Luis Muscolo. "Injuries to Polo Riders: A Prospective Evaluation." *British Journal of Sports Medicine*, 1999, 33:329–332.

Cotterell, Arthur. *Chariot: From Chariot to Tank. the Astounding Rise and Fall of the World's First War Machine*. Woodstock, NY: Overlook, 2005.

Craven, R.C. "The Red Star and the War Horse." *Breeder's Gazette*, July 18, 1918. 82–83.

Crist, Steven. "Data Debunking Myths Gets Buried." *Daily Racing Form*, August 22, 2008.

Cruise, David, and Alison Griffiths. *Wild Horse Annie and the Last of the Mustangs, the Life of Velma Johnston*. New York: Scribner, 2010.

Darnley-Smith, Jan, and Elwyn Hartley Edwards. *Horses, Their Role in the History of Man*, based on the original screenplay. London: Willow Books, 1987.

Davies, Gareth A., polo correspondent, August 18, 2015. http://www.telegraph.co.uk/sport/

othersports/polo/11809598/Modern-bulkier-polo-ponies-are-akin-to-impact-players-in-rugby-and-this-must-change-says-leading-official.html.

"Death and Disarray at America's Racetracks." *New York Times*, March 25, 2012.

De Barneville, Maurice F. "The Remount Service in the A.E.F.," *The Cavalry Journal*, 30, no. 123 (1921): 137.

Deheir, Jean-Claude, Jean-Paul Deleage and Daniel Hemery. *in the Servitude of Power. Energy and Civilization Through the Ages.* London and New Jersey: Zed Books, 1986, 1991. (Translation)

Delay, Cindy Pierson. "Understanding the Types and Classes of Horse Races." in About.com Horse Racing, 2013.

Denhardt, Robert Moorman. *The Quarter Running Horse.* Norman: University of Oklahoma Press, 1979.

Denison, Jennifer. "The Canine Crew." *Western Horseman*, August, 2012.

De Varila, Osborne. *The First Shot for Liberty, the Story of an American Who Went Over with the First Expeditionary Force and Served His Country at the Front.* Philadelphia: John C. Winston, 1918.

Dibner, Bern. *Alessandro Volta and the Electric Battery.* New York: Franklin Watts, 1964.

Dibner, Bern. *The Founding Fathers of Electrical Science.* Norwalk, CT: Burndy, 1954.

Dibner, Bern. *Oersted and the Discovery of Electromagnetism.* Norwalk, CT: Burnby, 1961.

Diego Jemio. "Argentina's Love Affair with Polo." *BBC News*, February 26, 2015. http://www.bbc/news/business-31602941.

Dinsmore, Wayne. "Army Horse and Mule Requirements." *Breeder's Gazette*, May 3, 1917. 924.

Dinsmore, Wayne. "Military Exports of Horses and Mules." *Breeder's Gazette*, April 25, 1918, 865.

Dista, B., G. Maldonado, H. Reid, B. Puschner, J. Maxwell, A. Agasan, L. Humphreys, T. Holt. "Acute Selenium Toxicosis in Polo Ponies." *J Vet Diagn Invest*, 2011 May; 23(3): 623–8. Doi: 10.1177/1040638711404142.

Drape, Joe. "As Concerns Over Drugs Mount, the Jockey Club Says It Will Pay for Testing." *New York Times*, August 12, 2013.

Drape, Joe. "Eight States Approve Medication Standards." *New York Times*, March 13, 2013. B13.

Drape, Joe. "Medication Is Cited in Horse Racing's Decline in U.S." *New York Times*, June 14, 2011.

Drape, Joe. "Study Raises Questions About Antibleeding Drug." *New York Times*, December 17, 2013.

Dunn. S. "Causes and Effects." *Breeder's Gazette*, September 1921, 372.

Eakin, Sarah. "Embryo Center Imports Argentine Expertise." *The Month in Polo Players' Edition,* http://www.poloplayersedition.com/new/art0306.html.

Editorial Viewpoints. *Journal of the American Veterinary Medical Association,* April 1, 1977, Vol. 170, Issue 7, 668.

Edwards, Everett E. "American Agriculture—The First 300 Years." *Farmers in a Changing World, The Yearbook of Agriculture.* United States Department of Agriculture. Washington, D.C.: U.S. Government Printing Office, 1940.

Ehrenfreund, Norbert, communication to the author, October 15, 2012.

Ellis, John. *Cavalry: The History of Mounted Warfare.* Barnsley, UK: Pen & Sword, 2004.

Encyclopædia Britannica. "Horse Racing: Bloodlines and Studbooks." Updated January 22, 2014.

Encyclopædia Britannica. "Horse Racing: The State of Racing." Updated January 22, 2014.

Encyclopædia Britannica. "Quarter-Horse Racing." http:/www.britannica.com/EBchecked/topic486381/quarterhorse-racing.

Equamore Foundation. 2014, www.equamore.org/portfolio/dancer/.

Erickson, John R. *The Modern Cowboy,* 2nd Ed. Denton: University of North Texas Press, 2004).

Essin, Emmett M. *Shavetails & Bell Sharps: The History of the U.S. Army Mule.* Lincoln: University of Nebraska Press, 1997.

Ethirajan, Anbarasan. "Concern Over Dwindling Number of Rare Indian Ponies." *BBC News*, July 13, 2015. www.bbc.com/news/world-asia-india-33308422.

Ewing, Sherm. *The Ranch, a Modern History of the North American Cattle Industry.* Missoula, MT: Mountain Press, 1995.

Fair, John S. "The Supply of Animals for the Army." Lecture, Quartermaster Reserve Corps, Washington, D.C., July 3, 1917. Washington, D.C.: Government Printing Office, 1917.

Fellenstein, Stephanie. "Drug Tests Begin for Polo Ponies." *Dvm360 Magazine,* June 1, 2010. http://veterinarynews.dvm360.com/drug-tests-begin-polo-ponies.

Fire Department. "Water Supply Systems." http://sf-fire.org/water-supplysystems.

Fire History. "A History of Horses in the Fire Service." http://firehistory.weebly.com/a-history-of-horses-in-the-fire-service.html.

"A Fire Pro-History of Fire Fighting." http://afirepro.com/history.html.

Firefighting History & Traditions. "Why Did Fire Stations Have Spiral Staircases?" *My Firefighter Nation.* http://my.firefightingnation.com/group/firefightingmrths.

Fitzsimons, Bernard, ed. *Tanks & Weapons of World War I.* New York: Beekman House, 1973.

Flink, James J. *America Adopts the Automobile, 1895–1910.* Cambridge, MA, and London: MIT Press, 1970.

Flood, Elizabeth Clair. *Old Time Dude Ranches Out West.* Salt Lake City: Gibbs-Smith, 1995.

Flores, Trudy, and Sarah Griffith. "Horse-Drawn Fire-Engine, 1913." *The Oregon History Project* 2002. https://oregonhistoryproject.org/articles/historical-records/horse-drawn-fire-engine-1913/#.WIeyvtBN38s.

"Four-Footed Experts in War." *Literary Digest*, 1, No. 5 (1915): 213.

Frank, Katie. "Learning to Downshift." *Western Horseman*, January, 2015. 70–76.

Freidel, Frank. *Over There: The Story of America's First Great Overseas Crusade.* Short Hills, NJ: Burford Books, 1964.

Frohm, Jack. "Your Riding Future: Colleges of Equestrian Knowledge." Quoted by Abbey, in *Horses and Horse Shows*, 264.

Fussell, Paul. *The Great War and Modern Memory.* London: Oxford University Press, 1977.

"Gain 100,000 Tons a Month in Ships." *New York Times*, July 31, 1918.

Gardner, Frank D. *Traditional American Farming Techniques.* Guilford, CT: Lyons Press, 2001. Originally published in 1916 as L.T. Myers, *Successful Farming.*

"General Orders: No. 34." *United States Army in the World War, 1917–1919*, vol. 16. 233.

"General Orders: No. 65." *United States Army in the World War, 1917–1919*, vol. 16. 297.

"General Orders: No. 66." *The United States Army in the World War, 1917–1919: General Orders, GHQ, AEF.* Washington, D.C.: Center of Military History, United States Army, 1992. vol. 16, 300. http://www.history.army.mil/html/books/023/23-22/.

Genung, A.B. "Agriculture in the World War Period," *Farmers in a Changing World, the Yearbook of Agriculture 1940.* Washington, D.C.: U.S. Department of Agriculture, 1940. 293–294.

Goddard, Stephen B. *Getting There, the Epic Struggle Between Road and Rail in the American Century.* New York: Basic Books, A Division of HarperCollins, 1994.

Goodwin, Dorothy C. "Brief Chronology of American Agricultural History." Compiled under Direction of Paul H. Johnstone, in *Farmers in a Changing World: The Yearbook of Agriculture, 1940.* Washington, D.C.: U.S. Department of Agriculture, U.S. Government Printing Office, 1940. Appendix A, 1184.

Govan, Thomas P., Capt. Historical Section, Army Ground Forces, "The Army Ground Forces, Training for Mountain and Winter Warfare." Study No. 23, 1946. http://www.history.army.mil/books/agf/agf23.htm.

"Government Attitude Towards Horse Buying." *Breeder's Gazette*, August 16, 1917. 211.

Gradenwitz, Alfred. "A Horses' Hospital: Work of the German Army Veterinary Surgeons." *Scientific American*, 114, no. 5 (1916): 126.

Grasse, Pierre Paul. *Larousse Encyclopedia of the Animal World.* New York: Larousse, 1975. 557.

Grasty, Charles H. "Allies See Victory Only in Defeat of U-Boats, and Look to America for Utmost Efforts." *New York Times*, March 17, 1918.

Grasty, Charles H. "U-Boat Sinkings Cut to 62,000 Tons in a Week." *New York Times*, September 24, 1917.

Gray, James R., and Wylie D. Goodsell. *Cattle Ranches, Organization, Costs, and Returns, Southwest Nonmigratory Grazing Areas, 1940–59.* Farm Economic Division, Economic Research Service, U.S. Department of Agriculture, in cooperation with Agricultural Experiment Station, New Mexico State University. Agricultural Economic Report No.1.

Grolier Educational. *Inventions and Inventors, Volume 4, Water and Pasture, Traditional Agriculture, Farming, Food & Biotechnology.* Danbury, CT: 2000.

Grolier Educational. *Inventions and Inventors, Volume 6, Animal Power, Land and Water Transportation.* Danbury, CT, 2000.

Grolier Educational. *Inventions and Inventors, Volume 10, Power and Energy.* Danbury, CT: 2000.

Gruber, Jacj. "New Horsepower for War Zones: Special Forces Saddle Up: U.S. Special Forces and Marines Train to Be Combat Ready on Horseback at the United States Marine Mountain Warfare Training Center (Mw Tc) Near Bridgeport, Calif." *USA Today*, June 22, 2014.

Gustafson, Sid, "Essay: Medication Continues to Stifle America's Triple Crown Hopes." *The Rail Blog, New York Times*, June 11, 2013.

Hagstrom's Atlas and Official Postal Guide of the City of New York Five Boroughs, 5th ed. New York: Hagstrom, 1947.

Halberstadt, Hans. *The American Fire Engine.* Osceola, WI: Motorbooks International, 1993.

Hall, Gregory A. "Eight Belles' Death at Derby Spurred Safety Reforms." *Courier-Journal*, May 2, 2009.

Hanson, Neil. *Unknown Soldiers: The Story of the Missing in the First World War*. New York: Alfred A. Knopf, 2006.

Hardy, Phil. *The Encyclopedia of Western Movies*. Minneapolis: Woodbury Press, 1984.

Harlan, C.L., C.A. Burmeister, and G.B. Thorne. *Department of Agriculture Yearbook of 1933*.

Harner, Joseph P. III, and James P. Murphy. *Planning Cattle Feedlots*. Department of Biological and Agricultural Engineering, Kansas State University, August, 1998.

Haskin, Steve. "The History of Drugs in America." Bloodhorse.com, July 1, 2012.

Haydon, F. Stansbury. *Aeronautics in the Union and Confederate Armies: With a Survey of Military Aeronautics Prior to 1861*. Cranbury, NJ: Scholar's Bookshelf, 2006.

Hayes, M. Horace, FRCVS. *Veterinary Notes for Horse Owners*. 18th Edition. New York: Simon & Schuster, 2002.

Haythornthwaite, Philip J. *A Photohistory of World War One*. London: Arms and Armour, 1995.

Hegarty, Matt. "Official Calls for U.S. to Ban Lasix in Stakes." *Daily Racing Form*, August 23, 2009.

Helliker, Kevin. "Rodeo Drive: Rich Urban Cowboys on Fine Horses Best Ranch Hands." *Wall Street Journal*, December 16, 2010.

Heninger, Allan T. *Present Sabres: A Popular History of the United States Horse Cavalry*. Tucson, AZ: Excalibur, 2002.

Henry, Marguerite. *Mustang, Wild Spirit of the West*. New York: Simon & Schuster, 1966.

Hersh, Marcus. "Giving Softer Whips a Crack." *Daily Racing Form*, November 19, 2009.

Hilberg, Karl. "Ethics in Our Sports," *Polo Players' Edition*, April 2016. 57.

Hilton, George W. *The Cable Car in America*, Revised Edition. Stanford University Press, 1997.

"History of the Equestrian Sport of Polo." SportPOLO corporation, 2013. http://sportspolo.com/History/default.htm.

"History of the Water Mains in New York City." https://www1.nyc.gov/html/dep/html/drinking_water/wood_water_pipes_history.shtml.

"The History of Water Hoose, Hoase, Hause, or Hose?" *Fire History*. http://firehistory.weebly.com/the-history-of-hoose-hoase-hause-or-hose.html

The Horse Council, "Number of Horses by Breed and Activity, in Most Comprehensive Horse Study Ever Reveals a Nearly $40 Billion Impact on the U.S. Economy." June 28, 2005.

"Horse Racing Fantasy: Simple Answers to Common Questions." *About Horses in General*, http//www.horseracingame.com/community content/stories/horseracing/28-09-2008.

"The Horses." http://www.engine3.org/Horses.html.

"The Horse's Gallant Part in the War." *Literary Digest*, 59, no.8 (1918).

"How Ya Gonna Keep 'em Down on the Farm After They've Seen Paree?" Lewis, Sam M and Joe Young, words, music by Walter Donaldson. New York: Waterson, Berlin & Snyder Co., Music Publishing, 1919.

Hurst, W.M., and L.M. Church. *Power and Machinery in Agriculture*. Washington, D.C.: U.S. Department of Agriculture, Miscellaneous Publications No. 157, April, 1933.

"The Indispensable War Horse." *Breeder's Gazette*, December 8, 1917, 1036.

Innes, C.M., and K.L. Morgan. "Falls and Injuries to Polo Players: Risk Perception, Mitigation and Risk Factors." *Sports Medicine-Open*, 2015.1:2. https://sportsmedicine-open.springeropen.com/articles/10.1186/s40798-014-0002-8.

Innes, C.M., and K.L. Morgan. "Polo Pony Injuries: Player-Owner Reported Risks, Perception, Mitigation and Risk Factors." *Equine Veterinary Journal*. School of Veterinary Science and Department of Musculoskeletal Biology, Institute of Ageing and Chronic Disease, University of Liverpool, UK, 2015. 47.

International Society for the Protection of Mustangs and Burros (ISPMB). "A Bit of History, BLM and Land Management." http://www.ispmb.org/history.html.

Iowa Beef Center. *Beef Feedlot System Manual*. Ames: Iowa State University, n.d. 1–27.

Jobe, Joseph, ed. *Guns: An Illustrated History of Artillery*. New York: Crescent Books, 1974.

The Jockey Club, *Annual Release of Report of Mares Bred Statistics*, 2008–2013.

Johnson, Paul C. *Farm Power in the Making of America*. Des Moines, IA: Wallace-Homestead Book Co., 1978.

Jordan, Terry G. *North American Cattle-Ranching Frontiers, Origins, Diffusion, and Differentiation*. Albuquerque: University of New Mexico Press, 1993.

Kane, Ed. "RCI Rules on Reducing Phenylbutazone Threshold." *DVM Newsmagazine*, December 1, 2010.

Kavanaugh, Jim. "Polo Ponies Are Pampered, Beloved, Hard-Trained Athletes." CNN.com. http://www.cnn.com/2009/US/04/21/polo.horses/index.html?eref=ib_us.

Kay, Alison C. "The Origins of Fire Insurance (& 'Lusty Able Body'd Firemen'). *Victorian Vestibule* Blog, March 11, 2011. http://www.

alisonkay.com/historyjunkey/fire-insurance/.
Keegan, John. *An Illustrated History of the First World War*. New York: Alfred A. Knopf, 2001.
Kilby, Emily R. "Demographics of the U.S. Equine Population." *The State of the Animals IV*, 2007. New York.
King, LeRoy O., Jr. *100 Years of Capital Traction: The Story of Streetcars in the Nation's Capital*. Dallas, TX: Taylor Publishing Company, 1989.
King, William T. *History of the American Steam Engine*. Mineola, NY: Dover Publications, 1896, 2001.
Kinoshita, June, and Nicholas Palevsky. *Gateway to Japan*, revised edition. Tokyo: Kodansha International, 1992.
Klein, Barry. "The World's First Insurance Company." https://www.irmi.com/articles/expert-commentary/the-worlds-first-insurance-company.
Koenig, Robert. *The Fourth Horseman: One Man's Secret Mission to Wage the Great War in America*. New York: Public Affairs/Perseus Books Group, 2006.
Laffaye, Horace A. *The Evolution of Polo*. Jefferson, NC: McFarland, 2009.
Laffaye, Horace A. *The Polo Encyclopedia*. Jefferson, NC: McFarland, 2004.
Laffaye, Horace A. *Polo in the United States: A History*. Jefferson, NC: McFarland, 2011.
"Lamar No. 1, 1907–2007." City of Lamar, Colorado. Rapid Fire Truck, City of Lamar. http://www.ci.lamar.co.us/index.asp?SEC=B45FE11F-D587-48C0-B6BD-0B59806BF135&Type=GALLERY.
Landers, T.A. *Insider's Guide to Horseracing*. Yardley, PA: Westholme, 2005.
Latham, Richard C. "Polo." *Encyclopædia Britannica*, www.britannica.com/sports/polo.
Lawrence, Robert G., and James M. Downes. *Costs and Returns of Maryland's Standardbred Breeders*. College Park: University of Maryland Agricultural Experiment Station, Eastern Shore Research Farms, MPS 963, July, 1981.
Lay, M.G. *Ways of the World: A History of the World's Roads and of the Vehicles That Used Them*. New Brunswick, NJ: Rutgers University Press, 1992.
Lecompte, Mary Lou. "The Hispanic Influence on the History of Rodeo, 1823–1922." *Journal of Sports History*, vol. 12, no. 1, Spring, 1985.
Leehrsen, Charles. *Crazy Good: The True Story of Dan Patch, the Most Famous Horse in America*. New York: Simon & Schuster, 2008.
Levin, Jonathan V. "Peru in the Guano Age." *The Export Economies: Their Pattern of Development in Historical Perspective*. Cambridge, MA: Harvard University Press, 1960.
Liu, Joanne S. *Barbed Wire: The Fence That Changed the West*. Missoula, MT: Mountain Press, 2009.
Livesey, Anthony. *The Historical Atlas of World War I*. New York: Henry Holt, 1994.
Louisiana Racing Commission. *Rules*.
MacDonald, James M. and William D. McBride. *The Transformation of U.S. Livestock Agriculture Scale, Efficiency and Risks*. Economic Research Service, Economic Information Bulletin Number 43, U.S. Department of Agriculture, January, 2009. 25.
Macdonald, Lyn. *1914*. London: Guild Publishing, 1987.
Macdonald, Lyn. *1915: The Death of Innocence*. New York: Henry Holt, 1994.
MacDonald, Lyn. *Somme*. London: Michael Joseph, 1983.
Malone, John Williams. *An Album of the American Cowboy*. New York: Franklin Watts, 1971.
Manhattan. *Breeder's Gazette*, August 16, 1911, signed. 250.
Manhattan. *Breeder's Gazette*, September 10, 1913, signed.
Manhattan. *Breeder's Gazette*, October 2, 1913, signed. 621.
Manhattan. *Breeder's Gazette*, November 20, 1913, signed. 992.
Manhattan. "Motor Trucks Supplementing but Not Supplanting Draft Horses, the Experience of Leading Firms in Chicago and New York." *Breeder's Gazette*, December 18, 1912.
Marine Corps Mountain Warfare Training Center. History. U.S. Marine Corps. http://www.29palms.marines.mil/mcmwtc/About/Historyaspx.
Marlin, D.J, and J.C. Allen. "Cardiovascular Demands of Competition on Low-Goal (Non-Elite) Polo Ponies." *Equine Vet. J.*, Sep. 31, 1999 (5).
Marshall, George C. *Memoirs of My Services in the World War, 1917–1918*. Ed. James L. Collins, Jr. Boston: Houghton Mifflin, 1976.
Marshall, Samuel L. A. and Edmund O. Stillman. *The American Heritage History of World War I*, ed. Alvin M. Josephy Jr. and Joseph L. Gardner. New York: American Heritage, 1964.
Maryland, Laws. Chapter 518, Section 4, Approved April 12, 1904 Maryland, Laws. Chapter 518, Section 4, Approved April 12, 1904.
Maryland, Laws. Chapter 449, Section 138, Approved April 3, 1906.

Masoff, Joy. *Fire*. New York: Scholastic Inc., 1998.

Mason, Carolyn. "Shakleford Horses Timeline: History on Hooves: The Horses of Shakleford Banks, Their Role in the Culture and History of Eastern North Carolina," November 17, 1997. http://www.shaklefordhorses.org/timeline.htm.

McBride, William D., and Kenneth Mathews, Jr. *The Diverse Structure and Organization of U.S. Beef Cow-Calf Farms*. Economic Research Service, Economic Information Bulletin Number 73, U.S. Department of Agriculture, March 2011.

McKnight, Dr. T. L. "Feral Livestock in America." *University of California Publications in Geography*, vol. 16. University of California Press, 1964. Quoted by Cruise & Griffiths, *Wild Horse Annie*.

McShane, Clay, and Joel A. Tarr. *The Horse in the City: Living Machines in the Nineteenth Century*. Baltimore: Johns Hopkins Press, 2007.

MedalMaclay.com. "Equitation Explained." 2008. http://www.medalmaclay.com/explained/sponsoredbybigeq.com.medalmaclay.com/eqresults/36.html.

Melina, Remy. "Why Are Dalmatians the Official Firehouse Dogs?" *Live Science*, May 19, 2011. http://www.livescience.com/33293-dalmatians-official-firehouse-dogs.html.

Michael 1XYZ. "History of Firefighting." Thread. http://www.firehouse.com/forums/t126027/.

Michigan State Polo Club. "Go Green! Go White! Go Polo: About the Team." http://www.msu.edu/msupolo/.

Midkiffe, Mary. "An Intuitive Edge." *Of Women and Horses*. Irvine, CA: Bowtie Press, 2000.

Milburn, Frank. *Polo: The Emperor of Games*. New York: Alfred A. Knopf, 1994.

Montreal Gazette, May 20, 1932. "Innovation for 'Double' Tickets." Quoted by *Wikipedia*.

Moore, Henry Charles. *Omnibuses and Cabs: Their Origin and History*. London: Chapman & Hall, 1902. 4. https://archive.org/details/omnibusescabsthe00mooruoft.

Morens, David M., and Jeffrey K. Taubenberger. "An Avian Outbreak Associated with Panzootic Equine Influenza In 1872: An Early Example of Highly Pathogenic Avian Influenza?" *Influenza and Other Respiratory Viruses*, 2010:4, 373–377.

Murnane, Thomas G. "James Law, America's First Veterinary Epidemiologist and the Equine Influenza Epizootic of 1872." Presented to the 2008 Annual Meeting of the American Veterinary Medical History Society in New Orleans, LA, July 21, 2008. Long Riders Guild Academic Foundation. http://www.lrgaf.org/medical/jameslaw-murnane.htn.

National Academy of Sciences. Office of News and Public Information. Washington, D.C., press release, June 5, 2013.

National Steeple Chase Museum. "The History of Steeplechasing." 2014. http://www.steeplechasemuseum.org/site/page/history.

National Steeplechase Association. "History." http://www.nationalsteeplechase.com/chasing//history. 2010–2014.

Nerenberg, Mark E., photograph.

"New Horse Buying Policy." *Breeder's Gazette*, November 22, 1917. 937.

New York Times, June 12, 1915.

Niedner. "What Is Water's Contribution in Putting Out Fires?" October 9, 2013. http://www.niedner.com/en/blog/water-contribution-in-firefighting.

Nunez, Claudia. "Horses Abandoned in Foreclosure Crises." Translated by Elena Shore. *La Opinion*. San Francisco, CA: New America Media. March 31, 2011.

O'Brian, Mitch. "How Fire Stations Evolved." *Fire Find*, 2009. http://fire-find.com/history-of-fire-stations/.

"Operating Instructions for L & H Freeze Branders." http://www.lhbrandingirons.com/Feeeze/Instructions.html.

Oswald, Paul. "Common Mistakes Seen in the Show Ring." Quoted by Abbey in *Horses and Horse Shows*.

Padget, Tim. "The Dead Ponies and Their Millionaire Owner." *TIME*, April 23, 2009, http://content.time.com/time/nation/article/0,8599,1893280,00.html.

Palazzo, Albert. *Seeking Victory on the Western Front: The British Army and Chemical Warfare in World War I*. Lincoln: University of Nebraska Press, 2002.

Parmeter, Irving. "The Horse in War Today and Yesterday." *Current History*, June 1928, 451.

Pate, J'Nell L. *Livestock Legacy, the Fort Worth Stockyards, 1887–1987*. College Station: Texas A & M University Press, 1988.

Patrascu, Daniel. May 29, 2009. http://www.autoevolution.com/news/fire-truck-history-7249html.

Pedrick, Don Harvey. "It's a Wrap!" *Polo Players' Edition*, September, 2003. *Victoria Polo Club Page*, http://carriagehousebandb.ca/wrap/html.

Pengra, Amy. "Polo Ponies: Horsing Around the Field—Luchese Bootmaker." https://www.lucchese.com/polo/article/polo-ponies-horsing-around-the-field/.

Pershing, John J. "Final Report to the Secretary of War." Paris, September 1, 1919. *United

States Army in the World War, 1917–1919: Reports of the Commander-In-Chief, AEF, Staff Sections and Services. Washington, D.C.: Center of Military History, United States Army, 1991, vol. 12, 17. http://www.history.army.mil/html/books/023/23-18/.

Pershing, John J. *My Experience in the World War.* New York: Frederick A. Stokes, 1931.

PETA, "Overbreeding and Slaughter," https://www.peta.org/issues/animals-in-entertainment/horse-racing-2/horse-racing-industry-cruelty/overbreeding-and-slaughter.

Peterson, Holly. "A Chance to Soar: For Young Equestrians, Commuting to Florida on Weekends Is a Commitment and a Goal." *New York Times*, March 26, 2015. D1, 8, 9.

Photographic History of the Civil War, Volume 2: The Cavalry: Decisive Battles. Secaucus, NJ: Blue and Grey Press, 1987.

Pinches, Harold E. "Revolution in Agriculture." *Power to Produce: The Yearbook of Agriculture, 1960.* Washington, D.C: U.S. Department of Agriculture, 1960. 1–7.

Pollen, Michael. "Power Steer." *New York Times Magazine*, March 31, 2002.

Polo Players' Edition Calendar, April, 1916. 64.

Polo Training Foundation. "The Future of Polo in America." www.polotraining.org/about/history.html.

Price, Steven D., and Charles Kauffman. *The Polo Primer: A Guide for Players and Spectators.* New York: Pelham Books, 1989.

prorodeohorses.com, classifieds.

Public Law 92–195, December 15, 1971.

Quartermaster General Annual Report, Fiscal Year 1915. Washington, D.C.: Government Printing Office, 1915. 62, https://catalog.hathitrust.org/Record/008607233.

Quartermaster General Regulations Governing the Purchase and Inspection of Animals for the Army. Washington, D.C.: Government Printing Office, 1917.

Quartermaster General Report to the Secretary of War, Fiscal Year 1916. Washington, D.C.: Government Printing Office, 1916. 62. https://catalog.hathitrust.org/Record/00860 7233.

Quartermaster General Report to the Secretary of War, Fiscal Year 1917. Washington, D.C.: Government Printing Office, 1917. 90. https://catalog.hathitrust.org/Record/00860 7233.

Quartermaster General U.S. Army Report to the Secretary of War 1919. Washington, D.C.: Government Printing Office, 1920. 44–46. https://catalog.hathitrust.org/Record/0021 38437

Quartermaster General U.S. Army Report to the Secretary of War 1920. Washington, D.C.: Government Printing Office, 1920. 50. https://catalog.hathitrust.org/Record/002138437.

Ratigan, W. J. "Taking Horses to War." *Breeder's Gazette*, August 5, 1915, 196.

Reynoldson, L.A., R.S. Kifer, J.H. Martin, and W.R. Humphries. *The Combined Harvester-Thresher in the Great Plains.* U.S. Department of Agriculture Technical Bulletin, 1928. 70.

Rizzo, Gwen. "Life Wish, Player Moves Forward After Serious Injury." *Polo Players' Edition*, April, 2016.

Rizzo, Peter J. "G.C. Shermans, Father and Son Volunteered Much of Their Time to the Sport." *Polo Players' Edition*, March, 2016.

Robertson, William H.P. *The History of Thoroughbred Racing in America.* New York: Bonanza Books, 1964.

Robinson, Roxana. "Heart's Desire." *What My Mother Gave Me: Thirty-One Women on the Gifts That Mattered Most.* Elizabeth Benedict, ed. Chapel Hill, NC: Algonquin Books, 2013.

Rodenbough, Theo F. "Cavalry of the Civil War: Its Evolution and Influence." *Photographic History of the Civil War*, vol. 2. 34.

Rommel, George M. Speech recorded in *Minutes of the Organization Meeting of the Horse Publicity Association of America* held at the Pennsylvania Hotel, New York, October 30–31, 1919, New York: Harris & Stacy Stenographic Reporters. 214.

Rowsome, Frank. *Trolley Car Treasury.* New York: Bonanza Books, 1956.

Rutstein, Milton, personal communication. April 24, 2010.

Ryden, Hope. *America's Last Wild Horses: The Classic Study of the Mustangs—Their Pivotal Role in the History of the West, Their Return to the Wild, and the Ongoing Efforts to Preserve Them.* Guilford, CT: Lyons Press, 2005.

Sanders, Ralph W. *Vintage Farm Tractors.* Stillwater, NM: Voyageur Press, 1997.

Satow, Julie. "A Socialite Met a Horse Trainer, and a Rare Horse Partnership Was Born." *New York Times*, May 31, 2015.

Sayles, G.O. *The Medieval Foundations of England.* Philadelphia: University of Pennsylvania Press, 1950.

Schaefer, Christina. *The Great War: A Guide to the Service Records of All the World's Fighting Men and Volunteers.* Baltimore, MD: Genealogical Publishing Co., 1998.

Schlebecker, John T. *Cattle Raising in the Plains, 1900–1961.* Lincoln: University of Nebraska Press, 1963.

Seal, Rector R. *Maryland Automobile History*

1900 to 1942. Chicago, IL: Adams Press, 1985.
Seals, Bob. "U.S. Army Captures World Polo Title." *Military History Online*. http://www.militaryhistoryonline.com/20th century/articles/polo, 12/29/2013.
Sellnow, Les. "Rodeo Horses." Friends of Rodeo, www.TheHorse.com, January 2002.
Simpson, Margaret, curator. "Horse-Drawn Fire Engines." Sydney, Australia: Powerhouse Museum. http://www.powerhousemuseum.com/collection/database/?irn=207677.
Smith, Bradley. *The Horse in the West*. New York: Leon Amiel, 1969.
Smith, D.J. *Discovering Horse Drawn Farm Machinery*. Aylesbury, Bucks, UK: Shire Publishing, 1979.
Smith, Dennis. *Dennis Smith's History of Firefighting in America: 300 Years of Courage*. New York: Dial Press, 1978.
Smith, Robert T. "The Father of Waters." *Water Trails West: The Western Writers of America*. New York: Avon Books, 1979.
Sokloff, Brian. "21 Polo Horses Die at Florida Match." *Huffpost Green*, http://www.huffingtonpost.com2009/04/20/21-polo-horses-die-at-florida-match.
Stand Up and Fight. MGM, Hollywood, 1939.
Stanley, Jerry. *Cowboys and Longhorns: A Portrait of the Long Drive*. New York: Crown, 2003.
Stanton, Doug. *Horse Soldiers: The Extraordinary Story of a Band of U.S. Soldiers Who Rode to Victory in Afghanistan*. New York: Scribner, 2009.
Starrs, Paul F. *Let the Cowboy Ride, Cattle Ranching in the American West*. Baltimore: The Johns Hopkins Press, 1998.
Steele, Christy. *Cattle Ranching in the American West*. Milwaukee, WI: World Almanac Library, 2005.
Steinkraus, William C., and M. A. Stoneridge. "Polo," in *The Horse in Sport*, foreword by H.R.H. Prince Philip, Duke of Edinburgh. New York: Stewart, Tabori & Chang, 1987.
Stowe, Dr. C. Gill. *2009–2010 American Horse Publications Equine Industry Survey*, 2010.
Suren-Pahlav, Shapour. "History of Chogan (Polo)," *Sport in Iran*, Iran Chamber Society, February 18, 2016, www.iranchamber.com/sport/chogan/chogan_history.php.
The Survey of Agriculture. 2007.
Terraine, John. *To Win a War: 1918 the Year of Victory*. Garden City, NY: Doubleday, 1981.
Thomas, Katie. "Polo Ponies Were Given Incorrect Medication." *New York Times*, April 23, 2009. B11.
Thornton, T.D. "For Horses' Safety He Thinks Outside the Hocks." *Boston Globe*, April 29, 2009.

Thoroughbred Charities of America, Thoroughbred Retirement Foundation, and The Jockey Club. "Joint Announcement." *Thoroughbred Daily News*, November 12, 2008, and *New York Times*, December 27, 2009.
Thoroughbred Daily News. "Round Table Focuses on Medication Issues." August 24, 2009, and "Driving Sustainable Growth for Thoroughbred Racing and Breeding," Selected Exhibits, August, 2011.
Thoroughbred Polo Ponies. "Engineered for Players." http://www.thoroughbred-poloponies.com/aboutus.html.
The Time Traveler's Guide to Medieval England, a Handbook for Visitors to the Fourteenth Century, A Touchstone Book. New York: Simon & Schuster, 2008.
Tolley, H. R., and L.M. Church. *Corn-Belt Farmers' Experience with Motor Trucks: A Study of 831 Reports from Farmers Who Own Motor Trucks*. Washington, D.C.: U.S. Department of Agriculture Bulletin No. 931, February 25, 1921.
Toth, Dr. Delphi M. "The Psychology of Women and Horses." *Of Women and Horses*. Irvine, CA: Bowtie Press, 2000.
Townsend, E.H. *Punch or the London Charivari*, February 9, 1916, 111.
"Training Polo Horses in Argentina." http://www.argentinapolo.com/gustavohorsetraining.html.
"Trial and Error: Breeders Look for the Best Formulas for Creating Top Ponies," *Polo Players' Edition*. http://www.poloplayersedition.com/new/art0306.html.
Truscott, Lucian K. *The Twilight of the U.S. Cavalry: Life in the Old Army, 1917–1942*. Lawrence: University of Kansas Press, 1987. xiv–xv. Cited in Bob Seal, "U.S. Army Captures Title."
Tucker, Spencer C. *The Great War: 1914–1918*. Bloomington: Indiana University Press, 1998.
United States Army in the World War, 1917–1919, vol. 12.
U.S. Department of Agriculture. *Overview of U.S. Livestock and Aquaculture Production in 2011*. National Agricultural Statistics Service, *Statistics on Major Commodities*.
U.S. Department of Agriculture Statistical Bulletin No. 5, *Horses, Mules and Motor Vehicles*, Washington, D.C January, 1925.
U.S. Department of Agriculture Yearbook—1919, 1920, 1921 and 1960
U.S. Department of Commerce, *Historical Statistics of the United States, Colonial Times to 1970, Part 1, Bicentennial Edition*. Washington, D.C.
U.S. Department of Commerce and Labor.

Thirteenth Annual Report of the Commissioner of Labor, Hand and Machine Labor, vol. 2. 1899. General Table, 427–1604.

U.S. Department of the Interior, Bureau of Land Management, National Wild Horse and Burro Advisory Board Meeting Minutes, September 9–13, 2013.

U.S. Department of the Interior, Bureau of Land Management, Rangeland and Herd Management, Wild Horse and Burro Program. Web page, May, 2014.

U.S. Department of the Interior, Bureau of Land Management. "Using Freeze Marks." https://www.blm.gov/wo/st/en/prog/whb program/adoption_program/freezemarks.html.

U.S. Department of the Interior, Bureau of Land Management. "Wild Horse and Burros Quick Facts." http://www.blm.gov/wo/st/em/prog/whbprogram/history_and_facts/quick_facts.html.

U.S. Equitation Federation Rule Book, 2013.

U.S. Government Accountability Office. "Horse Welfare, Action Needed to Address Unintended Consequences from Cessation of Domestic Slaughter." Report to Congressional Committees, June, 2011.

United States Polo Association. "Equine Drugs and Medications Rules of the United States Polo Association, 2015."

U.S. Trotting Association. *Harness the Excitement, Your Guide to the Sport of Harness Racing.* Columbus, OH, undated.

Unna, Warren. "'Last Roundup' Comes for Theater Animals: Horses and Mules Played Key Role in Combat Action," *India-Burma Theater Roundup*, 4, no. 27, March 14, 1946. http://www.cbi-theater.com/roundup/roundup031446.html.

"USPA Celebrates the 30th National Girls and Women in Sports Day." *News and Events,* February 2, 2016. https://uspolo.org/news-and-events/I/uspa-celebrates-the-30th-annual-n.

USPA Annual Report, 2015.

"USPA News. From CEO Duncan Huyler." *Polo, Players' Edition,* March, 2016. 6.

"USPA News." *Polo Players' Edition,* April, 2016.

Van Tuyl, G.E., and W.J. Bonelli. "Polo Ponies," *Iowa State Veterinarian.* Vol. 6, Issue 2, Article 8. http://lib.dr.iastate_veterinarian/vol6/iss2/8.

Varhola, Michael J. *Everyday Life During the Civil War: A Guide for Writers, Students and Historians.* Cincinnati, OH: Writer's Digest, 1999.

Vavra, Martin. "Livestock Grazing and Wildlife: Developing Compatibilities." *Rangeland Ecology & Management,* March, 2005. Vol. 58.

Volbehr, Ernst. *Das Gesicht Der Westfront: Ein Kriegsdocument Und Erinnerungbuch.* Potsdam: Athenaion, 1932.

Waldman, Louis. "Lessons in Labor Relations." Reprinted from *Labor Lawyer.* New York: E.P. Dutton, 1944. 19–38, in *Autobiographies of American Jews.* Compiled and with introduction by Harold U. Ribalow. Philadelphia: The Jewish Publication Society of America, 1968. 334.

The Wall Street Journal, May 3–4, 2014.

Waller, Anna L. "Horses and Mules and National Defense." Fort Lee, VA: Office of the Quartermaster General, 1958. 45. http://www.qmfound.com/horse.htm.

Wanless, Mary. "Living Your Love." *Of Women and Horses.* Irvine, CA: Bow Tie Press, 2000.

Ward, Fay E. *The Cowboy at Work, About His Job and How He Does It.* New York: Hastings House Publishers, 1958, 1976.

Washburn, R.S. *Cost of Producing Winter Wheat in Central Great Plains Region of the United States.* U.S. Dept. of Agricultural Bulletin, 1924. 1198.

"Waterboy, Danny Beg, and the Last Horse-Driven Engine of the New York Fire Department," posted January 24, 2015. http://hatchingcatnyc.com/2015/01/24/last-horse-driven-engine-of-new...

Watkins, Nicholas C. *The Western Front from the Air.* Stroud, UK: Sutton, 2000.

Webbe, Alex. "All About Polo Ponies." *About Polo Horses, Blogger,* January 19, 2010, http://polo101.com./about_polo/202.html.

Webbe, Alex. "Why Are They Called Polo Ponies?" in by Blogger "15 Questions You've Always Wanted to Ask About Polo." January 26, 2011, http://www.polo101.com/faq/15-questions-you-alwaysnted-t-ask-about-polo.

Weingroff, Richard. "The Rambler Sidebar: Bicycles and Automobiles in Central Park." Highway History Website. Federal Highway Administration. https://www.fhwa.dot.gov/.../stone.cp.pdf, Washington, 2010.

Wendel, C.H. *Encyclopedia of American Farm Tractors.* Osceola, WI: Motorbooks International, 1992.

Wendel C. H. *150 Years of J.I. Case.* Crestline Publishing Co., 1991.

Wentworth, Edward N. "Artillery Horse Routine." *Breeder's Gazette,* October 4, 1917. 554.

Wentworth, George E. "Losses of Army Horses." *Breeder's Gazette,* April 3, 1919. 786.

Wentworth, George E. Cook County, Illinois. *Breeder's Gazette,* May 12, 1921.

"What Breed Is A Polo Pony?" http://www.sportpolo.com/polo_pony/default.htm.

White, Lynn, Jr. *Medieval Technology and Social Change.* London: Oxford University Press, 1969.

Wik, Reynold M. *Steam Power on the American Farm.* Philadelphia: University of Pennsylvania Press, 1953.

Wilson, Dale E. *Treat 'Em Rough! The Birth of American Armor, 1917–20.* Novato, CA: Presidio, 1990.

WinningPoniesl.com. "Horse Racing History." 2013.

Wooden, Wayne S., and Gavin Ehringer. *Rodeo in America, Wranglers, Roughstock & Paydirt.* Lawrence: University Press of Kansas, 1996.

Woolcott, Alexander. "The Tanks." *The Command Is Forward: Tales of the A.E.F. Battlefields as They Appeared in the Stars and Stripes.* New York: Century, 1919. 158.

"Work Done by 1,500,000 Horses in France During the War." *Scientific American,* No. 2250, February 15, 1919. 105.

"Work of the Blue Cross on the Battle Front." *Literary Digest* 55, no. 20. 1917. 82, 84, 86.

Yearbook of Agriculture, 1960.

Yenne, Bill. *Tommy Gun: How General Thompson's Submachine Gun Wrote History.* New York: Thomas Dunne, 2009.

Zarzyski, Paul. "Good Horse Keeping," *Horsepeople: Writers and Artists on the Horses They Love.* Michael J. Rosen, ed. New York: Artisan, 2002.

Zobba, Rosanna, et al. "Physical, Hematological, and Biochemical Responses to Acute Intense Exercise in Polo Horses." *Journal of Equine Veterinary Science,* September 2011. Volume 31, Issue 9.

Index

abandoned horses 174, 176
Abbasid Caliph 151
Abilene 125
Achaemenid dynasty 151
Achaeminian monarchs 92
acre of wheat 117, 188–189
acrewall 123
Admiralty 24
adoption 8, 179, 180, 181
advertising 89
advisory boards 176
A.E.F. General Orders 41
Afghanistan 183
age of horse participation 138
aging of horse population 6, 90, 120, 121
Ahrens 97
Ahrens-Fox 101
Aibak, Sultan Qutabuddin 152
Aiken, South Carolina 161
Aisne 39
Albany 67
Aldeshot 153
Algeria 12
All-American Futurity 145
All Pro Polo League 171
Allan, Charles 86
Allies 3, 11, 14, 24, 51
allowance races 144
Al Quaida 183
Alton, Illinois 14
Amaral, Anthony 133
Ambulance Corps 45
American agricultural revolution 105, 112
American Association of Breeders & Importers of Belgians 89
American College of Veterinary Surgeons 149
American Expeditionary Force (A.E.F.) 24, 25, 32, 39, 40, 44, 46, 53, 54, 55
American Feed Manufacturers Association 89

American Fire-Engine Company 97
American horse functions in World War I 28–58; artillery 35–38; care 42–47; cavalry 29–31; diseases 4, 14, 15, 16, 20, 42, 43, 47; gas 34, 37, 38, 45, 51, 52; rations 16, 40–42; remount service 11, 12, 14, 15, 18, 19, 20, 23, 26, 46 54, 55, 56, 58, 59, 60; supply function 32–35, 41–42 ; surveillance 28, 30, 31; transportation 14, 16–17, 24–25
American horse population 3, 6, 8, 9, 11, 56, 60, 63, 90, 119, 120, 121, 122
American horse supply in World War I 3, 11–27; AEF from British 27; AEF from French 24–27; AEF from Spain 27, 57; Army purchases from dealers 22–24; Army purchases from farmers 22–24; Army sales in U.S. 56–57; Boer War precedent 11, 48, 119, 176; British horse draft 12, 19; Civil War precedent 11, 28; countries' supplies at outset 11–12; French and British purchases in U.S. 12–14; postwar sales of AEF horses in Europe 55; total by AEF 48, 103; U.S. Army purchases prior to war 21
American Humane Society 45
American Junior Rodeo Association 134
American La France Company 97, 101
American Quarter Horse Association 138
American Stud Book 142

American Tank Corps 39
American Veterinary Medical Association 17
American West 74, 165, 175
Ampere, Andre Marie 81
Andalusia 123
Anderson, W.W. 22
animal electricity 81
animal production cycle 119–121
Animal Transport Service 27
animals displaced by each tractor 119, 197
annual agricultural cycle 117–118
anthrax 14, 15
anti-gambling legislation 143
Apaloosas 161
Apennines 59, 184
Appleby, John F. 106
Appropriate Management Level (AML) 178, 179
Arabian racing's stud book 142
Arabian Sea 59
Arabian stallions 142
Arabians 142, 161
Arabs 151
arena polo 160, 172
Argentina 161, 162, 164, 165, 166, 167, 168, 170, 171
Argentine Criollos 161
Argonne 26, 29, 52
Arizona 164
armature 81
Armistice 27, 39, 43, 44, 46, 53, 55
armor-bearing stallion 104
Army 163
Army Championship 163
Army Council 54
Army Polo Association 163
Army Polo Committee 163
Army Regulations (Par. 1077) 41
Army Service Corps 34

229

Index

Army Waste Products Ltd. 54
Army's Horse Breeding Program 60
Army's Water Supply Service 42
Arras 37
artillery 13, 20, 22, 23, 25, 28, 29, 30, 31, 35, 36, 37, 38, 41, 47, 48, 49, 50, 51, 52, 53, 56, 57, 60, 61, 62, 163, 183
Artillery Brigade of the 26th Division 25
Asia 28, 152
ASPCA 102
asphalt 4, 65, 66, 67
Assam 152
Assateague Island 180, 182
Associated Manufacturers of Saddlery 89
Association of International Racing Commissioners 146
Atlantic coast 8, 180, 182
Augustus 91
Australia 161
Australian machine gunners 38
Austria 11, 28
Austro-Prussian War 29
automobile registration 71
automobiles, motor cars 9, 50, 70, 71, 73, 89, 117, 118, 120, 121, 122, 131
Autry, Gene 134
avian outbreak 76
axles 68, 115
Ayllon 182

B-Westerns 133
Baber 152
backgrounding facility 6, 129
Baker, A.D. 114
Baker, Newton 45
Baker Board 35, 37
Balada 156
Balfour, Lord 24
Ballin a Hone 157
Baltimore 14, 16, 75, 82, 96
bandaging 169–170
Barbaro 147
barbed wire 3, 6, 29, 39, 126–127
Bardon, Nicholas 92
bareback riding 134, 136
barge 14, 68
Barren Island 9
barrier islands 8, 182
Battery A, 7th Field Artillery 50
Battery B, 607th Field Artillery Battalion, 71st Infantry Division 62
Battery D of the 129th Field Artillery 51

Battery Park 85
beasts of burden 131, 139
bedroom communities 122
Beefmaster 128
Beery, Wallace 86
Belgian granite 67
Belgium 11, 28, 45, 47, 55, 58, 59, 62, 82, 84, 163
Belmont, August 154, 155
Belmont Park 140
Belmont Stakes 144
Belt Line System 85
belt pulley work 114, 115, 117
Bennett, James Gordon 153, 154
Bentley, Edward M. 82
Bergmann maschinenpistole 18 (MP18) 38
Berry, Charles A. 98
Best, Daniel 113
bevel gears 108
bicycles 26, 30, 64, 70, 89, 119
Big Brown 147
binder 8, 65, 106, 112, 188
Biodyl-type supplement 168
bitumen 65, 66
blacksmiths 8, 122, 186
blankets 8, 43, 186
Blasson, Harry 154
Bledso, Lieutenant e 50
Blizzard of 1887 126
Blue Cross 44, 45; dogs 45
Blyth, Ronald 2
Boer War 11, 48, 119, 176
bookmakers 143
Boston 4, 75, 91, 84, 93, 96, 97, 98
Boston's West End Railroad 84
Boundary (Florida Avenue) 84
Bozeman, Montana 131
Braine, Elgin 39
Braithwaite, George 95
brakes 68
Bramlage, Larry 149
branding 22, 128, 178, 179
Breeders' Cup Classic 144
Breeder's Gazette 1, 12, 15, 21, 57, 71, 86, 87, 90
breeding farm horses 119
breeds 126, 128
brick 64, 67, 92
Bridges, General 24
Brighton Polo Association 154
brine 81
British Commander-in-Chief 31
British Expeditionary Forces 17, 26, 55
British 46th Division 32
British highlands 123, 130

British Mark IVs 39
British Parliament 111, 112
British polo health study 169, 170
British polo rules 153, 155, 156
British ranchers 126
British Remount Directorate 59
British Royal Society's great magnet 81
British settlers 153
British tea or indigo planters 152
British thoroughbred racing 142
broadcasting by hand 104, 112
bronco busting 7, 132
Brooklyn 75, 78, 84, 102, 154
Brooklyn Bridge 78
Brown, George E. 89
bucking bronco 7, 132
bucking horse of the year 135
bucking horses 134–135
Buckingham, David E. 17
Budapest 84
Buenos Aires 161
buffalo 124, 127
Buffalo Country Club 154, 155
Buffalo, New York 131, 154, 155
buggy 69, 71, 73, 79, 86, 133, 186
bull-dozer 67
bull riding 134
bulldog 123
bullocks 64, 66
bulls 123, 128, 135
bunk feeding 6, 129
Bureau of Animal Industry 21
Bureau of Land Management (BLM) 7, 8, 176, 177, 178, 179, 180, 181, 182
Burford, Peter 2
Burlington Northern 131
Burma 58, 59, 62, 171
Burma military polo 171
Butazolidan (phenylbutazone) 146
Butler, W.H. 54
Buttermilk 134
Button 97
Byerly Turk 142

Cabinet edict 31
cable 1, 4, 9, 73, 77, 78, 79, 80, 82, 83, 84, 112, 113, 186
cable cars 1, 4, 9, 73, 77, 78, 79, 80, 82, 83, 84, 185
Calcutta 59, 66, 153

Index

Calcutta Polo Club 153
Caldwell 125
calf 6, 7, 129, 136, 137
calf-roper 136
calf roping 136
California 9, 18, 62, 72, 99, 113, 124, 127, 133, 155, 156, 163, 164, 184, 196, 197
calks, 121
Cambiaso, Adolfo 162
Cambrai 38, 39
Camp Carson 59, 62
Camp Hale 59
Camp Joseph E. Johnson 20
Canadian tracks 147
canals 68
Cane Pace 145
cantle 137
Caporetto 38, 41
Caribbean 4, 6, 76
Carranor Hunt and Polo Club 165
carriage horses 73
carriage painters 8, 186
cart 4, 49, 63, 67, 68
cartway 67
Case, John Increase 111
Case, J.I. Johnson company 109, 111, 113, 114, 116
Case Kerosene Tractor 116
case study of change 186
casinos 145
Cassidy, Hopalong 134
castrated cattle 123
Le Cateau 31
Caterpillar Company 113
cats 76, 82
cattle 6, 103, 108, 119, 123, 124, 125, 126, 127, 128, 129, 130, 131, 132, 133, 135, 136, 171, 176, 181, 186; dogs 130; drives 124–125; feed lots 129–130; at full weight 129; trailer 6, 129, 130; trails 127
cattle-herding horses 123, 129
cattle-raising origins 123–124
cavalry 133; charge 29, 31, 183
Cavalry Interests 89
Celts 63, 64
cement 4, 64, 65
Central America 4, 6, 76
Central Powers 11
central station plant 83
Central Virginia 149
chaise 69
Chamber of Agriculture 47
Champion 134
changing legs 166
Channing, William F. 93
chariot 28, 63, 64, 68, 103
Charles City, Iowa 114
Charlie 177
Charolais 128

Charter Gas Engine Company 114
Chengiz Khan 152
Chenglei 152
Chesler, Frankie 140
Chevy Chase 14, 15
Chianina 128
Chicago 102
Chicago 23, 67, 75, 77, 82, 86, 89, 96, 98, 102, 196, 111, 165
Chicago City Railway 77
Chicago Industrial Exposition of 1883 82
chickens 82, 176
children 5, 75, 88, 108, 122, 123, 134, 150, 177, 183
Chile 161
China 59, 60, 151, 152
Chincoteague Volunteer Fire Department 182
chlorine 37
Choral 147
chuck wagon 125
chukkers 158, 160, 161, 162, 166, 169, 172
Churchill Downs 144
Cincinnati 75, 90, 95, 96, 101, 165
Cincinnati Polo Club 165
Cinderella 156
Cinders 156
circuit 81, 82
Civil War 11, 14, 28, 29, 30, 36, 37, 44, 96, 110, 116, 119, 186
claiming races 144
Clapp & Jones 97
Clermont 111
Cleveland 82, 101
cloning 162
coach 4, 64, 65, 69, 73, 74, 110
coach horses 110
coal 65, 99, 113
coal gas 65
Coast Guard 58
cobblestones 4, 17, 49, 67
Cobnut 156
Code of Hammurabi 91
Cody, Buffalo Bill 132
Cold War 184
collection enclosure 177
Colonial Cup 145
Colorado 59, 62, 72, 196, 197
Colorado Rockies 59
Colorado Springs 62
Columbus 6, 124, 175
Commons 24
compaction 66
compass needle 81
compressed air cars 84
concrete 65, 66, 79
conduits 4, 77, 79, 84
Confederate 28, 30, 37

Congress 1, 7, 18, 19, 40, 74, 75, 84, 85, 88, 90, 99, 100, 116, 132, 147, 175, 177, 178, 181
Conn, George H. 23
Connecticut electric car lines 82
connecting rod 111
Conover 157
construction plows, scoops, scrapers, spreaders, leveling drags 66
contraception 181
Contributorship for the Insurance of Houses from Loss by Fire 92
converting reciprocal action to rotary action 111
Cook, A. (gunner) 49
Cooper, John S. 12–13
copper 81, 82; wires 82
corn 105, 114, 117, 125, 129, 189, 190, 196, 197; drills 105; shellers 114
corn belt farmers 117
Cornell 162
cost of keeping horses 118, 174, 190, 191
cotton farms 115
Cottontail 156, 167
cougars 125
Country Club in Westchester 154
cow and calf ranches 6, 129
cow horse 127–128
cow hunt 125
cow ponies 125
cowboy 6, 127–128, 130, 132, 133, 134, 135, 136, 137
Cowdray Park Gold Cup 171
cowgirls 134, 136
cradle 106, 107, 189
Crassus, Marcus Licinius 91
creosote 67
Creston, Iowa 13
Crestview Genetics 162
crop rotation 104, 105, 112
cross-breeds 161
Croton Reservoir 93
Crown Prince of Austria 11
crystals 80
Cuartelera 162
Cuba 24, 124
cultivating 110, 115, 117, 189
cultivators 105
Cup of Americas 161
cutting 136, 137, 150
cutting horse 127
Cypriot 59
Czechoslovakia 55

Daft, Leo 82
Daily Double 144
Daily Racing Form 7, 145, 149

Index

Daimler, Gottlieb 39, 113
Dakotas 126
Dalmatians 100, 102
Dancer's Image 146
Darby Arabian 142
Darius the Great 151
Dead Horse Bay 9
Deere, John 105
DeKalb, Illinois 126
DeKalb County fair 126
denial 88
Denison, Texas 155
Department of Agriculture 1, 21, 60, 90, 107, 116, 117, 118, 119, 120, 121, 175, 178, 190, 191, 192, 194, 196, 197
Department of Interior 178
department stores 87
depopulated rural landscape 122
Depression 165
Des Moines 13, 87
Detroit 17, 98
Devine, Andy 134
Dickel's Riding Academy 154
diesel 66, 67, 115
Dilger, Anton Casimir (alias Albert Delmar, Alberto Donde) 14–15
dime novels 7, 132
Dingee, W.W. 109
Dinsmore, Wayne 21
disking 117, 118
ditches 126
Dobbin 31–61
Dodge City 125
dogs 44, 45, 46, 82, 100, 108, 123, 130
Don Pepe Polo Farm 166
donkey 59, 76, 90, 103
double-features 133
doubles 133
draft animals 17, 25, 41, 46, 52, 56, 57, 89, 108, 110
draftees 19, 24
drawbar work 118
draymen 8, 186
dressage 137, 150
drugs 146–148
Dublin 157
Dude Ranchers Association 131
dude ranches 7, 131–132, 134; wagons 131
Duke 134
Dunlop, John 64
dynamo 4, 81

East-West Polo Match 165
Eastern Front 31, 32, 39
Eastern Intercollegiate Championship 164
Eaton's Custer Trail 131

Eclipse 142
Edison, Thomas 82–83
Egypt 151, 152
Ehrenfreund, Norbert 1
Eight Belles 147
1859 U.S. Fair in Chicago 111
1862 Homestead Act 126, 127
1871 Great Fire in Chicago 67
1873 DeKalb County fair 126
1879 Berlin Industrial Exhibition 82
Eisenhower, Dwight D. 40, 164
electric cars 82, 85
electric locomotive 82
electric motor 4, 81, 82, 185
electrical knowledge 80–82
electrocution 82
elevated lines 82
11th Cavalry 163
Ellsworth 125
embryo transfer 161
England 12, 19, 27, 40, 45, 54, 55, 65, 93, 100, 101, 112, 113, 118, 153–157, 161, 163, 164, 171
English Channel 17, 55, 162
English saddle 61, 137
epizootic 4, 75, 76, 98
Ericsson, John 95
Esfahan 152
Ettinger & Edmond 96
Europe 5, 6, 12, 14, 15, 16, 24, 28, 54, 56, 59, 61, 62, 63, 64, 68, 73, 90, 94, 103, 104, 132, 143, 154, 168, 171, 175
European Community 175
Evans, Dale 134
Exacta 144
exercise-induced pulmonary hemorrhaging (EIPH) 146
external combustion engine plows 113–114
extras 133
Extremadura 123

Fanshawe, Antony 162
Far East 175
Faraday, Michael 81
farm family size 122
farm horse functions 117–119
farm labor 116
farm population 121, 122
farm size 122
farm tractor improvements 114, 115
farm wage rates 116
farm workers 115–116; effect of tractors 116; numbers 115; wage rates 116
Farmall tractor 115
farmers' prices 116
Farming and Livestock Interests 89

farming, basic 103; ancient 103; inventions, U.K. 104–105; inventions, U.S. 105–108; introduction of horses 103; medieval 104; traditional 104
Fashion 143
fastest hands 136
Federal Aid Road Act of 1916 72
Federal Government 11, 116
feed grinders 114
Felton, Eddie 15
female equitation finals winners 140
female horse ownership 140
feminization 139–141
fences 100, 126, 127, 128, 129, 130, 137, 143; gate openings 127
feral horses 134 181
Ferguson, Harry 115
fertilizers 112, 129
The Field 153
5th Field Artillery 163
Final Report of the Assistant Chief of Staff, G-1 44
Finland 184
fire 1, 4, 5, 16, 67, 76, 86, 91, 92, 93, 94, 95, 96, 97, 98, 99, 100, 101, 102, 111, 182; brigades 93, 94, 95; departments 86, 98, 101; engines 76, 86, 96, 97, 101, 102; fighting 91–95; horse 91–102, 189; horse memorial 102; hose 94, 95, 96, 98, 101; house pole 98; houses 4, 98, 101; hydrant 93; insurance mark 92; as a social issue 91
fire control 91–102; Boston 91, 93, 98; New York 86, 93, 95, 97, 99, 101, 102; Philadelphia 91, 92, 93, 94; Roman 91–93
firepower 3, 29
First Aid for Horses 46
First Division 24, 25, 41, 51
first polo rules 153
Fitzpatrick, Lawrence J. 157
flail 104, 106, 112
Flanders 45, 53, 54
Florida 167
Flynn Dairy Company 87
flywheels 80, 114
Foch, Marshal 26, 39
Ford, Henry 9, 114, 115
Ford Corporation 115
Fordham Station 154
Fordson tractor 114–115
Forest Service 178, 182
Forester, Frank 69
Fort Keogh, Montana 19

Index

Fort Myer 163
Fort Reno, Darlington, Oklahoma 19
Fort Riley, Kansas 163
Fort Royal, Virginia 19
Fort Sill, Oklahoma 61
Fort Worth, Texas 13, 180
foul 159–160, 161
four-mule teams 125
Fowler, John 113
fox hunting 127, 154
France 11, 44, 45, 46, 47, 53, 55, 56, 62, 66, 69, 90
Francki Pharmacy 168
Franco-German War 29
Franklin, Benjamin 80, 91, 92–93
Franklin Circuit Court 146
"free wire" movement 127
freeze branding 179
freezemark 179
Freidel, Frank 2
French Fifth Army 51
French government 13, 14, 15, 16, 17, 24, 25, 26, 30, 31, 32, 34, 35, 36, 37, 39, 41, 42, 44, 46, 47, 49, 50, 51, 53, 54, 55, 59, 124, 154
French Minister of War 44
French Ministry of War 25
frequency of racing 149
Frick, George 111
friction 78
Friendly Society in Charleston, South Carolina 92
Froelich, John 114
fruit and vegetable man 88
fruit and vegetable wagons 88
Fulani 124
Fulton, Robert 111
Furosemide 146
Futurity 144

Gale, E. rifleman 49, 50
galvinometer 81
Garrard & Company of London 167
gas-traction engine 114
gas tractors 114, 116
gas warfare 34, 37, 38, 45, 51, 52
"gathers" 178, 179
gaucho 166
Gauss, Karl Friedrick 81
Geiser Manufacturing Company's Peerless steam plow 113
Gelbvieh 128
gems 80
General Accountability Office 175
General Land Office 176

General Motors 101
General Stud Book 142
generator 83, 185
Georgetown 84
Georgia 182, 196, 197
German 14, 15, 17, 19, 24, 26, 28, 29, 30, 31, 37, 38, 39, 47, 50, 52, 53, 55, 59, 62, 84, 113, 154
German Landsturm 47
German Rhineland 55, 163
German veterinary hospital 47
Germany 11, 12, 14, 19, 31, 40, 55, 84
Geronimo 61
Gettysburg 40
ghost towns 122
Gilbert, William 80
glanders 14, 15, 42, 43, 47
glass 80
Glidden, Joseph F. 126, 127
glue factories 90
goals 157–158
goats 108
Godolphin Barb 142
GonaCon 180
Goodyear, Charles 64
Gordon, Anne 2
GPS 183
grades 77, 80, 83
grain belt 8
Grand National 145
granite 67; setts 67
Grant, John 15
gravel 65, 67
Grayson County, Texas 155
grazing: competition 176; permits 176; rights 127
Grazing Service 176
Great Blizzard of January, 1887 126
Great Britain 11, 13, 44, 46, 90, 104, 105, 122, 142
Greece 80
Greek 62
Greener Pastures program 149
Greenfield Farm 14
Greyling 156
grip 77, 78, 79
gripman 77
grooms 8, 17, 48, 49, 61, 186
"ground hog" thresher 106
Grout, John 104
growth hormones 129
Guadalcanal 59
guano 75
Gulf of Mexico 13
gunpowder 5, 29, 103, 111
Guyton-Harrington federation 13

Haish, Jacob 126, 127
Hall of Fame 135
Hallidie, Andrew Smith 77
Hambletonian 142
Hambletonian (event) 145
Hamburg Fire Contract of 1591 92
Hamel 38
Hammurabi, Code of 91
hand pumps 4, 95
handicap races 144
handicaps 157–158, 160, 162, 172
Hanneman & Co. 97
harness makers 8, 186
harness racing: Pacing Triple Crown 145; Trotting Triple Crown 145
Haroon-al-Rashid 151
harrow 104, 112, 188
harrowing 115, 117, 188, 189
Hart-Parr Company 114
Hartopp, Edward "Chicken" 153
Harvard 162
harvesting machines 105
hauling 117, 118, 188, 189
Le Havre 32
Havre de Grace 143
hay and grain dealers 8, 186
hay rake 106
hazing 136
header 136
heavy draft horses 110
heavy drawbar work 118
Heavy Hardware Organizations 89
hedges 61, 126
heeler 136
Heidelberg University Medical School 14
hemp 77, 78
Henry, John C. 82
Henry, Marguerite 178
Hensch, Frederick 14–15
Herbert, Henry Lloyd 157
Herd Management Area (HMA) 178
herding dogs 123, 130
Hereford 126, 128
Herrenberg forests 51
Herrmann, Fred 15
Hilken, Paul 14–15
"hired assassins" 171
Hitler, Adolf 60
hobbles 123
Hodge, Paul Rapsey 95
hoe 104, 105
hogged manes 166
Holly water supply system 97
Hollywood 133
Holmes, C.B. 77
Holt, Benjamin 113

Index

Homestead Act of 1862 126, 127
Hong Kong 147
Horse Aid & Humane Association 89
horse-and-buggy doctor 186
horse and mule population 8, 118–119, 121
Horse Association of America 89
horse-drawn corn drills 105
horse-drawn grain drills 105
horse-drawn mowing machine 106
horse-drawn straddle-row cultivator 105
Horse-Hoeing Husbandry 105
horse markets 89
The Horse of Hurricane Hill 141
Horse Publicity Association of America 72, 89–90
horse-rendering plant 9
Horse Soldiers 184
horses: birth rate 90; clothing 186; maintenance costs 55, 118; population 131; prices 90, 118; shows 7, 44, 131, 134, 137–139, 150; slaughter for human consumption 90, 175; sweep 2, 5, 107, 108–110
horsecars 4, 8, 9, 64, 68, 75, 76, 77, 79, 80, 81, 82, 83, 84
horseless agriculture 122
horsemeat 54, 90, 175
horsepower definition 116
Horseshoe Manufacturers Association 89
Horseshoe Nail Manufacturers 89
horseshoers 20, 43, 44, 46, 89, 186
horseshoes 73, 103, 147, 185
horsey women 140
hostlers 8, 186
Hotel Pennsylvania 89
Hounslow Heath 153
House Judiciary Committee 177
Hudson River 14, 111
Hun 62
Hurlingham Club 153, 154, 155, 156, 157, 160

Iboudhou Marjing 152
ice wagons 87
iceman 1, 87, 88, 100
immigrants 4, 76
immigration bills 116
India 59, 63, 151–153, 157
Indian hunting trails 127
Indian reservations 181
Indians 124, 181

Indoor Polo Association 160
infantry (tanks) 40
influenza 4, 14, 15, 16, 20, 42, 76
Insider's Guide to Horseracing 148
Inspected by the U.S. Department of Agriculture 90, 175
insurance 91–95, 176; Code of Hammurabi 91; Genoa 92; Hamburg 92; London 92; New York 95; Persia 92; Philadelphia 92; South Carolina 92
Insurance Office for Houses at the Back of the Royal Exchange 92
integral three-point hitch 115
Intercollegiate Equestrian Federation 138
Intercollegiate Polo Association 163
internal combustion engine 4, 5, 9, 97, 101, 113, 186; plows 113–114
International Gay Rodeo Association 134
International Harvester Company 115
Interstate Horse Racing Act of 1978 145
Iowa State Fair 13
Iran 151
Ireland 115, 143, 156
iron 4, 63, 65, 64, 66, 67, 81, 105; plows with interchangeable parts 105; shod horses 66, 67; tires and wheels 64
Italian 14, 17, 41, 42, 59; Army 17, 41
Italy 11, 45, 58, 59, 62, 84

James River Work Center 149
Janus 142
Japan 68, 152
Jerome Park 154
Jockey Club 147, 148, 149
Joffre, Marshal 24
Johnson, Paul C. 108
Johnston, Velma 176, 177
Johnstone, "Jimmie" 13
Joker 134
Junior Championship 164
junk wagons 88
junkman 88

Kansas 125, 164
Kansas City 19, 23, 82, 163
Kansas Futurity 145
Keep the Boy in School 116
Kentucky 143
Kentucky Court of Appeals 146

Kentucky Derby 144, 146, 147
Kentucky Experiment Station 22
Kentucky Futurity 145
Kentucky State Racing Commission 146
Kenyon, David 98
Khosrov II Parvig 151
Kilby, Emily R. 140
King, William T. 96–97
Kitchener's Army 19
Knight, Walter H. 82
knightbearing horse 5
knuckle joints 110
Korea 184
Kunming 60

Ladana 147
ladies barrel racing 134, 136, 137
La Picaza 161
lariat or lasso 127, 130, 136, 150
Lashio 60
Lasix 146
La Souris 156
Latin America 168
Latta, Moses 95, 96
League of American Wheelmen (LAW) 70
leather buckets 93
Le Cateau 31
Lechuga Caracas 168
Le Havre 32
lend-lease 58–59
Leyden Jar 80, 81
library, first free 60
lifestyle ranches 129–130
light drawbar work 118
lightning 80
limestone 65, 66
Limousin 128
Lincoln, Pres. Abraham 30
Little Brown Jug 145
Little Mary 156
Liverpool 16, 51, 54
livery and boarding stables 72
livery men 8, 186
Lloyd, Edward 92
Lloyd's of London 16, 92
Locust Valley, Long Island 162
London 16, 54, 65, 67, 69, 73, 74, 77, 92, 93, 94, 95, 167
Lone Ranger 134
Long Branch, New Jersey 154
Long Drive 125, 133, 219, 227
Long Island 156, 162
long-term pastures 179
Longhorns 124, 125
Lord Marjin 152
Lorillard, Nathaniel Griswold 155

Index 235

loss of trails and riding areas 174
lotteries 145
Louisville 143
Lovely Sage 167
Low, J. (driver) 49
Lowe, Thadeus 39
Lucinda 126
Luxemburg 55

macadam 4, 65, 66, 67
Macdonald, Lyn 2, 47
machine guns 2, 29, 30, 31, 38, 39, 43, 52
Mack trucks 101
Macleod, R.A. (Rory) 48
Madison Square Garden 72
magnet 80, 81
magnetic field 81
magnetic force 81
magneto-electric machines 81
maiden races 144
mail wagons 86
Mallard 157
mallet and ball 166
mallet heads 155
Malta 153
Malta Polo Club 153
Manchester 43, 96
Manhattan 71, 72, 86, 93, 102, 154
Manhattan Company 93
Manhattan (letters by) 71–72
Manhattan Polo Association 154
Manipur 152–153
Mannheim, Germany 14
manure 8, 9, 23, 75, 117, 118, 141, 186, 189, 190; hauling 117; transporters 8, 186
manuring 105
Marco Polo Caravan Trail 60
Marines 184
Marmites Norvegienne 35
Marne 50
Marsh harvester 106
Marshall, George C. 2, 33, 34, 39–40, 41, 51, 52
Martin, Smokey Joe 102
Maryland 72, 86, 143, 146, 182, 196, 197
Master Horseshoers 89
mastic 65
Maures (Moors) 124
McAdam, John Loudon 65, 66
McCormick, Cyrus Hall 106
McCormick Company 114
McCormick reaper 5, 106, 107
McCrea, Joel 133
Meadow Brook Club 156, 157, 164, 165

meatpacking firms 130
mechanical reaper 106
mechanical thresher 5
Medical Corps 20
Medieval Europe 28, 29, 118
Medora, North Dakota 131
Memphis 16
Mensing, Private O. 46
Merial pharmaceutical company 168
Merkle, Andrew 106
Merrill, Frank (Merrill's Marauders) 59
Merryweather Company 101
Mesopotamia 63
Messenger Stakes 145
Meuse-Argonne 29, 52
Meuse River 29, 39, 52
Mexican cowboys in California 133
Mexico 4, 6, 13, 15, 20, 33, 76, 124, 150, 164, 175, 176
Michigan 76, 101, 163, 196
Michigan State Polo Club 163
Michler, General 51
Middle East 28, 63
Middle West 11, 89, 105, 113
Midkiff, Mary 140
Military Rodeo Cowboys Association 134
milkman 88
Millman, Carin 2
mines 77, 78, 186
Ming-Hung 151
Mississippi River 111
Missouri mules 59
Mix, Tom 134
Model T Ford 9, 114
Mohawk Chief 157
Montana 126, 135, 164
Morgans 161
mortgage foreclosure 174
Moscow 40
Moses, Robert 165
Moslem rulers 152
motorized fire engines 101–102
mowing machine 106
Mughal Empire 152
mules 1, 13, 14, 15, 17, 19, 20, 21, 22, 23, 24, 28, 33, 35, 37, 38, 41, 42, 43, 45, 46, 52, 53, 55, 56, 57, 58, 59, 61, 62, 76, 83, 115, 118, 119, 120, 121, 190, 191, 192, 195, 197; trains 59
Mustang Million 180
Mustang, Wild Spirit of the West 178
mustangs 7, 8, 124, 125, 154, 177, 178, 180, 184
mustard gas 34, 37
Mutual Fire Societies 91
Myanmar 152

Nagaland 152
nailed horseshoes 103
Napoleon 40
Narragansett Pier, Rhode Island 163
National Congress of American Indians 181
National Cutting Horse Association 134
National Equestrian Federation 138
National Firefighters Rodeo Association 134
National Grain Association 89
National Guard 19, 54
National Hay Association 89
National High School Rodeo Association 134
National Intercollegiate Rodeo Association 134
National Little Britches Rodeo Association 134
National Park Service 182
National Police Rodeo Association 134
National Pro Senior Rodeo Association 134
National Saddlery Manufacturers Association 89
National Twelve Goal Championship 164
National Velvet 141
NATO 184
natural predators 178
Navajo 181
Nebraska 126 164
Nejde 142
Nerenberg, Mark 1
Nery 49
Neuve Chappelle 31
Nevada 176, 180, 184, 196, 197
New Army 19
New Bridge Embryo Center 161, 162
New England 126
New Jersey electric car lines 82
New Mexico 145, 163, 164, 181, 196, 197
New Mexico Military Institute 163, 164
New Orleans 13, 16, 59, 75, 155
New York 1, 2, 4, 9, 67, 70, 71, 72, 73, 74, 75, 76, 82, 84, 85, 86, 87, 89, 90, 93, 94, 95, 96, 97, 99, 101, 102, 119, 131, 140, 142, 143, 144, 147, 153, 154, 155, 160, 183, 196, 197
New York City 9, 67, 82, 84, 85, 86, 93, 95, 102, 154, 160
New York Fire Department 101–102

New York polo 154, 160
New York racing 142, 143, 144, 147
Newcomen, Thomas 110
Newport, Rhode Island 154, 155
Newport News 15, 16
Newsham, Richard 94
1916–1917 Punitive Expedition into Mexico 20
1920s immigration bills 116
9th Lancers 153
Norddeutsch Lloyd's Neckar steamship 14
North American continent 176
North Carolina 142, 182, 196, 197
North Dakota 111
North German Lloyd shipping line 154
North Sea 3, 28, 29
North-South rivalry 143
Northern Alliance 183, 184
Northern Nevada Correctional Center 184
Northumberland Hussars 49
Northwestern Circuit Invitational Four-Goal Handicap Tournament 165
Norway 184
Norwich University 163
Novices' Cup 163

Oakley, Annie 132
oats 8, 14, 41, 104
Obeyran 142
Ocala, Florida 168
Ocracoke Boy Scouts 182
Ocracoke Island 182
octroi duties 42
Oelrichs, Hermann 154
Oersted, Hans Christian 81
Of Women and Horses 139
Officers Candidate School (OCS) 61
offside rule 153, 155
Ohio Percheron Breeders' Association 54
Ohm, George Simon 81
Oliver Company 115
Olympics of 1920 163
Omaha 23
omnibus 4, 8, 69, 73, 74, 75, 77, 86
on-the-farm hauling 117
onager 63
105mms 62
Onwentsia Polo Club 165
open hearth process 4, 78
open range 6, 126, 127, 128, 134
orchards 115

Oregon State University 162
Ostende, Belgium 163
OTTBs (off-the-track-thoroughbreds) 167
Otto, Nikolaus August 113–114
Otto Company 114
Our Dumb Friends' League 44
outer banks 182
overbreeding 174
overhead electric wires 84
Overture Cup 163
oxen 63, 66, 103, 104, 189

pacers 110
pack animals 30, 64
packinghouses 125, 128
paid professionals 171
Palaminos 161
palanquin 68
palenquear 166
Palm Beach Winter Equestrian Festival 140
Panama 40, 59
Panama Canal 59
Paree 116
pari-mutuel betting 144, 145
Paris 25, 53, 65, 66, 68, 74
patents 79, 84, 126
Patton, George S. 40, 164
Pau 154
Pearl Hose Co., No. 28 95
pedestrian herders 124
pen riders 129
Pennock, Abraham 94
Pennock, William 105
Pennsylvania 78, 89, 162, 196, 197
Pennsylvania Military Academy 162
Percheron 17, 21, 54, 89, 98
Percheron-Morgan hybrids 98
Percheron Society of America 21, 89
Pershing, John J. 24, 25, 26, 32, 50, 52
Persia 151
Peruvian guano 75
Petain, General 36
Petit Wasmes 48
petroleum 65, 113
Peytona 143
phaeton 69, 70
Philadelphia 75, 91, 92, 93, 94, 96, 98
Philadelphia Hose Company 94
Philippines 164
phosgene 37
La Picaza 161
Pickel Meadow Marine Camp 184

Pie 134
Pike's Peak 62
pink eye 16
Pintos 161
Piping Rock Club 162
piston, reciprocal, pumps 97
pitch 65, 66, 67
Pittsburgh 75, 82, 96
planting 117, 189
players' injuries 170–171
plow horse 104, 127
plow pit 84
plowing 5, 105, 110, 112, 115, 117, 118, 188, 189
plows 66, 104, 105, 113; all-metal 105; electric 84; gang 105, 112; iron with interchangeable parts 105; reversible 112; self-sharpening 105; steel 105; walking 105, 112; wheeled 105; wooden 104, 105
pneumatic tires 115
pneumatic tube car 84
Poland 11, 60
police work 150
Polish government 55; polo 151–173; health 167–171; rules 158–160, 167
at universities 162–163
Polo Association 157, 158, 160, 162, 164
Polo Museum 167
Polo Training Foundation 172
Pommer, Eugene 83
Pontiac, Michigan 101
pony express 9
A Pony for Jean 141
pony size 160, 167
porcine zona pellucida (PZP) 180, 181
Portland, Oregon, 90, 98, 102
posses 133
post roads 73
potassium permanganate 59
power equipment per farm worker 121
prairie soil 105
Preakness 144, 147
Prince of Wales 12
Princess Royal 12
Princeton 162, 164, 165
prison inmate rodeo programs 134
prison programs 134, 149, 180, 184
Professional Bull Riders Association 134
Professional Rodeo Cowboys Association 135
professionals 138–139

Index

proposed All Pro Polo rules 172
Prospect Park Parade Grounds 154
public animals 54
Public Forest lands 178
publicity campaign 89
pumps (hand) 4, 94, 95
purchasing boards 20, 23, 26

quarantine 54
quarter horses 161; racing 142, 161; triple crown 145
quartermaster 20, 22, 23, 33, 42, 54, 56, 57, 60
Queens County Hunt Club 154
Quenelle 144

racing 142–150
Radiant Emperor 151
radio commercials 88
railheads 6, 34, 37, 124, 125, 133
railroads 9, 29, 32, 33, 37, 40, 41, 53, 64, 68, 72, 73, 74, 78, 84, 86, 87, 110, 111, 124, 125, 127, 131, 184; engines 110
railway 12, 32, 45, 75, 77, 83, 86, 87
Rainbow Futurity 145
Ralla 157
ranch pickup trucks 6, 128, 129, 130
Ranelagh Club 163
range clearance 176
Rapid Motor Vehicle Company 101
Ratigan, W.J. 15–17
Reader's Digest 177
recreation barns 131
recreational partners and companions 131
Red Angus 128
Red Star Animal Relief 44, 45
Redford, Robert 181
regenerative braking 83
Regular Army 19
reining 137
S.S. *Rembrandt* 14, 16
Remount Division 56
Remount Purchasing and Breeding Program 58
Remount Service 20, 55, 58, 59, 60
remounts 11, 55, 56, 58, 59, 60, 136; depots 12, 19, 20, 23, 26, 55, 56, 59
"remuda" 125
Renault tanks 39
rendering 8, 9, 53, 90, 99, 176, 177, 186; workers 8, 186

Reno, Nevada 19, 176
requisition 26
Reserve Officers Training Corps (ROTC) 7, 60, 61, 62, 164
reversibility of function 81
Rhineland 163
Rice, Linda 140
Richardson, Bill 181
Richmond 4, 83, 96, 153
Richmond Park 153
ride-off 159
riding academies 71, 72, 73
"riding fences" 129, 130
Riga 38
right of way 159
Rip Van Winkle 142
road hauling 117
roadster 72
Robbins, S. Howland, Jr. 156
Roberts, Lord Frederick 157
Robertson, William H. P. 142
Robinson, Roxana 141
rodeos 7, 131, 133, 134, 135, 137, 138, 139; horses 134–137
Roebling, John 78
Rogers, Roy 134
roller 66, 83
rolling 66, 189
Roman 4, 62, 64, 66, 69
Roman roads 4, 64, 66; fire fighting 159; rendering 157
Rome 80, 90, 91, 93
rope pulley system 77
rotary motion, rotary power 106–110, 111
rotary pumps 97
ROTC 7, 60, 61, 62, 164
roundup 6, 127, 128
row crop tractors 115
Royal Service 12
Royal Society for the Prevention of Cruelty to Animals 44, 45
rubber tires 64, 115
rugby 154
Ruidoso Downs 145
Rumely, John 111, 114
Rumely, Meinrad 111, 114
Rumely steam tractor 114
Rumsey, Bert 131
runners 68
Russia 2, 11, 96, 109, 184
ruts 68

saddle-bronc riding 134, 136
saddle makers 8, 186
sagol kanjei 152–153; Imphal 152
St. Charles, Illinois 97
Saint Gertrudis 128
St. Louis 15, 23, 78, 163
St. Mihiel 52

St. Nazaire 16, 25
St. Paul, Minnesota 101
St. Petersburg, Russia 96
Saler 128
Salix 146
salt 123, 128
San Antonio 25, 125, 155
San Francisco 4, 67, 77, 93, 99
San Jose, California 99
San Lucas 62
Sapour II 151
Sarajevo 11
Saratoga 147
Sardinian 59
Saskatchewan 111
Schenectady 67
Scott, Randolph 133
Scott, Winfield 30
Scout 134
scythe 104, 106, 107
Seagram company 101
seasonality 118
2d Armored Division's 2d Armored Brigade 40
2d Cavalry 29
sedan 52
seed drill 8, 104, 105
selective service law 19
selenium 168
self-polishing plow 105
self-sharpening steel plowshare 105
Sellers, James 94
Serbia 11, 55
75 millimeter howitzer 62
shays 69
sheep 103, 108, 119, 130, 162
Sheffield Farms 88
Shepherd, Carol 139
Sherer, Joseph Ford 153
shipping fever 14, 20, 42, 43
Shire Association 89
Shirin 151
short-haul versus long-haul division 87
Shorthorn 128
Sicily 59, 184
sickle 107, 112
Sidalia, Missouri 124
Siemens, Werner 82
Siemens-Halske 84
Silchar polo club 153
silent movies 133
Silsbury 97
silver 81, 157, 167
Silver (the horse) 134
Silver Snaffles 141
Simmental 128
simulcast gambling 145
Sioux City 23
Sir Archy 142
Sitting Bull 132

Index

6th Division (Gordon) 52
6th Field Artillery 163
slaughter 7, 90, 119, 129, 130, 150, 174, 175, 176, 181
slaughterhouses 175, 176
slots 146
small towns 6, 100, 122
smart bombs 183
Smith, George 93
sod wall 126
solenoid 81
Solitaire 156
Somme 39
sorrel 137
La Souris 156
South Africa 11
South Atlantic 16 32
South Carolina 126
South Dakota 111
South Pacific 59
Southwestern Intercollegiate Championship 164
Spain 15, 26, 27, 123
Spanish land grants 127
specialty horses 133
speed limits 71, 87
spiral staircases 98
Sprague, Frank Julian 83–84
Sprague Electric Railway and Motor Company 83
springs 69, 74, 82, 83
stagecoach 9, 69, 73, 74, 86, 133
stakes races 144
stand-ins 133
Standardbred 70, 142, 149
Stanford 162, 164
star movie horse 133
Staten Island 87
static electricity 80, 81
steam 110–114
steam engine 5, 78, 80, 91, 97, 101, 102, 111, 112, 113, 114, 185; plowing 112; self-propelled 111; steering 111
steam fire engine manufacturers 95–97
steam fire engine pumps 95–97; opposition 95–96; preparation and use 96, 97, 101
steam-gas competition 113–115
steam, invention 110–11; expansion 110
steam plow 5, 112–114; improvements 113; weight 112–113; wooden tracks 113
steam-powered thresher 110–111
steam pressure limits 97
steam rollers 66
"steam tackle" 112–113
steam traction engine 66, 111, 112

steamboats 110, 111
steel plate 68
Steele 133
steeplechase 143, 145, 150, 154
Steeplechasing's triple crown 145
steer roping 134
steer wrestling 134, 136
steering 68, 111, 114, 115
steroid 147
Stewart, Jimmy 134
Stewart, Robert 153
Stilwell, Joseph 59
Stilwell Road 60
stock contractors 134–135, 136
stock pens 20
stocking or backgrounding facilities 129
stockyards 13, 15, 20, 42, 87
stones blocks 65, 66, 67, 68, 152; broken 64, 65; setts 67
storage battery cars 84
straddle-row cultivator 105
street lighting 65
streetcar 83, 84
stud farms 150
studded metal wheels 115
stunt horses 133
submarine 3, 14, 15, 19, 24, 32
Subway 85
sulky 70, 105, 142
sulphur 80
Summerall, General 51
super dreadnaughts 16
Superfecta 144
Supply Company of the U.S. 16th Infantry 33
SUVs (sports utility vehicles) 130
swayback 133
sweep power 108
Swift & Company 87
Swiss border 3
Switzerland 28, 55
Sylhet Light Infantry 153
Syrian seals 64

T.A. Landers 148, 149
Tajikistan 183
Taliban 183
Tam the Untamed 141
tanks 39, 40, 50, 62, 66
Tanoira, Javier 171
tar 65, 66, 67, 78
tarmac 65, 66
Taureg 124
tax on slave purchases 91
Taylor, Robert 86, 133
Taylor Grazing Act 176
team roping 134, 136
teamsters 8, 13, 20, 33, 43, 186
telegraph 9, 29, 30, 93

television 145
Telford, Thomas 65
Temple Gwathmey 145
The Ten Pound Pony 141
10th Cavalry 24
10th Hussars 153
Terrabusi, Carlos Reyes 166
Terraine, John 51
Texan independence war 124
Texas 154, 155
Texas A & M 163
Texas Polo Club 155
Theodosius 103
therapeutic horses 150
Third Army 55
third rail 82
Thompson, John Talieferro 38
Thoroughbred & Racing Interests 89
Thoroughbred Safety Committee 147
thoroughbreds 7, 142, 148, 149, 150, 160, 161, 167
three-field system of crop rotation 104
Three Horse Tread Power 107, 108
three-point hitch 115
thresher 5, 8, 104, 106, 108, 110, 112, 113, 117, 188, 189
thresher sweep power 107, 108–110
threshing machine 106–110, 117
Throw out your buckets 93
tie-down roping 134, 136
Tiffany 156
Tiger 182
Timurlane 152
tires 63, 64, 115
toe grabs 147
Toiyabe National Forest 184
Tokaido 68
Tommy Gun 38
Tonto 134
Tony 134
Tooke, Ernest 135
Topper 134
Toth, Delphi M. 141
traction 66, 67, 77, 111, 112, 113, 114, 117
traction engine steering 111
tractors 5, 9, 66, 89, 112–115, 116, 117, 118, 119, 121, 128, 129, 186, 191, 197; belt function 117; invention of term 114; road travel 115; weight 113
trail riding 150
Trainer Incentives Program 180
training barns 7, 138, 139, 148
training race horses 148–149

Index

transporting burden 86
treadmill thresher 106–108
treadmills 106, 108, 110
trench broom 38
trenches 3, 28, 29, 30, 31, 33, 34, 35, 36, 37, 38, 39, 48
Trevithick, Richard 111
Trifecta 144
Trigger 134
Triple Crown Races 144
Tritton, Sir William 39
trollers 82
trolley cars 4, 9, 73, 80, 82, 84, 85
Trolley Dodgers 84
troopers 133
tropical West Africa 123
trotters 110
trough or "bunk" feeding 129
Truck & Transfer Companies 89
trucks 4, 5, 9, 33, 34, 37, 39, 45, 52, 60, 61, 62, 86, 87, 101, 117–118, 119, 121, 128, 135, 176, 184, 188
Truman, Harry S. 51–52
Truscott, Lucian K. 164
tsetse fly 124
Tucson 163
Tull, Jethro 104–105
tumbling rods 108, 109, 110
Tunisia 59
Twelve Goal Inter-Circuit Championship 164
twilight of Army horses 1, 3, 60
Twin Trifecta 144
twine binder 106, 107, 112

Union Fire Company 91
Union Pacific 131
Union wagon train 37
U.S. Army 14, 24, 42, 43, 57, 183, 184
U.S. Army Bulletin 43
U.S. Equestrian Federation (USEF) 139, 168
U.S. Fair in Chicago in 1859 111
U.S. First Division 41, 51
U.S. Food and Drug Administration 168
U.S. 4th Cavalry regiment 163
U.S. Inspected and Passed by the U.S. Department of Agriculture 90
U.S. Military Academy 163
U.S. Naval Academy 83
U.S. Open Championship 164, 167, 168, 171
U.S. Patent Office 126, 127
U.S. polo health study 170

U.S. polo rules 153
U.S. Special Forces 183
U.S. Supreme Court 127
U.S. Women's Open 173
United States Polo Association (USPA) 158, 160, 164, 165, 172, 173; affiliated clubs 165; Board of Governors 168; Girls' National Interscholastic Championship 173; Gold Cup Championships 162; handicap levels 172; membership 172; Polo Pony Welfare Committee 168; President's Cup 168
University of Arizona 163, 164
University of Missouri 160, 163, 164
University of Oklahoma 162, 164
University of Southern California 163, 164
University of Utah 162, 164
unwanted horses 174

Van Depoele, Charles J. 82
Van der Heyden, Jan 93–94
Van der Heyden, Nicolaas 93–94
vaquero 6, 127
Vargas, Victor 168
vehicles 63, 68–88
Venezuela 168
Vera Cruz, Mexico 15
Verdun 52
veterinarian 12, 15, 16, 17, 54, 64, 69, 147, 149, 150, 168
Veterinary Corps 20, 44, 45, 46
Vieille 29
Villa, Francisco (Pancho) 20
Villers Tournelles 33
Virginia 4, 14, 19, 83, 96, 142, 149, 162, 177, 182, 196, 197
Virginia (barge) 14
Virginia City, Story County 177
Virginia Military Academy 162
Viviani, M. 24
V-J Day 58
Vold, Harry 135
Volta, Alessandro 81
voltaic pile 81
von Guerricke, Otto 80
von Hutier, Oskar 38
von Kleist, E.G. 80
Vosges Mountains 51

wagon 1, 4, 9, 28, 33, 34, 36, 37, 46, 48, 63, 64, 67, 68, 72, 78, 86, 88, 89, 98, 99, 100,

101, 109, 125, 132, 133, 188; ammunition 28; covered 9; fruit and vegetable 88; ice 87, 88; junk 88; milk 88
wagon trains 28, 37, 132
Walla Walla, Washington 163
Wang, Xingchi 2
Wanless, Mary 139
War Department 22, 24, 25, 26, 54
Ward, Fay E. 128
Washington 14, 20, 24, 27, 58, 72, 75, 84, 149, 163, 164
Washington (state) 163
Washington Post 149
Washington, D.C. 14, 20, 24, 27, 58, 72, 75, 84, 149, 163, 164
water 5, 15, 16, 17, 20, 31, 35, 41, 42, 45, 49, 65, 80, 93, 94, 95, 96, 97, 99, 101, 104, 108, 110, 111, 114, 124, 137, 141, 146, 176, 181, 188; carts 35; points 42
Watrous Engine Works 101
Watson, John 153
Watson, John Henry 155
Watt, James 111
wax 80
Wayne, John 133
wealthy patrons 171
Webb Fire Apparatus Company 101
weekend rodeo-cowboys 135
weight 67, 68; added to racehorses 145, 149; steam engine 113; vehicle limited 68
Wellington, Florida 167–168
West Indies 124
West Point 163
West Texas 124, 125
Westchester Cup 156, 157, 164, 167
Westchester Polo Club 154, 155
Western Front 26, 28, 31, 37, 38, 46, 62
western range horse blood 167
western saddle 61, 137
What My Mother Gave Me 141
wheat 5, 12, 105, 106, 112, 113, 117, 188, 189
wheel 4, 22, 36, 48, 63, 64, 67, 68, 69, 73, 78, 79, 82, 85, 185; solid 63; spoked 4, 63, 185
wheel-rutting 68
wheelwrights 8, 186
whips 8, 147, 186
Whitfield, Fred 136
Whitney, Harry Payne 156, 161

Wholesale Saddlery Associations 89
Wichita 125
Wild Free-Roaming Horse and Burro Act 7, 178
wild grasses 125
Wild Horse Annie 177
wild west shows 7, 132, 133
Williams, Fred M. 72
Williams, W.H. 114
Willis Hartman Award 167
Wilson, Pres. Woodrow 52
windmills 128
Wingate, Orde 59
Winn, Molly B. 2
winnowing 106, 188
Winstrol 147
winter feeding 126, 129
wire cable 78

wire-cutting 127
wire tie binder 106
wolves 125
women herding cattle 123
Women's Championship 173
Women's National Intercollegiate Katydid Farms Trophy 173
Women's Professional Rodeo Association 134
Wood, Jethro 105
wood blocks 65, 67
Woodbury, Daniel 108, 109
Woodbury Power of the Dingee Pattern 109
Woodbury Sweep Power 109
wooden saddles 183
Woollcott, Alexander 53

work distribution by age group 121
World Trade Center 183
World War II 3, 7, 38, 59, 60, 62, 120, 128, 129, 132, 140, 164, 171, 184
wrangler 125
Wyoming 126

Yale 162, 165
yearlings 138, 180
Yonkers Trot 145
Young, H.M. 97
Ypres 37

Zarzyski, Paul 137
zebra 76
Zebu 124
zinc 81

www.ingramcontent.com/pod-product-compliance
Ingram Content Group UK Ltd.
Pitfield, Milton Keynes, MK11 3LW, UK
UKHW041940140426
5217IPUK00014B/585